THE TROJAN KINGS OF BRITAIN

THE TROJAN KINGS OF BRITAIN

Caleb Howells

First published 2024

Amberley Publishing
The Hill, Stroud
Gloucestershire, GL5 4EP

www.amberley-books.com

Copyright © Caleb Howells, 2024

The right of Caleb Howells to be identified as the Author of this work has been asserted in accordance with the Copyright, Designs and Patents Act 1988.

All rights reserved. No part of this book may be reprinted or reproduced or utilised in any form or by any electronic, mechanical or other means, now known or hereafter invented, including photocopying and recording, or in any information storage or retrieval system, without the permission in writing from the Publishers.

British Library Cataloguing in Publication Data.
A catalogue record for this book is available from the British Library.

ISBN 978 1 3981 1275 9 (hardback)
ISBN 978 1 3981 1276 6 (ebook)

1 2 3 4 5 6 7 8 9 10

Typesetting by SJmagic DESIGN SERVICES, India.
Printed in the UK.

Contents

List of Illustrations	7
Introduction	8
1. The Authenticity of the *Historia Regum Britanniae*	11
2. Chronological Issues Concerning the Trojan War	34
3. The True Date of the Trojan War	50
4. The Characters of the Trojan War	83
5. The Historical Trojan War	113
6. The Founding of Rome	131
7. Brutus of Britain	158
8. The Migration from Italy	178
9. The Migration to Gaul and Britain	194
Appendix 1: A Small Adjustment in Assyrian and Egyptian Chronology	229
Appendix 2: The Descent from Brutus	239
Notes	253
Bibliography	276
Index	280

List of Illustrations

1. Amarna letter
2. View of Jerusalem
3. Ruins of Megiddo
4. Donation stela of Osorkon I
5. Bust of Ramesses II
6. Assyrian relief from Nineveh
7. Lachish letter
8. Mycenean axe
9. Baths of Aphrodite, Cyprus
10. View of Tarragona
11. Tombs of the Kings, Cyprus
12. Ruins at Paphos
13. Ruins of the Roman Forum
14. Etruscan pottery
15. Montefortino helmet
16. La Tène sword
17. Cissbury Ring
18. Inscription of Nebuchadnezzar II

Introduction

More or less every nation has a foundation story. It is natural, after all, to want to know one's own origins. Many of these foundation stories are quite easily verifiable, such as those of the USA or the Soviet Union. But these are modern examples. Generally speaking, the further back in time we go, the more shrouded in mystery the facts become. The USA was founded about 250 years ago, but if we consider a nation whose foundation story is based 2,500 years in the past, then establishing the facts is quite another matter.

Many different foundation stories have been written about Britain. However, by far the most famous version is the one that connects it to Greek myth in a most spectacular way. Easily one of the most famous legends in Greek mythology is the account of the Trojan War. This was the conflict that resulted from Paris Alexander eloping with the renowned Helen and taking her back to his city of Troy. The Greeks did not take kindly to this, the story goes, and so they set sail with their armies to try to reclaim Helen and defeat the Trojans for their treachery. The story famously reaches its peak when the Greeks pretend that they have gone home, leaving behind an enormous wooden statue of a horse. The horse is then taken inside the city of Troy by the Trojans, who believe it to be a gift to the gods left by the Greeks. However, inside the statue are Greek soldiers, waiting until nightfall to emerge from their hiding place and take the city. The plan works, and Troy falls.

This is a very well-known legend, but what is not so well known is that this, supposedly, is directly connected to the foundation of Britain. The link between Troy and Britain is not present in the ancient Greek accounts; ostensibly, the earliest surviving source

Introduction

for the British legend is the *Historia Brittonum* (*HB*), a document written in Britain about the year 828 CE. The story subsequently appeared in a considerably expanded form in the *Historia Regum Britanniae* (*HRB*), written by Geoffrey of Monmouth in *c.* 1137 CE. This work was much more popular than the earlier one, and it was from this source that the legend became widely known.

To provide a brief summary, the legend states that after the fall of Troy, a Trojan prince named Aeneas sailed away on a voyage which eventually brought him to Italy. Once there, he and his family had a hand in founding the city of Rome, or rather its precursor. His grandchild (or great-grandchild, depending on the version) was named Brutus. This child ended up unwittingly causing the deaths of both of his parents, for which reason he was exiled from Italy. On his travels, he met up with a large group of Trojan refugees being held captive in Greece. Eventually, he became their leader, freed them from captivity, and led them through the Mediterranean until they finally arrived at an island called Albion. Brutus established his rule over that island, naming it 'Britain' after himself, and his descendants along with the other Trojans named themselves 'Britons' in his honour.

That is the most famous foundation story that Britain possesses. And for many years, it was accepted as historical fact. Although Geoffrey of Monmouth's *HRB* did have some contemporary critics, the overwhelming majority of Britons believed it. It was used as a reliable source for numerous scholarly works in subsequent centuries. For example, *Holinshed's Chronicles*, written in the sixteenth century, drew heavily on the *HRB*. However, it was around this time that some scholars started questioning the existence of Brutus, and this scepticism only increased with time. For the last few centuries, the story of the Trojan migration to Britain under Brutus has been widely discarded as nothing more than a medieval myth.

Today, virtually no serious scholar even entertains the idea that Brutus may have been real or that some Trojans might have ended up in Britain. The closest is archaeologist Miles Russell, who has proposed the apparently radical idea that the story might have originated in Britain as far back as Roman times rather than medieval times. But, nonetheless, the story itself is still regarded as a myth.

Could it be that the legend of the Trojan migration to Britain actually has a basis in fact? Despite the overwhelming consensus that says otherwise, the purpose of this book is to demonstrate that this legend is supported by copious amounts of evidence. Both the migration itself and the fact that the kings of ancient Britain were descended from the Trojans are backed up by ancient written sources that have been completely overlooked. It will be shown that the archaeological record clearly testifies to this migration. And it will be shown that many of the characters involved in these legends – not just the British origin story, but the associated Greek ones – can be identified as real people, attested in ancient historical records.

1

The Authenticity of the *Historia Regum Britanniae*

One key element in the issue of whether or not the legend of Brutus and his Trojan refugees is true is the question of whether or not sources like the ninth-century *Historia Brittonum* (HB) and the twelfth-century *Historia Regum Britanniae* (HRB) are accurate. The latter normally gets greater attention than the former, because it was much more famous in its own time and is therefore a far more influential work. It is also considerably more voluminous than the former. When determining the reliability of British legends found in these two works, it might be assumed that all that is really needed is an analysis of the *Historia Brittonum*, on the basis that the later *HRB* simply derived its stories from this earlier work. However, such a conclusion is based on a false premise – that the *HRB* really was derived from the *HB*.

Consider the implications of the aforementioned premise. If Geoffrey of Monmouth, the writer of the *HRB*, was simply using the *Historia Brittonum* as a source for his stories and then greatly expanding them using his own imagination, then all of the details about the Trojan migration, and all the dozens of kings descended from Brutus, that are present in the *HRB* but not the *HB* can be dismissed as fictional, nothing more than the inventions of Geoffrey's mind. It would also mean, as said before, that the most sensible thing would be to examine the *HB* for trustworthiness, and the judgement that comes from such an investigation would then apply to the *HRB* as well. If the *HB* is inaccurate, then the *HRB* must be correspondingly untrustworthy.

On the other hand, if we reject the premise that Geoffrey used the *HB* as a source, then this leads us to completely different conclusions. It would mean that any criticisms of the *HB* would not at all necessarily apply to Geoffrey's *HRB*. It would mean that the *HRB* can be judged on its own merit. It would also mean that there would be no basis for automatically assuming that the details present in the *HRB* but missing from the *HB* were invented by Geoffrey – rather, they could well be accurate historical details that the compiler of the *HB* simply did not include in his work.

So, what does the evidence indicate? Did Geoffrey use the *HB* as a basis but then greatly expand on it? Or did he have a totally separate source that did include all the many details and kings that he wrote about but are not found in the *HB*? According to Geoffrey of Monmouth himself, his *Historia Regum Britanniae* is actually a translation of a pre-existing work. He claimed at the start of his tome that Walter, archdeacon of Oxford, had given him a 'very ancient book written in the British tongue'. He then translated this work into Latin, thus producing the *Historia Regum Britanniae*. But the vast majority of scholars today do not believe this claim. They view it merely as a fictional backstory given to make his historical work seem more reputable.

The actual evidence from a comparison of the *HRB* with the *HB* points to quite a different conclusion. One of the greatest demonstrations of this is found in the descriptions of the Roman era in both works. The writer of the earlier work, the *Historia Brittonum*, provides an outline of the Roman era of Britain by giving a brief description of each Roman emperor who spent time in Britain, in chronological order. Let us examine this account of Roman Britain and compare it to Geoffrey's much more detailed version, and see if the latter could reasonably have been derived from the former.

The Roman Era of Britain in the HB *and the* HRB

The first Roman emperor with a connection to Britain was Julius Caesar. Historically, he invaded Britain twice, first in 55 BCE and then in 54 BCE. Here is the beginning of the description of Julius Caesar found in the *HB*:

> Julius Caesar, the first who had acquired absolute power at Rome, highly incensed against the Britons, sailed with sixty vessels to the mouth of the Thames, where they suffered shipwreck whilst he fought against Dolobellus, (the proconsul of the British king, who was called Belinus, and who was the son of Minocannus who governed all the islands of the Tyrrhene Sea), and thus Julius Caesar returned home without victory, having had his soldiers slain, and his ships shattered.

The Authenticity of the Historia Regum Britanniae

There are a number of details to be seen from this passage. One detail is the fact that Caesar had sixty vessels. It is the only piece of numerical information in this brief passage, yet it is not found in the *HRB* (even though plenty of numerical information is found throughout that work). Next, there is the detail that the Roman ships suffered shipwreck. This does not happen in Geoffrey's *HRB*. The leading commander of the Britons, according to the *HB*, was a certain 'Dolobellus', and the king of the Britons was named Belinus. In contrast, in the *HRB*, Dolobellus does not appear. Belinus appears, but he is the commander of the British army rather than being the king. The king in Geoffrey's account is named Caswallon. Belinus's father, Minocannus, whom the *HB* says governed the islands of the Tyrrhene Sea, does not appear in the *HRB*, nor does any dominion of the Tyrrhene Sea by the Britons. Finally, the description of Caesar being beaten and leaving Britain does appear in the *HRB*, but there is again no mention at all of any damage being done to his ships.

In all, it can be seen that almost every single detail contained in the *HB*'s brief description of Julius Caesar's first invasion of Britain is completely different in the *HRB*. By no reasonable logic can the *HRB*'s account be seen as an expansion of the *HB*'s account. The only similarities that exist are the result of both works discussing the same historical event. Also, it is significant to note that the king of the Britons according to Geoffrey was Caswallon – in other words, Cassivellaunus, the historical opponent of Julius Caesar in Britain. This historical figure does not appear in the *HB*, but he does accurately appear in the *HRB*.

Let us see how the next section of the *HB* compares to the *HRB*. This is the description of Caesar's second invasion of Britain as found in the *HB*:

> But after three years he again appeared with a large army, and three hundred ships, at the mouth of the Thames, where he renewed hostilities. In this attempt many of his soldiers and horses were killed; for the same consul had placed iron pikes in the shallow part of the river, and this having been effected with so much skill and secrecy as to escape the notice of the Roman soldiers, did them considerable injury; thus Caesar was once more compelled to return without peace or victory. The Romans were, therefore, a third time sent against the Britons; and under the command of Julius, defeated them near a place called Trinovantum.

So, this event happened three years after the previous event, according to the *HB*. According to Geoffrey's *HRB*, it was only two years (in reality, it was just one). Thus, that detail is different. The number of ships is also not mentioned by Geoffrey, despite him putting plenty of numerical information in his work elsewhere. The 'same consul' who placed iron pikes in the river is the Dolobellus mentioned earlier. Yet, he does not appear in the *HRB*'s version of events. Rather, the *HRB* accurately attributes the iron pikes to Caswallon (the historical Cassivellaunus).

One significant similarity between the *HB* and the *HRB* is the fact that they both incorrectly portray Julius Caesar as leaving Britain after the incident with the iron spikes and then returning for a third time. In reality, the Romans won the battle involving the iron spikes and continued on their march through Britain. It is unclear as to what exactly led to this mistaken belief, but the fact that it appears in both the *HB* and the *HRB* does not in any way prove or even indicate that the latter was derived from the former. It could easily be the case that both works were influenced by a common source which contained the mistake, or that this mistaken tale had started circulating among the Britons hundreds of years prior to either source being written down and thus it found its way into both sources.

Regarding the final statement in this passage, which says that Caesar defeated the Britons near a place called Trinovantum, this also differs in the *HRB*. The place known as Trinovantum appears numerous times in Geoffrey's *HRB* (and it is identified as London), yet it does not appear here. Rather, Geoffrey's work places the defeat of the Britons at Dorobernia, that is, Canterbury.

So again, almost every detail in the *HB*'s version of events is either not reflected or completely contradicted by the *HRB*. The only specific similarity which might make one think that they were textually related is the detail about the Romans invading three times, rather than just twice. But as has already been explained, this is easily and satisfactorily explained as deriving from a common source. The rest of the accounts are so different that it beggars belief that anyone could think that Geoffrey used the *Historia Brittonum* as a source for his account of Julius Caesar's invasion.

An additional point to take into consideration is the fact that Geoffrey's account is generally more accurate than the *HB*. Remember, the *HB* refers to a character who does not seem to have ever existed: Dolobellus. And it mistakenly calls the king of the Britons 'Belinus', also making him the son of someone who supposedly ruled over islands in the Mediterranean. The *HRB* does not contain these errors, but accurately names the leader of the Britons 'Caswallon' (simply a later development of the ancient name Cassivellaunus). This is a very important point to note; when stripped down to the same level of brevity as the *HB*, the *HRB* is by far the more accurate version. So if we accept the current consensus that Geoffrey used the *HB* as the basis for his account, we arrive at the remarkable and quite frankly ridiculous conclusion that he took the *HB*'s account, embellished it, and in the process accidentally made it more accurate. Obviously, this did not happen.

Now, this raises an important question. If Geoffrey did not use the *HB* as a source for this account, then what did he use? It is clear that the two accounts are textually related to *some* degree – that is, they both mistakenly describe the Romans as invading three times, which did not happen and thus is not present in by far the majority of sources. It does not appear in any non-British sources. Therefore, we can logically conclude that Geoffrey used a British source, but from what we have just considered, this source could not have been the *Historia Brittonum*. So he must have had a different source, one which evidently no longer survives other than through his *Historia Regum Britanniae*.

For some reason, most scholars today seem to want to avoid arriving at the conclusion that Geoffrey may well have been telling the truth when he claimed that his work was a translation of an otherwise lost source. But, despite the preferences of the majority, this conclusion is nonetheless the one that the evidence supports. To confirm that this is the case, let us continue our comparison of the *Historia Brittonum* and the *Historia Regum Britanniae* as they describe the Roman era.

The *HB* goes on to describe what happened to Julius Caesar after his invasion of Britain:

> In honour of him the Romans decreed the fifth month to be called after his name. He was assassinated in the Curia, in the ides of March.

This does not appear in the *HRB*. And it is not the case that Geoffrey simply decided not to write about what happened to Caesar after this invasion, because he does devote a small passage to what then became of Caesar. He refers to Caesar's war against Pompey. Did he take this from *HB*'s account? No, because it is not mentioned in the *HB*.

Describing Claudius, the Roman emperor who did finally conquer Britain, the *HB* says:

He carried with him war and devastation; and, though not without loss of men, he at length conquered Britain. He next sailed to the Orkneys, which he likewise conquered, and afterwards rendered tributary.

This broadly agrees with the *HRB*'s account, but only because they are both describing the same historical event. There are no specific details here which uniquely match details found in the *HRB*. There are not even any names of specific individuals mentioned (other than Claudius). Geoffrey devotes a lot of attention to a Roman general whom he names Lelius, which is almost certainly a reference to one of the leading Roman generals involved in this historical event, whose name was Aulus. Geoffrey also spends quite some time on Vespasian's involvement in the conquest of Britain. Yet these characters do not appear in the *HB*, so where did Geoffrey get his information?

Here is the next part of the *HB*'s description of Claudius:

> No tribute was in his time received from the Britons; but it was paid to British emperors.

This is a bizarre statement that has no parallel in Geoffrey's *HRB*. There are no 'British emperors' in his account. If Geoffrey was using the *HB* as his basis for this era and greatly expanding on it, we would expect to find a section devoted to explaining who these British emperors were and what they did, but no such section exists. They are not even mentioned. Clearly, the *HRB*'s description of events was not derived from the *HB*. This conclusion is strengthened by the following information provided in the *HB* about Claudius:

> He reigned thirteen years and eight months. His monument is to be seen at Moguntia (among the Lombards), where he died on his way to Rome.

None of this information is found in the *HRB*. The next part of the *HB* describes an event which is often thought to be fictional. It is not known from contemporary accounts of the era. However, it is not unique to the *HB* and the *HRB*, for there are records of it that go back at least as early as the sixth century. Here is the passage as found in the *HB*:

> After the birth of Christ, one hundred and sixty-seven years, king Lucius, with all the chiefs of the British people, received baptism,

The Authenticity of the Historia Regum Britanniae

in consequence of a legation sent by the Roman emperors and pope Evaristus.

While this same basic story of King Lucius being baptised is found in the *HRB*, almost every single detail is different. Geoffrey does not say what year it was when Lucius was baptised, but he does say when he died. He gives the year as being 156 years after 'the Lord's Incarnation', which would be 156 CE. On the other hand, the *HB* here gives the year of Lucius' baptism as 167 CE, which is an obvious contradiction. Why would Geoffrey not only *not* use the date from the *HB*, but provide information that actually *contradicted* it? This is easily explained if the *HB* and the *HRB* are only loosely textually related, but it is completely illogical if the former was actually the source of the latter.

The next detail that does not match between the two sources is the fact that the *HB* says that the Roman emperors were involved in Lucius being baptised, while the emperors have nothing to do with it in Geoffrey's account. Furthermore, the pope in Geoffrey's account is not Evaristus but Eleutherius. As well as being a difference between the two accounts, this is also an example of Geoffrey's greater accuracy. Evaristus died right at the beginning of the second century, well before the year given by the *HB*. On the other hand, Geoffrey's account is far more plausible. He claimed that Lucius died '156 years after the Incarnation of the Lord'. Eleutherius, for his part, is known to have been pope from the 170s to the late 180s. Obviously, this does not quite work, for this would mean that Lucius was already dead before Eleutherius became pope. However, this is easily explained by the fact that a not-too-uncommon mistake in these medieval British records was to get the 'Incarnation' (birth) of Jesus mixed up with his 'Passion' (death) when relating dates.

In other words, it is perfectly possible that Geoffrey's statement that Lucius died 156 years after the Incarnation of Jesus was actually dated from his Passion, and the use of the word 'Incarnation' is an error. This would place the true date some thirty-three years later, or about 189 CE. This alternative date for Lucius' death fits perfectly with the information about Lucius. On the other hand, no such simple explanation is possible for the statement in the *HB*. Applying the same logic to that record, this pushes Lucius even further apart from the pope mentioned there (Evaristus). So that does not work. Alternatively, if we apply that same logic but assume that 'Evaristus' is a mistake for 'Eleutherius', the thirty-three-year adjustment pushes Lucius' baptism to beyond Eleutherius' death. Therefore, the information in the *HB* is simply wrong, as records often were, while the information in the *HRB* appears to have simply suffered from replacing 'Passion' with 'Incarnation'.

Let us now move on to the next part of the Roman era of Britain as found in the *HB*. This is a description of Septimius Severus' dealings with the island:

> Severus was the third emperor who passed the sea to Britain, where, to protect the provinces recovered from barbaric incursions, he ordered a wall and a rampart to be made between the Britons, the Scots, and the Picts, extending across the island from sea to sea, in length one hundred and thirty-three miles: and it is called in the British language, Gwal.

Once again, we find that almost all the specific details in this account are different in the *HRB*'s version of events. In Geoffrey's work, Severus is not described as an emperor but a senator (this is a mistake that he makes multiple times in the *HRB* for some reason). Furthermore, the *HB* claims that he built a wall and a rampart, but the *HRB* only mentions a wall. In reality, Severus built neither. Yet, numerous ancient sources credit Severus with the building of Hadrian's Wall, and on this basis, as well as archaeological evidence, it is generally believed that he did perform significant reconstruction work on the wall.[1] However, there is no evidence at all that he built or reconstructed the rampart in that area. Therefore, this is another example of the superior accuracy of the *HRB*, in that it does not include the inaccuracy found in the *HB*.

There is another inaccuracy in this passage of the *HB*. It gives the length of the wall as 133 miles. In reality, Hadrian's Wall is about 84 miles. This erroneous figure is not found in the *HRB*'s version of events. Furthermore, while the *HB* mentions the Scots being involved in this event, the *HRB* makes no mention of them. A final difference between this passage and the *HRB* is that the last statement about the name of the wall and rampart in the British language does not appear in any form in the *HRB*. These differences between the *HB* and the *HRB* are hardly what one would expect if Geoffrey was using the *HB* as his core source for this era. The rest of the account about Severus is as follows:

> More over, he ordered it to be made between the Britons, and the Picts and Scots; for the Scots from the west, and the Picts from the

north, unanimously made war against the Britons; but were at peace among themselves. Not long after Severus dies in Britain.

As mentioned before, the *HRB* makes no mention of the Scots despite the fact that they are mentioned three times in the *HB*'s brief passage about these events. In addition, the *HB* claims that the wall was built to protect the Britons from the Picts and the Scots, while Geoffrey's account more accurately portrays the situation as being a case of the Romans fighting against the natives, rather than the Picts and Scots fighting against the Britons.

Let us now move on to the next part of the *HB*, which describes the usurpation of Carausius:

> The fourth was the emperor and tyrant, Carausius, who, incensed at the murder of Severus, passed into Britain, and attended by the leaders of the Roman people, severely avenged upon the chiefs and rulers of the Britons, the cause of Severus.

This brief account is notable for its inaccuracies. It suggests that Carausius was an emperor before he arrived in Britain, and it explicitly says that he went there to avenge Severus's death. Not a word of this is accurate. In reality, Carausius was a Roman officer who was called to Rome due to charges of misconduct. In response, he withdrew into Britain and declared himself emperor, defying Rome. This is accurately related in Geoffrey of Monmouth's account. Furthermore, Carausius's rulership had nothing whatsoever to do with Severus, yet this inaccuracy in the *HB* notably does not appear in the *HRB*. Geoffrey of Monmouth's version, yet again, is by far the more accurate one.

The next part of the *HB* deals with Constantius, the father of the famous Constantine the Great:

> The fifth was Constantius the father of Constantine the Great. He died in Britain; his sepulchre, as it appears by the inscription on his tomb, is still seen near the city named Cair segont (near Carnarvon). Upon the pavement of the above-mentioned city he sowed three seeds of gold, silver, and brass, that no poor person might ever be found in it. It is also called Minmanton.

After the statement that 'he died in Britain', none of the rest of the information appears in the *HRB*. Given that this makes up by far the majority of the information provided about Constantius in the *HB*, we would fully expect this grave to be described in the *HRB* if Geoffrey was using the *HB* as his source for this era. The fact that he does not offer a single word about it heavily argues that he was not, in fact, using the *HB* as a source.

The next part of the *HB*'s account of the Roman era is particularly interesting, for it discusses an emperor who did not even really exist:

> Maximianus was the sixth emperor that ruled in Britain. It was in his time that consuls began, and that the appellation of Caesar was discontinued: at this period also, St. Martin became celebrated for his virtues and miracles, and held a conversation with him.

Around this time, there was an emperor who ruled in Britain named Magnus Maximus. However, he is described in the following part of the *HB*, so this 'Maximianus' is generally held to be a phantom character, a duplicate of the historical Maximus mentioned subsequently. If Geoffrey used the *HB* as his source for the Roman era of Britain, we would fully expect to find this phantom Maximianus and these associated events in the *HRB*. Yet, none of this information is found in the *HRB*. Yet again, the *HRB* shows itself to be more accurate than the *HB* when considered from the same level of brevity.

The next part of the *HB* describes the historical Magnus Maximus with numerous correct pieces of information, many of which do appear in the *HRB*. Yet, the *HRB* uses the name 'Maximianus' when describing this historical individual. So what was it that occurred? Did Geoffrey use the name from one emperor in the *HB* but then combine it with the information about the next emperor? This is hardly logical. A more logical conclusion is that Magnus Maximus was incorrectly named 'Maximianus' in some records circulating in Britain, while other records used the correct form of the name, 'Maximus'. The compiler of the *HB* evidently found some records describing an emperor named 'Maximianus' who came after Constantius, while finding other records describing an emperor named 'Maximus'. Evidently the compiler did not realise that it was the same man, so he wrote about both.

On the other hand, the compiler of the *HRB* evidently only used sources that referred to the man as 'Maximianus'. Or, alternatively, the compiler simply realised that he was the same as Maximus and so he did not accidentally split him into two people, as did the compiler of the *HB*. Clearly, Geoffrey of Monmouth did not get his information from the *HB*, but it is clear that the *HRB* does derive from British

The Authenticity of the Historia Regum Britanniae

sources, because continental sources did not refer to Maximus as 'Maximianus' (while the *HB* proves that Maximus was known by that incorrect name in some British records).

The next emperor that the *HB* speaks about is another one who does not seem to have ever existed:

> The eighth was another Severus, who lived occasionally in Britain, and sometimes at Rome, where he died.

There is no independent evidence of this emperor's existence, and it is therefore impossible to determine with any degree of certainty if this reference in the *HB* has any historical basis. There is a distinct possibility that this is a fictional emperor based on some misunderstanding of the available records at the time. Notably, no such emperor appears in Geoffrey's *HRB*, showing once again how he clearly did not use the *HB* as the basis for his account about the Roman era of Britain.

The *HB* next describes an emperor by the name of 'Constantius' who ruled Britain for sixteen years, until he was treacherously murdered in the seventeenth year of his reign. This does find a parallel in the *HRB*. Geoffrey wrote about a ruler of Britain named Constantine who ruled in Britain for upwards of ten years, before being murdered by a Pict in his service. However, there are distinct differences. The *HB* portrays him as the last of the line of Roman emperors who ruled Britain, whereas Geoffrey portrays him as the first of the new line of Brittonic kings after the Romans left. This is a major difference in viewpoint which does not make any sense if the *HRB* used the *HB* as a source.

On the other hand, consider a scenario which makes more sense. Let us suppose that Constantius was the Brittonic ruler who expelled the Romans from Britain in 409 (as described by Roman historian Zosimus).[2] However, he continued ruling in a Roman fashion, perhaps even styling himself as 'emperor'. After he was murdered, his successor, who would likely have been the infamous Vortigern, totally abandoned the Roman form of administration. Thus, in some sources, Constantius could have been viewed as the last of the line of Roman emperors who ruled Britain. Logically, this was the viewpoint taken by the source used by the *HB* for this piece of information. But from another point of view, Constantius could be viewed as coming after the Romans as a Brittonic ruler of Britain. This was evidently the viewpoint taken by the writer of the source for this part of the *HRB*. This would also explain the difference in spelling, with the *HRB* spelling the name as 'Constantine' rather than 'Constantius'.

What is the significance of all of this? As we saw at the start of this chapter, the majority of scholars conclude that Geoffrey of Monmouth did not translate one particular, otherwise unknown, book. Rather, they conclude that he simply used the few sources that we still have available to construct his own historical account, with copious amounts of imagination to fill in the gaps. His source for the Roman era is generally held to have been the *Historia Brittonum*. Yet, the *HB* includes copious amounts of information that is not present in Geoffrey's *HRB*, or information which the *HRB* directly contradicts. To believe that Geoffrey used the *HB* as his source for this era simply flies in the face of all the available facts. Almost every similarity that does exist between them can be put down to the fact that they were both generally describing historical events. And the very occasional specific similarities that exist are readily explained by the simple fact that historical errors generally circulate within regions, and the *HB* and the *HRB* are both British sources.

Flaws in the Common Arguments for Derivation
Before we go on to consider other evidence that the *HRB* is a genuine translation of a now-lost work, and not simply a compilation of sources that were available to Geoffrey of Monmouth, let us first delve into more detail regarding the supposed evidence that the *Historia Brittonum* was used as a source, so as to see why this evidence is invalid.

As we have observed already, there are a small number of errors that are unique to the *HB* and the *HRB* (ignoring subsequent records). We have discussed the one regarding Caesar mistakenly being described as leaving Britain after the battle on the Thames. Another example is connected to the character of Belinus, whom the *HB* incorrectly portrays as the king of Britain at the time of Caesar's invasion. According to scholars, this character was fictional, and the development of this character can be seen in the records leading up to – and culminating in – the *Historia Brittonum*. If so, then Geoffrey of Monmouth must have taken the character from the *HB*, therefore proving that he took details from the sources available to him rather than translating one particular authentic source.

There are many flaws in this conclusion. One flaw is the last conclusion mentioned, that the 'fact' that the character originated with the *HB* must mean that Geoffrey was taking details from the *HB* and was therefore not telling the truth about translating one particular book. It could easily be the case that Geoffrey was telling the truth, and it was actually the original compiler of Geoffrey's 'very ancient book' who took this particular piece of information from the *HB*. After all, the *HB* was written more than 300 years before the *HRB*, so the compiler of the 'very ancient book' could have used it just a decade or so later, and it would still have been about three centuries old by Geoffrey's time. We see numerous examples of how Geoffrey's *HRB* influenced works written just a few years after its publication, so there is no reason why the *HB* could not likewise have influenced works that were compiled immediately afterwards.

Perhaps the reader is wondering why it makes a difference whether it was Geoffrey or the hypothetical author of the 'very ancient book' who took this piece of information from the *HB*. It certainly does make a difference. If the hypothetical author of Geoffrey's source took certain details from the *HB*, then there is nothing wrong with this. It is to be expected that a scribe would examine various different documents available to him to create as accurate a history as possible. While no historian is completely accurate, this means that we would be able to put about as much confidence in the *HRB* as we would for any other historian of this era, like Gildas, Bede or the author of the *HB*.

On the other hand, if Geoffrey was the one who took this detail about Belinus from the *HB*, then this means that he was lying when he claimed that his *HRB* was a translation of a 'very ancient book written in the British tongue'. If he lied about this, then there is no reason to assume that he deserves our trust as a historian. He could have been simply inventing parts of his 'history' from his own imagination, as he is generally believed to have done. This is why it is so significant to note that it could easily be the case that the original author of Geoffrey's book was the one who took this detail about Belinus from the *HB*.

But the argument from conventional researchers on this topic gets even worse when one examines the evidence in closer detail. According to scholars, the course of transmission went from the Roman historian Suetonius, to the Roman historian Orosius, to the author of the *Historia Brittonum*. Suetonius wrote a line in his *Twelve Caesars* which contained the following words:

Adminio Cynobellini Britannorum regis filio

Then Orosius, in his *Historia Adversus Paganos*, evidently used this line but misunderstood the words, writing:

Minocynobellinus Britannorum regis filius

It is then believed that the author of the *HB* further misunderstood this, creating 'Bellinus, filius Minocanni' – Bellinus the son of Minocannus. On the face of it, this seems like a fairly reasonable conclusion. However, the problem lies in the dates for these sources. Suetonius was writing in the early second century CE. Orosius was writing in the early fifth century. The author of the *Historia Brittonum* was writing in the ninth century, over 500 years after Orosius. There are no intermediate sources to show the course of transmission between Orosius's work and the *HB*. The speculation that it was the author of the *HB* who misunderstood Orosius's line and created 'Bellinus son of Minocannus' is totally lacking any actual evidence. It is pure speculation. There is a 500-year gap between the two sources, so there is no reason why it could not have been an earlier scribe who made the mistake, which mistake then found its way into the *HB* many years, if not centuries, later. From an earlier source, that mistake could have made its way into Geoffrey's 'very ancient book' completely independently of the *HB*.

Another flaw in the reasoning of most researchers regarding this point is the fact that there is reason for concluding that the Belinus who appears in the *HRB*'s account of the Roman invasion is not actually related to the apparently fictional Bellinus who appears in the *HB* – at least, not directly. Let it be noted that there are two key differences between the Belinus who appears in the *HRB* and the Bellinus who appears in the *HB*. Firstly, *HRB*'s Belinus is described as the chief of the army of Britain, 'by whose counsel the whole kingdom was governed'. On the other hand, the *HB*'s Bellinus is described as the king of Britain at the time of Caesar's invasion. Furthermore, the name of the father of Belinus is not mentioned in the *HRB*. In reality, later Welsh texts use the name 'Beli ap (meaning 'son of') Manogan (another spelling of 'Minocannus')' for a totally different character in the *HRB*, not this Belinus.

Also significant is the fact that the original line in Suetonius's *Twelve Caesars* that supposedly led to 'Bellinus son of Minocannus' was not referring to the time of Julius Caesar. Rather, it was referring to the time of Claudius, almost a century later. The line refers to Cunobelinus, a king of Britain who did not fight a war against the Romans. It has been observed that the author of the *HB*, for some unknown reason, identified the 'error-created Bellinus' (as we shall now call him) as the much earlier Cassivellaunus, the king who did fight against the Romans in Caesar's time, rather than identifying him with the king who was actually the subject of Suetonius's and Orosius's lines.

The Authenticity of the Historia Regum Britanniae

There is an explanation that clarifies this confusing fact, as well as the differences between the *HB*'s Bellinus and the *HRB*'s Belinus. Consider for a moment the possibility that the commander of the army at the time of Julius Caesar's invasion really was a man named Belinus, and he did hold an extremely powerful position over the Britons, just like the *HRB* describes. This would explain why the author of the *HB* misplaced the 'error-created Bellinus' into the position of Cassivellaunus rather than Cunobelinus. Evidently the author read accounts about a powerful man named Belinus who held power over Britain during the time of Julius Caesar, and then mistakenly assumed that he was the same as the 'Bellinus son of Minocannus' that he found in one of his other sources. This explains why this 'error-created Bellinus' was not placed in the time of Cunobelinus in the *HB*, as we would expect if it was simply a case of the *HB*'s Bellinus coming from the aforementioned scribal mistake.

It would also explain the differences between the Bellinus who appears in the *HB* and the Belinus who appears in the *HRB*. The latter was a historical figure and was unrelated to Orosius's scribal error. On the other hand, the Bellinus in the *HB* was, if this theory is correct, a combination of that historical Belinus and the fictional Bellinus that resulted from Orosius's scribal error.

However, Geoffrey's character of Belinus is not the only supposed piece of evidence that the *HRB* was created by Geoffrey from the sources available to him. Another supposed piece of evidence is seen from some of the descriptions found in the *HRB*. One notable example is seen from the passage in the *HRB* dealing with the activities of Magnus Maximus, a largely successful usurper of the Western Roman Empire in the late fourth century. After describing how he came to power, there is a small section of the *HRB* which provides an overview of his reign. It states the following:

> The seat of his empire he made at Triers, and fell so furiously upon the two emperors, Gratian and Valentinian, that he killed the one, and forced the other to flee from Rome.

Maximus killed Gratian in 383, while Valentinian was forced to flee from Italy (actually from Milan, not Rome) in 387. The following year, Maximus was defeated. What is interesting about this evident overview of Maximus's reign as emperor is that it is quite clearly taken from the brief comments about Maximus made by Gildas, a sixth-century writer in Britain whose *De Excidio* has survived until today.

He does not go into a great deal of detail about the events involving the usurper, but what he does say is that Maximus 'fixed the seat of his unholy government at Treves [Trier], and so furiously pushed his rebellion against his lawful emperors that he drove one of them out of Rome, and caused the other to terminate his most holy life'.

Note the clear similarities between the two sentences. There is the statement that Maximus established the seat of his power at Trier. There is also the juxtaposition of the fates of the two emperors placed immediately after this statement about Trier. There is also the same inaccuracy that one of them fled from Rome, whereas in reality it was from Milan.

Many researchers would look at that and think that this is clear evidence that Geoffrey created his own history by using the various different sources he had available to him, such as Gildas's *De Excidio*, from which the aforementioned quotation is taken. This conclusion bypasses a very simple alternative. It could easily have been the case that it was not Geoffrey who took this line from Gildas's *De Excidio*, but it was the original author of the work which Geoffrey translated. Obviously the author must have worked from the sources that were available to him to have been able to record so much verifiable history (such as the usurpation of Magnus Maximus, to cite just one of countless examples). The narrative in the *Historia Regum Britanniae* continues to the end of the seventh century, so it is obvious that Gildas would have written his work over a century prior to the earliest possible date for the composition of the original version of the *HRB*. As was explained before, while Geoffrey using lots of different sources available to him would mean that he was lying and therefore his history would be inherently untrustworthy, there is nothing wrong at all with the original author of the work that Geoffrey was translating having used Gildas's work.

This is a simple and straightforward explanation for the similarity between Gildas's *De Excidio* and Geoffrey's *HRB*, but it appears that researchers and scholars have been so eager to accuse Geoffrey of lying about the existence of the 'very ancient book' that they have overlooked many simple solutions to apparent problems.

Naming Evidence
Now, let us examine some more evidence that actively indicates that Geoffrey's claim about the 'very ancient book' was true, besides the dissimilarities between the *Historia Brittonum* and Geoffrey's *HRB* that we have already considered. One significant piece of evidence is seen in the use of names in Geoffrey's account. If the *HRB* was the

work of Geoffrey's own research, we would expect the forms of the names of individuals mentioned therein to correspond to the forms that Geoffrey would have known. On the other hand, if he really was translating an old book, then the forms of the names found therein could easily be very different from those of the sources that were commonly known about and used in Geoffrey's time.

For example, the *HRB* tells us about a king who ruled Britain when the Romans invaded in 43 CE under Emperor Claudius. This Brythonic king is described as the son and successor of Cunobelinus (spelt 'Cymbeline' in the *HRB*). As such, he is clearly identifiable as the historical Togodumnus. He is also described in the *HRB* as dying during the initial invasion by the Romans, which also fits the historical Togodomnus. Yet, the name of this king is not spelled 'Togodumnus' in Geoffrey's account. Rather, it is spelled 'Guiderius'. Although these names are quite different, it is possible to see how the historical name of the king could have evolved into 'Guiderius' over time. A name being clipped of its beginning or ending is not too unusual in the records. As an extreme example, the name of an Anglo-Saxon king who fought against the Britons in the late sixth century appears in a Welsh poem as 'Ulf', a shortening of 'Freothulf'. Here, most of the name has been clipped, with only the ending remaining. Therefore, it would not be unusual for the beginning of 'Togodumnus' to have been clipped, leaving 'Godumnus'. From this form, general oral corruptions or scribal corruptions (such as mistaking the 'n' for 'ri') could have twisted this into the 'Guiderius' that appears in Geoffrey's *HRB*.

But note that this explanation *only* works if we allow many centuries for the corruption to have taken place. Geoffrey certainly would not have taken the name 'Togodumnus' and corrupted it into 'Guiderius' in one fell swoop. This form can only be explained if Geoffrey was using a source which contained the story of Togodumnus after having gone through many centuries of transmission. No existing source outside of the *HRB* contains such a corruption of the historical king's name, so the logical conclusion is that Geoffrey was using a source to which we no longer have access, other than through the *HRB*.

There is another example from the section covering the first century CE. When describing the initial invasion of Britain, the *HRB* portrays the Romans as being led by an officer whose first name was 'Lelius'. Historically, the invasion of Britain in 43 CE was led by a Roman whose first name was 'Aulus'. It is evident that Lelius is meant to represent the historical Aulus. Just as with the previous example, it is possible to see how, with time, the historical name 'Aulus' could have been corrupted into the name as it appears in the *HRB*, 'Lelius'. However, this would clearly not happen instantly. It would require the story to have been transmitted over a substantial period of time for scribal and oral corruptions to transform one into the other.

This is perfectly acceptable when working from the assumption that Geoffrey's account of the Roman invasion did not come directly from the classical Roman sources available to Geoffrey, but came from a British account that had gone through centuries of transmission before finally appearing in the *HRB*. On the other hand, dismissing Geoffrey's claim about his 'very ancient book' and concluding he got the information from the surviving classical Roman sources and produced his own account does not in any way explain the change of name from 'Aulus' to 'Lelius'.

Consider yet another example. The historical usurper Magnus Maximus features extensively in the *HRB*. Yet, his name is not written as 'Maximus', but 'Maximianus'. Why would Geoffrey have changed the name, given that the records available to him definitely referred to Maximus by his historical name? It is true that the name 'Maximianus' appears in the ninth-century *Historia Brittonum*, but as a separate individual to Magnus Maximus, who is then described in the following section under his historical name. As mentioned before, it appears that the 'Maximianus' here is nothing more than an accidental duplicate, but the short passage mentioning him does not describe his usurpation and thus could not be the source of Geoffrey's account.

As mentioned previously, the only conclusion that makes sense of this information is that some accounts circulating in Britain described Maximus using his correct name, while other records used the similar but mistaken form 'Maximianus'. The author of the *Historia Brittonum* evidently saw both categories of records and did not realise that they described the same man, so he wrote about both. On the other hand, Geoffrey's source book evidently derived directly from one of the sources that used the form 'Maximianus'. Concluding that Geoffrey did *not* have access to a source that we no longer have but simply created his account from the commonly known sources we have today along with his own imagination (thereby meaning his *HRB* is of no historical value) does not adequately explain why Geoffrey used the form 'Maximianus' rather than 'Maximus'.

Other Evidence

Consider yet more evidence that Geoffrey really was translating one particular book rather than constructing his own historical account.

The Authenticity of the Historia Regum Britanniae

This piece of evidence is related to something which has long puzzled researchers. At the very beginning of the *HRB*, Geoffrey notes that he was not able to find in the works of Gildas or Bede any information about the kings who lived before the Roman era, nor many of them who lived during it, nor the great Arthur himself. Yet, at several points deep into the book, there are references to certain events being described in more detail by Gildas.

For example, at the end of 'Book One', which deals with the Trojan migration to Britain, there is a brief reference to an event in the time of Julius Caesar involving two royals quarrelling over the name of a city. The account in the *HRB* then says that 'Gildas the historian has given a full account' of the event in question. This is notable, given that such an event does not appear in Gildas's *De Excidio*, the only work of his that survives until today and was available in the medieval era. It also does not appear in the *Historia Brittonum*, which was sometimes mistakenly attributed to Gildas. But it is especially interesting because Geoffrey had specifically noted, at the beginning of his book, that he could not find any information at all from Gildas about the kings of the pre-Roman era.

In Book Two of the *HRB*, which deals with the activities of various pre-Roman-era kings, there is another reference to Gildas having written about what the account had just described. Throughout the rest of the *HRB*, we find other references of a similar nature, references to Gildas writing about something which does not appear in the *De Excidio*, or about something which Geoffrey specifically said at the start of the *HRB* that Gildas did not write about.

These references are bizarre and inexplicable to most researchers, because of the underlying assumption that Geoffrey was not actually translating a book but was creating his own history. Therefore, these references to Gildas are taken to be the words of the author, Geoffrey himself offering some explanation in the middle of his narrative. But as we have seen, this viewpoint gives nonsensical results. On the other hand, what does make perfect sense is concluding that these references to Gildas are the words of the *original* author, whose words Geoffrey is simply translating along with the rest of the narrative. Therefore, the original author was referring to works of Gildas's which were available in his time but which had not survived to Geoffrey's time. This conclusion makes perfect sense of the comments that appear in the *HRB*. Thus, these comments indicate that Geoffrey really was translating one particular book. On the other hand, if Geoffrey was taking pieces from various different sources available to him and creating his own history, these references to Gildas make no sense at all.

Another piece of evidence is related to a name that appears in the *Historia Brittonum*. As noted earlier, in the account of Julius Caesar's invasion of Britain as found in that ninth-century work, there is a reference to the leader of the Brythonic army being a man by the name of 'Dolobellus'. There is no record of such a man ever having existed, and the information provided in the *HB* about this initial invasion is generally very inaccurate. As we have already seen, the *HRB*'s version of events is much more accurate, while still evidently having come from British accounts rather than the contemporary Roman accounts.

Interestingly, in the *HRB*, the various leaders of the Brythonic tribes are described as convening with Cassivellaunus at a city named Dorobellum. It is here that they discuss how to deal with the Roman invasion around the time in which Caesar first lands in Britain, before they have engaged him in battle. Some researchers have suggested that 'Dorobellum' is Canterbury, whose Latin name in Roman times was 'Durovernum'. In medieval times, the Latin name was 'Dorobernia'. This is relatively similar to 'Dorobellum', but the problem is that the *HRB* also makes a reference to 'Dorobernia' later in the account. The fact that Canterbury appears under its correct Latin name makes it very unlikely that 'Dorobellum' is also a reference to that same city. In reality, it is much more likely that Dorobellum is a corruption of 'Durolevum', the name of a more obscure Roman settlement in the same general vicinity.

This being the case, note how similar the place names 'Durolevum' and its corrupted form 'Dorobellum' are to the personal name 'Dolobellus'. There is every reason to believe that Durolevum could have had a part to play during the invasion of Britain, such as actually being the site at which the Brythonic leaders gathered to discuss how to deal with the invasion, like the *HRB* describes. Julius Caesar's eyewitness account of the invasion confirms that such a conference occurred. Of course, the site would only have been known by that name in later times, after the Romans had established themselves in the country and had given Latin names to various localities. But in a record written hundreds of years after the fact, there is no problem with this.

On the other hand, there is no evidence at all for the existence of the *Historia Brittonum*'s Dolobellus. The logical conclusion, therefore, is that this character was accidentally created due to a misunderstanding of the place name 'Durolevum' or 'Dorobellum' in the account about Caesar's invasion. Despite being a logical and elegant solution to the otherwise inexplicable Dolobellus, this conclusion relies on the *HRB* containing accurate information about the invasion that is not found anywhere else – namely, that the place that would come to be known as Durolevum was involved in the events. This could not be the case if Geoffrey was filling in the extra details from his imagination, but it could perfectly well be the case if he really was translating a book that contained information which has not come down to us from other records.

Consider another argument that Geoffrey's ancient book in the British tongue was genuine. In the part of the *HRB* that deals with King Arthur, there is a description of Arthur's special coronation after his victories against his enemies. Several dozen kings, nobles and other important individuals are described as attending this coronation. Many of these individuals can be identified from surviving Welsh genealogies. Examples include Urien, Cador, Danaut and Peredur. As was noted by Arthurian researcher Mike Ashley, almost all the individuals who can be identified from other records date from the mid- to late sixth century.[3]

This ties in with numerous other pieces of evidence that place King Arthur's reign in the middle of the sixth century, as argued extensively in the book *King Arthur: The Man Who Conquered Europe*. However, consider the full significance of this information as it concerns the authenticity of Geoffrey's book. It is commonly claimed that Geoffrey of Monmouth must have delved into the genealogies available to him, such as the *Harleian MS 3859* from the tenth century. He certainly could have taken some names from that document if he had wanted to.

However, the big problem with this conclusion is that there is no way for him to have known which individuals were contemporary with each other. The lists do not all contain the same number of names, nor do they start and end in the same time period. For example, some of the lists start from the tenth century and go back to the first century. Others start from the tenth century and go back to the third century. Some start from the ninth century and finish at the fifth. Still others start at the beginning of the seventh century and only go back about 100 years. The point is that they all start and end in different centuries, meaning that there is no way of comparing them easily without additional information.

It is only with a detailed examination and comparison of numerous different sources, such as the *Lives of the Saints* (a collection of biographies of important religious figures from the medieval era), the *Annales Cambriae* (a chronicle that was produced in the tenth century), countless famous and obscure Welsh poems, and other records, that it is possible to discern a plausible chronological scheme for each list.

If Geoffrey of Monmouth had done such a thing and thus managed to successfully invent an account which almost exclusively named individuals who really were contemporaries of each other, this would probably be one of the greatest scholarly feats of the medieval era.

The reality is that Geoffrey obviously did not do such a thing. If he had even attempted to achieve such a feat, there would not be so many contradictions between the *HRB* and the earliest and best records of the events concerned, such as Julius Caesar's eyewitness account of the invasion of Britain. Rather, it is clear that Geoffrey was simply translating the book that he had in front of him.

Consider one example of an individual mentioned in the *HRB*'s account of Arthur's coronation whose appearance there defies explanation. In the *HRB*, his name appears as 'Cathleus map (son of) Catel'. This is clearly the same as the 'Catleu ap Catel' who appears in the *Harleian MS 3859*. The line of individuals in which he appears has proven extremely difficult to pin down, even for modern scholars. Yet, there are some indications that he lived in the sixth century. There is a very obscure Welsh poem by a late sixth-century poet named Aneirin in which a person named 'Catlew' is mentioned. The name is extremely rare, possibly only being used in the *Harleian* genealogies and in this poem, suggesting that it is likely the same person. The individual in the poem is stated to have survived the Battle of Catraeth, an event which is believed by modern scholars to have occurred at the turn of the seventh century. This would definitely place Catlew, or Catleu, in the middle of the sixth century, where he could have attended Arthur's special coronation.

Yet there is virtually no way for Geoffrey to have worked that out himself. Are we really to believe that he just plucked a name out of a list of over a dozen individuals and just so happened to pick the one that was contemporary with all the other individuals whose names he had picked? And that he did this over and over again? It is true that not *all* of the names in the coronation scene are identifiable as sixth-century figures, and there are a few who seem to be anachronistic – unless there were multiple people with the same names from different time periods – but the individuals in this part of the *HRB* are accurate far too often for it to be a coincidence.

Conclusion

So far, we have seen that there is very good evidence that the current consensus regarding Geoffrey of Monmouth is completely incorrect. Rather than having plucked different pieces of information from the

The Authenticity of the Historia Regum Britanniae

numerous different sources that he had available to him, and filling in all the gaps with his imagination, the evidence supports the conclusion that he really did translate a genuine historical work from several centuries before his time. We have seen this from the fact that the only viable source for the Roman era would have been the *Historia Brittonum*, but the account in the *HRB* was most certainly not derived from that work. Furthermore, the *HRB* is almost consistently more accurate than the *Historia Brittonum*, which is ludicrous if the *HRB*'s account was derived from it.

Additionally, we have seen that the spelling of names in the *HRB* also indicates that Geoffrey's account was not derived from the various sources available to him. This conclusion is also supported by the otherwise inexplicable references to Gildas throughout the work. Furthermore, the fact that most of the names in the description of Arthur's special coronation in the *HRB* are of individuals who really were contemporaries with each other shows that the account cannot have been invented in later times – certainly not by the twelfth century – but was almost certainly from a genuine tradition of the event which must have found its way into Geoffrey's source.

The significance of all of this is quite simple: Geoffrey of Monmouth's *Historia Regum Britanniae* is a valuable source of historical information. It is not full of invented stories from the imagination of a twelfth-century cleric. No, rather, it is a genuine translation of a bona fide historical work, just as valid as the works of Gildas or Bede, the *Historia Brittonum*, or any other medieval historical account.

This does not mean that it is perfectly accurate. It is demonstrably not. But what it does mean is that there is no valid reason for just dismissing as fictional any story that appears in the *HRB* that is not found in other sources. Such stories should be considered and weighed on their own merit, as they would be if they appeared in any other medieval historical source. This means that there is genuine reason for looking into Geoffrey's account of the pre-Roman era of Britain, including the story of the Trojan migration to Britain, to see whether there is evidence that it preserves genuine traditions from that time period. Such an investigation is exactly what is going to be done in the following chapters of this book. But first, some groundwork needs to be laid in order to make any kind of progress regarding determining the historical basis for the legend. We will see what that is in the next chapter.

2

Chronological Issues Concerning the Trojan War

To determine whether or not the story of the Trojan migration into Britain really took place, it is absolutely vital to establish when the Trojan War occurred. After all, if the Trojan War has been misplaced by a significant amount, then inevitably no evidence of the migration will be found, regardless of whether it really happened or not. For example, if historians in later centuries misdated the Roman invasion of Britain to 300 BCE, then they could well conclude that it never happened, on the basis that there is no archaeological evidence for a Roman invasion of Britain in 300 BCE. For this reason, the following few chapters will examine the evidence regarding when the Trojan War really took place. However, we first need to address some existing theories on the subject.

Traditionally, the Trojan War has been assigned a date of somewhere around 1200 BCE. The ancient Greeks believed that it took place this far in the past, as evidenced by ancient sources such as the Parian Chronicle. However, there have been many researchers in modern times who have challenged this traditional view. Examples include Peter James, David Rohl and Immanuel Velikovsky. Although the last of those three proposed theories which were very different to those of the first two, they all suggested that the Trojan War took place several centuries later than the Greeks believed. Some of their arguments can seem quite compelling, but there is something fundamental about these proposals, and similar ones, that must be addressed. Invariably, the researchers proposing a major revision of the date of the Trojan War argue that the entire archaeological record of the ancient Middle East needs to be revised accordingly. This is a massive claim, and any version of it is invariably rejected by the general academic community.

Chronological Issues Concerning the Trojan War

The Dating of the Middle East

Consider an example: the generally accepted chronology for the Near and Middle East places Ramesses the Great in the thirteenth century BCE – about the same century, supposedly, as the Trojan War. However, revisionists such as James or Rohl would argue that he actually ruled about two or three centuries later. This has far-flung repercussions, because the chronology of much of the rest of the Near and Middle East is tied to Egyptian chronology.

For example, suppose a city in Syria is excavated. As the archaeologists dig down the layers of the ancient city, one particular layer is found to possess many artefacts that have the name of Ramesses written on them or can be identified with the particular style of Egyptian art that was prevalent in Egypt during his reign. Therefore, the archaeologists logically conclude that the layer of the city in which those artefacts were found dates to the time of Ramesses. This conclusion can then be used to help date other cities in which no datable Egyptian artefacts are found. The archaeologists can examine the style of pottery found in the layer of the city with the artefacts from Ramesses' reign. Using the knowledge that this was evidently the style of pottery in common use during Ramesses' time (for pottery styles changed with some frequency, as they do today), the archaeologists can look for this same type of pottery at other sites which do not have any datable Egyptian artefacts. Upon finding them, they can logically conclude that the layers of these other cities in which they are found must also date to the same time period: Ramesses' reign.

This logic is generally sound, provided it is based on a sufficient number of samples and not just a few isolated pottery finds. However, the key problem is that it relies on the currently accepted chronology for Ramesses, or whichever Egyptian king is used, being accurate. If the Egyptian chronology is out by two centuries, then the chronology of all regions that are dated by means of Egyptian chronology will also be out by two centuries, as will all regions that are, in turn, dated by means of those regions.

Egyptian history is not the only foundation used when dating cities. Historical records do exist for other empires and kingdoms, and these can often be dated relatively independently. However, Egyptian chronology is the single most commonly used foundation because of the unparalleled length of time during which it consistently exerted a strong cultural influence on the rest of the Middle East and nearby areas of the Mediterranean, in addition to the great number of ancient written sources about Egypt.

It might be thought that modern scientific dating methods, such as radiocarbon dating, would be able to settle matters of chronology beyond all doubt. However, the situation is unfortunately more complicated than that. Radiocarbon dating is dependent on the amount of carbon-14 in the atmosphere at the time that the sample died (for example, the sample might be a bone or a piece of wood), because it involves measuring the remaining quantity of carbon-14 in the sample to ascertain how much time has passed since the organic material died, since it decays over time at a known rate.

However, the problem with this is that the quantity of carbon-14 in the atmosphere has not remained perfectly constant throughout history. For example, if there was slightly less carbon-14 in the atmosphere during the time of Ramesses the Great than there is now, an analysis of a sample from his time would give the impression of being older than it really is. On the other hand, if there was slightly more carbon-14 in the atmosphere in Ramesses' time, then a sample analysed today would appear to be younger than it really is.

Scholars attempt to solve this problem by using items of 'known date' and adjusting the radiocarbon results accordingly. For example, if a bone from Ramesses' time produces a radiocarbon date of 1000 BCE, then scholars will assume that there was slightly more carbon-14 in the atmosphere than there is today, hence why the sample appears to date from 1000 BCE when it must actually date from *c.* 1250 BCE, the time of Ramesses' reign. In turn, any other sample from that region which also gives a radiocarbon date of 1000 BCE will likewise be adjusted to *c.* 1250 BCE. In other words, Egyptian chronology is used to calibrate the radiocarbon dates.

There is no inherent problem in using objects of known date to calibrate radiocarbon records, since it is without question that carbon-14 levels have not remained perfectly consistent throughout history.[4] However, the potential problem is what scholars consider to be objects of 'known date'. The reality is that Egyptian chronology is taken for granted as being correct, so it is used to calibrate radiocarbon dates from Egypt itself as well as other areas in that region. Therefore, because of its impact on radiocarbon dating and traditional dating methods, it is exceedingly important to establish the correct chronology of the kings of Egypt.

The Dating of Troy

Let us now consider how this affects our investigation into the timing of the Trojan War. Troy was located in Anatolia (roughly equivalent to modern-day Turkey). The empire which had the most direct impact on this city during the traditional time of the Trojan War was the Hittite Empire. The chronology of this empire is directly tied to Egypt, for the two nations had lots of interactions with each other, most notably at the famous Battle of Kadesh, involving Ramesses the Great. In turn, the archaeology of Turkey is largely determined in relation to Hittite remains, including the archaeology of Troy itself. This includes a layer of the city displaying evidence of destruction, which has been dated to the traditional time of the Trojan War, roughly 1200 BCE.

Furthermore, there are contemporary documents that record apparent conflicts in the region of Troy involving a nation known as the Ahhiyawa, lying to the west of the Hittite Empire. It is generally understood that the Ahhiyawa were the Achaeans, the ancient Greeks.[5] The documents mentioning conflicts in the area of Troy involving this nation are dated to the traditional date of the Trojan War, *c.* 1200 BCE. Thus, this has been taken as evidence that the Trojan War was a historical event. It also serves as evidence that the traditional date for the war is correct, though it is rarely used in this capacity because so few researchers doubt the traditional date in the first place.

Of course, the revisionists who argue that Egyptian chronology should be reduced by about two or three centuries would argue that these Hittite documents actually date to the eleventh or tenth centuries BCE. If so, then this would support the conclusion that the Trojan War actually took place in *c.* 1000 BCE or even *c.* 900 BCE. Thus, as already noted, it is extremely important to address this issue of Egyptian chronology and determine whether the revisionist viewpoint is the most convincing one. Otherwise, we could be looking in the wrong century for evidence of the Trojan migration to Britain.

Evidence for Traditional Egyptian Chronology
Entire books have been written about the revisionist point of view, and it would be futile to attempt to address all the arguments that have been raised in one chapter of this book. However, to help ascertain which chronology is correct, we will consider one specific line of reasoning. It is often claimed by revisionists that their chronology fits the Bible's record better than the generally accepted chronology. The Bible, despite the criticisms it receives, does present a full, specific, continuous chronology for the entire time span it covers. Secular evidence broadly confirms its account of the history of Israel from at least the time of King Omri (*c.* 900 BCE) down to the end of the Biblical narrative at the

close of the first century CE. Therefore, there is good reason for giving credence to its presentation of events during the preceding centuries. If the Bible account appears to favour one particular chronology over another, then that chronology would obviously be the preferable one, at least in terms of the Biblical evidence.

Therefore, in this section, we will examine which chronology really fits the Biblical information better. We will start with the account of Joseph in Egypt through to the time of Solomon, since that section of the Biblical narrative covers the period in question.

Let us start at the furthest end of this period of Bible history: Joseph's experience in Egypt. In the Bible, Joseph is described as one of the twelve sons of the patriarch Jacob. Due to his brothers' jealousy, Joseph was sold as a slave into Egypt. Years later, after being sent to prison on false accusations, he impressed the king of Egypt so greatly that he was raised to the position of Vizier of Egypt, second only to the king. One detail in this story that helps to date it is the price for which Joseph is sold by his brothers. According to the Biblical account, he was sold for twenty pieces of silver, likely meaning silver shekels. Just like in the modern-day world, inflation existed in ancient times. The price of things rose as time went on, including the price of slaves. So, we need to establish two things. First, when is the story of Joseph set? Second, at what point in the chronology of Egypt was the price of a slave twenty silver shekels?

The answer to the first question is quite clear because, as is the case in almost every instance, the Bible presents some rather direct information about its chronological sequence. While there are several different interpretations of the chronological information contained therein, there is universal agreement that the reign of Solomon dates to about the turn of the tenth century BCE, or a little before. In the passage found in 1 Kings 6:1, the Biblical account tells us directly that the temple in Jerusalem, which was built in the fourth year of King Solomon, was built in the 480th year after the Israelites' departure from Egypt; in other words, there were 479 full years between the Exodus and the construction of the temple. Counting back 479 years from Solomon's reign takes us to about the year 1500 BCE. According to the Biblical evidence, the Israelite entry into Egypt, which took place not long after Joseph was taken there, happened 215 years before the Exodus.[6] This means that Joseph must have been taken to Egypt in about the middle of the eighteenth century BCE.

So, at what point in Egypt's history – which is archaeologically connected to the history of much of the rest of the Near Eastern world – was the price of a slave twenty silver shekels? Was it during the part of Near Eastern history which is generally held to be the eighteenth century BCE, or was it during an earlier period, indicating that the chronology of Egypt and the rest of the Near East should be brought forward? The evidence from available records – of which there are many – is that the price of a slave was indeed twenty silver shekels during the period that is traditionally dated to the eighteenth century BCE.[7] Perhaps the most famous record which confirms this is the Code of Hammurabi, dated to the middle of the 1700s BCE, exactly contemporary with Joseph's time if the currently accepted dating of the Near East is correct. The fact that the price of a slave according to this and other records from that same time period was the same as the price for which Joseph was sold clearly supports the traditional dating for the Near East.

The fact that this is not just a coincidence is seen from the fact that later in the Bible, in the law code given by Moses to the nation of Israel (known as the Mosaic Law), the price of a slave is given as thirty pieces of silver. This was just after the Exodus, meaning that this should have been the price of a slave in c. 1500 BCE. Secular records that are traditionally dated to that time period do indeed agree that this was the price of a slave at that time.[8] So, the Biblical information regarding the price of a slave matches the currently accepted chronology regarding the eighteenth century BCE and the sixteenth century BCE. This gradual rise in the price of a slave is seen throughout the rest of the Bible, and in every case it matches the price of a slave in that same time period according to the currently accepted chronology, but not according to any of the revised chronologies.

What about the period between Joseph and Moses? This is the period in which the Israelites lived in Egypt for 215 years, having moved there from the land of Canaan. The Bible says that they settled in the land of Goshen, widely understood to be in the Delta region of Egypt – that is, the north of Egypt, where the Nile River separates and spreads out dramatically and flows into the Mediterranean Sea. So, is there historical and archaeological evidence for extensive Semitic settlement of Egypt during the periods of Egyptian history that are traditionally dated to the eighteenth to sixteenth centuries BCE? Or is there better evidence for this in an earlier period of Egypt's history, indicating that the history of Egypt would work better with the Bible if it was brought forward by several centuries?

As with the previous point, the currently accepted chronology works best with the Bible, rather than the revised chronologies. It is widely accepted that the period given by the Biblical narrative for the time of the Israelite sojourn in Egypt is exactly the period in which Semites are known to have extensively inhabited the country. To put it in the words of Egyptologist James K. Hoffmeier: 'For a period roughly from 1800 to 1540 B.C., Egypt was an attractive place for the Semitic-speaking people of western Asia to migrate.'[9]

Unfortunately, it is very difficult to distinguish between Israelites and other Semitic peoples from the same region in the archaeological record. Nonetheless, a sizeable amount of archaeological material has been identified as specifically coming from Canaan, the country from which the Israelites emigrated to Egypt according to the Bible.[10] In any case, this evidence is the best that we have, and it is consistent with the Biblical data. And let it be noted that the Biblical account does not present Joseph's family as the only one which moved to Egypt at this time. It portrays a scenario in which many peoples from Canaan and that general region were flocking to Egypt to escape the effects of famine, meaning that we should fully expect to find a great mix of Semitic nations inhabiting Egypt at that time.

One example of evidence for extensive Semitic occupation of Egypt during these centuries is the fact that as many as twenty Semitic settlements have been discovered by archaeologists in the north of Egypt.[11] There is also a fascinating document which has been discovered from southern Egypt which dates to the same time period as these Semitic settlements (albeit in a different part of the country). This document records the names of dozens of slaves for just one particular household. Over forty of these names are Semitic, and some of them are recognised as forms of Israelite names that appear in the Biblical account concerning this very time period, such as Issachar and Shiphrah. Given the fact that such a great number of Semitic slaves were present in southern Egypt, yet the archaeological evidence clearly shows that they were far more prevalent in northern Egypt, it is evident that the number of those in northern Egypt must have been extremely large indeed.[12]

In line with the statement from James K. Hoffmeier quoted earlier, the evidence also shows that such Semitic occupation of Egypt was significantly reduced after the sixteenth century BCE. Thus, the archaeological and historical evidence strongly supports the Bible's claim that Egypt was extensively inhabited by Israelite and other Semitic peoples from the eighteenth century until the sixteenth century BCE, but then a large portion of this foreign population (according to the Bible, the Israelites) left at the end of this period.

Chronological Issues Concerning the Trojan War

The revised chronologies that have been proposed, which bring forward the chronology of Egypt by two or three centuries, would completely destroy this correspondence between the evidence and the Biblical information. These chronologies would have us believe that the Israelites and other Semitic families inhabited Egypt when there is no evidence for their presence in the country, and then the Israelites departed just before the evidence for Semitic occupation actually starts to appear. When we combine this archaeological evidence with the perfect correspondence regarding the price of a slave at the start of this period, in Joseph's time, and the price at the end of this period, in Moses' time, we can see that there is an extremely convincing case to be made that the chronology of Egypt should stay more or less exactly as it is, at least for these few centuries.

We can add to this the fact that war chariots feature prominently in the account of the Exodus. This is significant, for it is widely agreed that war chariots were not introduced to Egypt before the seventeenth century BCE. If, once again, the revised chronologies are correct and the chronology of Egypt should be brought forward, meaning an earlier period of Egypt's history is actually equivalent to the sixteenth century BCE, then this means that the Exodus took place during a period of Egypt's history in which chariots were not used. This, of course, does not work with the Biblical information. The presence of war chariots in the account strongly indicates that the currently accepted chronology is correct, at least as far as correspondence with the Biblical narrative is concerned.

Yet another piece of evidence that the Exodus could not belong to an earlier period of Egypt's history is the fact that the term 'pharaoh' is used throughout Genesis and Exodus. According to the Bible's own claims, these books were written by Moses shortly after the Exodus, therefore about the year 1500 BCE. According to the available records, the term 'pharaoh' was first used as a title for the king from about 1500 BCE.[13] Thus, the use of the term 'pharaoh' in documents that have their origin in the sixteenth century BCE is consistent with the evidence. On the other hand, if an earlier period of Egypt's history should be dated to the sixteenth century BCE, then the term 'pharaoh' would not have been used.

Therefore, we can see that all the evidence available strongly supports the currently accepted chronology of Egypt for the era covered by the story of Joseph until the Exodus. Now, let us consider the following two centuries: the fifteenth and fourteenth centuries BCE, the period covered by the Israelite conquest of Canaan according to the Bible.

Egyptian history overlaps considerably with Canaan during this time period, for many of the Canaanite kings were subject to Egypt, and many letters between the two nations have been discovered. Therefore, does the currently accepted chronology of the archaeology of Canaan correspond to the Biblical information?

As it happens, a number of specific cities that the Bible says were destroyed during the Israelite conquest of Canaan can be confirmed by archaeology as having been destroyed at this time. Consider an example of this. The city of Hazor is described in the Bible as being burnt down by Joshua during the early part of the Israelite conquest – in other words, at some point around the middle of the fifteenth century BCE. As it happens, the current archaeological scheme places a significant destruction layer at Hazor to the period between 1450 and 1400 BCE, precisely matching the Biblical account.[14] On the other hand, if the archaeological sequence were shifted forward by several centuries, this would remove this connection and it would also mean that Hazor continued to be ruled by Canaanite kings loyal to Egypt long after the Bible claims that the Israelites had conquered it.

The fact that the archaeological sequence is ideal as it is can be further seen by the subsequent archaeological layers of the city of Hazor. In a layer dated to about the tenth century BCE, archaeologists have uncovered a distinctive six-chambered gate and casemate system at Hazor. Identical structures, down to the design and measurements, have also been identified at the cities of Megiddo and Gezer, also dating from the same era.[15] This perfectly corresponds to the fact that the Biblical account claims that Solomon, who ruled about this time, 'built up' Hazor, Megiddo and Gezer. Given that information, it would be a remarkable coincidence if these gates actually dated from a later time.[16] The correspondence with the Bible's account is strengthened by the fact that the six-chambered gate at Gezer is found immediately above a layer of destruction at the city, which matches the fact that the Bible states that Solomon built up the city after it had been conquered, destroyed and then gifted to him by a pharaoh.

Returning to Egypt, the current chronology continues to match the Bible in regard to Solomon's time when we look at Pharaoh Shishak. This Egyptian king, mentioned in the Bible, has long been identified as the secularly recorded Pharaoh Sheshonk. Shishak is described in the Bible as having invaded Israel and raided Solomon's great wealth almost immediately after that Israelite king's death. Archaeologists have discovered Egyptian monuments recording Sheshonk's raid of Israel, generally accepted as confirming the Bible's account.

Chronological Issues Concerning the Trojan War

According to revisionists such as James or Rohl, Sheshonk was not the Pharaoh Shishak of the Bible's account. According to them, Shishak was actually an earlier pharaoh. Rohl, for example, identifies him with Ramesses II, who did also attack the country. Arguing that he ruled about three centuries or so later than commonly believed, Rohl claims that his campaign into Canaan is the origin of the Biblical account of Shishak's invasion into Israel (Canaan being the earlier name for Israel).

But again, despite the fact that proponents of the revised chronologies argue that their schemes fit the Biblical data better, the opposite is the case. Firstly, there is a very specific detail regarding the use of the word 'pharaoh' which only works according to the currently accepted chronology. In every single reference in the Bible up until the mention of Shishak, the word 'pharaoh' appears by itself. For example, there is the Pharaoh who interacted with Joseph, and the Pharaoh of the Exodus. Their personal names are never given. However, from the time of Shishak onwards, the term 'pharaoh' is almost never used by itself, but is almost always used in conjunction with the king's personal name (such as 'Pharaoh Necho' or the equivalent form 'King Shishak'). It is known that this title was indeed used by itself when it first started to be used (around the time of Moses, which fits its usage throughout the Torah). But when was it first used in conjunction with the king's personal name? The earliest evidence for this comes from the time of an Egyptian king traditionally dated to the tenth century BCE, shortly before Sheshonk.[17]

So in other words, the Bible consistently uses the term 'pharaoh' in isolation throughout the period in which it really was used in isolation, and then within the same century in which it evidently started to be used in conjunction with the king's name, the Bible begins to do the same (sometimes using 'pharaoh' and sometimes using 'king'). This is a perfect correspondence. It is an extremely specific detail which surely cannot be dismissed or put down to coincidence. Yet, this correspondence would be broken if the chronology of Egypt were shifted forward by several centuries.

There is additional evidence in favour of the current consensus regarding Egyptian chronology that can be seen from the Biblical Pharaoh Shishak. As stated earlier, he was said to have carried away the great wealth of Solomon from Jerusalem. Solomon, as is well known, is described in the Bible as having been an exceedingly rich king. As it happens, there is considerable evidence that Sheshonk came upon an almost unfathomable amount of wealth when he raided Israel. His raid into Israel occurred almost at the very end of his reign; Egyptologists argue as to whether he died the same year or one or two years later. In any case, there was hardly any time between his invasion of Israel and his death. The archaeological evidence shows that during that small window of time, he suddenly engaged in grand building projects all over Egypt, the likes of which had not been seen since the time of Ramesses the Great. The renowned Egyptologist Kenneth Kitchen described it as seeming as if Sheshonk had just won the lottery.[18]

After Sheshonk died, his son Osorkon I succeeded him. Within the first few years of that new monarch's reign, Osorkon is recorded as having made an extraordinarily large donation of silver and gold to the Egyptian temples amounting to 383 tons. This is astonishing, given that the second-largest donation seen from surviving Egyptian records, which dates from the time of Thutmoses III, was 13 tons. Furthermore, Sheshonk II, the successor of Osorkon I, was found by Egyptologists to have been interred in a solid silver coffin.[19] This is an exceptionally rare find, given that silver was actually more precious than gold in ancient Egypt.

What could possibly explain this extraordinary display of wealth seen from Sheshonk I through to Sheshonk II? Sheshonk I's sudden lottery-style spending immediately after his campaign into Israel, Osorkon I's phenomenally large contribution to the Egyptian temples, Sheshonk II's solid silver coffin – this all makes perfect sense if Sheshonk I really was the Shishak of the Bible, who plundered Solomon's great wealth several years after that Israelite king's death. On the other hand, if we conclude that Sheshonk actually lived later than commonly believed, and the Shishak of the Bible was actually an earlier Egyptian king, such as Ramesses II or Ramesses III, then this sudden increase in the wealth of the Egyptians in Sheshonk's time becomes inexplicable, and we are left with no clear trace of Solomon's wealth in the archaeological and historical record.

From this examination of the evidence from the time of Joseph right down to the time of Solomon, it is abundantly clear that the Bible works far, far better with the currently accepted chronological scenario of Egypt and the Levant than it does with any of the revised chronologies. Therefore, it must be stated emphatically that this book does *not* make any attempt whatsoever to revise the currently accepted chronology of the Near East, as do certain other books that purport to reveal the 'truth' about the Trojan War. It is important to emphasise this point, because many books that attempt to re-date the Trojan War (placing it in *c.* 900 BCE, *c.* 800 BCE or even 650 BCE) do so on the basis that the entire chronology of the Near and Middle East should be brought forward by the corresponding amount. As we have seen, this position is unsustainable, on the basis of the great deal of evidence that the currently accepted chronological scheme for the Near East is correct. Therefore, these theories that attempt to bring forward the Trojan War are invariably rejected by the vast majority of scholars.

A Weak Foundation

However, an inescapable issue is that the reason why so many researchers are intent on removing the Greek Dark Ages and bringing down Egyptian chronology by hundreds of years when they try to revise the date of the Trojan War is because of the common viewpoint that events described in documents traditionally dated to *c.* 1200 BCE describe the Trojan War. For example, as mentioned earlier, there are Hittite documents from that era which describe the 'Ahhiyawa' campaigning in western Anatolia. These Ahhiyawa are generally identified with the Achaeans, the Greeks who fought in the Trojan War. On the basis of these documents, many would argue that the Trojan War clearly occurred in the time period in which these documents were written, meaning that the dating of the Trojan War is fixed by the dating of these documents (and therefore, the war definitely occurred in *c.* 1200 BCE). Let us examine this argument in its entirety and see why it does not work.

In addition to mentioning that the Ahhiyawa, or Achaeans, were campaigning in western Anatolia, the Hittite documents also make specific mention of a conflict over a place called 'Wilusa', indicated by the documents to be in north-west Anatolia. This is usually understood to be an ancient Hittite form of the later Greek 'Ilios', the name of the city of Troy in north-west Anatolia. In the Hittite records, this location is also associated with the place name Taruiša, which has been linked with 'Troy'. This does appear to be a reasonable identification. This being so, we can conclude that there was a conflict of some kind involving the Greeks and the city of Troy in *c.* 1200 BCE. So far, so good. What is more, these Hittite documents appear to mention certain characters who feature in the tales of the Trojan War. For example, there appears to be a mention of Paris Alexander, the prince of Troy; Priam, the king of Troy; Eteocles, the king of Thebes in the generation before the Trojan War; and Atreus, the father of Agamemnon and Menelaus.

At first glance, this might appear to be a very convincing case. However, the case falls apart when it is examined closely. Let us first consider the supposed identifications of figures mentioned in the Hittite documents with characters from Greek legend.

Firstly, we have Paris Alexander. In the Greek legend of the Trojan War, he was the Trojan prince, the son of King Priam. It was Paris Alexander who kidnapped Helen and ran away with her to Troy, thus initiating the war between the Trojans and the Greeks. In the Hittite documents, there is a mention of a king of Wilusa named Alaksandu, and many scholars believe this to be the Hittite approximation of the ancient Greek spelling of Alexander. This does seem like quite a reasonable conclusion. But was this Alaksandu the Paris Alexander of Greek legend? One problem with this identification is that Paris Alexander is never presented as the king of Troy, or Ilios. His father Priam is always portrayed as the active king right up until the end of the Trojan War. In contrast, Alaksandu is definitely called the king of Wilusa, and it is he who is described as making treaties with the Hittite kings. This does not neatly match the information about Paris Alexander, nor does it leave any room for Priam's prominent role in the story of the Trojan War.

In addition, Alaksandu is described as making a treaty with Muwatalli II, and this treaty also implies that he had a treaty with Muwatalli's father, Mursili II. The latter is believed to have reigned from 1321 to 1295 BCE, while Muwatalli reigned from 1295 to 1272 BCE. Therefore, Alaksandu belongs to the *c.* 1300 BCE period. This is far away from *c.* 1200 BCE and especially far away from the most popular dates for the Trojan War, which are *c.* 1194 to 1184 BCE. However, some ancient Greek estimates did place it that far back, so perhaps it is simply the case that one of the less common Greek estimates is correct, and the Trojan War actually happened in the early thirteenth century. Does this conclusion work? Well, it may work for Alaksandu – if we ignore the fact that Paris Alexander was not actually the king of Troy – but the other supposed identifications still do not work.

Let us now take Priam, the legendary father of Paris. He was said to have been the king of Troy for decades leading up to the Trojan War. He has been tentatively identified by many with a figure in the Hittite documents known as Piyama-Radu. This figure appears quite prominently in the records, and he is described as causing significant trouble in western Anatolia. Could this be the mighty King Priam? The answer is a definitive 'no'. There are several completely insurmountable problems with such an identification. Firstly, Piyama-Radu is never described as a king. There are suggestions by some scholars that he may have been attempting to carve out a kingdom for himself by all his raiding efforts, but nonetheless, he is nowhere described as being a king. If he was attempting to carve out a kingdom for himself, he evidently was not able to do so. He was simply a troublesome war leader who was active in western Anatolia, which does not fit the character of King Priam.

The second major obstacle to this identification is that, beyond never being described as a king, Piyama-Radu is also never suggested to have come from Wilusa, or Troy. One common suggestion among modern researchers is that he came from the kingdom of Arzawa, which was in the south-west corner of Anatolia.[20] This is admittedly speculative, but it illustrates the point that there is nothing which associates him specifically with Wilusa.

The third major obstacle to this identification is that Piyama-Radu's activities go completely contrary to Priam's role in the legends. During the Trojan War, nations from all over western Anatolia are described as joining Troy in the war against the Greeks. In contrast, Piyama-Radu is described as raiding all over western Anatolia, making himself the enemy, not the ally, of those nations who appear in the *Iliad* as allies of the Trojans. In fact, Wilusa – Troy – is specifically one of the cities that Piyama-Radu is described as attacking in the Hittite records. What is more, he is actually portrayed as allying himself with the king of Ahhiyawa and fighting against the Hittites. In other words, he fought *with* the Greeks *against* the nations and city-states of western Anatolia, including against Troy itself. The idea that he was Priam, the king of Troy, is ludicrous.

As if it were even necessary, a fourth obstacle to his identification with Priam is the fact that he is shown to have been active in the first half of the thirteenth century through to the middle of that century, with his last known appearance being in *c.* 1250 BCE. This makes him a younger contemporary of Alaksandu, the king of Wilusa who had a treaty with Mursili II, who reigned from 1321 to 1295 BCE. Therefore, it is impossible for Piyama-Radu to have been the father of Alaksandu, as would have to have been the case if Piyama-Radu was Priam and Alaksandu was Paris Alexander.

Let us now examine Atreus. According to Greek legend, he was the king of Mycenae, the father of Agamemnon and Menelaus. According to some researchers, he was likely identical to a figure in the Hittite records named Attarsiya. He is portrayed as a leader of the Ahhiyawa, the Achaean Greeks. He was said to have engaged in many military campaigns against the Hittites in western Anatolia. There is no particular connection with Atreus in this regard, since he himself is not portrayed in the Greek legends as fighting in Anatolia. However, since Atreus' sons did famously engage in a campaign in that region, this could be viewed as compatible with the legends.

However, the major problem with this identification is that the letters which describe Attarsiya's Anatolian campaign are dated to about 1400 BCE or shortly thereafter. If Attarsiya was Atreus, then we would have to accept that he was active shortly after 1400 BCE, and then his sons fought a war against Troy well over 100 years later. That is clearly impossible.

Finally, let us consider Eteocles. In Greek legend, he was one of the sons of Oedipus. He was also the king of Thebes in Greece. After the death of his father, Eteocles and his brother Polynices jointly ruled Thebes, but they did not do so peacefully, and they eventually killed each other in battle. The hypothetical ancient form of the name of this character is 'Etewoklewes'. In one of the Hittite documents, there is a letter which speaks of a man named Tawagalawa. It is commonly believed that this is the Hittite form of the hypothetical 'Etewoklewes'. Not much is revealed about this man, apart from the fact that he was the brother of the king of Ahhiyawa. This is arguably a match for Eteocles, inasmuch as his brother Polynices was the joint ruler of a Greek kingdom.

Yet, as with the other identifications, this supposed connection with the Greek stories has a serious flaw. The mention of Tawagalawa comes from a letter dated to about 1250 BCE. That places it after the time of Alaksandu. Yet, Eteocles lived in the generation *before* the Trojan War. Therefore, it is not possible for Tawagalawa to have been Eteocles, unless the Trojan War happened in about 1200 BCE or a little later. But if that were the case, then we would have to reject Alaksandu as Paris Alexander.

Therefore, the sum of all this is that none of the identifications work with the legends. The only two that make any degree of sense are Alaksandu as Paris Alexander and Tawagalawa as Eteocles, but these two identifications are mutually exclusive for the chronological reasons just described. Thus, only one, at most, of the supposedly multiple identifications can actually be correct.

Regarding the records of a conflict or war over Wilusa, this also does not fit the legends. In the Tawagalawa letter, mention is made of a war between the Hittites and the Ahhiyawa (the Greeks) over Wilusa. While many have attempted to relate this to the Trojan War, the letter refers to the fact that this conflict ended up being settled amicably. This is completely incompatible with the description in the Greek legends of Troy being utterly devastated by the victorious Greek army after their ploy with the Trojan Horse, with most of the inhabitants being massacred. This was not settled amicably. Therefore, the conflict mentioned in Hittite sources cannot be the same as the Trojan War of Greek legend.

It is true that there is archaeological evidence of a destruction of the city of Troy due to warfare in *c*. 1180 BCE, but this was not the conflict involving the Greeks mentioned in Hittite sources, as is evident for chronological reasons and because the conflict mentioned in the Hittite sources was settled peacefully, not with the destruction of the city. Therefore, there is no evidence that the destruction in *c*. 1180 BCE had anything to do with the Greeks. In fact, there is reason to believe that the destruction of *c*. 1180 BCE was caused by Balkan invaders, on the basis of the style of material culture found at Troy immediately after that destruction layer.[21] Furthermore, archaeology has revealed that the city of Troy was destroyed numerous times over the centuries. The fact that one destruction layer happens to coincide with one of many disparate estimates for the date of the Trojan War can simply be put down to coincidence.

Conclusion

In summary, we have seen that there have been many attempted revisions of the dating of the Trojan War, but they all require revising the chronology of the entire eastern Mediterranean and the Middle East. As such, these chronologies are invariably rejected by the majority of scholars. Indeed, we have seen that there is substantial evidence that the currently accepted chronology of the Near and Middle East is correct, at least from about 1800 BCE to about 1000 BCE, which encompasses the supposed era of the Trojan War. However, this currently accepted chronology being correct does not necessarily mean that the currently accepted dating of the Trojan War is correct. Indeed, we have seen that the supposed connections between the Greek legends and the Hittite records from the supposed era of the Trojan War are completely unconvincing.

Thus, it could easily be the case that the Trojan War has been misdated in isolation. The fact that the currently accepted chronology for the Near East is evidently correct does not in any way require the Trojan War to have taken place in *c*. 1200 BCE, as is commonly believed. The Trojan War can and should be dated on its own merit, and this is what the next chapter will attempt to do.

3

The True Date of the Trojan War

Now that we have established that there is no convincing evidence from contemporary records or archaeology that the Trojan War occurred in the date popularly assigned to it, let us examine what the ancient sources actually say about the Trojan War and see if there is a different date which fits the documentary evidence and is actually supported by contemporary records.

Is the Traditional Date Reliable?
Firstly, let us consider the reliability of the dates given by the ancient Greeks. After all, the Parian Chronicle explicitly places the Trojan War in the thirteenth century BCE. In addition, Herodotus stated that it took place about 800 years before his own time, which would also place it in the thirteenth century BCE.[22] Ctesias of Cnidus, a contemporary of Herodotus, also dated the Trojan War to that same century. Surely these sources cannot all be wrong? A closer examination of these sources will reveal how much confidence can be placed on these dates.

First, consider Herodotus. It is true that he explicitly dated the Trojan War to about 800 years before his own time. However, he also dated the Ethiopian king of Egypt named Shabaka to the same era – over 750 years before his own time. This is seen from his comments in *The Histories*, 2.137–140. In this section, Herodotus describes the Ethiopian king 'Sabacos' (clearly the Ethiopian Shabaka) conquering Egypt and ruling it for fifty years. After these fifty years, Anysis, a native ruler whom he had driven out, returned to Egypt to continue his rule. During those fifty years of exile, he had been residing on an island named Elbo. Herodotus then claims that the Egyptian kings

The True Date of the Trojan War

after Anysis had searched for the island for more than 700 years until the time of Amyrtaeus, a ruler of Sais contemporary with Herodotus. Therefore, if the subsequent kings of Egypt had searched for it for more than 700 years since the time of Anysis, yet Sabacos (Shabaka) began his rule fifty years before Anysis returned to Egypt (which he, in turn, then ruled for an unspecified period of time), then Herodotus is placing the start of Sabacos' dominion of Egypt more than 750 years before his own time.

The problem with this is that Shabaka is believed to have begun his reign in *c.* 700 BCE, only about 250 years before Herodotus. Thus, the fact that Herodotus placed the Trojan War about 800 years before his own time is not, in itself, necessarily any more reliable than his placement of Shabaka in almost exactly the same era, when Shabaka actually only lived in *c.* 700 BCE. If Herodotus' exaggerations are consistent, then this actually indicates that the Trojan War could have occurred around 700 BCE. Of course, this is not necessarily a safe assumption, but it can be taken as indicative. The point is that it is clear that Herodotus was capable of extreme exaggerations in his chronology. The case of Shabaka is a clear example of this; even the reign length given to Shabaka is excessive. Herodotus states that he ruled for at least fifty years, yet scholars today generally assign him a reign of only fifteen years, from 705 to 690 BCE.

Another example of this is seen from Herodotus' comments about Cadmus, a figure from Greek legend. Herodotus stated that Cadmus lived some 1,600 years prior to his own lifetime, which would place Cadmus' life at the very start of the second millennium BCE. Yet all other information from Greek tradition and genealogies indicates that he lived less than two centuries before the Trojan War, as we will see in more detail later in this chapter. So even if the traditional date of 1200 BCE for the Trojan War is used, Herodotus' estimate for Cadmus' lifetime is clearly too extreme by many centuries. A gap of about two centuries between Cadmus and the Trojan War has evidently been exaggerated to eight centuries.

Thus, Herodotus' comments about how long ago Shabaka lived, his comments regarding the length of his reign, and his comments concerning how long before the Trojan War Cadmus lived, all display serious exaggeration on the part of Herodotus' chronological estimates. This same principle is also seen from many more of his statements (for example, Herodotus places Homer 400 years before his own time, which would be in the ninth century BCE, yet most scholars today place Homer in the eighth century or even the seventh century BCE).

Therefore, it would actually be *uncharacteristic* for his date for the Trojan War to be accurate. In reality, the very fact that he stated that it occurred about 800 years before his own time is evidence that we should look for it several centuries more recently than that – perhaps even as late as *c.* 700 BCE, as in the case of Shabaka.

The reason why Herodotus' estimates are generally exaggerated is probably partly due to the natural distortion of records over time, and also probably due to a desire on the part of the ancient Greeks to emphasise their antiquity. Scholar Nikos Kokkinos observed that in the time in which Greek historians were attempting to determine the precise year in which the Trojan War took place, 'the Greek past must at all costs have been kept as antique as possible to match the heavy competition from the newly discovered histories of the Eastern kingdoms'.[23]

However, while these two factors might go some way to explaining why this momentous event in Greek history was pushed back in time, it seems likely that other factors were involved as well. Many scholars in recent years have highlighted the fact that certain ancient chronologists evidently used an estimate of forty years per generation, which is absurd. Nikos Kokkinos, along with others, claims that the majority of genealogical evidence points towards the tenth century BCE for the date of the Trojan War. It appears that these scholars tend to use thirty-three years per generation, which is surely still too high. An average of twenty to twenty-five years is surely more probable. This would bring the date of the Trojan War even further forward than the tenth century BCE. It is evidently the ancient use of excessively long generation lengths that contributed to the twelfth- or thirteenth-century BCE date for the Trojan War reached by most ancient historians. In fact, it is very likely that this is the main factor, influenced by the first two principles mentioned in this section – the natural distortion of records and the desire to exaggerate the antiquity of one's nation.

The example of Ctesias demonstrates this principle of excessive generation lengths very well. He placed the fall of the Assyrian Empire eight generations after the Trojan War.[24] The last Assyrian king ruled until the second half of the seventh century BCE, meaning that this information would place the Trojan War in about 800 BCE, or in other words, roughly 160 to 200 years before the fall of the last king of Assyria if we assume twenty to twenty-five years per king. However, Ctesias himself claimed that there were more than 360 years between these two events.[25] He must have been using an average generation length of forty-five years to be able to achieve this result. This highly implausible reckoning would place the Trojan War in the first half of the tenth century BCE. However, the situation gets worse, because Ctesias' chronological scheme placed the fall of Nineveh, during the last Assyrian king's reign, in 907 BCE.[26] So the Trojan War, which he separated from the fall of Nineveh by about 360 years despite there apparently being only eight generations between the two events, would be placed in about 1267 BCE. So while his information about the separation between the last Assyrian king and the Trojan War would actually indicate that the latter event occurred in about 800 BCE, Ctesias' chronological scheme actually placed it in the thirteenth century BCE.

It appears that this excessively early date for the fall of Nineveh was quite a commonly held belief in the ancient period (itself attesting to how an event could be accidentally moved back by hundreds of years), due to the strong influence of Ctesias' chronological scheme. Eratosthenes, a mathematician who famously placed the Trojan War in 1183 BCE, seems to have arrived at his somewhat later date for the Trojan War partly by dating the fall of Nineveh slightly later than Ctesias did, and partly by using slightly reduced generation lengths between the fall of Nineveh and the fall of Troy.[27]

It is impossible to state with certainty what the exact process was in every instance that led to various different ancient historians placing the Trojan War in *c.* 1200 BCE, since they rarely explained their exact methods of arriving at their dates. Ctesias is one of the only historians who provided enough information to be able to actually assess his calculations. Yet, it is very likely that the answer can be explained by a combination of these principles. To summarise: the antiquity of events has a tendency to be exaggerated in any setting where there are not reliable chronological records, where the events are transmitted largely by oral tradition; the Greek historians had a natural desire to create a more ancient history for themselves, extending it back as far as the available information would allow; motivated by this desire, they had a tendency to use excessively lengthy generational gaps in their estimates, often as long as forty years or more; other historical events that the Trojan War was dated in relation to were, at times, demonstrably misdated by centuries, such as the fall of Nineveh.

In addition to this, we may add the fact that many 'genealogical' lists may actually contain instances of a 'son' in the list actually being an unrelated successor, or perhaps an uncle or brother who succeeded to the throne. This would mean that the number of generations in the list should actually be reduced. Furthermore, in some instances in which Greek king lists were used, it may have been the case that multiple kings ruled at once, rather than strictly one after the other. This would also distort the estimates of the ancient historians.

For primarily these reasons, and perhaps some other ones that have yet to be identified, the ancient Greek historians miscalculated the date of the Trojan War and pushed it back to the thirteenth or twelfth century BCE. This miscalculation is demonstrable in the case of Ctesias, and in the case of Herodotus it is strongly indicated by the fact that his other chronological estimates are demonstrably exaggerated. When we consider the information Ctesias was actually working with, a date around 800 BCE is indicated, and Herodotus' exaggeration of Shabaka's antiquity indicates that the Trojan War could have even been as late as *c.* 700 BCE. Frankly, it is remarkable that the date of *c.* 1200 BCE has managed to gain the popularity that it has in modern times, given its demonstrably flawed foundations.

What the Evidence Really Indicates

As we noted, the information Ctesias provided about the number of generations between the fall of Troy and the fall of Nineveh indicates that the Trojan War occurred in about 800 BCE. However, we can also calculate the date of the Trojan War by working from the other direction. According to Ctesias, the legendary first Assyrian king was Ninus, credited with conquering Babylonia and carving out an empire. The description of his activities appears to match the historical Tukulti-Ninurta I, although in an exaggerated form.[28] For this reason, it is generally accepted that Ninus is a legendary version of Tukulti-Ninurta I.[29] He was a king who lived in the thirteenth century BCE and made Assyria a great power. The connection between him and the legendary Ninus appears to be confirmed by Herodotus' more accurate chronological scheme.[30]

Ctesias places the Trojan War twenty-one generations after Ninus. The historical Tukulti-Ninurta I is believed to have begun his reign in *c.* 1240 BCE, meaning he was probably born in about 1270 BCE. If we assign twenty to twenty-five years per generation, then counting forward twenty-one generations would place the birth of the king who reigned during the Trojan War somewhere between 850 and 745 BCE. Assuming that the king was between twenty-five and sixty-five years old at the time of the Trojan War, this places the Trojan War between 825 BCE at the earliest and 680 BCE at the latest. This is broadly consistent with the date derived from counting back from the fall of Nineveh, though it seems to indicate a somewhat later date. This is possibly explained by the fact that there was a cluster of short-lived kings leading up to the fall of Nineveh, and they may have been mistaken for successive generations in Ctesias' list. This would mean that there were not actually eight full generations separating that event from the Trojan War.

Let us now consider the writings of Flavius Josephus, a Jewish historian who lived in the first century CE. In his work *Against Apion*, he asserts that the history of the Greeks does not stretch back particularly far at all. In Book 1, chapter 16, Josephus provides some information to support this claim. One point of particular interest is the fact that the Greek alphabet, according to tradition, was supposed to have been introduced into Greece from Phoenicia by a man named Cadmus. This was said to have occurred long before the time of the Trojan War. Scholars agree that the Greek alphabet does come from the Phoenician one, so this legend is consistent with the evidence in that regard. However, as Josephus himself notes, there is no evidence at all that the Greek alphabet had been around for all that long. In fact, it is widely accepted by scholars today that there is no evidence that it was in use before the ninth century BCE, with 900 BCE being the earliest possibility considered by most authorities.[31]

So if the evidence indicates that the Phoenician alphabet was only adopted by the Greeks in *c.* 900 BCE at the very earliest, and yet Greek records claim that it was introduced into Greece by Cadmus quite some time *before* the Trojan War, this would indicate that the Trojan War took place *after* the ninth century BCE. This is consistent with the date indicated by the information Ctesias provided, and also with Herodotus' claim when we assume that he exaggerated the date as much as he did in the case of Shabaka.

Information about the ancient Olympic Games also helps us to date the Trojan War. According to ancient sources, this festival was founded in the year 776 BCE. This date was so firmly established that the Olympic Games were often used in ancient records as a chronological reference (for example, an event might be dated to the 'second year of the fifty-sixth Olympiad'). It is notable, then, that the early fifth-century BCE writer Pindar claimed that Heracles was the one who founded the Olympic Games.[32] Pindar was the earliest writer to describe the origins of the Olympic Games, so this is a valuable reference. Heracles was said to have sacked the city of Troy during the youth of the boy who later grew up to be the elderly King Priam at the time of the Trojan War. Assuming that Heracles was about thirty years old when this event occurred, then given that there must have been some fifty or more years between this event and the Trojan War, we can conclude that Heracles must have been born at least eighty – or possibly even ninety or more – years before the war. Since the Olympic Games were founded in 776 BCE, this would place the birth of Heracles in *c.* 800 BCE. Counting forwards eighty or ninety years to the Trojan War takes us to the end of the eighth century, around 720 or 710 BCE. This fits perfectly well with the information that we have looked at so far from Ctesias, Herodotus and Josephus.

The fact that Heracles did actually live in the eighth century BCE is supported by details surrounding his contemporaries. For example, one of his associates was Jason, the leader of the famous Argonauts (in fact, Heracles himself was said to have been one of these Argonauts). One of the first things that he was said to have done upon being tasked with retrieving the Golden Fleece was speak to the Oracle of Delphi, a renowned source of wisdom in the ancient world. Yet, archaeological evidence indicates that there was no sanctuary – and thus no evidence of an oracle to visit – at Delphi before the ninth century BCE.[33] This would mean that the story of Jason could only have taken place at that time or later, perfectly in line with his contemporary Heracles being the founder of the Olympic Games in 776 BCE. And it is important to note that the Oracle of Delphi appears in several other Greek tales based around this time. For example, the Greek king Agamemnon was said to have visited her before setting off to attack Troy. Both Oedipus and his father, likewise, were separately said to have consulted the Oracle, yet they lived several generations before the Trojan War.

We arrive at the same conclusion when considering Theseus. One of the most fundamental points about the legend of Theseus is that he was the one who united Attica under the rule of Athens. This is referred to as the synoecism of Attica. Yet from a historical point of view, it is acknowledged that this unification actually occurred at about the end of the eighth century BCE.[34] And when was Theseus supposed to have lived? Well, his son Demophon was the king of Athens during the Trojan War. Therefore, Theseus lived just before the Trojan War. Since the unification of Attica is historically held to have occurred at the end of the eighth century BCE, yet Theseus was the one who was said to have done this, then that places the Trojan War right at the end of the eighth century BCE or the very beginning of the seventh.

Genealogies of individuals from the ancient period provide additional evidence for this late date. For example, the last king of Macedon descended from Alexander the Great's general Antigonus was a king known as Perseus of Macedon. According to Livy, a Roman historian of the first century BCE, there were twenty kings between Caranus – the legendary first king of Macedon – and this Perseus.[35] Perseus of Macedon was born in *c.* 212 BCE. If we assume an average of twenty to twenty-five years per king, then Caranus must have been born between 612 and 712 BCE.

However, the situation with the dynasty of Macedon is more complicated than this. In the earliest account of the founding of Macedon, which is found in the writings of Herodotus, the founder of the dynasty is definitely said to be Perdiccas I.[36] Thucydides also agrees with this, by stating that Perdiccas II was the eighth king of Macedon, and other lists agree that Perdiccas II was eighth in line from Perdiccas I.[37] But in later records, Caranus is introduced as the founding figure, first as the father of Perdiccas I and then as his great-grandfather in even later records. Perhaps some might attempt to explain this away by suggesting that Caranus was the true founder but that Perdiccas was considered the founder in some traditions because he may, for example, have consolidated his family's power in the area. This potential explanation is refuted by the fact that Herodotus' account of Perdiccas explicitly presents him as coming from Argos to Macedon with his brothers and founding the dynasty there. He does not present his family as already being in Macedon, as would have been the case if Caranus really existed and founded the dynasty.

For that reason, scholars generally believe that Caranus was a fictional character inserted further back in the genealogical records of the kings of Macedon for political reasons.[38] The two figures separating Caranus from Perdiccas I in later records are likewise fictional figures. It is clear that Perdiccas was originally held to be the founder of Macedon, being the one who migrated to that territory from Argos.

With this in mind, when did Perdiccas I live? This is not too difficult to answer, since there is a firm chronological anchor point just five generations later. His descendant King Amyntas I became a vassal of the Persian king Darius I in *c.* 512 BCE. The start of his reign is commonly given as 547 BCE, which is not inconsistent with the date in which he became a vassal of Darius. Assuming that he was about twenty-five years old when he became king would place his birth in *c.* 572 BCE. Counting back five generations to the birth of Perdiccas I takes us to *c.* 672–697 BCE. This is quite close to the estimate of 612–712 BCE for Caranus' birth when counting back from Perseus of Macedon.

How was Perdiccas related to the characters of Greek legend? In Herodotus' account of the founding of Macedon, he connects Perdiccas and his two brothers with Temenus, the great-great-grandson of Heracles, explicitly calling them 'sons of Temenus'.[39] Supporting the fact that Perdiccas was the son of Temenus is the fact that another early version of the story – the fifth-century BCE play *Archelaus* by Euripides – explicitly presents the founder of Macedon as the son of Temenus, although the name of the founder was changed into Archelaus, obviously to honour Archelaus I, the reigning king of Macedon at the time the account was written. Additional supporting evidence is seen from the fact that a historian of the first century BCE, Pompeius Trogus, explicitly placed Perdiccas at about the time of the Trojan War, which would only make chronological sense if he was the direct son of Temenus, given that Temenus lived a few generations after Heracles.[40]

Therefore, the fact that Perdiccas was the son of Temenus means that he was the great-great-great-grandson of Heracles. If Perdiccas was born in *c.* 672–697 BCE, then that would place Heracles' birth in *c.* 772–822 BCE. This fits well with the other information we have looked at so far.

Now consider evidence from the ancestry of the famous Greek scientist Pythagoras. He is believed to have been born around the year 570 BCE. According to Pausanias, he was the great-grandson of a man named Hippasus.[41] This Hippasus, according to Pausanias, opposed a Dorian man named Rhegnidas. Rhegnidas, in turn, was said to have been the great-great-great-great-grandson of Heracles. This means that Rhegnidas came six generations after Heracles. And, as we have just noted, he was the contemporary of Hippasus, the great-grandfather of Pythagoras. Because it is not possible to know the exact age difference between Hippasus and Rhegnidas, let us assume that they were essentially the same age. If Pythagoras was born in *c.* 570 BCE, then using an average of twenty to twenty-five years per generation, his great-grandfather Hippasus should have been born between 630 and 645 BCE.

Now recall that Hippasus was a contemporary of Rhegnidas, the great-great-great-great-grandson of Heracles. If we assume that Rhegnidas was born at more or less the same time as his contemporary enemy Hippasus, then counting back six generations from 630–645 BCE takes us to 750–795 BCE for the birth of Heracles. As we can see here, the ancestry of Pythagoras clearly points towards an early eighth-century BCE birth for Heracles, which fits in very well with the estimate derived from the number of generations between Heracles and Perseus of Macedon, as well as the one derived from the number of generations between Heracles and Perdiccas I.

Another example of a genealogical record which supports this dating is one that was found on the island of Chios, near Turkey. It dates to the fifth century BCE, though the exact year in which it was composed is unknown. It lists the genealogy of a certain Heropythos of Chios, going back fourteen generations to the founding of the island.[42] The Greek settlement on the island was supposed to have been founded by a figure known as Oenopion, the brother of two of the Argonauts.[43] If we count back fourteen generations from the fifth century BCE, we should be able to ascertain when Oenopion – and thus the Argonauts, along with Jason and Heracles – lived. Once again assuming twenty to twenty-five years per generation, fourteen generations from *c*. 450 BCE takes us to 730–800 BCE. This perfectly matches the aforementioned genealogies and other pieces of information which indicate that Heracles, Jason and their companions lived in the first half of the eighth century BCE.

Notable also is the example of Pheidon, the tyrant of Argos. He is interesting to historians because there is considerable debate as to when he lived. The earliest chronological references to him, which come from Herodotus, definitely place him in the sixth century BCE. Some modern scholars accept this as the most likely date.[44] However, later records place him earlier than that, in the early seventh century BCE. It is quite possible that there were two Pheidons, explaining these chronological discrepancies.

Yet importantly, the information provided by Herodotus definitely makes the Pheidon of the sixth century BCE the father of a man named Leocedes, or Lacedas.[45] This Lacedas was one of the suitors of Agariste of Sicyon, a mid-sixth-century BCE noblewoman. Significantly, Pausanias mentions a son of Lacedas named Meltas, whom he says is the tenth in descent from Medon of Argos.[46] From other records, we know that this Medon was the grandson of Temenus, the great-great-grandson of Heracles mentioned earlier.[47] Although Pausanias calls Meltas the tenth in descent from Medon, he was actually the tenth *king* from Medon. In terms of descent, the available records show that he was not a descendant of Medon at all. Rather, he was a descendant of Temenus through a different grandson. Here is the line of descent to Pheidon as recorded by Diodorus Siculus:

Temenus→Cissius→Thestius→Merops→Aristodamus→Pheidon[48]

And then when we include the information from Herodotus and Pausanias, we can complete this genealogical record by adding Pheidon's son Lacedas and his grandson Meltas.

What is the significance of this? Since Lacedas was definitely a mid-sixth-century BCE figure, we can count back the generations to get to Temenus, the great-great-grandson of Heracles. If we suppose that Lacedas was born in *c.* 580 BCE, which is reasonable given that he was a suitor of Agariste of Sicyon, then counting back six generations to get to Temenus' birth takes us to 700–730 BCE. This is broadly consistent with the estimated range of 670–695 BCE derived from the information about Pythagoras' ancestors, and it is especially consistent with our estimate for the birth of Perdiccas I, the son of Temenus, in 672–697 BCE. This, in turn, is consistent with placing Heracles' birth at the beginning of the eighth century BCE.

Pausanias explicitly makes Pyrrhus, the famous king of Epirus who fought a war against the Romans, a twentieth-generation descendant of Achilles. Pyrrhus was born in 319 BCE. Allowing for twenty to twenty-five years per generation would place Achilles' birth between 819 and 719 BCE. The lower end of this is consistent with the other genealogies thus far considered, placing the Trojan War towards the end of the eighth century BCE.

Some available genealogies indicate a slightly earlier date for these characters but still indicate that they lived far later than commonly believed. For example, the genealogy of a rich Athenian family known as the Philaids goes back thirteen generations from a man named Miltiades, who was born in the early sixth century BCE, to Ajax, one of the warriors who fought in the Trojan War. This would indicate a date of somewhere in the ninth century BCE for the Trojan War. This does not match the estimate we have made from the other genealogies, but it fits the general timeframe in contrast to the tradition of *c.* 1200 BCE, and it is possible that the genealogy has been accidentally expanded by, perhaps, some brothers being listed as father and son.

On the other hand, there are some records that indicate an even later date for the Trojan War. For example, the city of Byzantium was said to have been founded by a man named Byzas. According to the earliest known writer to mention Byzas, Diodorus Siculus, he was a contemporary of the Argonauts.[49] Recall that the Argonauts were active some fifty years or so before the Trojan War. Thus, Byzas is supposed to have reigned before the time of the Trojan War by roughly half a century. Yet with that in mind, it is significant to note that Byzas was alleged to have founded Byzantium in *c.* 658 BCE.[50] This would mean that the Trojan War should have occurred roughly half a century later, near the end of the seventh century BCE.

The True Date of the Trojan War

So although there are some genealogies that point to a ninth century BCE date for the Trojan War, there are other records, such as this one, which point to a date much later than that. Therefore, the genealogies which place the war in *c.* 700 BCE represent a reasonable middle ground, and they are backed up by specific chronological references in the legends, such as Heracles being the one who founded the Olympic Games and Cadmus introducing the Phoenician alphabet to Greece long before the Trojan War.

Additionally, although they are very late sources, it is interesting to consider the fact that a number of British and Norse genealogies also point to the conclusion that the Trojan War happened in the early Archaic era rather than the Mycenaean era. We will examine this point in greater detail in a later chapter, but for now, suffice it to say that Geoffrey of Monmouth's list of the kings of Britain from Brutus to the first century BCE appears to include many additional kings taken from later eras. However, there are a number of different British genealogies which provide far fewer names. For example, the text known as *Hanes Gruffydd ap Cynan* provides just twenty-three kings between Aeneas, a prince of Troy at the time of the Trojan War, and Beli ap Manogan. The dating of this Beli is somewhat difficult to ascertain with certainty, but he is probably to be identified with Beli the legendary father of Caswallon, the Cassivellaunus who battled Julius Caesar in 54 BCE. This would place Beli in 100 BCE at least.

This being so, the twenty-three kings between Beli and Aeneas would place Aeneas' birth somewhere between *c.* 580 BCE at the latest to *c.* 700 BCE at the earliest, using twenty to twenty-five years per generation. In the *HB*, there is a record of another version of the descent from Aeneas to Brutus, which adds several more generations, so this genealogy could potentially go back just a little further. But the point is, it definitely supports this revised date for the Trojan War, while it is completely unworkable with the *c.* 1200 BCE date of the Trojan War. Additional British genealogies exist which are essentially the same as the one just discussed, to within a few generations.

We achieve essentially the same result when we look at the legendary descent of the kings of the Norse. Like the British, they claimed descent from the Trojans. In the *Prose Edda*, a famous collection of Norse mythology compiled in the thirteenth century CE, Odin and the other Norse gods are portrayed as real people who were descended from King Priam of Troy. The line of descent from Priam to Odin is given, and then Odin is described as travelling with his people from Anatolia to Scandinavia. The *Prose Edda* provides us with eighteen names from Tróán, daughter of Priam, to Odin. So, what is now important to establish is when Odin is supposed to have lived in this tale. It is generally believed that the story of Odin fleeing his home around the Black Sea region due to Roman military forces driving him out is tied to the historical Roman conquest of much of western Asia. This occurred in the first century BCE. In fact, the *Prose Edda* confirms this timing by stating that Odin's son Skjold succeeded his father in the time when Augustus 'secured peace throughout the whole world. That was when Christ was born.' Augustus became the emperor of Rome in 27 BCE, so these events are definitely set in the first century BCE. Odin's birth was likely near the beginning of that century.

Therefore, if we count eighteen generations back from 100 BCE, we should arrive at the birth of Priam's daughter Tróán. Using our normal twenty to twenty-five years per generation, this only takes us back to 460–550 BCE. In truth, it appears that the normal generation lengths of the Norse kings were longer than other dynasties. This is indicated by analyses of the generations counting backwards to Odin from Halfdan the Black, a person of known date from the ninth century CE. Using 27.5 years per generation, as indicated by this analysis back from Halfdan to Odin, for the eighteen generations from Priam's daughter to Odin would take us back to 595 BCE. This is still too early for our estimate for the Trojan War. To get us back to the late 700s BCE, each generation from Priam's daughter to Odin would have to be thirty-four years in length. This is decidedly lengthy, but not impossible. It is also possible that a handful of names have been accidentally omitted simply due to the passage of time before this list was committed to writing. In any case, we can see from this legendary source that the alleged genealogy of the Norse kings from Priam is only sufficient to go back to our estimate for the Trojan War, while it is completely incompatible with the traditional date of *c.* 1200 BCE.

In summary, what we can see so far is that despite the fact that certain ancient sources claimed that the Trojan War took place around 1200 BCE, the majority of the details and available genealogies indicate that it must have actually occurred closer to about 700 BCE, given the evident timing of other characters, events and features that surround the war.

Evidence from the Legends of Troy
Now, consider some additional evidence from details that are specific to the story of the Trojan War itself. Herodotus records a legend that Helen of Troy and her lover, Paris Alexander, visited the Egyptian city

The True Date of the Trojan War

of Heracleion before they arrived at Troy, having been blown off course during their journey from Greece. Yet, Heracleion was not founded until the eighth century BCE, which would mean that this event mentioned by Herodotus could not have taken place before that century at the earliest.[51] The same phenomenon is to be noted regarding a number of other settlements and nations that are mentioned in Homer's *Iliad* and other accounts of the Trojan War. Consider some more examples.

Tyndareus, the father of Helen, was said to have been the king of Sparta. Yet there is no archaeological evidence that Sparta existed prior to *c*. 950 BCE.[52] And its rise to prominence is generally dated by modern historians to the late eighth century BCE.[53] Yet Tyndareus in the legends is said to have been one of the most powerful kings of his day. This only matches the period around the late eighth century BCE at the very earliest.

The sister of King Priam of Troy was a woman named Aethilla. She was said to have been captured by the Greeks after the fall of Troy and taken away with many other captives from the city. When the Greeks stopped off at the peninsula of Pallene, Aethilla and her companions burned the Greek ships, escaping from their captives, and founded there the city of Scione.[54] Thus, according to this legend, the city of Scione should have been founded around the time of the Trojan War. Yet, the evidence is clear that the city of Scione was founded in *c*. 700 BCE.[55] This suggests, of course, that the fall of Troy occurred around that year, as the rest of the evidence that we have thus far considered also indicates. Similarly, the city of Metapontum in Italy was said to have been founded by a Greek king named Nestor on the way back from the Trojan War.[56] Yet, it is widely agreed that this city was actually founded in *c*. 700 BCE, just like Scione.[57]

The city of Naples in Italy also has an origin story connected to the Trojan War. Its founding was said to have been related to the voyage of Odysseus on his journey back from Troy. He was said to have broken the heart of a siren named Parthenope, whose dead body then washed ashore. A city was then founded on that site, taking its name from the siren.[58] Another account attributes the founding of Neapolis (ancient Naples) to one of the Argonauts, which would push its founding back by roughly half a century.[59] In fact, these may represent distinct foundings, given that Neapolis and Parthenope were actually distinct settlements, despite being closely connected.[60] Significantly, archaeology has shown that Neapolis was founded in the eighth century BCE, while Parthenope was founded in the seventh century BCE.[61] This conforms perfectly to a mid-eighth-century BCE date for the Argonauts and a late eighth- or early seventh-century BCE date for the Trojan War.

Perhaps the city whose founding has the most famous connection to the Trojan War is Carthage. In a well-known legend recorded by the Roman writer Virgil, Carthage was said to have been founded in the time of Aeneas, the Trojan prince, in the aftermath of the Trojan War. Aeneas was said to have met Dido, the famous Phoenician princess who, according to legend, was the founder of the city of Carthage. It has long been noted that the dates for the Trojan War do not tie in at all with the founding of Carthage. The most popular date for the founding of that city is 814 BCE. However, the reality is that the ancient sources provide us with a variety of different estimates as to the founding of the city. Many of these ancient sources agree with the popular 814 BCE date to within one or two decades. However, many others indicate a time in the middle of the eighth century BCE. For example, the Roman historian Cicero states that Carthage was founded 600 years before its destruction, which would indicate a date of 746 BCE. Several other sources, such as Marcus Porcius Cato, Lucius Cincius and Quintius Fabius agree with a mid-eighth-century BCE foundation for the city. Therefore, the date of 814 BCE certainly cannot be viewed as definitive.

In reality, though, a plausible explanation for the discrepancy between the dates given by these various sources is that different writers referred to different traditions regarding what constituted the 'founding' of the city. For example, it is often said by modern sources that there is no archaeological evidence at all for a settlement at Carthage prior to the middle of the eighth century BCE at the very earliest.[62] This would tie in with the aforementioned ancient sources which place the city's foundation in that very time period. However, one modern source notes that although 'Greek Geometric pottery, which was found at Carthage, indicates the city's founding is no earlier than 760 B.C.E., some radiocarbon dates based on bovid bones were slightly older than 800 BCE', thus lending a small degree of support to the popular 814 BCE date.[63] In addition, Princess Dido herself, as the sister of King Pygmalion of Tyre, definitely belongs to the ninth century BCE, not the eighth century. But even if a settlement was established there in the late ninth century BCE, it was clearly not significant and evidently was not built up until the middle of the eighth century BCE at the earliest, as shown by the archaeology. Thus, some traditions may have viewed the 'founding' of Carthage to have been the time in which it was built up and fortified, which evidently was in about 750 BCE, while other traditions considered the founding to have been when Dido first arrived and established a small settlement there. This appears to be the most elegant solution to the discrepancy between the dates provided by the ancient sources, as well as the discrepancy between some of these dates and the archaeological data.

But even so, 750 BCE is not 700 BCE. So how does this evidence tie in with our revised date of *c.* 700 BCE for the Trojan War? Well, although the most famous connection between the founding of Carthage and the Trojan War places the founding of the Phoenician city in the years just after the war, with Aeneas as a contemporary of Dido, this is merely the most famous version of the story to modern readers. It is not at all the earliest account. Virgil wrote his *Aeneid* in the latter part of the first century BCE. It is noteworthy that the legend of Dido was already well known by the time of Virgil, and the previous versions of the legend do not make any mention of Aeneas, thus making it likely that the connection between Dido and Aeneas is an invention on the part of Virgil.

Significantly, other connections between the founding of Carthage and the Trojan War do not make them exactly contemporaneous, but make Carthage slightly older. For example, a very early source, Philistus of Syracuse of the early fourth century BCE, places the founding of Carthage several decades before the fall of Troy. This is supported by Eudoxus of Cnidus, another Greek historian from the same century.[64] A different, later source – Appian of the second century CE – specifies that Carthage was founded 'fifty years before the capture of Troy'.[65] The fact that this has earlier support than Virgil's version, combined with the total absence of Aeneas in earlier accounts of the legend of Dido, indicates that the founding of Carthage did actually predate the fall of Troy by about half a century, rather than post-dating it by a few years as in Virgil's *Aeneid*.

This being the case, the archaeologically established date of *c.* 750 BCE for the founding of Carthage would indicate that the Trojan War must have occurred near the end of the eighth century BCE, probably around *c.* 700 BCE in particular. This is in harmony with all the other evidence thus far considered.

It is also enlightening to see where the ancient Greek writers placed the Trojan War in their histories. Strabo, for instance, seems to place it just before the rise of the Cimmerians in western Anatolia. He describes the history of that area around the time of the Trojan War, and then he states the following:

> After the Trojan War the migrations of the Greeks and the Trerans, and the onsets of the Cimmerians and of the Lydians, and, after this,

of the Persians and the Macedonians, and, at last, of the Galatians, disturbed and confused everything.⁶⁶

According to this, the Trojan War was followed by 'the migrations of the Greeks and the Trerans, and the onsets of the Cimmerians and of the Lydians'. The fact that Strabo specifically states 'after this' before going on to mention the Persians, as well as stating 'at last' before mentioning the Galatians, indicates that all the ones he mentioned before the Persians evidently occurred at roughly the same time, without large gaps of centuries between them. The rise of the Cimmerians and the Lydians in that region occurred in the first half of the seventh century BCE. The 'Trerans' are an obscure people, but according to Strabo himself they were either another name for the Cimmerians or were a Cimmerian tribe. So his reference to the arrival of the Trerans presumably refers to the Cimmerian raids in that region right at the start of the seventh century BCE, with 'the onset of the Cimmerians' referring more to their subsequent rise to power, with the height of their power having been in about 652 BCE. Regarding the Greeks, archaeology has demonstrated a surge of Greek migrations to western Anatolia in about 700 BCE.⁶⁷ Therefore, it is significant that Strabo places the Greek migrations, the Cimmerian raids and their rise to power, and the rise of the Lydians apparently immediately after the Trojan War.

Similarly, the historian Thucydides could relate almost no history at all between the Trojan War and the history of the seventh and sixth centuries BCE. He spoke about the Trojan War and then described a few migrations that supposedly occurred within the following century. And then, in the space of a few lines with no indication whatsoever of the passing of centuries of history, Thucydides refers to Ameinocles the Corinthian visiting Samos 'nearly three hundred years' before the end of the Peloponnesian War, which ended in 404 BCE.⁶⁸ This places Ameinocles' visit to Samos around the start of the seventh century BCE. So regardless of what Thucydides believed about the date of the Trojan War, he knew of almost no history at all to speak of between that war and events of the seventh century BCE.

Although it is true that Thucydides does explicitly place about a century of events between the Trojan War and Ameinocles' expedition to Samos near the start of the seventh century BCE, there is good reason for thinking that this has been exaggerated due to the same reasons that the date of the Trojan War itself was exaggerated. Thucydides states that the 'Dorians and the Heraclids became masters of the Peloponnese' eighty years after the Trojan War. Other records

The True Date of the Trojan War

claim that it was Temenus in particular who led the Dorians to supremacy during the event known as the Return of the Heracleidae. Temenus was supposedly the great-great-grandson of Heracles. As we established previously, the information about Heracles sacking Troy when Priam was a child indicates that Heracles was born at least eighty or ninety years before the Trojan War.

Counting forwards four generations from Heracles to Temenus takes us to between eighty and 100 years later. In other words, Temenus must have been born around the time of the Trojan War or shortly afterwards. This means that the rise of the Heraclids that Thucydides refers to, which was led by Temenus, could have occurred as soon as twenty-five or thirty years after the fall of Troy. This is supported by the fact that the king defeated by Temenus was supposedly Tisamenus, grandson of Agamemnon. The descent went through Agamemnon's son Orestes, who was already an adult and betrothed at the time of the Trojan War. This would mean that, like Temenus, Tisamenus would likely have been born around the time of the fall of Troy, supporting the conclusion that the rise of the Heraclids (when Tisamenus was overthrown) likely occurred just twenty-five or thirty years afterwards. Thucydides' claim that it was eighty years later is surely based on calculations using excessive generation lengths.

In summary, then, although Thucydides places a little more than eighty years of history between the Trojan War and Ameinocles' expedition to Samos, the reality would seem to be that this should be reduced to just approximately three decades at the most. The exact date of the latter event is not known, with Thucydides simply saying that it occurred nearly 300 years before the end of the Peloponnesian War, which would take us to 704 BCE. His very next sentence states that 'the earliest sea-fight in history was between the Corinthians and Corcyraeans; this was about two hundred and sixty years ago, dating from the same time'. The fact that he dates this to 'the same time' as the aforementioned event, Ameinocles' trip to Samos, indicates that his reference to 'nearly three hundred years' may actually be about 260 years. This means that Ameinocles' trip to Samos could have occurred closer to 664 BCE rather than 704 BCE. In any case, Thucydides' temporal references are explicitly approximate. The point is that the paucity of history that Thucydides was able to place between the Trojan War and Ameinocles' voyage supports a date of *c.* 700 BCE for the Trojan War, just like we see in Strabo's writings.

Evidence from Homer's Writings

Homer provides us with a very long list of participants in the war, both on the Greek side and the Trojan side. He also refers to the cities that these participants ruled. The Greek version is known as the Catalogue of Ships, whereas the Trojan version is called the Trojan Battle Order. One of the cities that Homer mentions in the Catalogue of Ships is Corinth. This city was uninhabited during the Mycenaean era (1600–1200 BCE), only being founded in the second half of the tenth century BCE.[69] Therefore, its appearance in this list in the *Iliad* has to be dismissed as a mistake if one holds that the Trojan War happened in *c.* 1200 BCE, whereas it can be accepted without any issues if the war took place in *c.* 700 BCE.

Another example of this is the city of Argura. On the basis of ancient descriptions of its location, this is commonly identified with an archaeological site known as Gremnos Magoula, in Greece. Aside from some evidence of occupation in Neolithic times, it appears that the earliest artefacts discovered at this site date from the Geometric period of Greek history, which lasted from about 900 BCE to 700 BCE.[70] Therefore, the evidence indicates that the city of Argura was founded no earlier than that period, which would require the Trojan War to have occurred no earlier than this. In like manner, the city of Gyrton, mentioned in Homer's Catalogue of Ships, appears to have been built no earlier than the Archaic period, which began in the eighth century BCE.[71] This particularly ties in with the fact that its founder was said to have been Phalerus, one of the Argonauts, just two generations or so before the Trojan War.[72]

To be sure, scholars have not missed the fact that there are many settlements mentioned in the Catalogue of Ships which did not exist until hundreds of years after the traditional date of the Trojan War. One modern historian, Catherine Morgan, expressed her agreement with 'recent commentators in believing that the *Catalogue* in general describes an Early Iron Age/early Archaic, rather than a Bronze Age, state of affairs'.[73] In line with this, John Kinloch Anderson, a professor of Classics and Ancient History, proposed that the Catalogue of Ships was the work of a poet of the late eighth century BCE.[74] Similarly, Jonas Grethlein, a professor at the University of Heidelberg, wrote that 'there are strong correspondences between the Catalogue of Ships and Greece of the seventh century'.[75] Therefore, there is general agreement among scholars that the Catalogue of Ships points towards a date in the late eighth century or early seventh century BCE – the early Archaic period, not the Mycenaean period.

The True Date of the Trojan War

Nonetheless, this is normally dismissed as simply being due to Homer's *Iliad* being composed hundreds of years after the events in question. While this is a tempting excuse, it is perhaps preferable to accept the evidence as it is and see where it leads us. In this case, the description of the world in the *Iliad* leads us to a date of about 700 BCE for the setting of this story about the fall of Troy. It is valuable to consider just how extensive the evidence is for Homer's world in general – beyond simply the Catalogue of Ships – matching the period around 700 BCE.

Historian Irene de Jong, in Volume II of *Homer: Critical Assessments*, states that 'all recent studies agree' that the geography found in Homer 'largely mirrors the landscapes and settlements of the late eighth or seventh century, despite earlier attempts to show that it corresponds to the geography of Mycenaean Greece'.[76] For instance, the *Odyssey*, Homer's second most famous work after the *Iliad*, set just after the Trojan War, refers to the Sicilians as trading partners of the Greeks. Jong argues that this description only fits the period after the first Greek settlement on Sicily, which was in about 735 BCE. In addition, both of Homer's works suggest that the region of Messenia was within Spartan territory, which was only the case after about 725 BCE. She also highlights the fact that one of the characters refers to the temple of Apollo at Delphi when referring to amazingly wealthy places. As we have already mentioned, there is no evidence for any sanctuary at Delphi prior to the ninth century BCE.

There is one piece of evidence concerning the geography of Homer's *Iliad* which is often highlighted when arguing that the Trojan War must have occurred in the Mycenaean era. This is the fact that Agamemnon, the leader of the Greek forces against Troy, is described as the king of Mycenae. He is not shown to be the king of all Greece, but he is nonetheless shown to be the most powerful king of that nation. Yet, the only time in which Mycenae was the most powerful city in all of Greece was in the Mycenaean era – hence the name of the era. This might appear convincing at first, but remember that all the other evidence concerning the geography of Homer's description best fits the early Archaic period, as we have just seen. When this issue of Mycenae's prominence is investigated further, the case falls apart.

Firstly, let it be noted that the city of Mycenae most certainly still existed in 700 BCE, so there is no reason why an Agamemnon of the late eighth century BCE could not have been the king of that city. It was not as mighty nor as powerful as it had been in the Mycenaean era, but it was certainly still in existence, and its famously grand walls

The Trojan Kings of Britain

were still standing. In fact, archaeology has revealed that restoration work was done on its walls in the eighth century BCE.[77] So the reference in the *Iliad* to Mycenae as a 'great citadel' is not out of place.

Secondly, Professor Jonas Grethlein wrote that 'the borders of Mycenae ... that we can reconstruct on the basis of Linear B tablets do not correspond to the descriptions in Homer'.[78] This supports the idea that it is not the Mycenae of the Bronze Age, the Mycenaean era, that features in the *Iliad*.

Thirdly, while attention has been focused on Mycenae as the domain of Agamemnon due to the belief that the Trojan War took place in the Mycenaean era, the reality is that Mycenae is actually almost never mentioned in the *Iliad*. There are only a handful of references to it, and fewer still of it being Agamemnon's domain. In reality, the *Iliad* refers to Agamemnon's domain far more frequently as 'Argos'. In *Book I*, the king himself even refers to Argos as 'my home'. In another place, in *Book II*, Agamemnon is described as the 'lord of Argos and many isles'. He is described as sailing from Argos. In several places in *Book IX*, Agamemnon refers to returning not to Mycenae but to Argos.

It is important to note that the cities of Argos and Mycenae are right next to each other. When Argos was powerful, it had control over a large region, encompassing Mycenae and many other parts of the surrounding territory. So although Agamemnon is described as the king of Mycenae, evidently meaning the city itself (perhaps because that is where his family was based), his domain is the kingdom of Argos, which, at the time, took in not just the city of Mycenae but probably the entirety of the Argolis and, according to the *Iliad*, some islands as well. Now, if the city of Mycenae was truly the dominant force of the time and the genuine centre of Agamemnon's kingdom, why would the name of the kingdom be 'Argos' rather than 'Mycenae'? The fact that Agamemnon's kingdom is never referred to as 'Mycenae' but only as 'Argos' would suggest that it was actually an Argive kingdom, though Agamemnon apparently chose the city of Mycenae as his residence.

Other records tell us that a certain Diomedes was the king of Argos at the time of the Trojan War. This is evidently in the sense that he was the king of the city itself, similar to a local governor, while Agamemnon was evidently the high king of the entire city-state of Argos and all the territory that it controlled, hence why he is referred to as the 'lord of Argos and many isles' in the *Iliad*.

So, when in history did Argos become especially powerful? Scholars agree, largely on the basis of archaeology, that Argos became a powerful kingdom in the eighth century BCE.[79] However, this period of Argive dominance did not last long. As the *Encyclopaedia Britannica* states, 'Árgos was the dominant city-state in all the Peloponnese until the rise of Spartan power.'[80] As stated earlier, Sparta started becoming prominent in the late eighth or early seventh century BCE. Thus, the period in which Argos was the most powerful Greek kingdom was fairly brief, covering the latter half of the eighth century BCE through to the early part of the seventh. In fact, it appears that the period immediately either side of *c.* 700 BCE is the only era in Greek history in which Argos was the dominant power in Greece but Sparta was also a comparably powerful city-state. As we have seen, this is exactly what we find in the legend of the Trojan War, with Agamemnon the king of Argos being the supreme king of the Greeks, but Tyndareus the king of Sparta also being described as one of the most powerful kings of his day.

The material culture described in the *Iliad* also predominantly fits the same time period, the late eighth or early seventh century BCE. For example, the type of common house described, with a central hall with a pitched roof, is consistent with this time period, although it is also found in the Dark Ages. Decorations and clothing also match this era, though they were not specific to it. What was specific to this early Archaic period was the presence of 'older forms of dress and housing coexisting with newer forms of armour and communal architecture, and it is this state of affairs that we find predominantly reflected in the epics', as Irene de Jong explains.

There is a grand total of two pieces of material culture in the *Iliad* which appear to fit the Mycenaean period better than any other. One is a type of helmet which was made from boar tusks, and the other is a special golden cup with bird ornaments on the handles. Both of these uniquely fit artefacts from the Mycenaean period. Is this evidence, then, that the Trojan War really took place at the traditional time of *c.* 1200 BCE, and that these descriptions are a remembrance of the material culture from that time? This has, at times, been claimed, but there are serious problems with this conclusion. Firstly, the artefacts that these two items match do not appear to have been used after *c.* 1400 BCE, about two centuries prior to the traditional date of the Trojan War; there is certainly no evidence that the war occurred *that* early.

Secondly, these two items are described in the *Iliad* in excessive detail, which is illogical if they were common in the time period in which the events took place. The very fact that they are described in such detail is evidence that they were not common to the time period in which the characters actually lived. As Irene de Jong suggests, it may well be that Homer was simply inspired to include some remarkable items in his poem based on recent discoveries from Mycenaean graves or paintings, the ancient Greeks having no way at all of knowing which era these graves and items were from.[81] Nonetheless, by far the majority of material culture is consistent with and at times even requires a late-eighth or early-seventh century BCE date.

Another category of evidence which supports an early Archaic period date for the Trojan War is the description of warfare found in the *Iliad*. The modes of battle, along with styles of armour, used by the Greeks varied throughout history. Because the battle descriptions in the *Iliad* are rather detailed, we can see which period best fits the modes of battle and armour styles that Homer appears to have been describing. Historian Hans van Wees has noted that Homer's warfare descriptions match the warfare of Homer's own day, the early Archaic period, and not the earlier Mycenaean period. In fact, he believes that it can be pinpointed to the era between 700–650 BCE in particular. The following is a summary of some of this evidence.

After 650 BCE, the Greeks regularly used the phalanx mode of combat, in which the soldiers formed an organised, tight body of combatants rather than all the men spreading out over the battlefield. This phalanx formation is not how the Greek armies are described in the *Iliad*, so it appears that the battle descriptions do not fit the post-650 BCE era.

On the other hand, vase paintings from the Geometric period of Greek art, from 900 to 700 BCE, are not consistent with the *Iliad* in terms of which weapons were most common. In Homer's account, the spear is by far the most common weapon mentioned. Yet in the Geometric vase paintings, bows and arrows are shown as being used far more than spears. And swords are shown as being the most commonly used weapon, yet they are the least commonly used weapon in Homer's description of the Trojan War. In contrast, vase paintings from just after the end of the Geometric period, in *c.* 700 BCE, do depict the different types of weapons with almost exactly the same level of frequency as Homer mentions them. Spears are by far the most common type of weapon shown, while swords are almost never shown, in complete contrast to the preceding era of Greek art but in perfect correspondence to Homer's writings. This indicates that the *Iliad*'s battle scenes belong to the period from *c.* 700 BCE at the earliest, but before *c.* 650 BCE, on the basis of the complete absence of anything resembling the phalanx formation.[82]

Regarding the armour used by the Greek troops, Homer's descriptions appear to match the style of armour used by the Greek hoplite soldiers.[83] This type of armour was not developed until the end of the eighth century BCE.[84] This fact has been recognised by many scholars before but has been dismissed as an anachronistic feature of the *Iliad*. Of course, this is due to the *a priori* belief that the Trojan War took place in *c*. 1200 BCE. Simply accepting the evidence as it is would lead us to the conclusion that it actually occurred no earlier than when this style of armour was first developed.

As well as the hoplite style of armour, we must also note the circular shields that the Greek soldiers are often described as carrying in the *Iliad*. In Mycenaean times, this was not the common style of shield used.[85] Rather, shields were rectangular or oblong 'figure-of-eight' shapes. It was only in the eighth century BCE that the Greeks were, as a matter of course, using large, round shields like the ones described in the *Iliad*.[86] In addition, as pointed out by historian Irene de Jong, the descriptions of narrative art (art which depicts a narrative) on the shields of the Greek soldiers would only match the shields used from the middle of the eighth century BCE onwards, when narrative art first appeared in the Greek world.[87]

A slightly more complicated issue, but one which gives the same result, concerns the belts described by Homer. He refers to the soldiers as wearing a 'zoster', which several verses in the *Iliad* indicate was a rather broad type of belt, extending up to the middle of the stomach and covered with metal. Yet the soldiers are also described as wearing a corslet, a piece of armour covering the entire upper torso down to at least the middle of the belly. Scholars have contended that it would be impossible to wear both at the same time. This may well have been true in the Mycenaean period, yet in the eighth century BCE, the Greeks developed what is known as a 'bell-corslet', which extends outward slightly at the end.[88] This would allow for a broad metal zoster to overlap slightly with the bell-corslet, allowing a soldier to wear both, as described in the *Iliad* and depicted on certain vase paintings.[89] This does not fit the Mycenaean period. In fact, there is no archaeological evidence for the existence of any broad metal belt of this sort in the Mycenaean period, and certainly not a corslet that could have accommodated one. Historian Irene de Jong concurs that the military equipment used by the characters in the *Iliad*, from the helmets on their heads to the greaves on their legs, was standard Greek military equipment in the Archaic period, but is not found before *c*. 720 BCE.[90]

Hans van Wees has further noted that Homer's descriptions of the use of spears likewise best fits a later period rather than the

Mycenaean era. In the *Iliad*, some combatants are described as using single spears, while others are shown to have been using two spears at once. Pairs of spears were not very common in the Mycenaean period, apparently only being used for hunting. They were extremely common during the Greek Dark Ages, but it is only later, just after 700 BCE, that both single spears *and* pairs of spears were common, in line with Homer's descriptions.[91] In addition, the bronze helmets worn by Homer's Greek soldiers are described as having tall crests on them. This is characteristic of the Archaic period, while there is no evidence at all that this style of helmet was used by the Greeks of the Mycenaean period or the Dark Ages.[92]

The only examples of weaponry present in the *Iliad* that might be claimed to match the Mycenaean era are the especially long spears and the bronze weapons; by the eighth century BCE, long thrusting spears were no longer in use and weapons were predominantly made of iron, not bronze. However, the heroes in Homer's works are regularly depicted as superhuman, at times throwing entire boulders with one hand. Thus, the presence of exceptionally large spears is not necessarily a reflection of the reality of the Mycenaean era and can simply be attributed to the fact that Homer would logically describe the weapons in a manner appropriate to his superhuman heroes. Similarly, regarding the presence of bronze weapons, researchers ignore the fact that Homer also describes his characters as using weapons made of gold, silver and tin, none of which fit any historical era. These are evidently nothing more than examples of artistic licence, Homer describing a more glamorous world than the real one. The bronze weapons can be assigned to this category. Notably, the tools described in the *Iliad* are made of iron, not bronze, which fits the Archaic period, not the Mycenaean period.

Thus, on the basis of these reasons and others, Hans van Wees argues convincingly that the warfare depicted in the *Iliad* definitely belongs to the period from *c.* 700 BCE to *c.* 650 BCE. This ties in perfectly with our estimated date of *c.* 700 BCE for the Trojan War (let it be noted that Hans van Wees does not believe that the Trojan War itself took place in that era, but merely that Homer was using descriptions of warfare from his own era). It is also worth noting that, in harmony with the aforementioned statement from Catherine Morgan that the Catalogue of Ships best fits the early Archaic period, Hans van Wees points out that a number of scholars have stated that the general political, social and economic structure of the world seen in the *Iliad* matches well with the eighth century BCE, although Hans van Wees himself argues that it is also compatible with the seventh century.[93] As we saw earlier, such a claim is largely corroborated by Irene de Jong, regarding the landscape and settlements portrayed in the *Iliad*.

Irene de Jong also comments specifically about the political world of the *Iliad*, noting that it is consistent with the politics of 'early Greece', in contrast to the earlier Mycenaean era.[94] It is interesting to note that even in certain very specific details, Homer's tale matches the reality of the late eighth or early seventh century BCE. For example, Athens is said to have raised fifty ships for the Trojan War, and that is exactly the number of ships that it is attested as being able to deploy in the seventh century BCE. The general political scene of decisions being made by largely informal public gatherings, though with aristocrats in leading positions who occasionally took the decision-making process to private meetings, exactly matches the general practice in the late eighth century BCE.[95]

A less subtle example of the politics of the *Iliad* matching the eighth century is the fact that the story presents the Phrygians as possessing a prosperous kingdom in Anatolia, yet the Phrygian kingdom did not emerge until some point during the eighth century BCE.[96] Thus, the presence of the Phrygian kingdom in this story and other Greek legends based around the same time shows that these stories cannot be based any earlier than the eighth century BCE, when the Phrygian kingdom first emerged. In fact, even without a kingdom, the Phrygians as a people did not even arrive in Anatolia until after the traditional date of the Trojan War.[97] And the Cimmerians appear in the *Odyssey*, yet they do not appear in the historical record until almost the end of the eighth century BCE.[98]

In contrast, the mighty Hittite Empire, which controlled most of Anatolia during the traditional Trojan War era, is never mentioned in any record about the Trojan War. On the other hand, Ctesias' account of the Trojan War claims that Priam of Troy was a vassal king of the Assyrians, and that the Assyrians assisted the Trojans during their war with the Greeks.[99] This claim is also found in the writings of Plato, of the late fifth, early fourth century BCE.[100] The Assyrians never had any contact at all with Anatolia until the time of the Neo-Assyrian Empire, which began in the ninth century BCE and ended in the seventh. Thus, this information about the Trojan War once again supports our revised date, and does not work at all with the traditional date.

One notable difference is that the communities in the Homeric tales tend to be ruled by kings rather than elected, fixed-term magistrates, whereas it appears that the monarchies in most parts of Greece had been replaced by aristocrats by the end of the eighth century BCE. However, Irene de Jong argues that the actual description of the kings in the tales, with their notably unstable positions of power and an evident desire to do whatever necessary to maintain them, fits well with the positions of power that the aristocrats of the late eighth and seventh centuries BCE often carved out for themselves.[101] In fact, there are examples of figures from the middle of the seventh century BCE setting themselves up as hereditary rulers as opposed to simple magistrates. It may, therefore, be that the leaders of communities in the Homeric tales are portrayed as hereditary monarchs, or dynastic kings, partially due to artistic licence. And, of course, it should be remembered that it is not the case that elected magistrates had replaced the monarchies in *all* areas of Greece by the end of the eighth century BCE.

The existence of artistic licence in the tales is evident by the description of all the different regions of Greece being united under the leadership of one ruler, Agamemnon, and the reference to the Greeks forming the united 'Panakhaians'. This does not match the reality in any period prior to the *Iliad* being composed, whether the Mycenaean era or the eighth or seventh centuries BCE. Different regions of Greece had always been independent of each other, and there is not even a tradition of Greece being united at any time prior to Homer, other than in the *Iliad* itself.[102] Yet, it is known that by the end of the eighth century BCE, the Greeks did start to view themselves in a united sense, in contrast to non-Greeks. For example, there were a number of sanctuaries and festivals developing at that time that were attended by all the Greeks, and only the Greeks. Thus, the description in the *Iliad* of a unified Greece is an evident example of artistic licence, yet is most easily explained in the context of the world of the late eighth century BCE. In fact, Irene de Jong states the following concerning the politics, material culture and geography of the tale of the Trojan War: 'So far as we can tell, the epic picture is in almost all respects a reflection of the poets' own world.'[103]

Of course, this historian is not intending to suggest that the Trojan War happened in the late eighth or early seventh century BCE, but this statement most certainly does support that conclusion.

So far, we have seen that there are various pieces of evidence from surrounding Greek legends that indicate that the Trojan War happened about five centuries later than commonly believed. The evidence from Ctesias' chronological information indicates a date at some point in the eighth century BCE. The Phoenician alphabet being brought over to Greece evidently occurred no earlier than 900 BCE, yet Greek legend

The True Date of the Trojan War

places it some two centuries before the Trojan War. We have seen that the earliest source about the founding of the Olympic Games makes its founder Heracles, who was born about ninety years or so before the Trojan War, yet it is known that the Games were founded in 776 BCE. There are also the many references to the Oracle of Delphi, despite the fact that there was no sanctuary at Delphi prior to the ninth century BCE.

We have also seen that there are a number of genealogies which place Heracles and his associates in that same time period, the early eighth century BCE, such as the genealogy of Pythagoras, that of the kings of Macedon, that of the kings of Argos, and that of the inhabitants of Chios. In addition, there are also a number of cities mentioned in the *Iliad* and other records of the Trojan War which were not founded until about the eighth century BCE, such as Heracleion. At least one in particular, Scione, was specifically said to have been founded just after the Trojan War, yet the evidence shows that it was founded in *c*. 700 BCE. The evidence from Neapolis and Parthenope also supports this dating. Furthermore, we have now seen that the entire world portrayed in the *Iliad*, from the military equipment and forms of warfare to the political and economic landscape and the material culture, all match in almost all respects the period around 700 BCE. Could it be, then, that the Trojan War occurred in *c*. 700 BCE? This does indeed seem to be the conclusion that is best supported by the evidence. But let us consider one more line of reasoning to reaffirm this conclusion.

Evidence from the Dating of Homer

If the Trojan War took place about the year 700 BCE, this means that Homer, the author of the *Iliad*, would have had to have lived after that year at the very earliest. Given the testimony from ancient writers, he most certainly could not have lived much later. Most researchers conclude he was probably an eighth century BCE poet, although there is considerable evidence that he lived as late as the middle of the seventh century BCE. For example, the ancient writer Demetrius of Magnesia claimed that Homer lived at about the same time as another poet called Thaletas.[104] Another source of antiquity, the Byzantine *Suda*, claimed that Homer lived a little after Thaletas.[105]

So, when did Thaletas live? According to Plutarch, he lived in the generation after a different poet named Terpander. There is some specific dating information available concerning Terpander, because he was said to have won the twenty-sixth Olympiad, which was in the 670s BCE. If Thaletas lived in the generation after Terpander, that means that he would have lived no earlier than the middle of the seventh century BCE. Recall that Thaletas was said to have lived at about the same time as, or even a little before, Homer. So this would place Homer in the latter half of the seventh century BCE. Supporting this dating for Thaletas is the fact that an ancient authority named Glaucus of Rhegium, from the fifth century BCE, informs us that Thaletas was born after Archilochus, another Greek poet.[106] Yet Archilochus is widely accepted as having lived in the middle of the seventh century BCE, having been a contemporary of King Gyges of Lydia, whose reign is generally dated from the 680s to the 650s BCE.[107]

So in summary, Thaletas was a younger contemporary of Archilochus, who lived in the early to mid seventh century BCE. He lived in the generation after Terpander, who won the Olympic Games in the 670s BCE, reaffirming that Thaletas must have lived no earlier than the middle of the seventh century BCE. This is, indeed, the generally accepted dating for Thaletas today.[108] Bearing this in mind, we have seen that certain ancient sources place Homer at about the same time as, or a little later than, Thaletas. If this information is correct, it indicates that Homer was a poet of the latter half of the seventh century BCE. This date is supported by Strabo, who said:

> The writers of chronicles make it plain that Homer knew the Cimmerians, in that they fix the date of the invasion of the Cimmerians either a short time before Homer, or else in Homer's own time.[109]

The Cimmerian invasion of Anatolia occurred in the first half of the seventh century BCE. Thus, according to Strabo, 'the writers of chronicles' placed Homer at this time or shortly afterwards (who these writers were is unclear). A date in the seventh century BCE is also supported by Theopompus, a fourth century BCE writer, and Euporion, a third century BCE writer.[110] Not all ancient sources support a date that is quite this late – some sources make Homer himself a contemporary of Archilochus – but all things considered, placing Homer in about the middle of the seventh century BCE seems probable. Although it is not currently the majority opinion, there are a growing number of scholars who support such a date, such as Hans van Wees, Irene de Jong, Walter Burkert, Martin L. West and many others, some of whom even favour a date in the second half of that century.[111]

With this being the case, the conventional chronology of the Trojan War would create a roughly five-century gap between the

Trojan War and Homer. On the other hand, our revised dating of the Greek legends would make Homer almost a contemporary of the events he was describing. While the existence of a large gap of many centuries is supported by a few ancient writers, there were many others who placed Homer very close to the fall of Troy. For example, Eratosthenes of Cyrene, of the third century BCE, placed Homer just 100 years after the capture of Troy. Many other ancient writers placed Homer somewhat over one century after the war. In fact, most ancient sources placed him between fifty and 150 years after the Trojan War.[112]

But there are a number of ancient sources that place him even closer to that event. For example, Crates of Mallus, of the second century BCE, claimed in one place that Homer was a contemporary of the war, though in another place he concluded that he may have lived up to eighty years after it.[113] Tatian, of the second century CE, accepted that Homer may have been a contemporary of the Trojan War.[114] Pseudo-Plutarch's account about Homer, probably of the second or third century CE, states that 'some say he lived at the time of the Trojan War and saw it personally'.[115] Diodorus Siculus reports that a certain Dionysius 'writer of cycles' claimed that Homer lived at the time of the Trojan War, and that 'countless others' agree with this.[116] It has also been argued that Hellanicus, a historian of the fifth century BCE, dated Homer to the time of the Trojan War.[117]

So we can see that the majority viewpoint of the ancient writers was that Homer was active fifty to 150 years after the Trojan War, though a reasonable number of sources actually make him a contemporary of the war itself. Relatively few, in contrast, place a large gap between Homer and the Trojan War (and this would be easily explained if they knew roughly when Homer lived but were influenced by the popular date of *c.* 1200 BCE for the Trojan War). Therefore, the available evidence definitely supports the viewpoint that Homer lived close to the time of that event. Given that the evidence is clear that Homer likely lived in the middle of the seventh century BCE or thereabouts, this supports the conclusion that the Trojan War itself took place in about 700 BCE, as all the other evidence so far examined has indicated.

A writer of perhaps the second century CE, in a work attributed to Lucian known as the *Encomium of Demosthenes*, expressed his uncertainty as to whether Homer belonged to the 'Heroic period' or the 'Ionian period', the former being the era in which the Greek heroes such as Heracles and Agamemnon lived, and the latter being the era in which figures such as Hesiod and Homer were generally placed, in 'later' Greek history.[118] This reinforces the fact that Homer did not live long after the 'Heroic period' at all, but that the line between the two periods was actually quite blurred.

Other lines of evidence which support the conclusion that Homer was a near-contemporary of the Trojan War are details concerning his family and his contemporaries. There were lots of different ideas in the ancient world about Homer himself, many of which are contradictory. Nonetheless, they do shed light on when he was believed to have lived in relation to certain other figures. For example, one account which does not specifically comment on chronology makes Homer the son of Telemachus, a character who appears in Homer's *Odyssey*.[119] Given that the *Odyssey* is a story about the journey back from Troy upon the end of the war, this would make Homer part of the generation immediately after the Trojan War. Another tradition makes Homer's father Thamyris, another character who appears in Homer's own works.[120] Again, while there are many sources which contradict each other on the details and ascribe different parents to Homer, this does show when the writers of these particular sources believed Homer lived in relation to the characters in his works – in other words, they show that Homer was believed to have lived in the generation after the events that he wrote about. So these can be added to the list of ancient sources that considered Homer to be a contemporary or near-contemporary of the Trojan War.

Other genealogical information also confirms that Homer lived only very shortly after the time of the fall of Troy. Several ancient writers, such as Hellanicus and Damastes, both of the fifth century BCE, claimed that he was a tenth-generation descendant of a legendary figure named Orpheus.[121] Using our standard twenty to twenty-five years per generation, this would indicate that there were about 200–250 years between Orpheus and Homer. So, when did Orpheus live?

There is not much datable information about Orpheus. However, one important piece of information is that he had a brother named Linus.[122] This Linus was said to have lived during the time of Cadmus, the same Cadmus who supposedly brought the Phoenician alphabet to Greece. Later, his life ended when he was accidentally killed by one of his young pupils, Heracles. We have already seen that Heracles attacked the city of Troy about sixty years or so before the Trojan War. Therefore, Linus' death, which occurred when Heracles was just a child, could have occurred perhaps as much as one century before the Trojan War. If we assume that Linus was quite elderly when he died, this places his birth about 180 years or so before the war. The further back in time we place his birth, the better, given the great span of time that is usually given between Cadmus (Linus' contemporary king) and Heracles, such as in Herodotus' writings. There is no information about the age difference between Linus and his brother Orpheus, but if Linus was born some 180 years before the Trojan War, then we could potentially place the birth of Orpheus as far back as 200 years or so before the war.

As we said before, ten generations from Orpheus would indicate that Homer was born about 200–250 years later. If Orpheus was born roughly 200 years before the Trojan War, and Homer was born about 200–250 years after him, Homer must have been born at some point within the first fifty years after the war. If this legendary genealogy of Homer's is even roughly correct, this supports the view that Homer was a near-contemporary of the events he describes in the *Iliad*.

Another piece of evidence comes from the fact that Homer was said to have met Medon, the first archon of Athens (although some records call him the last king).[123] His father was Codrus. Codrus, in turn, was the son of the previous king, Melanthus. This king was not the son of the previous one, but merely succeeded him, forming a new, albeit extremely short-lived, dynasty. The king whom he succeeded was named Thymoetes, the son of Oxyntes, the son of Demophon, who fought in the Trojan War. So, Medon, the ruler of Athens whom Homer met, was roughly four generations after Demophon (remembering that Thymoetes' successor, Melanthus, was not his son, so he may well have been similar in age to Thymoetes himself).

If we suppose that Demophon was about thirty years old at the time of the Trojan War, then that would place his birth in *c.* 730 BCE according to our chronology. Counting forward four generations for the birth of Medon would take us to 650–630 BCE. This would easily allow for Medon to have met Homer, if the latter was born somewhere in the first half of the seventh century BCE. Therefore, this information about Homer meeting Medon clearly supports the conclusion that the Trojan War took place in about 700 BCE.

Regarding why Herodotus placed Homer some four centuries before his own time, one suggestion is that Homer actually lived ten generations before Herodotus. The Greek historian then decided to give the maximum possible estimate for how far back Homer lived, using forty years per generation.[124] The fact that he makes a point of saying that Homer lived 'no more' than 400 years before his own time indicates that he was indeed trying to give a maximum figure.

Allowing a more realistic twenty to twenty-five years per generation would place Homer's birth between *c.* 700–650 BCE. While this ten-generation theory is only a suggestion, it does nicely explain why Herodotus' estimate is so out of harmony with the other evidence about the date of Homer's lifetime.

Conclusion

In conclusion, we can see that in addition to all the details from the Greek stories concerning Troy and related myths concerning characters of that era pointing towards the conclusion that the Trojan War occurred in *c.* 700 BCE, the information about Homer also supports such a conclusion. We have seen that most ancient sources placed his life to between fifty and 150 years after the war, with a fair number of sources placing him even closer than that. Diodorus Siculus, Pseudo-Plutarch, Tatian, Crates of Mallus and possibly even Hellanicus all attest to Homer having actually been a contemporary of the fall of Troy. Many traditions about Homer himself support the conclusion that he lived very near to the events he wrote about. He was, in several places, claimed to be the son of certain characters who appear in his works. We have also seen that the strong tradition about Homer being a tenth-generation descendant of Orpheus supports the conclusion that he lived not long after the Trojan War, as does the tradition about Homer meeting Medon, the ruler of Athens. Given the strong evidence for Homer having lived in the seventh century BCE, this supports a date for the Trojan War around the beginning of that century or the end of the previous one.

Given all of the information analysed so far, we feel confident in placing the Trojan War in *c.* 705–695 BCE, the birth of Homer in *c.* 680 BCE, and the composition of the *Iliad* likely around 650 BCE or thereabouts.

The fact that this revised date for the Trojan War is correct is shown by the fact that multiple characters – well over a dozen, in fact – from the *Iliad* and other Greek myths based around this era can be identified with historical or at least semi-legendary individuals from the eighth and seventh centuries BCE. Many of the events described in the legends can be identified with historical events that took place at this time, and even the Trojan War itself is supported by the archaeology of this period. We will analyse all of this additional, much more specific, evidence in the following two chapters.

4

The Characters of the Trojan War

The previous chapter established that the evidence from the legends and many other sources concerning the Trojan War indicate that this famous conflict must have occurred about the year 700 BCE. This means that Homer and all the many other ancient writers who spoke about the Trojan War and the surrounding Greek legends were not talking about events in the distant past, centuries upon centuries before their own time. No, rather, this means that the events in question occurred just a few centuries, or just decades in some cases, before being recorded. For example, in addition to Homer's works, there is a vase dated to *c.* 675 BCE, called the Mykonos Vase, which depicts the famous Trojan Horse, the cunning method by which the Greeks finally overthrew the city of Troy. While previously this could be dismissed as a distorted memory of a battering ram, or whatever other suggestion that researchers have made, now we must acknowledge that it is attested just decades after the event in question, meaning it must be accepted as probably historical.

This is the consequence of revising the date of the Trojan War to *c.* 700 BCE. We are forced to accept that these famous Greek legends are actually recorded very soon after their supposed occurrence. As with any historical event, the closer the records are to the events they describe, the more likely it is that the records are accurate. Scholars already suggest that there may be some historical event at the foundation of Homer's *Iliad*, but given the evidence for when the Trojan War really took place, there can be absolutely no doubt whatsoever that it is historical.

Throughout this chapter, we will see that all the major events from the time of Heracles through to the aftermath of the Trojan War can be clearly identified in the historical and archaeological record, as can numerous characters featured in these legends. To begin with, let us examine Heracles and some of his contemporary legendary figures.

Heracles

The idea of Heracles – or Hercules, as he is more commonly known – being a historical figure might seem quite bizarre and overly optimistic. After all, he was said to have been a demigod, the son of Zeus. He was a hero with phenomenal superhuman strength, said to have fought monsters and travelled all over the world, defeating the multi-headed Hydra and killing the Nemean Lion, to name just a few of his feats. But despite these dramatic legends, he is actually one of the easiest characters to pin down. First, we must establish two important facts. One of them was already outlined in the previous chapter – that is, the fact that Heracles evidently lived in the first half of the eighth century BCE. The second is the fact that the rulers of the Dorians, the descendants of Heracles, were said by Herodotus to have been of Egyptian descent.[125] Elsewhere, Herodotus explicitly states that Heracles' parents were 'both of Egypt by descent'.[126] Therefore, although it was not mentioned often, there was an early tradition that Heracles' family was originally Egyptian.

With these facts in mind, it is extremely revealing to look at the Egyptian king list composed by Manetho, an Egyptian priest of the early third century BCE. In the part of this list concerned with the eighth century BCE, Manetho mentions a king named 'Osorthon'. This is generally held to be Pharaoh Osorkon III. However, given that Manetho specifically mentions that he ruled at Tanis, there is a good argument to be made that this 'Osorthon' is actually Osorkon IV, and there are a number of scholars who do accept this identification.[127] This latter figure did rule at Tanis, while the earlier Osorkon III was a king of Upper (southern) Egypt and never ruled over that northern city. Osorkon IV is usually believed to have ruled from about 730 BCE to about 715 BCE. However, as shown in Appendix One, Egyptian chronology for this era should be shifted back by thirty-one years. This would place the reign of Osorkon IV from about 761 to 746 BCE. This ties in with the fact that his predecessor in Manetho's list, named Petubastes, was said to have ruled when the Olympic Games were first founded. There was a king named Pedubast who is believed by many scholars to have been the immediate predecessor of Osorkon IV, and this would match the 'Petubastes' of the list.[128] He most likely would indeed have been ruling when the Olympic Games were founded, allegedly in the 770s BCE. In contrast, an earlier king named Pedubast, who historically came before Osorkon III, was not the *immediate* predecessor of that earlier Osorkon, and he would have ruled well before the start of the Olympic Games.

Why is it so significant to determine which Osorkon is the subject of Manetho's entry, and when it was that he ruled? Because immediately after mentioning the name of this eighth century BCE Egyptian king, Manetho's king list includes the comment: 'the Egyptians called him Heracles'.

It is almost shocking how direct a statement this is, yet there it is. In plain words, there is a statement that this historical figure, from precisely the right time period and of the right nationality, was known as Heracles. Obviously, most researchers have not paid any attention to this due to the pervasive belief that Heracles belonged to the Mycenaean era. But having established the correct chronology of the Greek legends, and the fact that the descendants of Heracles, along with Heracles himself, were believed to have actually been of Egyptian descent, there is no reason at all to question that Osorkon IV, the mid-eighth-century BCE Egyptian king who is recorded as being known by the name Heracles, was the Heracles of the Greek tales.

If this is the case, then can any events from Osorkon's life be connected with the legends of Heracles? Before we answer this, something that needs to be established first is that ancient historians were quite convinced that there were actually multiple figures called Heracles, and that stories from the lives of these other figures had become attached to 'their' Heracles, the one of the Trojan War era. Although not all ancient writers agreed on which particular stories had been taken from earlier figures, there is good evidence that the majority of Heracles' famous Twelve Labours, though not necessarily all, were taken from Egyptian mythology of a much more ancient era. While it goes beyond the scope of this book to delve into the exact origins of these famous accounts, it does appear that the 'original' Heracles was an Egyptian god whose stories, as the ancient Greek historians claimed, became attached to the later figure of the era just before the Trojan War.

This being the case, we can remove most of the Twelve Labours (such as the defeat of the Hydra and the Nemean Lion, the capture of the Cerynian Hind and the Erymanthian Boar, the cleaning of the Augean Stables, and a few others) from our consideration of the historical Heracles of the eighth century BCE. They can be attributed to an Egyptian god. It appears that the less famous stories concerning

Heracles are the ones which apply to Osorkon IV, such as his attack on Troy, his journey with Jason and the Argonauts and several others. These explicitly take place in the era just before the Trojan War and cannot be attributed to earlier myths.

Unfortunately, there is not a great deal of information about Osorkon's life and what he did during his reign, but the fact that he ruled at Tanis, a city in the Delta region of Egypt, means that it is reasonably plausible that he could have had some impact on affairs in Greece and other areas on the northern coast of the Mediterranean. After all, the reverse happened less than a century later, in the time of Psamtik I; Greek soldiers arrived in Egypt and entered the service of the king. This king was also said to have negotiated some kind of alliance with Gyges of Lydia, so evidently there was a reasonable amount of communication and, by necessity, travel between Egypt and western Anatolia in this general period. King Gyges was even said to have sent troops to Psamtik in Egypt.[129] It would hardly be shocking for Psamtik to have done the same for Gyges if the situation had called for it, though in this particular instance that does not seem to have happened. Yet, it does seem that it was Psamtik who had taken the initiative to form the alliance with Gyges, meaning that he was the one who must have sent men to Anatolia, albeit not a division of soldiers.

The point is, given the evident growing communication and travel between Egypt and at least some of the Aegean shores at about this time, it would not be at all shocking or extraordinary for the slightly earlier Osorkon IV to have done something similar. While he himself is not likely to have travelled to Anatolia, there is nothing unbelievable about concluding that he may well have been in communication with Greeks or others in that area, just as Psamtik was in communication with Gyges of Lydia. Heracles was said to have assisted Laomedon, the king of Troy, after that king had employed the services of Poseidon and Apollo in fortifying the city of Troy. Laomedon had ended up refusing their wages, which caused them to attack the city and send a sea monster against it. The king of Troy called on Heracles to help him, which he did, slaying the monster. However, Laomedon then refused to pay Heracles what they had agreed, leading Heracles to attack Troy himself. He slew the king, but left the young boy Priam alive as his successor.

As we have just considered, given the communication and exchange of soldiers between Psamtik and Gyges of Lydia just a few decades later, there does not appear to be anything unbelievable about concluding that Osorkon IV perhaps sent a small body of troops to that land to aid the king of Troy. There is no direct evidence of this, although Egyptian artefacts dating to the eighth century BCE have been found at a variety of locations in western Anatolia, demonstrating, if nothing else, an Egyptian connection of some kind with that region in the pertinent era.[130] Nonetheless, at the time of Heracles' alleged raid of Troy – the middle of the eighth century BCE – archaeologists at Troy have uncovered a surge in building work and general activity at the site, including fortification work performed on the gates and the city walls.[131] This most likely corresponds to the legendary fortification of the city by Poseidon and Apollo in Priam's youth. There is no evidence of destruction at this time that we might attribute to Heracles, or Osorkon, but it appears that Heracles' attack was more of a fleeting raid to kill the king and his associates, rather than an actual attempt to destroy the city. The fact that he was said to have attacked the city with just six ships indicates that it was not a dramatic affair.

Regarding Heracles' alleged voyage with Jason to the land of the Golden Fleece to help him in restoring his rightful place on the throne, it is again quite possible that Osorkon IV may have offered his assistance in some way to this Greek prince. It is known on the basis of archaeology that the Greeks had managed to restore contact with the north of Egypt by the eighth century BCE.[132] Many Egyptian artefacts have been found in Greece in eighth-century BCE contexts, proving that there was a connection of some kind between the two lands at this time.[133] These artefacts might just be attributable to trade, but on the other hand, they might preserve evidence of an Egyptian presence in the country. In any case, they prove that there were relations between Greece and Egypt as early as the eighth century BCE, a fact which is now widely accepted by scholars. This strongly supports the case that Osorkon IV, a ruler of northern Egypt just like Psamtik, could have sent soldiers to Greece or at least in some way been involved – even just financially – in activities occurring in that land at that time, helping to see how he became the Heracles of Greek legend.

In fact, Egyptian artefacts from the eighth century BCE have also been found in Italy. Perhaps these are connected with Heracles' alleged sojourn in that country.[134]

But is it really plausible that the stories of Heracles came from an Egyptian ruler? Well, although the Greek legends portray him as living in Greece, there is nothing unusual about one culture taking stories from a foreign location and adapting them to fit into the local setting. For example, it is widely believed that the Greek myth of Aphrodite and her lover Adonis comes from the Middle East, from stories about

Inanna and her lover Tammuz.[135] Yet stories about the Greek deities are explicitly placed in locations within the Greek world: Cyprus, with exact spots on the island being specified in the myths. Thus, there is nothing implausible about stories of Heracles being moved from Egypt to Greece.

There is one particular event which happened in Heracles' legendary life which we may be able to relate directly to an event in Osorkon's life. As noted before, there is not a considerable amount of information regarding Osorkon's activities, but one thing that is known is that, very shortly after he came to the throne, he faced an invasion by the forces of Piye, king of the Kushite Dynasty of Egypt. Osorkon joined a coalition of other regional kings of Lower Egypt and set out to fight against Piye. However, the Kushite king's forces were too powerful, so the kings of Lower Egypt, including Osorkon, submitted to his rule. Osorkon actually took the initiative to go and personally pay homage to the king. After this, the other kings in the coalition followed suit. This pleased King Piye, and he returned to his own lands, having nominally subjected northern Egypt. In reality, the northern kings were now free to reign in their territories as they pleased. In a sense, then, Osorkon IV's actions in this episode led to the rescue of Lower Egypt from Piye's rage, resulting in him turning away. From a certain point of view, this could be viewed as a victory for Osorkon IV.

What we find in the legend of Heracles is a story which might have come from a distorted memory of this event. Just as the aforementioned episode in Egyptian history occurred just after Osorkon became king, the event in Greek legend that we will now discuss is said to have happened just after Heracles reached manhood; it was his first major adventure in the legends.

A king named Erginus, king of the Minyans, waged war against Thebes, the Greek city which is presented as being Heracles' home. Heracles gathered the young men of the city and stirred them into joining him in fighting against Erginus. They successfully defeated the invading army, actually killed Erginus and then razed his capital to the ground.

Although it is not exceptionally similar, this Greek legend does have certain key similarities to the Egyptian events. Both Heracles and Osorkon were said to have faced an invading army heading towards their homeland right at the start of their careers. Heracles' home, the Grecian Thebes, likely represents the Egyptian Tanis, the home of Osorkon IV. The fact that Osorkon was part of a coalition of kings facing up against this invading force likely led to the description of

Heracles stirring up the young men and getting them to join him in his fight against their enemies. And the victory that Heracles was said to have received at this battle could have come from Osorkon's successful halting of Piye's campaign by taking the initiative to submit to Piye, which ended up turning the invader away back to his lands. In fact, Osorkon is specifically noted as travelling to a temple, the Temple of Ra at Heliopolis, to submit to Piye. So Osorkon's successful dealing with the invasion came about due to him travelling to a temple, and this could well be related to the fact that Heracles' victory was likewise connected to him going to a temple – he was said to have gone to the temples in the area and taken suits of armour that were affixed to the walls. So although the details differ, both accounts share the concept of the invading force being halted due to the hero having gone to a temple. Also, it is worth noting that at least one version of the Greek legend, recorded by Pausanias, claims that Erginus was not actually killed during this event but made peace with Heracles and lived for a long time afterwards, which would tie in with him being Piye.[136]

It is clear that there are substantial differences between these two accounts, but the Greek records of this event are all recorded hundreds of years after the fact, most of them coming from the first century BCE or later. So whatever the origin of this Greek myth, it is perfectly acceptable to suppose that it went through a considerable amount of corruption and distortion over the centuries, especially if it was taken from a foreign nation and adapted to a local Greek setting. The reason for the enemies being turned into Minyans, a real ethnic group in the Aegean, is unclear. There was a city in Middle Egypt known as Minya, which name comes from the ancient Egyptian 'Menat Khufu', which would have been under the control of Piye at the time of his attack against Osorkon and the other northern kings. The similarity between 'Menat' – which we know for a fact eventually evolved into 'Minya' – and the Greek 'Minyans' may well have led to this confusion. Or, perhaps less likely, the mistake may have derived from the name of the capital of Piye's kingdom, Meroe.

There are only two more events in the life of Osorkon IV which we know about, and one of them is possibly connected to the legend of Heracles. This event appears in Assyrian records, where Osorkon IV is referred to by the form 'Shilkanni'. The Assyrian Empire, under Sargon II, came against Egypt. Osorkon wished to avoid a confrontation, as the Assyrian king was far more powerful than he was, so he met Sargon near the border of Egypt and gifted him twelve large horses, which the Assyrian records describe as being 'without equal in Assyria'. In appreciation for this gift, Sargon did not attack Osorkon's realm.

It appears that this might be the origin of the story of Heracles' capture of the Mares, or horses, of Diomedes. These were said to have been ferocious, man-eating beasts. Heracles captured them (there are many conflicting accounts as to how this was done) and then offered them to King Eurystheus. This king was the one ordering Heracles to engage in all of the famous Twelve Labours. Osorkon taking some exceptionally mighty horses and gifting them to an otherwise antagonistic king may well be the origin of this Labour, written hundreds of years after the fact. This is not to say that the legendary Eurystheus comes from Sargon, but merely that the otherwise unknown foreign king in this story was substituted in the later Greek version of events for the probably historical King Eurystheus, someone who was far more familiar to the Greeks.

The only other event in Osorkon's life that we know about is his attempt at helping King Hanno of Gaza in his rebellion against Sargon, years prior to the aforementioned event involving Osorkon gifting horses to Sargon. Osorkon was said to have sent aid to King Hanno, but the rebellion was completely quashed and Osorkon's ally, Hanno, was burned alive. The only conceivable connection that this has to the story of Heracles is the fact that Heracles himself was said to have been burned alive, but it is very unlikely that there is any genuine connection here.

One more account in the legendary life of Heracles is worth talking about. Heracles was said to have travelled to Egypt and fought against a king there named Busiris. Although there is no direct record of it, this could easily have come from a real incident involving Osorkon and any one of the independent rulers of parts of the Delta region at that time. In fact, it is possible that Busiris was actually King Bocchoris. Evidence of his presence has been found at Osorkon's former capital, Tanis, after Osorkon himself disappears from the historical record.[137] On this basis, it is thought that Bocchoris may have fought against Osorkon at the end of the latter king's reign. This is not to say that the name 'Busiris' came from a corruption of 'Bocchoris', but rather, the name 'Busiris' had an independent origin derived, in part, from the name 'Osiris', as generally believed by scholars, but then the Greeks applied this name to 'Bocchoris' as an alternative form, due to the similarity of the names.

So in summary, we can see that the historical Heracles was very likely Osorkon IV. It is quite possible that he may have lent his support to certain rulers in the Aegean, just as he sent troops to Hanno in Palestine. We have seen that there is evidence of increasing connections between Egypt and the Aegean in the eighth century BCE, with Egyptian artefacts from this period being found in Greece, western Anatolia and Italy, the same regions in which Heracles was said to have been active. And as we have seen, the fact that the rulers of the Dorians were said to have been of Egyptian descent, as well as Heracles himself supposedly being of Egyptian descent, ties in with Heracles being identical to this historical Egyptian king. Furthermore, we have seen that two of the three known events in Osorkon's life were likely the origin of two events in Heracles' life – him repelling an invading force from his homeland and his taking and giving mighty horses to an otherwise antagonistic king. A third event in the life of Osorkon – his conflict with Bocchoris – is not directly recorded but is considered likely by historians, and this may well have led to the story of Heracles' conflict with the Egyptian king Busiris.

With this identification in mind, it should be noted that it seems extraordinarily unlikely that the kings of Argos, Macedon and other kingdoms were actually descendants of Heracles. Nonetheless, there is nothing unusual in ancient records about claiming descent from a famous figure, even when no genuine connection existed.

Pygmalion

Another character who can be identified clearly is Pygmalion of Cyprus, the legendary king famous for having fallen in love with a statue. His chronological placement in the legends is somewhat inconsistent, though he is essentially made a contemporary of Heracles. One way of chronologically fixing him is the fact that Heracles was said to have had relations with Parthenope, the daughter of Stymphalus.[138] This Stymphalus, for his part, was the son of a woman named Laodice, the daughter of Cinyras, a king of Cyprus.[139] Cinyras, meanwhile, is said to have married Metharme, the daughter of Pygmalion.[140] Here is a list to make the genealogical relationship easier to follow:

Pygmalion→Metharme→Laodice→Stymphalus→Parthenope (lover of Heracles)

This would place Pygmalion four generations before Heracles, who was, in turn, about two generations before the Trojan War. However, Pygmalion's son-in-law Cinyras (the husband of Pygmalion's daughter Metharme) was said in the *Iliad* to have been the king ruling over

Cyprus at the time of the Trojan War. This makes the chronology quite awkward. Perhaps we could suppose that Parthenope was quite young at the time of her interaction with Heracles, conceivably being as young as fifteen years old at the time. Since Osorkon IV, the historical Heracles, likely died in the 740s BCE, we could estimate that Parthenope was born in about 760 BCE. Her father, Stymphalus, could have been born in *c.* 780 BCE. Stymphalus' mother, Laodice – if we assume that she was also young at the time of her son's birth – could have been born in *c.* 798 BCE. Then her mother, Metharme, could have been born in *c.* 816 BCE. This would then give a birth date of *c.* 836 BCE for Pygmalion. Would this allow Cinyras to have been king at the time of the Trojan War? Well, if he was born at the same time as his wife Metharme, then he would have had to have been over 100 years old at the time of the war.

In reality, it appears that these genealogies are not totally accurate; they are flawed and somewhat inconsistent, but they generally agree that Pygmalion was an older contemporary of Heracles. Another demonstration of this is the fact that Heracles was said to have travelled to Egypt and killed King Busiris. According to the story, Busiris had been advised to sacrifice foreigners by an advisor named Thrasios, portrayed as either the brother or son of Pygmalion.[141] This would make Pygmalion a contemporary or older contemporary of Heracles. Thus, if the Trojan War took place around 700 BCE, then the legendary Pygmalion of Cyprus should have lived at the very beginning of the eighth century BCE or the very end of the ninth.

With this is mind, which figure from the early eighth century BCE could have been the origin of Pygmalion of Cyprus? This is not a difficult conundrum. There was a well-known king of Tyre named Pygmalion who also had control over parts of Cyprus, whose reign is generally considered to have stretched from about 831 BCE to 785 BCE.[142] Regarding the legend about his son or brother Thrasios being an advisor to King Busiris, there is really nothing unlikely about a member of the royal family of Tyre being present in Egypt in the eighth century BCE, given the extensive connections that have always existed between those two regions. A brother or son of Pygmalion of Tyre could well have been present in Egypt, perhaps as an elderly advisor or soothsayer of some kind, at the time of Osorkon IV's reign in Egypt.

In any case, the identity of the Pygmalion who lived shortly before this episode in Heracles' life is undoubtedly the historical Pygmalion of Tyre of the late ninth, early eighth century BCE.

Iphitos

The character we will now discuss is quite a minor one in Greek legend, but it does appear that he can be identified with a historical figure from the eighth century BCE. In legend, Iphitos is another person who belongs to the era of Heracles. He was said to have lived in Elis, an ancient district in Greece. He was killed by a man named Copreus; his killer then fled from Elis and was received by Heracles' enemy King Eurystheus.[143] So this legendary Iphitos of Elis was definitely a contemporary of Heracles. That is all the information that the legends provide about this character.

In other ancient records, there are reports of a certain 'Iphitos king of Elis' who allegedly played an important part in establishing the Olympic Games.[144] As we have already noted, the Olympic Games were said to have been founded in 776 BCE. Therefore, this Iphitos king of Elis was definitely a figure of the late ninth, early eighth century BCE. Beyond that, nothing is known about him. It seems likely that the Iphitos of Elis who was killed by Copreus in the time of Heracles was the same as Iphitos the king of Elis who lived in the early eighth century BCE and had a hand in founding the Olympic Games in 776 BCE. No additional information is known about either the legendary Iphitos or the historical Iphitos to compare them in any greater detail.

Sesostris

Another figure from this general era who can be identified as a historical person is Sesostris. This pharaoh is first mentioned by Herodotus, later being mentioned by Diodorus Siculus and Strabo. King Sesostris is described as leading a mighty campaign from Egypt through the Middle East and all the way over to Thrace, just across the Bosphorus from Anatolia. It should first be noted that no Egyptian king ever conquered such a vast area. Evidently this story is a greatly exaggerated account of a real king who engaged in notable military campaigns. Significantly, Manetho's king list records a king named 'Sesostris', seemingly aiding us in identifying the king in question. The Sesostris of Manetho's list occupies the place of the historical Senusret III. And this historical king did engage in a number of significant campaigns, invading and conquering parts of Canaan.

However, there are a few serious problems with the identification of this king with the Sesostris of Herodotus' account. Herodotus places this pharaoh just two generations before the Egyptian king who was ruling at the time of the Trojan War. This would make him a contemporary of Heracles. According to the traditional dating of the Greek legends, this would mean that he would have to have been a figure of the thirteenth century BCE. However, Senusret III is believed to have lived in the nineteenth century BCE, many centuries too early even for the traditional date of the Trojan War. Thus, it does not appear that Senusret III could be the Sesostris whom Herodotus was describing. What is possible, though, is that the name 'Sesostris' came from a Greek version of 'Senusret' – as indicated by Manetho's use of the name in the place of Senusret III – but then this name came to be applied to a different pharaoh with a sufficiently similar name, somewhat similar to how the name 'Maximianus' was mistakenly applied to Magnus Maximus in British records.

With the Trojan War really having occurred in *c.* 700 BCE, Herodotus' Sesostris should have been one of the kings who ruled Egypt in roughly the middle of the eighth century BCE. He should be a king with a similar name and who engaged in activities which could plausibly have developed into the legend as recounted by Herodotus and later writers.

The pharaoh who fits this description is Shebitku. He is believed to have ruled from about 713 to 704 BCE, although his reign must really have continued for at least three more years to encompass the siege of Jerusalem, for reasons we will see in a moment. However, as is shown in Appendix One, these conventional Egyptian dates should be moved back by thirty-one years. This would make Shebitku's actual dates 744-732 BCE. This is a perfect fit for our estimate regarding when Sesostris would have lived. Furthermore, his name is sufficiently close to 'Sesostris' for the identification to work. When we compare the Greek forms in the surviving versions of Manetho's king list with the contemporary Egyptian forms, we can see that there are regularly dramatic differences. For example, another king from around this era was named Taharqa, yet the form used in Manetho's list is 'Tarakos'. Another king, Tefnakht, is called 'Stephinates'. This king's son was named Bakenranef, yet the Greek form was 'Bocchoris'. So although 'Sesostris' and 'Shebitku' are not identical, they are surely similar enough that an ancient Greek historian might have mistakenly believed that 'Sesostris' was the Greek name for this king. For comparison, one legend about Shebitku, which is also recorded by Herodotus, uses the form 'Sethos', perhaps a form from which someone might have conflated it with 'Sesostris'.[145]

This legend about Shebitku recorded by Herodotus is the next piece of the puzzle. This Egyptian monarch is described as facing an invasion from Sennacherib, king of Assyria. Despite overwhelming odds, Sethos (Shebitku) defeated the invading Assyrian army with divine help. This legend evidently has its origin in the fact that Shebitku really did face off against the Assyrians, notably at about the time of the Assyrian siege of Jerusalem, traditionally dated to 701 but actually in 732 BCE (see Appendix One). He sent an army to the Levant, apparently under the command of his brother Taharqa, who seems to have been the ruler or co-ruler of Kush (Ethiopia) at the time.[146] The exact outcome of the battle is unclear, though it evidently did not halt the Assyrians in any significant way, although they were soon after driven out of the region. But whatever actually occurred, the legend of Sethos recounted by Herodotus proves that it came to be remembered as an Egyptian victory.

It was pointed out earlier that no Egyptian king ever actually performed the feats attributed to Sesostris. Yet, Shebitku is perhaps one of the best possible candidates in this regard, because his legendary defeat of the Assyrians could quite logically have evolved into exaggerated tales of him conquering them, which then, by the time they reached Herodotus, could have evolved into tales of this Egyptian king conquering the territory from Egypt through to Asia Minor, which was the territory of the Assyrian Empire at the time (the description of 'Sesostris' reaching Thrace would only be a slight exaggeration of the extent of the Assyrian Empire, and the subsequent versions which have him going even further than that, as far as Spain, are demonstrably later exaggerations). This is the most elegant solution to the problem of Sesostris' legendary campaign, rather than dismissing it simply as an extremely exaggerated version of a real campaign that did not reach further than the land of Canaan, which is a feat that numerous Egyptian kings achieved.

Evidence that this is actually what happened is found in the writings of Strabo. He refers to Sesostris, recounting an even grander version of the legend than the one Herodotus wrote about, saying that he went as far as Spain.[147] However, it is extremely significant to note that in this same passage, in conjunction with Sesostris, Strabo also mentions that 'Tearco the Ethiopian' led his army as far as Europe, even reaching 'the Pillars', meaning the Pillars of Hercules, at the entrance to the Mediterranean – in other words, Spain. So here we have direct proof that Taharqa ('Tearco the Ethiopian', as scholars universally accept him as being) was credited with leading his army from Egypt all through the Near East, right up through Anatolia, all the way through Europe as far as Spain. And in fact, Strabo claims that this information came from Megasthenes, a Greek historian of the fourth century BCE, meaning that it existed in this form at least as early as just one century after Herodotus wrote about Sesostris.

Of course, it is obvious that Taharqa did not actually do any of this. The only possible origin for this legend could be when he led Shebitku's army into battle against the Assyrian Empire, which then must have become distorted and exaggerated into claims that he had defeated them, thus evolving into claims that he had conquered all of their territory, thereafter exaggerated to include even more than their territory. Regardless of how unlikely this might appear to the modern reader, the account recorded by Strabo proves that this must have happened. And if it happened in accounts concerning Taharqa, then it logically could also have occurred in accounts concerning Shebitku, the one who actually sent the army and was king of Egypt at the time.

So in summary, we can see that the legendary Sesostris who ruled approximately two generations before the Trojan War was almost certainly Shebitku, the king of Egypt from 744 BCE to about 732 BCE. He ruled at the right time, his name could plausibly have been viewed as sufficiently similar to 'Sesostris' for a writer to mistakenly apply that to him as the Greek form of his name, and the incredible conquests of Sesostris, going all the way up into Asia Minor, could have quite naturally derived from exaggerated accounts originating in his supposed victory against the Assyrian Empire, as evidently occurred in the case of the commander of the army, Taharqa.

Pheron

Herodotus states that the pharaoh who came after Sesostris was Pheron. Modern scholars are in general agreement that 'Pheron' is not a genuine name, but simply derives from the title 'Pharaoh'. Thus, the name provided by Herodotus gives us no clues as to his actual identity. However, there is one defining and specific characteristic of this Pheron which Herodotus tells us about: he was blind. So, was there a king of Egypt in the latter half of the eighth century BCE who was blind? According to Herodotus himself, there was indeed a king who fits this description. In a separate part of his account, he tells us about a king named Anysis who ruled at the same time as 'Sabacos', but in another part of Egypt. Sabacos is obviously Shabaka, the historical successor of Shebitku.[148] It is known that Shabaka, the king of the Kushite Dynasty of Egypt, ruled most of the country, while there were a number of independent rulers in the north. It appears that

Herodotus' Anysis must have been one of these, and the fact that he is said to have lived for a considerable period on a small island in Egypt supports this conclusion, inasmuch as there were many small islands in the Delta region, along the north coast of Egypt.

There is no universal agreement as to the identity of Anysis, but a reasonable suggestion would be a king recorded in Manetho's king list as Ameres, or Ammeris. He is perfectly placed chronologically, for Herodotus places the blind king Anysis just before Shabaka, but with their reigns largely overlapping. Ammeris, for his part, is thought by scholars to have been installed as the ruler of his small territory of Sais by Shebitku, the immediate predecessor of Shabaka. This places Ammeris' accession just before Shabaka, and their reigns are believed to have largely overlapped. Egyptologists assign Ammeris the years *c.* 715–*c.* 695 BCE, while Shabaka is assigned the years *c.* 704–690 BCE (note that all these dates should really be moved back by thirty-one years). Thus, Ammeris' reign started before Shabaka's, but there was an extensive period of overlap. So Ammeris is virtually certain to be the Anysis of whom Herodotus wrote, and one of the names could easily be a corruption of the other.

In truth, whether Ammeris really was Anysis or not is not exceptionally important. The origin of the story of Anysis could lie with a different minor ruler in northern Egypt at about this same time. But Ammeris certainly seems to be the most likely candidate. In any case, the vital point is simply that according to Herodotus, there was indeed a tradition of a blind king of Egypt in the late eighth century BCE. This is exactly the time which our *c.* 700 BCE date for the Trojan War would require, in accordance with the legend of Pheron the blind king of Egypt ruling just before the Trojan War.

However, one more point needs to be made regarding Pheron. As we have seen, his 'name' is simply the title 'Pharaoh'. In addition, the story of Pheron involves the detail that he eventually recovered from his blindness. Thus, it is possible that Pheron is actually an amalgamation of two kings – primarily Anysis, or Ammeris, the blind king installed by Shebitku, and then his successor Tefnakht. The first was blind, but the second was not, hence explaining the story of Pheron being blind but then recovering. Notably, some versions of Manetho's king list portray Ammeris as the founder of the Twenty-Sixth Dynasty of Egypt, while other versions do not mention him but instead portray Tefnakht as the founder of the dynasty. The fact that there were evidently conflicting traditions as to whether Ammeris or Tefnakht was the founder of the dynasty would nicely explain how the two might, under the distorted title 'Pheron', be conflated into one character.

Proteus

The Egyptian king who was said to have been reigning at the time of the Trojan War is Proteus. He is the king who received Helen and Paris Alexander when they were blown off course from Greece to Troy and arrived in Egypt. As with Pheron, his name is generally accepted to not really be a name, but a title; it is considered likely to be the Greek form of an Egyptian title meaning 'the high doors'.[149] This was a title used by the Egyptian kings in general, so his 'name' does not help us in identifying him. However, he was the successor of Pheron according to Herodotus. Therefore, if Pheron was a conflation of Ammeris and Tefnakht, then logically Proteus would be the successor of Tefnakht.

The successor of Tefnakht is a somewhat awkward matter to establish. According to Manetho's king list, the king who came after Tefnakht was a certain 'Nechepsos'. However, there is no independent evidence for a king of Sais by this name at this time. On the basis of the evidence as a whole, since there are some mentions of Nechepsos in other records, it is generally accepted now that this is a distortion of 'Necho the Wise', a reference to Necho II from the second half of the seventh century BCE.[150] In which case, Nechepsos should be removed from his place just after Tefnakht in Manetho's list. If this conclusion is correct, as appears to be quite well accepted now among Egyptologists, then the successor of Tefnakht would have been, in reality, his son Necho I.

Therefore, we can conclude that Necho I was the historical Proteus. The fact that Necho was a king of Sais, in the western Delta region of Egypt, ties in well with the fact that Proteus was said to have lived in this general area of Egypt. He was associated in the legends with the island of Pharos in particular.[151] In contrast, most Egyptian kings throughout history ruled from Memphis. But Necho's capital at Sais fits in well with the legend about Proteus and with the idea of him receiving Helen and Paris Alexander, who obviously arrived by sea, naturally reaching the north of the country first. However, Herodotus tells us that Proteus also ruled over Memphis. Necho is also understood to have ruled over Memphis.[152]

There are no additional details about Proteus that can aid in identifying him with any more certainty than this. But given that Necho I was apparently the successor of Tefnakht and ruled in the same parts of the country as Proteus and ruled at the same time as him according to our revised date of the Trojan War, this identification does seem to be correct. His reign has traditionally been dated from 672 BCE to 664 BCE. When we apply the necessary adjustment of thirty-one years, this becomes 703–695 BCE. However, given that his 'predecessor' Nechepsos is misplaced in Manetho's list, meaning that Necho I actually came directly after Tefnakht, it appears that Necho I's reign actually started six years earlier, in 709 BCE, but still ran to 695 BCE (this final year cannot be moved because it is connected to independent Assyrian records, as explained in Appendix One). Since the evidence indicates that the Trojan War took place from *c.* 705 BCE to *c.* 695 BCE, this makes Necho I perfectly placed to be Proteus.

Thuoris

This next king, Thuoris, is not mentioned by Herodotus. He appears in Manetho's king list, where his name is accompanied by the statement that he is the Polybus mentioned by Homer, the husband of Alcandra. Homer mentions this Polybus as the king of Egypt during the time of the Trojan War. This appears to conflict with the records about Proteus being the king of that country at that time, but Polybus is specifically said to have lived at Thebes, which is in southern Egypt.[153] So evidently, while Proteus was ruling in the north of the country, at Memphis and part of the Delta region (fitting Necho I), there was another king ruling southern Egypt, which was exactly the case in Necho I's time. In contrast, in the traditional period of the Trojan War, around 1200 BCE, there was only one king of Egypt, and the seat of government was in the Delta region, not Thebes. Therefore, the general picture of Egypt depicted in the legends matches the eighth or seventh century BCE, not the thirteenth or twelfth century BCE.

To return to the main point, who was Polybus, or Thuoris? Manetho's king list places him in the position of a figure known to Egyptologists as Twosret. It does seem very plausible that 'Thuoris' is a distorted Greek form of 'Twosret'. This historical pharaoh is believed to have lived in the early twelfth century BCE – incidentally, this could be taken as evidence by some that the traditional date of the Trojan War is correct, instead of our revised date. However, there is a serious problem with Manetho's placement of this king. Twosret was actually a woman, not a man. Therefore, she certainly cannot have been the Polybus mentioned by Homer, despite what Manetho said. Also, as a minor point, she did not rule from Thebes, like Polybus was said to have done, and this would also not allow space for Proteus as a different, concurrent king of Egypt.

What appears to have happened is this. 'Thuoris' is indeed the Greek distortion of 'Twosret', so Manetho's Thuoris quite simply is Queen Twosret, pharaoh of Egypt in the twelfth century BCE. However, the reference to this being the Polybus mentioned by Homer is a mistake on Manetho's part, based on a confusion between 'Thuoris' and the actual name of the king of Thebes at the time of the Trojan War. Evidently the name of that king was something quite similar to 'Thuoris', and so Manetho mistakenly described his Thuoris – the historical Twosret – as being that king, when it was actually a different king with a similar name.

So, was the king of southern Egypt, based at Thebes, in the late eighth and early seventh centuries BCE a figure with a name whose Greek form was similar to 'Thuoris'? When we take into consideration the necessary thirty-one-year adjustment, we find that the king of Thebes from 721 to 695 BCE was Taharqa. His name takes on a few different forms in the records; in some versions of Manetho's king list it appears as 'Taracus', in others it appears as 'Tarcus', while in Strabo's account it appears as 'Tearco'. And, of course, the actual contemporary Egyptian spelling was 'Taharqa'. It certainly appears that this name could have been seen as similar enough to 'Thuoris' for a record about him being Homer's Polybus to have been mistakenly thought to apply to Thuoris.

Nothing else appears to be known about Polybus which would help to identify him with any greater certainty, but everything points to Taharqa as this legendary king's historical alter ego. He ruled from Thebes during our estimated years for the Trojan War while a different king, Necho, ruled Memphis and parts of the Delta region, just as Polybus was said to have ruled from Thebes while Proteus ruled Memphis and other areas of the Delta region. Taharqa's name, too, could easily be mistaken in Greek for another form of 'Thuoris', explaining Manetho's mistake in identifying Queen Twosret as King Polybus.

Agamemnon
Let us now move away from Egypt and address the main Greek character in the legend of the Trojan War: Agamemnon. Can this Greek king be identified with a historical figure from the eighth century BCE? In fact, this is the easiest identification of them all. There is actually a direct reference to a king named Agamemnon giving his daughter in marriage to Midas, king of Phrygia in the late eighth or early seventh century BCE.[154] This historical Agamemnon of the late

eighth century BCE is perfectly chronologically placed to have been the Agamemnon of Greek legend, portrayed as already having adult daughters by the time of the Trojan War.

This eighth-century Agamemnon is referred to as 'Agamemnon of Cyme', or 'king of the Cymeans', Cyme being a Greek city in Anatolia. It is partway down the western coast of that country, not too far from Troy. It is entirely possible that this was established by the Greeks around the time they were attacking Troy and the Trojans' allies. In fact, Strabo claimed that this city was founded by Greeks who found the locals 'in bad plight because of the Trojan War', indicating that it was indeed founded at about the time of that war.[155] And there is nothing about this historical Agamemnon being termed 'of Cyme' that is incompatible with him being the Agamemnon of legend. He could easily have been the king of Argos, but also ruled this newly established Greek city during his exploits in western Anatolia. To be sure, Cyme was the most important of all the Greek cities of the north-western corner of Anatolia.[156] Furthermore, Agamemnon being referred to as 'of Cyme' is simply because Cyme was the territory he ruled over that was by far the closest, and therefore the most relevant, to the royal family of Phrygia.

In fact, the ruling class of Cyme was believed to have been descended from the legendary Agamemnon, as Strabo himself noted.[157] Archaeology has also shown that the first coins minted in Cyme, in the early sixth century BCE, depict a horse on them, which has been understood by some scholars to be a reference to their victory at Troy, involving the Trojan Horse. So the association of the legendary Agamemnon with Cyme is definitely backed by the available evidence, meaning that everything points to the historical, late eighth-century BCE Agamemnon of Cyme being the same person as the Agamemnon who waged war against Troy in Greek legend.

Midas

It seems logical now to move on to a figure who was closely connected to Agamemnon of Cyme. As noted, the daughter of Agamemnon was said to have married Midas, king of Phrygia. Unlike Agamemnon of Cyme, researchers generally have not failed to notice the apparent connections between this king and the legendary king Midas from Greek legend, the one who could turn anything into gold simply with a touch. A few authorities actually accept the identification of the Midas of Greek legend with this historical king of Phrygia, such as the *Encyclopaedia Britannica*, which refers to Phrygia in the late eighth century BCE as coming 'under the rule of the legendary king Midas'.[158] The fact that the Midas of Greek legend really was the same as this eighth-century BCE ruler is shown by Herodotus recording that King Gyges of Lydia was the first foreign king after Midas, son of Gordias, to send a gift to the Oracle of Delphi. As mentioned several times before in this book, it is widely accepted that the Oracle of Delphi did not exist until the ninth century BCE at the earliest, there being no evidence at all of a sanctuary there before that time. This means that this 'Midas, son of Gordias' of Phrygia would have had to have been a king of Phrygia by that name who lived no earlier than the ninth century BCE but before the early seventh century BCE, when Gyges of Lydia ruled. The Midas of Phrygia of the late eighth century BCE must be the right one.

This is significant because the Midas of Greek legend was also 'son of Gordias'. This would certainly appear to confirm the identification, already acknowledged by the *Encyclopaedia Britannica*, that the historical Midas of the eighth century BCE was the Midas of Greek legend. While many scholars and researchers accept this identification, few seem to have realised the repercussions of this for the chronology of the rest of Greek mythology.

It is true that Midas does not appear extensively in the accounts of other legendary events in Greek history – probably because he lived in Phrygia in Turkey, which, by and large, was far away from most of the other events taking place in Greek legend. For this reason, it is not immediately obvious which period he was supposed to belong to, because it is almost as if he lived in isolation from the other legends. However, he *is* connected to the other figures of Greek legend in some records, rare though these records may be. For example, he was said to have been educated by Orpheus.[159] We already spoke about Orpheus as the brother of Linus, a contemporary of Cadmus and the tutor of young Heracles. This would place Orpheus' birth almost two centuries before the Trojan War, as we established before. However, in reality, it appears that there were two figures around this general period named Orpheus. One was the brother of Linus, and one was a young student of Linus.[160] While the record about Midas being tutored by Orpheus does not allow us to say with certainty which Orpheus is meant, if it was the younger Orpheus (the contemporary of Heracles), this would make his student Midas an adult at the time of the Trojan War. This reaffirms his identity as the historical Midas of the late eighth century BCE, if there was any doubt.

This general chronology is supported by later legends which speak of Heracles killing the illegitimate son of Midas named Lityerses.[161]

The chronology is tight, but it would be possible if Lityerses was born while Midas was still a teenager (made more likely by the fact that he was said to have been illegitimate) and it was near the end of Heracles' life when he killed him. Justin, a historian of the second century CE, also supports this chronology by explicitly placing Midas in the time of the Trojan War.[162]

However, one potential issue that might be raised with this is that Midas is not named by Homer in his account of the Trojan War, despite the fact that he specifies that the Phrygians were allies of Troy and were involved in the war. One thing to note regarding this, however, is that those who are said to lead the different troops from the nations that were allied to Troy were not necessarily the kings of those respective nations. The leaders of the Phrygians are said by Homer to have been Phorycs and Ascanius, neither of whom are called kings, and who may well have just been military commanders or perhaps princes. There is also a mention of a king of Phrygia named Mygdon, but he is portrayed as ruling some decades before the Trojan War. He was also specifically said to have been killed by Heracles, confirming that he died many years before the Trojan War. His son Coroebus is mentioned in some sources as participating in the siege of Troy, but he is not described as a king.

In some other sources, a Phrygian king named Dymas is mentioned, but he was the father-in-law of Priam, and thus would have lived quite a few decades before the Trojan War, probably even before Mygdon. Thus, it appears that Homer, and other writers who spoke about the Trojan War, simply did not mention the king of Phrygia at the time of the war, meaning that there is no inconsistency in concluding that it was Midas. Incidentally, his father Gordias was said to have been a lowly farmer who became king, explaining why there does not seem to be any connection between Gordias and Midas and the earlier kings of Phrygia mentioned by Homer and others.[163]

Mopsus

Another character in Greek legend connected to this area is Mopsus. He is most famous as a seer, but he was also said to have been a ruler of certain parts of Anatolia.[164] Further, he was recorded as having founded and ruled the city of Colophon, a city on the western coast of the country.[165] Several cities on the south coast of Anatolia were supposedly founded by him.[166] He, like Agamemnon and Midas, is made a contemporary of the Trojan War in the Greek myths. One of his opponents was Calchas, the seer of the Greeks during the war.[167]

Another contemporary of his was Amphilochus, an Argive prince at the time of the Trojan War.[168] So Mopsus was definitely supposed to have been a contemporary of the Trojan War. Is this character identifiable with a historical figure in the late eighth century BCE?

Indeed he is. Just like Agamemnon, Mopsus appears in records explicitly concerning the eighth century BCE. He is mentioned by Nicolaus of Damascus, a historian of the first century BCE. According to this historian, a king of Lydia in the late eighth century BCE named Meles was overthrown by a figure named 'Moxos'.[169] An inscription from this time, known as the Karatepe bilingual, shows that 'Moxos', or 'Moksas', was an alternative form of 'Mopsus'. Thus, the 'Moxos' who usurped the throne of Meles the king of Lydia in the late eighth century BCE is almost certainly the Mopsus of Greek legend who was active in that area of Anatolia at the time of the Trojan War. This eighth-century BCE 'Moxos' is specifically said to have accomplished many great deeds and to have been famed in Lydia for his courage, which would definitely be consistent with the idea that he was the same as the character found in the Greek legends.

Hector

Hector was said to have been a prince of Troy, one of Priam's sons. He features prominently in the tales of the Trojan War, especially Homer's *Iliad*, for he is depicted there as being the military leader of the Trojans. Appropriately, he was said to have been the best fighter among the Trojans. Unlike with the previous characters discussed, the identification of Hector with a specific figure of the late eighth century BCE is not completely certain. However, there is a distinct possibility as to his identity. It was mentioned earlier that a genealogy of a fifth-century BCE inhabitant of Chios places the birth of the founder of the island, Oenopion (a brother to some of the Argonauts), in *c.* 800 BCE. According to a historian of the fifth century BCE named Ion of Chios, Oenopion's great-grandson was a certain Hector, the ruler of Chios.[170] His great-grandfather Oenopion being born in *c.* 800 BCE would place Hector's lifetime at the end of the eighth century BCE, perfectly chronologically placed for him to be the Hector of the Trojan War. Although these legends about Hector do not describe him as the son of Priam or as a Trojan prince, there are a few reasons for considering him to be the Hector of the *Iliad*.

Firstly, there is the simple fact that he had the right name and he lived at the right time. It appears that 'Hector' was an extremely uncommon name in the ancient Mediterranean. In fact, most reference works only speak of one Hector, the prince of Troy, and those that include others only add Hector of Chios. The fact that it appears to be a name that was only used by the Trojan prince and by this ruler of Chios supports the conclusion that they were actually the same man. It would certainly be a striking coincidence for two men who both lived at the same time to have both had such a unique name.

A second reason to believe that he may have been the Hector of the *Iliad* is that details about his life fit the idea that he was on the side of the Trojans. It is true that he was said to have been the descendant of Oenopion, a Greek who had migrated to Chios from Crete along with many others. However, Greek legend indicates that the Trojans themselves were simply Greeks who had migrated from elsewhere several generations before the Trojan War, and had perhaps intermingled with the natives (this will be examined in greater detail later). One legend in particular, found in Virgil's *Aeneid*, states that Teucer, one of the founders of the city of Troy, migrated to that area from Crete with many others accompanying him. It could easily be the case that this migration from Crete, which was said to have been motivated by a famine, is the same one in which Oenopion partook. And then after this migration from Crete, we find, both on the Trojan side and the Chios side, a prince named Hector just a few generations later. This is a peculiar coincidence, and it points towards it being the same Hector.

It is known from archaeology that Trojan influence in the late eighth century BCE extended at least as far as several nearby islands, such as Thasos, Samothrace, Tenedos and others.[171] Therefore, it would not be surprising if Troy also had a degree of power over Chios, which is another island that is relatively nearby.

In line with the idea that, although being descended from the Greeks, Hector of Chios was actually the Trojan prince is the fact that the records about Hector of Chios describe him as fighting against Carians and against Abantes, a people from Euboea in Greece who are said to have settled in Chios a few generations previously. In Homer's Catalogue of Ships, the Abantes are described as being part of the Greek expedition against Troy. Thus, it would make some sense for Hector of Chios, who is specifically described as fighting against the Abantean inhabitants of that very island, to have been the same as Hector of Troy. Perhaps at some point during the ten-year siege of Troy he went on an expedition against Chios due to its inhabitants participating in the attack on Troy, thereafter becoming the ruler of the island.

Although it is true that Hector of Chios is also described as driving Carians from the island, while Carians were described by Homer as allies of Troy, this is not without explanation. The Carians were said to have lived in Miletus, which was definitely a Greek colony, the Greeks evidently having intermingled with the natives. Thus, it is remarkable to hear that the Carians were Trojan allies. It is likely that this was exceptional, and that other Carians, such as those living on Chios and elsewhere, did not side with the Trojans but sided with the Greeks. Strabo affirms that the Carians regularly intermingled and associated with the Greeks.[172] Thus, the description of Hector battling against Abantes and Carians on Chios could plausibly fit Hector of Troy.

With this possibility in mind, we may explain Hector's supposed descent from Oenopion as simply being a mistake in the later records derived from the fact that he succeeded one of Oenopion's descendants as king of the island. However, it is also interesting to note that the available records do not seem to ever state exactly *how* Hector of Chios was the great-grandson of Oenopion, only that he was. This leaves open the possibility that there is no mistake in the account of Hector of Chios, and that he was the son of Priam of Troy but was also descended from Oenopion through his mother or grandmother.

It must be remembered that the surviving accounts of Hector of Chios are, themselves, very late records and are regarded as little more than legends. So we should not expect perfect correspondence between the records of Hector of Chios and those of Hector of Troy to be able to equate the two. Nonetheless, there are enough similarities to conclude that it is at least a distinct possibility that the two figures are identical. In summary, 'Hector' was an extremely uncommon name, these two Hectors possibly being the only figures from Greek legend to be recorded with it. They both lived at the same time, the end of the eighth century BCE. It is known from archaeology that Troy at this time exerted influence of at least some sort over several nearby islands in the Aegean, so it is not unbelievable for it to have sent an expedition against Chios. It may be that Priam sent his son Hector on an expedition against the Abantes of Chios in retaliation for their part in the campaign against Troy, resulting in Hector becoming the ruler of the island and becoming 'Hector of Chios' in local legend centuries later.

Memnon

Memnon is an intriguing character from Greek mythology. He is famous for being the Ethiopian king who marched all the way over

The Characters of the Trojan War

to Troy to aid the Trojans in their fight against the Greeks. During this campaign, he was said to have also conquered Egypt, as well as essentially all the Middle East as far as Iran.[173] Interestingly, there is only one period of history in which the Ethiopians ruled Egypt, and it was in the eighth and seventh centuries BCE, exactly the period in which the Trojan War actually took place. We also know that at least one king of that Ethiopian dynasty, Taharqa, was described as conquering all the territory between Egypt and Troy, and even beyond. This seems to be an excellent correspondence. However, as remarkable as it may seem, it appears that this is simply a coincidence.

The reason for saying this is that there is evidence that the 'Ethiopians' over whom Memnon was king were not actually the Ethiopians of Africa. Although some ancient sources describe them as being from Africa, other early sources describe them as being a different group of Ethiopians, ones who lived in the east. These eastern Ethiopians are mentioned, among other places, in Herodotus' description of Xerxes the Great's army that he took against Greece in 480 BCE. Given that the Ethiopians of Africa were far more famous than the Ethiopians from the east, it is easy to see how the latter group could have been misidentified as the former, whereas the reverse is not such a natural mistake.

The fact that Memnon actually came from the east, and not from Africa, is shown by the fact that Susa – a city in Iran – was referred to as 'the city of Memnon' at least as far back as the writings of Herodotus in the fifth century BCE.[174] The writings of Ctesias are even more specific. As recorded by Diodorus Siculus, the fifth-century BCE historian Ctesias described Memnon as actually being sent by the king of Assyria on his conquests, starting out from Susa in Iran.[175] This would most certainly seem to confirm that Memnon hailed from the east, and that the Ethiopians over whom he was the king were the lesser-known eastern Ethiopians, rather than those of Africa. Supporting this conclusion even further are the legends about Memnon's father, Tithonus. As early as the seventh century BCE, there are legends about Tithonus being abducted by Eos (the mythical mother of Memnon), the goddess of the dawn.[176] As the goddess of the dawn, she was believed to have lived in the east. Later legends about Tithonus concur that he fathered Memnon after travelling far to the east, into Asia.[177] In short, the weight of evidence definitely supports the conclusion that Memnon was originally believed to have come from the east, in the region of Susa in particular, and was only later associated with the Ethiopians of Africa.

Interestingly, when we look into the description of Memnon's campaign, something becomes quite clear. He was said to have conquered all the land between (and including) Egypt and Susa, and yet he also campaigned as far as Troy in Anatolia. The description of Memnon's conquests almost perfectly matches the Assyrian Empire at its peak, in *c.* 700 BCE, although it had not quite reached Susa by that point, nor did it ever conquer as far as Troy, though it is known to have reached as far as the allies of Troy, such as the Phrygians and the Lydians. The fact that Memnon was specifically said to have been sent out by the king of Assyria solidifies the conclusion that this is really a description of an Assyrian campaign in *c.* 700 BCE.

A number of Assyrian kings launched campaigns into Egypt and Anatolia, but when we get the chronology of Assyria properly established, it becomes clear which campaign was Memnon's. He was said to have come to Troy's aid after Hector was killed by Achilles, which was in the final year of the siege. According to our revised chronology, that would be in approximately 695 BCE. Was there an Assyrian campaign into Egypt and then Anatolia at this time? First of all, remember that the traditional dates of the Assyrian kings in this period are out by thirty-one years, as established in Appendix One. Therefore, a campaign which took place in 696 BCE would be misdated in most modern sources to 665 BCE. As it happens, the recorded activities of the Assyrians in that era excellently match the legend.

Assyrian king Ashurbanipal led two successful campaigns into Egypt about this time – one dated by modern scholars to 667 BCE and one dated to 665 BCE (these dates should be adjusted by thirty-one years to 698 BCE and 696 BCE).[178] Either one of these could have been the origin of the story of Memnon conquering Egypt. Also supposedly in 665 BCE (actually 696 BCE), there is a record of King Gyges of Lydia requesting assistance from Assyria due to attacks from the Cimmerians. The Assyrians did send help, and two Cimmerian chieftains were taken back to the Assyrian city of Nineveh.[179] Of course, this is not the same as a campaign to help Troy, but the Assyrians historically never got as far as Troy, so this legend recorded by Ctesias simply cannot be completely accurate. Nonetheless, Lydia was one of Troy's allies according to the *Iliad*, so an Assyrian campaign to support one of Troy's allies in the final year of the Trojan War could very easily be distorted into a campaign to support Troy itself in later accounts. Undoubtedly, helping one of Troy's main allies in any form would have, by extension, aided the Trojan cause.

The Characters of the Trojan War

This is not to say that Memnon was Ashurbanipal himself. The legends are clear that Memnon was sent *by* the king of Assyria, not that he was the king of Assyria himself. Since he was associated with Susiana (Elam), it seems likely that he can be identified as a descendant (possibly the son) of a king of Elam named Menanu, who reigned in the eighth century BCE. Relations between Assyria and Elam were good in the years leading up to 696 BCE, so such a man could plausibly have served as a commander in the Assyrian military. But in any case, we can see that Memnon's legendary Assyrian-backed expedition in which he conquered Egypt and then travelled to Anatolia to support Troy evidently came from the historical activities of a military commander who participated in one of Ashurbanipal's campaigns into Egypt (either in 698 BCE or 696 BCE) and then travelled to Anatolia to aid King Gyges of Lydia.

Phemius

Phemius is a fairly minor character compared to the others thus far considered. He appears in Homer's *Odyssey* as a poet who sings for the suitors of Penelope, the wife of Odysseus. Not many details are known about him, other than that he was from the Greek island of Ithaca. Interestingly, ancient biographies of Homer's life speak of a figure named Phemius. According to Pseudo-Herodotus' *Life of Homer* and Pseudo-Plutarch's *Life of Homer*, Homer's mother married this Phemius, a schoolteacher who lived in a Greek city on the western coast of Anatolia. He was said to have taught literature and music.

It is very likely that this Phemius is identical to the Phemius who appears in the *Odyssey*. The legendary character is a poet, or bard, while the probably historical Phemius of Homer's time was a schoolteacher who taught music. Evidently his career as a schoolteacher would have happened much later in his life, but the topic he taught would have reflected his career as a poet. Furthermore, the timeline is logical, for he is shown to be fairly elderly in Homer's childhood. When Homer reached adulthood, Phemius died and the school was passed on to Homer. Phemius could have been relatively young when he served as an official poet, or bard, perhaps being around twenty-five years old in *c.* 700 BCE, which would have made him about sixty-five years old in *c.* 660 BCE, when Homer probably reached adulthood. And although Phemius was not living in Anatolia in the *Odyssey*, there is no reason at all why he could not have moved later in life.

Mentor

Another character who is mentioned in Pseudo-Herodotus' *Life of Homer* is Mentor. Not much information is given about him, but he is someone whom Homer is described as meeting, and he is presented as being from Ithaca. The Mentor of this record concerning Homer is undoubtedly identical to a character named Mentor in Homer's *Odyssey*. This latter figure is presented by Homer as a friend of Odysseus. The Mentors of both the *Odyssey* and the *Life of Homer* are both described as 'the son of Alcimus', which would be a truly remarkable coincidence if they were not the same Mentor. And just like the probably historical Mentor of the *Life of Homer*, the Mentor of Homer's *Odyssey* is from Ithaca. As with Phemius in the previous section, it is perfectly possible for Mentor to have been fairly young at the time of the events described in the *Odyssey*, and to have been quite old when he then met Homer.

Tychius

There is yet another character mentioned in Pseudo-Herodotus' *Life of Homer* who can be identified with a character in one of Homer's works. In the *Iliad*, Tychius is described as the leatherworker who created a shield for Ajax, made from seven ox-hides along with a plate of brass. The passage describing this is the only time Tychius appears in Homer's works. In Pseudo-Herodotus' *Life of Homer*, there is mention of a Tychius who worked as a shoemaker when Homer was young and had only just started performing poetry. Just like with Phemius the bard, we can easily imagine Tychius being fairly young at the time of the Trojan War, perhaps in his mid-twenties, and then working as an elderly shoemaker when Homer was a young adult. The profession of shoemaking involves leatherworking, so this detail supports the identification of the Tychius in the *Iliad* with the Tychius who met Homer.

Theoclymenus

This next character does not appear in Homer's works. In fact, he only appears in one ancient work regarding the Trojan War, but it is a relatively early source, so it is worth investigating. The work is Euripides' *Helen*, a play written in the fifth century BCE. It is based on a variant of the story of the Trojan War which claims that Helen was never actually taken to Troy, but that the 'Helen' whom Paris took to Troy was a fake, created by the gods. The real Helen, meanwhile, stayed in Egypt. During her time in Egypt, she was protected by King Proteus, mentioned in other records including Herodotus. In this play,

Proteus dies and is succeeded by his son Theoclymenus. He intends to marry Helen, but then Menelaus, her husband, arrives after returning from the Trojan War.

There are a number of clues that help us to identify King Theoclymenus of Egypt. Firstly, his name is potentially useful to us, because it does not appear to be derived from a title, like 'Proteus' and 'Pheron' evidently are. Rather, it seems to be like 'Sesostris' – that is, a corruption of the king's genuine Egyptian name, perhaps influenced by another name which was better known to the Greeks (since 'Theoclymenus' appears as the name of another, Greek, character in Greek legend). Secondly, King Theoclymenus is described as having a habit of killing Greeks, and that surely cannot be a description that matches many historical pharaohs of this early period. Thirdly, recall that we identified Proteus with Pharaoh Necho.

Using this information, we can identify the historical Theoclymenus. We are looking for a king who came after Pharaoh Necho, who killed Greeks, and whose name could have become 'Theoclymenus' to the Greeks. The historical figure who matches this legendary character would appear to be Pharaoh Tantamani. What are our reasons for saying this?

Firstly, consider his name. 'Theoclymenus' is obviously not identical to 'Tantamani', but it is reasonably close. When we place the Greek ending on the name of the historical pharaoh, we get 'Tantamanus'. The second half of the name, 'amanus', is manifestly similar to 'ymenus', although the vowels are different. The first half of the name, 'Tant', is not too similar to 'Theocl', but they become slightly more similar when we transform the 'T' into a 'Th' for the Greek form (as in 'Twosret' becoming 'Thuoris'), creating 'Thant'. The second 't' can be associated with the 'c' in Theoclymenus' name without too much difficulty, because these two sounds historically have a tendency to become exchanged for one another. For example, the legendary first king of the Hyksos in Egypt is recorded in some traditions as 'Salitis', and a number of Egyptologists have proposed that he should be identified with a king recorded in a more contemporary document as 'Shalek'.[180] Notice the 'k' in the place of the 't'. Therefore, it would not be surprising for the second 't' in 'Tantamani' to have become the 'c' in 'Theoclymenus'. Of course, this is not to say that 'Tantamani' could have become 'Theoclymenus' on its own, but rather, the point is that it is perfectly possible to see how the Greeks could have taken the name of this pharaoh and viewed the closest approximation in their language as 'Theoclymenus'.

Now let us consider the timing of his reign. Theoclymenus was said to have succeeded Proteus. In reality, Proteus – that is, Necho I – was succeeded by his son Psamtik. However, in the same year in which Necho died and Psamtik became king of northern Egypt, Tantamani ascended to the throne of southern Egypt. The year was 695 BCE (664 BCE as it appears in modern reference works, without the thirty-one-year adjustment). Thus, although he was not the son of 'Proteus', he was a king who came immediately after him.

What about the detail that he had a habit of killing Greeks? This matches Tantamani, because Psamtik is known to have had Greek mercenaries in his army – a practice which started with Psamtik.[181] Tantamani and Psamtik fought on occasion, meaning that Tantamani must, inevitably, have killed Greeks. So, on the basis of his name, on the basis of the timing of his rule, and on the basis of the fact that he did kill Greeks just like Theoclymenus was said to have done, it appears that Tantamani was indeed the historical figure behind the legendary character of Theoclymenus.

Conclusion
Now that we have uncovered the true identities of many of the characters involved in the Trojan War and the events surrounding it, we will proceed to examine the war itself. We will discover what actually happened and how it ties in with known history and archaeology from the late eighth and early seventh centuries BCE.

5

The Historical Trojan War

In this chapter, we will review the historical events that led to the legendary tales of the Trojan War. We will see how the various characters discussed in the previous chapter all played a part in the wider events that occurred in the eastern Mediterranean in the ninth through to the seventh centuries BCE. We will also see that many Greek legends are easily discernible in the archaeological record from this period, including the Trojan War itself and the events surrounding it.

The Prelude to the Trojan War
Cadmus, a Phoenician prince, allegedly brought the Phoenician alphabet to the Greeks, who then adopted it as their own. We cannot confirm the details of this legend, but evidently something like this happened, since the Greeks did adopt the Phoenician alphabet. As we have already established, the archaeological evidence shows clearly that this must have happened no earlier than $c.$ 900 BCE. Cadmus may have done this while relatively young, perhaps thirty years old or so. One of his contemporaries is Orpheus, whose brother – probably a much younger brother – is Linus. Linus grows up and becomes a music teacher. During the middle of his life, there is a king of Tyre named Pygmalion who has power over Cyprus. This is the famous Pygmalion of Cyprus of Greek legend. Pygmalion's sister, Dido, sails to north Africa and founds Carthage in the last quarter of the ninth century BCE. At this time, it is only a very small village, leaving few archaeological remains.

Near the end of Linus' life, perhaps at around seventy or eighty years old, he becomes the tutor of the young Heracles. We are now in the early eighth century BCE. In this century, Osorkon IV lived and ruled at Tanis in northern Egypt. He was known by the name 'Heracles' and is evidently the Heracles of Greek legend. This conforms to fairly early records claiming that Heracles was of Egyptian descent. Archaeology reveals Egyptian artefacts in Greece in the eighth century BCE, the time of Osorkon IV, indicating a connection of some kind between the two countries. Perhaps they were simply connected through trade at this point, but evidently travellers did journey from one country to the other. It may be that the tale of Linus tutoring Heracles – that is, Osorkon IV – is simply a legend with no historical basis, but it is not out of the question that a king in Egypt may really have asked for a famous tutor from Greece to travel to Egypt to tutor his son.

Around the time of Osorkon's youth or early adulthood, the Olympic Games in Greece were founded. It is unlikely that this Egyptian king had anything to do with the founding of them, but he, as Heracles, ends up being credited with such a feat in some later records. More plausible records attribute the Olympic Games to Iphitos of Elis. This Iphitos of Elis who allegedly had a hand in founding the Olympic Games in 776 BCE was likely identical to the legendary Iphitos of Elis who was killed by Copreus in the time of Heracles.

As an adult, Osorkon evidently had some contact with Greece and became famous there as Heracles, with tales of his life being modified to fit the local geography, as has happened throughout history with countless other myths and legends. Yet, he most likely did travel, or send troops or some other kind of support, to many of the places that Heracles is described as visiting in the legends. Such places include Italy and western Anatolia, where some eighth-century BCE Egyptian artefacts have been discovered. The fact that troops are known to have been sent between Lydia and Egypt in the following century proves that this is not implausible.

Right at the start of Osorkon's reign, King Piye from the south of Egypt embarked on a campaign against him. Osorkon rallied the other minor kings of the north of Egypt and fought against him. Piye's forces were too powerful, so Osorkon took the initiative to approach him at a temple and submit to him, prompting the other rulers to do the same. In response, Piye accepted their submission and returned to the south, having nominally subjected the north but in reality leaving it to its own devices. These events evidently led to the much later Greek legends of Heracles facing a large invading force against his homeland at the start of his career. Heracles rallied the young men of the area and was able to defeat the invading force by going to a temple and using the armour found there.

The Historical Trojan War

At this time, as per the legends, Laomedon the king of Troy engaged in grand construction work on the city of Troy. Archaeology shows significant construction work at Troy at this time, in about the middle of the eighth century BCE. Laomedon was then said to have got into trouble with those involved in the construction (allegedly the gods Poseidon and Apollo – the historical origin of this story is unclear) because he refused to pay their wages. However, the story claims that Heracles happened to be passing through the country at this time and was able to save Laomedon from the wrath of these two gods. Heracles had supposedly been in the region because he was waging war against the Amazons. As mentioned before, eighth-century BCE Egyptian artefacts have been found in western Anatolia, supporting the conclusion that some Egyptian troops really were in the region at this time. This would be similar to how Psamtik sent men to Gyges of Lydia and requested military support in the early seventh century BCE. Osorkon may have sent men to the region for some reason, perhaps to assist in a war against the Amazons as the legends claimed, and then his troops would have been in a position to assist another king in the area. Aid was apparently given, but then when the king of Troy did not uphold his end of the deal, Osorkon's troops killed the king, but evidently did not devastate the city.

At this time, Jason and the Argonauts went on their famous voyage to Colchis at the eastern end of the Black Sea to find the legendary Golden Fleece. Archaeology reveals that the eighth century BCE is when the Greeks entered the 'Age of Expansion', with evidence of Greek presence being found on the coasts of the Black Sea.[182] Thus, the evidence supports the story of Jason having a historical origin in this time period.

And around this same time, *c.* 750 BCE, Carthage experienced a surge of major construction work, this being recognised by many later historians of antiquity as marking its foundation. As claimed by certain Greek historians, this was about one generation or so before the Trojan War. Argos, meanwhile, rose to the ascendancy among the Greek nations in the Peloponnese, setting the stage for its prominence in the *Iliad*.

Near the end of Osorkon's reign, in about 747 BCE, Osorkon's realm was threatened by Sargon, the king of Assyria. To appease the king, Osorkon gathered twelve large horses and gave them to Sargon, who described them as being without equal in all Assyria. This likely led to the tale of Heracles capturing the mighty Mares of Diomedes and handing them over to the otherwise antagonistic King Eurystheus.

A few years later, a member of Pygmalion's dynasty – perhaps a brother or, more likely, a son of Pygmalion – was apparently active in Egypt and served as an advisor. As per the legends, he contributed to a conflict between Heracles and Busiris, most likely the conflict between Osorkon IV and Bocchoris that some scholars believe probably occurred.

Shortly after this, from 744 to 732 BCE, Pharaoh Shebitku reigned in Egypt. His battle against the Assyrian Empire became remembered as a great victory, evolving into tales of him conquering the territory of that empire, all across the Levant through to Anatolia. Thus, he became memorialised by Herodotus and later historians as the mighty King Sesostris who engaged in far-reaching military campaigns even as far as Thrace. Shebitku then installed a king later recorded as Ammeris on the throne of Sais in northern Egypt. He was evidently the same as King Anysis mentioned by Herodotus as a king of the north of Egypt at this time. He was allegedly blind, and evidently is the primary origin of the legendary blind king Pheron. In reality, this legendary king is most likely a combination of Anysis (Ammeris) and his son Tefnakht, since Pheron was said to have recovered from his blindness, indicating that the second part of his life is taken from the following historical king.

After Tefnakht, Necho I succeeded to the throne of Sais and other parts of the north of Egypt, including Memphis. He became known in Greek legend by the name 'Proteus', derived from one of his Egyptian titles. He was the king of Egypt during the Trojan War.

The Archaeology of the City of Troy

Now that we have examined the historical events involved in the Greek legends leading up to the legend of the Trojan War, let us turn to the city itself. As we have already mentioned, there is evidence of the city having had refortification work performed on its city walls in the eighth century BCE, which fits in with the legend of Laomedon, the king of Troy, fortifying the city.[183] Prior to that, in roughly 800 BCE, there was an earlier construction phase after about a century or two of very little activity at the site (but not total abandonment, as previously believed).[184] This would correspond to the 'founding' of the city of Troy by Ilus, the father of Laomedon.

Beyond just the timing of these archaeological construction events fitting in with our revised chronology of the Greek legends, the culture displayed by the inhabitants of Troy in this period also matches the legends. According to Virgil's *Aeneid*, a figure named Teucer migrated from Crete to the area of Troy along with many companions. This is supported by a work known as *The Alexandra*, usually attributed to Lycophron of the third century BCE. This work makes a passing reference to Dardanus having married into Crete's royal house.[185] Dardanus is the person who married the daughter of Teucer according to Greek legend, and he was the great-grandfather of Ilus, father of Laomedon. Therefore, this supports the conclusion that the origin of the Trojans did lie, at least in part, with Crete. But Dardanus, the one who married Teucer's daughter and formed a new kingdom that may be considered a continuation of Teucer's own, was said to have come from somewhere else. He is never described as a native of Anatolia, yet he was not one of the Cretans either. According to Dionysius of Halicarnassus, Dardanus came from Greece.[186]

This means that the origin of the Trojan people partially lies with Greece and partially lies with Crete. And Crete itself had been taken over by the Mycenaean Greeks by the middle of the fifteenth century BCE. So really, the claim in the legends is that the Trojan people, ultimately, were Greeks. Dionysius of Halicarnassus even directly stated that 'the Trojans were a nation as truly Greek as any'.[187] This agrees with the way that the *Iliad* portrays the Greeks and Trojans as having essentially the same culture, religion and language. Of course, they had been cut off from Greece itself for a century or two and had most likely intermingled with the natives of western Anatolia to a large degree, so they appear to have no longer had any sense of shared identity with the original Greeks. Nonetheless, this origin is significant. In the Mycenaean era, the archaeology of Troy shows no significant evidence of Greek culture. On the other hand, the Troy of the Archaic Era displays such a strong level of Greek culture that, for many decades, it was considered to be a bona fide Greek colony. It is now understood that it stood separate from the Greek colonies still in contact with the mainland, partly on the basis of chemical analyses showing that the Greek-style pottery found at Troy was made locally, rather than being imported. Nonetheless, it is evident that Greek settlers arrived around 900 BCE.[188] Therefore, this fits perfectly with the legendary arrival of Greek settlers in the time of Teucer, six generations before Priam (an elderly king at the time of the Trojan War).

What can we say about the importance and power of Troy in this period? Although some have claimed that the Troy of the Archaic Period was little more than a backwater village, more recent research has completely overturned that viewpoint. In fact, it is now understood that the Troy of the late eighth century BCE was an important sea-port town, much like it had been in the Mycenaean era. Part of the evidence for this is the fact that analyses of pottery in the surrounding region has revealed that pottery on Samothrace, Thasos, Lesbos, Tenedos and Lemnos in c. 700 BCE originated in Troy.[189] This proves that the Troy of this era was an important trading city in that region at that time. One researcher in 2006 described the Troy of c. 700 BCE as being 'a port-town ... whose main purpose was to service maritime trade into and out of the Aegean and Euxine [Black] seas'.[190] One reference work from 2020 suggested that 'Troy probably lost its position as a regional center' only in the late seventh century BCE, meaning that it still had it at the start of that century.[191] Notably, the grand city wall described by Homer was still standing and still in use at this time.[192] The fortifications of most other contemporary Greek cities 'must have seemed slight by comparison', as one modern work explains.[193] Therefore, although the city was probably not as large or as powerful as the Troy of the Mycenaean era, we can still say that the city of Troy in c. 700 BCE does match what we would expect from the city in the time of the Trojan War.

The Trojan War

Let us now examine the wider events that occurred around this time that led to the war, as well as the events involved in the siege of Troy itself. As noted earlier, Argos became the dominant power in the Greek world in about the middle of the eighth century BCE. Thus, Agamemnon the king of Argos was perfectly positioned to lead the war against Troy at the end of that century. By that time, Sparta had also risen to become a powerful state in Greece, as described in the legends and confirmed by the history of the Archaic Period. Menelaus, the brother of Agamemnon, ruled over Sparta.

Meanwhile, in Anatolia, Phrygia was the main power in the region. It was a small empire encompassing almost the entire western end of Turkey, and undoubtedly Troy was part of that empire or at the very least was a close ally. Priam, the king of Troy, even married a Phrygian princess.[194] Lydia, however, must have been a powerful state within the Phrygian Empire, similar to how Babylonia was a powerful state within the Assyrian Empire. This would explain how Lydia immediately rose to the ascendancy after the fall of Phrygia near the beginning of the seventh century BCE. Although it is uncertain, it appears that Troy was possibly within – or maybe just outside – the sphere of the Lydian state, with the Phrygian Empire as the overall power over the whole region.

The war between the Greeks and the Trojans was not limited to just the city of Troy. It might be imagined by the modern audience that the

Trojan War was simply a case of the entire Greek army encamped by the Trojan city, engaged in battle against the forces of that city there for ten long years. That is not the situation described in the legends. Rather, the war took place over a much wider area and involved far more than just the inhabitants of the city of Troy against the entire Greek army. The Trojan Battle Order in the *Iliad* shows that numerous cities and nations all over western Anatolia were involved in the war. The Phrygians and the Lydians fought on the side of the Trojans, but so did the Paphlagonians in north central Anatolia. In addition, the Carians in the south-western corner of Anatolia also fought for the Trojans, as did the Lycians, slightly further south-east than the Carians. The Thracians were also allies of the Trojans in this war, on the north-western side of the Dardanelles.

Connected to this is the fact that the Greeks were said to have attacked far more than just the city of Troy. Again, the idea that the siege of Troy was really a case of all the Greek forces surrounding Troy for ten years is a misconception. In fact, the Greeks did not initially land at the right city. According to legend, they first landed at nearby Mysia by mistake and began raiding that land.[195] Then, during the war against Troy, the Greek forces only presented a united attack on the city of Troy during the first year of the siege and during the last year of the siege. During all the years in between, the forces from Greece went their separate ways and raided the surrounding land, particularly the land of the allies of Troy. The ancient historian Thucydides notes that the Greeks could have taken Troy easily if they had stuck together – which surely would have been the case – but due to a lack of wealth and provisions to keep them going, they took to raiding the surrounding areas.[196] This, really, is what most of the Greeks were doing during the majority of the ten-year siege of Troy.

This is not just a claim found in later tradition, because even in the *Iliad* itself we find the claim that Achilles, one of the most powerful Greek warriors, conquered eleven cities during the Trojan War.[197] According to Apollodorus, a Greek historian of the second century BCE, he captured numerous cities along the western coast of Anatolia, such as Smyrna and Cyme.[198] After this, he captured Side, a city along the middle of the southern coast of Anatolia. Note that he was said to have captured these cities; he did not simply sack them and move on. And if Achilles alone conquered so many cities, we can conclude that the total number of cities and regions conquered by all the Greek leaders involved in the Trojan War must have been immense.

Let us combine this information with something else that Thucydides pointed out. He analysed the figures given by Homer for the number of ships sent out from Greece, and the number of men per ship, and he concluded that the 'expedition was indeed greater than those that went before it but yet inferior to those of the present age'.[199] So according to him, the expedition against Troy was actually smaller than the foreign campaigns in which the Greeks were engaging in his own time. Summarising the situation, Thucydides stated that 'it will appear that the whole number of men considered as sent jointly from all Greece were not very many'.[200]

So in other words, when we look at the situation as a whole, we can see that the Trojan War was not just a siege against the city of Troy. Rather, it involved a large – but not excessively large – army of Greeks travelling to western Anatolia and spreading out across much of that region, engaging in raiding and conquering various cities and territories. And, of course, the city of Troy itself was besieged, but this was merely part, albeit a key part, of the wider events occurring in western Anatolia. The scenario of thousands of Greeks sailing over to Anatolia and conquering various parts of that region is exactly what occurred in the Archaic Era. It is true that there were Greek migrations to Anatolia between Mycenaean times and the Archaic Period (however, the extent of these migrations is largely based on Greek tradition about migrations subsequent to the Trojan War, so modern references to these migrations must obviously be treated with caution). But it is known that it was at the very end of the eighth century BCE that a new surge of migrations occurred.[201] As the *Encyclopaedia Britannica* notes, 'Archaeological finds indicate considerable Greek colonizing activity on the south coast of Anatolia in the 8th century BCE and on the north coast in the 7th century.'[202]

Countless Greek cities were established in Anatolia in this era and afterwards. This fits exactly with the description of the sizeable Greek forces spreading out and conquering much of western Anatolia at the time of the Trojan War. Note also what Thucydides stated after his section on that war:

> For also after the Trojan war the Grecians continued still their shifting and transplantations; insomuch as never resting, they improved not their power. For the late return of the Greeks from Ilium caused not a little innovation; and in most of the cities there arose seditions, and those which were driven out built cities for themselves in other places.

The Historical Trojan War

So according to this source, the Greeks continued their migrations even after the Trojan War. This, again, is exactly what the archaeological record reveals about the era from the late eighth century BCE through to the following century.[203] Although some Greek cities did exist in Anatolia prior to the Archaic Period, it was from the end of the eighth century BCE onwards that there was a sudden, prolonged surge of colonisation. From the evidence of Homer and Thucydides, it is evident that the Trojan War was the catalyst for this sudden surge of colonisation and migration. With this in mind, the archaeological evidence is in complete agreement with the Trojan War being at the end of the eighth century BCE.

Colonisation is not the only aspect of the legends confirmed by archaeology. It is also known that there was fighting between the Greeks and certain nations in the legends specified to be allies of the Trojans. For example, Assyrian inscriptions dated to the end of the eighth century BCE and the beginning of the seventh record conflicts with the Greeks, sometimes just in sea battles but also in coastal raids.[204] Furthermore, Gyges of Lydia is recorded as warring against the Greeks in the Troad right at the beginning of the seventh century BCE.[205] It is possible that the Trojan War was actually a part of this very conflict. This is uncertain, however. Part of the reason that this is uncertain is because the exact dating of this conflict is unknown, though it is generally dated to the 690s BCE. Another reason to doubt that it was actually the conflict of which the siege of Troy was a part is the fact that it is reported to have been primarily a case of Lydia conquering the Greeks rather than the other way around.

On the other hand, there are records of the Greeks founding a number of cities in the Troad at the beginning of the seventh century BCE, despite Gyges having gained control over the entire Troad by the beginning of that century. This might indicate that there was a degree of back-and-forth between the Greeks and the Lydians at this time, which fits well with the legend of the Trojan War. The Greeks had established themselves in the Troad before Gyges' conquests in the 690s BCE, which likely corresponds to the initial attack on the Troad by the Greeks, right at the start of the Trojan War. Gyges' conquest of that region may, therefore, have been part of the efforts of Troy's allies to fight back against the Greeks (especially if the dating of this conquest to the 690s BCE can be trusted). The fact that a number of Greek cities are recorded as being founded right around this time and just after may demonstrate that the Greeks fought back against Lydia and managed to regain footholds in the area, just as the Greeks were successful in fighting back against Troy and its allies in the legends of the Trojan War.

Whether this exact scenario is correct or not, or whether Gyges' conquests occurred just after the fall of Troy rather than before, the records are clear that the Greek colonisation of much of western Anatolia in this era was not a peaceful process. There was notable warfare between the Greeks and those recorded as allies of the Trojans, such as the Assyrians and the Lydians.

The Destruction of Troy
But if the Trojan War really did take place in *c.* 700 BCE, we would expect there to be a destruction layer discernible in the archaeology of the site dating to that time. And is that what we find? It is indeed. There is a destruction layer that has been dated to about 650 BCE.[206] This date must be taken as only approximate, since it is entirely founded on pottery finds, which are, by their nature, almost always approximate. In reality, the destruction could be dated to several decades either side of 650 BCE, as reference works freely admit. The destruction is said by some academic sources to have occurred at some point between 675–625 BCE.[207]

In any case, a twenty-year difference in the upper date given by archaeologists to this destruction and our date for the Trojan War cannot be viewed as significant when the archaeological date is established solely by pottery styles. This is especially so when we consider that the type of pottery found at Troy in this time period (known as G2/3 Ware) is also found on many islands in the region, as was mentioned before. If Troy was producing pottery (G2/3 Ware) that was imported to these other islands, but then Troy was destroyed, then obviously the production of new pottery at Troy would have stopped. The inhabitants of the islands which had been getting their pottery from Troy would thus have ceased receiving new pottery from that city, and therefore they may have continued using the G2/3 Ware for a few decades after it had stopped being produced, due to Troy having been destroyed. Thus, the G2/3 Ware in these other locations may well be found by archaeologists in slightly later contexts than when they were originally produced, thus causing scholars to misdate them by a few decades. Since the destruction layer at Troy is dated based on this G2/3 pottery, this could mean that the archaeologists have misdated the destruction by a few decades.

Therefore, this destruction layer is a good fit for our date of 695 BCE for the final year of the Trojan War. Although it is possible that this was caused by an earthquake, there are scholars who argue that an attack is a more likely explanation.[208] It was followed by a period of either total abandonment or at least a seriously decreased population. This fits in with the ancient descriptions of the Greeks completely massacring the inhabitants of the city after their machination with the Trojan Horse. At the end of this period of abandonment or decreased population, in *c.* 625 BCE, the material culture of the site completely changed. It is at this point that it became a true Greek colony.

In summary, we can see that the archaeology of Hisarlik, the site of the ancient city of Troy, fits perfectly with the legends when we examine the remains from the Archaic Period. Greek settlers appear to have arrived in the area in *c.* 900 BCE, just as Teucer was said to have arrived from Crete. After a long period of very little activity at the site, there is renewed building work in *c.* 800 BCE, corresponding to the founding of Troy by the legendary figure 'Ilus', four generations after Teucer. Then, we find additional construction work – including fortification work – in *c.* 750 BCE, corresponding to the fortification of the city during the reign of Laomedon, the son of Ilus. This occurred while Priam was young. By the end of the century, Troy had become an important trading city in the region, fitting the requirement for Troy to have been important at the time of the Trojan War. Its grand Bronze Age walls were still standing and in use. Then, dated to *c.* 675–625 BCE but possibly slightly earlier, there was widespread destruction and then a period of possibly total abandonment, corresponding to the destruction of the city and the massacre of its inhabitants at the hands of the Greeks in 695 BCE.

Aftermath of the War
After the destruction of Troy and the massacre of its citizens, what happened next? In ancient Greek literature, the subject of the Greek forces returning from Troy was a topic about which much was written. A book in the same vein as the *Iliad* and *Odyssey*, called *Nostoi* (meaning 'Returns'), was written at around the same time as Homer's works, though it is now lost to us. Still, we are aware of the basic contents from references contained within other literature, and there are also many other references by Greek historians to the events that occurred after the fall of Troy, perhaps taken directly from the *Nostoi* in some cases, though not necessarily all.

According to this ancient literature, the Greek gods were enraged over the impious acts performed during the sack of Troy. For this reason, they decided that most of the Greeks would not be allowed to return to their homes. Agamemnon was one of the few who did, but most of the others were scattered to various different lands as they attempted to journey home. In this section, we will examine this legendary scattering of the Greeks after the Trojan War, and we will see how this event is discernible in the archaeological record.

Cyprus

The famous archer Teucer (not the ancestor of the Trojans, but a different man by the same name) is said to have landed in Cyprus and founded the city of Salamis.[209] In reality, it appears that this 'founding' was more of an expansion, since there is evidence that Salamis had been inhabited for many centuries prior to the Trojan War. But in the Archaic Period, archaeologists have noticed a surge of Greek artefacts, generally dated to the late eighth and early seventh centuries BCE. This is the case for Cyprus in general, and Salamis in particular.[210] Thus, the idea that some of the Greek forces that had been campaigning in Anatolia during the Trojan War ended up settling in Cyprus in general, and Salamis in particular, is clearly consistent with the archaeological record.

Paphos was also said to have been founded at this time. The Greek commander Agapenor was said to have settled on Cyprus and founded Paphos. There were actually two cities in Cyprus called Paphos. One is known as Old Paphos, and the other is known as New Paphos. The former is now known as Kouklia, while the latter is the modern city called Paphos. The foundation story regarding Agapenor is specifically about New Paphos, but it is now widely thought that this is a mistake, since that city is now understood to have been founded in the fourth century BCE.[211] Therefore, Old Paphos must be the subject of the legend about Agapenor. In truth, this 'founding' was probably not a genuine one, but simply an expansion of the settlement, since King Cinyras was said to have lived in Paphos even before the Trojan War. In any case, it is significant that, at Old Paphos, 'epigraphical testimonies confirm the rule of Greek *basileis* (kings) as early as the 7th century' BCE.[212] Thus, the archaeological evidence supports the essential veracity of this tradition.

Spain

As well as Cyprus, Teucer was also said to have travelled to Spain, to the region of Gades (modern-day Cadiz) in particular.[213] Interestingly, the earliest archaeological traces of the Greeks in Spain date back to about 700 BCE.[214] These Greek artefacts were found in Huelva, which is just next to Gades. Therefore, this strongly supports the legend of the Greek archer Teucer settling in the region of Gades after the Trojan War.

Italy

Many of the Greeks were said to have settled in Italy. Specifically, they were almost exclusively said to have settled in the south of Italy. It is widely known that, historically, the Greeks did extensively settle southern Italy. In fact, the Romans even had a name for the coastal regions of southern Italy specifically based on this fact; they called it Magna Graecia, meaning 'Great Greece'. But when did this settlement actually take place? It is universally accepted that this settlement took place in the Archaic Period, generally dated to the eighth and seventh centuries BCE. Nothing in the sources says that the Greeks who arrived there after the Trojan War were the very first to settle there, so there is no issue with the fact that a number of Greek colonies were apparently founded in about the middle of the eighth century BCE, and therefore several decades before our revised date for the Trojan War. In fact, certain traditions explicitly note Greek settlers arriving in Italy about half a century prior to the Trojan War, such as a Greek king named Evander.[215] But the sudden wave of settlers arriving after the fall of Troy, after 700 BCE, is evident in the archaeological record.

The fact that there was a particularly strong period of Greek settlement after 700 BCE is the reason why some modern sources refer to the settlement of Magna Graecia as 'a process that began in the 7th century' BCE.[216] Others similarly refer to Magna Graecia as being 'inhabited by Greek settlers from roughly 700 BCE'.[217] Thus, we can see that the archaeological record is definitely consistent with the settlement of southern Italy by the Greek forces on their way back from Troy, just after 700 BCE.

Libya

According to Apollodorus, a Greek commander in the Trojan War named Guneus went to Libya after the Trojan War.[218] A later source specifies that he settled near the Cinyps River, which is in the historic region of Tripolitania.[219] Interestingly, according to a separate tradition (first recorded by Herodotus), the Greek colony of Cyrene was founded in the seventh century BCE.[220] Herodotus reports that the first king of the newly founded colony of Cyrene was a man named Battus. However, Battus himself is said to have been sent out by a king of Thera named 'Grinnus'.

It is very probable that these two traditions about the Greeks founding a colony in Libya are connected. Herodotus' 'Grinnus' is most likely the same as the 'Guneus' in the late traditions about the Trojan War. Guneus' founding of a Greek colony 'near the Cinyps River' is quite possibly a reference to Cyrene itself, or another colony slightly further west of Cyrene founded by the same settlers. In the account about Grinnus and the founding of Cyrene, the whole process from deciding to settle in Libya to Cyrene finally being established is said to have taken a number of years. The date of the beginning of Battus' rule in Cyrene is commonly given as *c.* 630 BCE, but Herodotus' account is too vague to be able to date it with any precision. Furthermore, archaeology has shown that Greek finds at Cyrene actually date back to the *first* half of the seventh century BCE.[221] In any case, given the approximate nature of this '*c.* 630 BCE' date and the fact that Grinnus could have been young at the time of the Trojan War but old at the time of Battus finally establishing the colony of Cyrene and beginning to rule there, we can see that this is compatible with the tradition of Guneus founding a colony in Libya after the Trojan War.

Egypt
Another place to which certain Greeks were said to have travelled after the Trojan War is Egypt. In particular, Menelaus and his men were said to have blown ashore there on their journey home. This was not a fleeting visit, for he was said to have stayed in that country for some eight years.[222] According to some versions of the story, Helen of Troy was actually in Egypt all along, and was never in Troy at all. This is the version recounted by Herodotus. However, Homer's more contemporary tale – along with many others – definitely portrays her as being in Troy for the duration of the Trojan War. This earlier version is the preferable one, and we may perhaps suggest that the idea of her being in Egypt came from distorted and poorly understood accounts of her being in Egypt with Menelaus after the Trojan War.

A small division of the Greek forces being blown ashore in Egypt after the Trojan War is directly corroborated by independent records. These records have, of course, been completely missed, much like the identification of Heracles with Osorkon, because of mistaken beliefs about the timing of the Trojan War. When it is placed in its correct chronological position – that is, starting and ending within a decade either side of the year 700 BCE – then this event in Egypt is easily identifiable. We have already established that Necho I, probably the historical Proteus, actually died in 695 BCE. In the south of Egypt, where Thebes was the capital, Tantamani ascended to the throne in this same year. As we established in the previous chapter, Tantamani is very probably the historical origin of Theoclymenus, the king of Thebes at the time of Menelaus arriving in Egypt according to the fifth-century BCE poem *Helen*. But since Homer presents Menelaus as meeting Polybus the king of Egypt, whom we have identified with Taharqa, Menelaus must have arrived in Egypt before his death, which was in 695 BCE as well. Given the fact that *Helen* portrays Proteus as having just recently died and Theoclymenus as the new king of Egypt when Menelaus was present in the country, it seems virtually certain that 695 BCE was the year in which Menelaus arrived in Egypt. He must have arrived before Taharqa's death that year, to have been able to meet him as Homer's 'Polybus'.

With those facts in mind, consider the fact that the successor of Necho I after his death in 695 BCE was his son Psamtik I. Herodotus has much to say about this next king. According to this fifth-century BCE historian, something notable happened at the start of the reign of Psamtik. Herodotus reports:

> Ionians and Carians, voyaging for plunder, were forced to put in on the coast of Egypt, where they disembarked in their armor of bronze; and an Egyptian came into the marsh country and brought news to Psammetichus (for he had never before seen armored men) that men of bronze had come from the sea and were foraging in the plain.[223]

So according to this report, Greeks (Ionians) and Carians were forced ashore on the coast of Egypt. And they were not traders, but were definitely soldiers and had been 'voyaging for plunder'. This perfectly matches the record about Menelaus and his men being forced ashore on the coast of Egypt shortly after the Trojan War. Granted, the story of Menelaus does not mention Carians, but their presence does not contradict the story of Menelaus either. And in addition, many modern reference works say that the presence of Carians in Psamtik's army came from direct communication between the Egyptian king and Gyges, king of Lydia, as noted previously. In this case, it may be that the presence of Carians in Herodotus' account of the soldiers that were blown ashore is a mistake. But in any case, as we have noted, there is no contradiction with the account of Menelaus if the Carians really were there.

In conclusion, we can see that the legend of the Greeks being scattered to many different locations around the Mediterranean in the aftermath of the Trojan War – such as Cyprus, Spain, Italy, Libya, and Egypt – is firmly supported by the archaeology and history of the early seventh century BCE.

Trojan Migrations

The Greeks were not the only ones who were said to have been dispersed after the fall of Troy. The Trojans themselves were also said to have migrated to other lands after the fall of their city. The most famous of these is the migration to Italy, led by Aeneas, a prince of Troy. This is the one which has the most direct connection to British legend and the story of Brutus founding Britain, so we will leave that one for last. For now, we will examine some of the lesser-known legendary migrations and see how these are evident in the historical and archaeological record.

Sicily

One location that was said to have been settled by Trojans after their defeat at the hands of the Greeks was Sicily. There are a few different versions of this legend, but essentially all attribute it to the leadership of a man named Elymus, the brother of Aeneas.[224] He was said to have been the forefather of the Elymians, an ancient tribe that inhabited Sicily. Interestingly, it is noted that the Elymians are not easily identifiable in the archaeological record even as late as the eighth century BCE.[225] It is not until the seventh century BCE that a distinct material culture, which had strong Greek influences, appears at Elymian sites.[226] Could it be that the Elymians are not distinguishable in the archaeological record prior to that time simply because they were not actually there? That would certainly be a logical conclusion. And the fact that their material culture displays evidence of Greek influence would tie in perfectly with the legend of the Trojans arriving there, given that the Trojans of the Archaic Period themselves were originally Greeks, still with a Hellenised material culture and religion at the time of the Trojan War.

One specific city which was said to have been founded by Elymus was Segesta. Although modern reference works acknowledge that this city was, according to legend, founded by remnants of the Trojans, it is also tacitly acknowledged that it was only really founded centuries after the Mycenaean era. Although its exact date of founding is impossible to establish, it is generally placed in the eighth century BCE.[227] For example, the earliest pottery remains found at Segesta are Elymian ware, 'dating from the eighth and seventh

1. One of the Amarna letters, recording correspondence between Egyptian pharaohs and various Canaanite vassal kings. These letters demonstrate that any major revision of the chronology of Egypt that would bring it forward by many centuries, such as the revised chronology proposed by Velikovsky, cannot be correct. Such a revision would place these Canaanite vassal kings in the period in which the Biblical record shows that the Israelites had already long since displaced them. (Courtesy of the Metropolitan Museum of Art)

2. A view of modern Jerusalem. Where an Islamic shrine now stands, King Solomon had constructed a richly-adorned temple which was plundered by Pharaoh Shishak shortly after his death. The Biblical record places this in the tenth century BCE. In line with this, Egyptian monuments record a king known as Sheshonk I engaging in a campaign against Israel, and the conventional Egyptian chronology places this in the tenth century BCE. This correspondence with the Bible supports the conventional chronology of Egypt.

Above: 3. Ruins of Megiddo. This ancient city in Israel is described in the Bible as being fortified, along with the cities of Gezer and Hazor, by King Solomon. In line with this, archaeologists have unearthed identical six-chambered city gates at those three cities, all dating to the tenth century BCE. This correspondence with the Biblical record supports the conventional chronology of the archaeology of the Near East.

Left: 4. A donation stela from Osorkon I, who gave by far the largest ever recorded donation of gold and silver to the Egyptian temples. This inexplicably large donation occurred just a few years after Sheshonk I's campaign into Israel, supporting the conclusion that Sheshonk I really should be identified with Shishak, the king who plundered Solomon's wealth. (Courtesy of the Metropolitan Museum of Art)

Above left: 5. A bust of Ramesses II. He is believed to have ruled from 1279 to 1213 BCE. The conventional date of the Trojan War places it in the time of this pharaoh, or a few decades later by some estimates. However, there is abundant evidence that the Trojan War actually occurred many centuries after the time of Ramesses II. (Courtesy of the Museo Egizio under Creative Commons 2.0)

Above right: 6. A great battle depicted on an Assyrian relief housed in what Sennacherib called the 'Palace Without Rival' in Nineveh. The fall of Nineveh is vitally important to the dating of the Trojan War, because the fifth-century BCE historian Ctesias misdated Nineveh's fall to about 900 BCE, when it actually occurred more than two and a half centuries later. This is significant, because Ctesias dated the Trojan War relative to the fall of Nineveh, and it seems that his chronology became highly influential among later Greek historians.

7. One of the Lachish letters. It is an excellent example of the alphabet used by the Israelites, which was essentially identical to the Phoenician alphabet. This alphabet was adopted by the Greeks in about 900 BCE, and Greek legend firmly places the adoption of this alphabet *before* the time of the Trojan War. (Courtesy of the Dutch National Archives under Creative Commons 0)

Above: 8. A Mycenean bronze axe head. The traditional date of the Trojan War places it in the Mycenaean era, and many people believe that Homer's descriptions match that era because he refers to bronze weapons. However, his references to bronze weapons need not be taken as any more historically significant than his references to weapons made of gold, silver, and tin, which do not match any historical era. (Courtesy of the Metropolitan Museum of Art)

Below: 9. The Baths of Aphrodite, Cyprus. According to Greek legend, this was the location where Adonis first saw and fell in love with Aphrodite. This demonstrates the fact that legends can be taken from one country and applied to specific locations in a different country, since the story of Adonis and Aphrodite originally came from the story of the Sumerian deities Tammuz and Inanna.

10. A view of modern Tarragona, Spain, with the ruins of a Roman amphitheatre in the foreground. One tradition states that Tarragona got its name (which was 'Tarraco' in ancient times) from 'Tearco the Ethiopian', a king of Egypt who was said to have campaigned through Europe as far as Spain, according to Greek legend. Scholars widely acknowledge that Tearco is the historical Taharqa of the late eighth century BCE, and his legendary campaign evidently came from his historical campaign against the mighty Assyrian Empire.

11. The Tombs of the Kings, Cyprus. This massive burial ground contains the tombs of many Greek and Roman high officials of Cyprus. According to Greek legend, Cyprus was settled by Greeks after the end of the Trojan War. In line with the revised chronology of the Trojan War presented in this book, archaeologists have noted a surge of Greek artefacts in Cyprus from about 700 BCE.

Above: 12. Roman ruins at Paphos, Cyprus. According to Greek legend, Paphos was founded by the Greek commander Agapenor after the Trojan War. The earliest evidence for Greek kings at Old Paphos (about 16 kilometres from the modern city of that name) dates to the early seventh century BCE, supporting a date of about 700 BCE for the Trojan War.

Below: 13. Ruins of the Roman Forum. The earliest evidence for the construction of public buildings in the Forum dates to the latter half of the seventh century BCE. This supports the conclusion that Romulus should be dated to about that time, about one century later than the traditional date.

Top left: 14. Etruscan pottery. It is said that the Etruscans imitated Greek pottery. This is consistent with attributing the origin of the Etruscans, in large part at least, to the Trojans, who were actually Greek descendants. It also helps us to see that the 'Greek' influences in La Tène art can be attributed to the Etruscans rather than the Greeks directly. (Courtesy of the Metropolitan Museum of Art)

Above left: 15. A Montefortino helmet of the Roman army. It would have held a plume on the central knob, and such a design is consistent with ancient Celtic helmets from the La Tène era, supporting the conclusion that La Tène culture emerged due to the arrival of Italic settlers in Celtic lands, led by Brutus. (Courtesy of the Metropolitan Museum of Art)

Above right: 16. La Tène sword. These are commonly found in graves from the La Tène culture, whereas swords and other weapons and armour are generally absent from graves from the preceding Hallstatt culture. This is consistent with the conclusion that the La Tène culture was formed by Brutus and his fellow Etruscans settling in Gaul and forming a new ruling class, since Etruscan graves are also characterised by weapons and armour. (Courtesy of the Metropolitan Museum of Art)

17. Cissbury Ring, Worthing. This large hill fort underwent a major expansion in the fifth century BCE. This was just one of many hill forts in Britain and Gaul that were substantially enlarged and fortified in that century. This phenomenon was almost certainly the result of Brutus and his followers bringing with them their Etruscan settlement styles.

18. An inscribed cylinder from the reign of Nebuchadnezzar II. Establishing the true dates for his reign is of vital importance to establishing the date of the Trojan War. The evidence from the Biblical record and from an astronomical tablet dated to Nebuchadnezzar's thirty-seventh year indicates that his reign should be placed twenty years earlier than the dates commonly ascribed to him by most scholars. (Courtesy of the Metropolitan Museum of Art)

centuries'.[228] Of course, bearing in mind the inherent imprecision of dating based on pottery finds, this is compatible with this Elymian ware dating to just after 695 BCE, after the Trojan War.

Tenea

Another location that was said to have been inhabited by survivors of the Trojan War is Tenea. This is a city in Greece, and it was said by Pausanias to have been built by Trojan prisoners, having been taken captive after the fall of their city and permitted to build a new city for themselves.[229] Tenea has only been uncovered by archaeologists very recently. Excavations in the area began in 2013, but it was not until 2018 that actual buildings from the city itself were discovered. The city does not go back to the Mycenaean era. In fact, the earliest remains found in the area do not even come from these excavations themselves, but rather from discoveries of individual artefacts in the decades prior to these excavations. For example, a number of statues dating to the sixth century BCE were found in the era. However, it seems that the very earliest artefact from this site that has yet been discovered is a sarcophagus containing a female skeleton. This has been dated to the late seventh or early sixth century BCE.[230] Given that this appears to be the earliest artefact yet discovered at Tenea, this is consistent with the idea that it was founded soon after the Trojan War of *c.* 700 BCE.

Evidence that Tenea really was built by the Trojans has been uncovered by the recent excavations. The leader of these excavations, Elena Korka, certainly believes as much, for she stated in an interview regarding her discoveries, 'The people here were different – they were Trojans. They had their own identity.' This statement is based on the fact that although Tenea appears Greek in many ways, its material culture and practices have been found to be distinct from the surrounding Greek territories. For example, the inhabitants of this city had different pottery styles and burial customs from the peoples around them, indicating that they had a separate identity. Thus, we can see that the claims that Trojan prisoners built this city for themselves after the Trojan War of *c.* 700 BCE is supported by the available evidence.

Conclusion

In summary, we can see that there is bountiful archaeological and historical evidence for the events leading up to the Trojan War, as well as for the Trojan War itself. Rather than the city of Troy being the only object of the Greeks' attacks, in reality, they were campaigning all over western Anatolia. This is exactly what the archaeological and historical evidence demonstrates for the late eighth and early seventh centuries BCE. The city of Troy itself displays a destruction layer which fits our estimate of *c.* 695 BCE for the fall of Troy. In addition, archaeology confirms many of the events which were supposed to have happened after the fall of Troy, such as the dispersion of the Greeks and the settlement of the Trojans in a number of different locations around the Mediterranean.

However, there is one particular location to which the Trojans were said to have migrated which is worthy of much deeper examination. This is the migration which is directly linked to the later British legend of Brutus.

6

The Founding of Rome

One of the most significant and influential nations to have ever existed was that of the Romans. The founding of Rome, therefore, is an event of extreme importance. According to legend, this city was founded by Trojans after they migrated from their homeland after the fall of Troy. These Trojans were said to have been led by Aeneas, the Trojan prince who allegedly also led some of his people to Sicily. Given the close proximity between Rome and Sicily, this makes sense. However, there are many misconceptions about the Trojan founding of Rome. It is very important that these are cleared up, because they interfere with being able to identify the evidence for this event.

The True Chronology of the Founding of Rome
One of the biggest misconceptions regarding the legendary arrival of the Trojans in the area of Rome is the matter of when it was in relation to the founding of Rome itself. It is commonly claimed that the Trojans arrived in the area under the leadership of Aeneas and founded a city called Alba Longa soon after their arrival. Centuries later, two princes who descended from Aeneas named Romulus and Remus ended up founding a nearby city, which became Rome. This was said to have been in 753 BCE. Since Aeneas was said to have lived centuries before Romulus and Remus, this would place the Trojan War long before 700 BCE.

However, much like with the claims that Aeneas was contemporary with Dido and the founding of Carthage, this chronology of Rome and its relation to the Trojan War is based on later records, such as Virgil's *Aeneid* in particular. As well as the *Aeneid*, this chronology is also found in the records of the Roman historian Livy, a contemporary of Virgil. However, as with the claims about Aeneas and Carthage, it is vital that we look at the earliest records available. It would be very misleading to follow later records that just so happen to be more famous today. This is a trap that many modern researchers have fallen into. So, what do the earliest available records claim about the connection between the Trojans and Rome?

The reality is that there were many different claims about the founding of Rome, but the overwhelming majority of them agreed that it was connected to the Trojans. And unlike the later Roman records, which placed centuries of history between the Trojans arriving in Italy and the city of Rome being founded, these earlier Greek records usually connected the arrival of the Trojans directly with the founding of the city, or they separated the two events by only a few generations rather than many centuries. Professor Nicholas Horsfall noted that the earliest Greek historians, with just one exception, placed the founding of Rome no later than three generations after the fall of Troy.[231] Hellanicus of Lesbos and Damastes of Siguem, both of whom were of the fifth century BCE, described Rome as being founded jointly by Aeneas and Odysseus. Plutarch recorded one tradition that Romulus, the eponymous founder of Rome, was the 'son of Aeneas and Dexithea the daughter of Phorbas', as well as a different tradition that he was the son of 'Aemilia, the daughter of Aeneas and Lavinia'.[232] One ancient Greek writer who placed the founding of the city somewhat later was Alcimus, of the third or fourth century BCE, who made 'Rhomus', the eponymous founder of Rome in this version, the grandson of Romulus, son of Aeneas. Numerous other Greek historians between the fifth and first centuries BCE presented views that fit between these two versions – either it was founded in the time of Aeneas himself, or shortly after him, up to three generations later.

One ancient historian, Dionysius of Halicarnassus, helpfully compiled a record of various different claims about the founding of Rome. One historian he mentions is Cephalon of Gergis, seemingly of the late third century BCE. He reported that Rome was founded in the second generation after the Trojan War by Romus, a son of Aeneas. Dionysius states that historians Demagoras, Agathyllus and many others agree with this version.[233] He goes on to report numerous other Greek versions which, although conflicting, all agree that the city was founded in the time of Aeneas or only as much as three generations later. A modern historian, Henry A. Sanders, composed an even more comprehensive list demonstrating the same thing.[234] In fact, his list references at least twenty-four ancient sources placing the founding of Rome in this period.

What can be seen from this analysis is that the idea that Rome was founded in or just after the time of Aeneas was by far the most popular belief in ancient times. It just so happens that the alternative belief – that it was founded centuries after Aeneas arrived in Italy – came to be more famous due to its presence in the very popular *Aeneid*. Really, this later, less-supported version was almost certainly created in an attempt to harmonise the native beliefs about the date of the founding of Rome with the popular estimates for the date of the Trojan War. This is reaffirmed by evidence that the legendary kings between Aeneas's children and Romulus and Remus were invented by later Roman writers, as we shall see next.

Invented Kings

Alba Longa itself, the city said to have been established by Aeneas' son Ascanius, is known to have been real. However, the lineage between the kings of Alba Longa and the kings of Rome is widely believed to have been invented. One historian in the nineteenth century wrote the following regarding them:

> The empty catalogue of the kings of Alba Longa – names, and nothing more – which fills a few sentences in the third chapter [of the first book of Livy], may safely be dismissed.[235]

This basic sentiment is shared by numerous other scholars. It has been noted that many of them appear to be inventions based on place names in the region of Rome. For example, one legendary king was named Tibernius. In one of the accounts that does provide some information about a few of the kings of Alba Longa, we find that Tibernius supposedly drowned in the river that flows past Rome. It is from him that it was said to have received its name, the Tiber. A later king was named Aventius. Legend states that he gave his name to the Aventine Hill, where he was buried. Another source from the nineteenth century states directly:

> The line of Alban kings are mere phantoms, invented – as an examination of the chronology proves – to fill the interval between the fall of Troy and the foundation of Rome.[236]

Similar statements can be found from more recent scholars, such as the renowned Margaret Hubbard in her book *Propertius*, as well as

Howard Hayes Scullard in *A History of the Roman World from 753 to 146 B.C.* Mary Beard described this list of kings as being, 'even by Roman standards, flagrantly fictional'.[237] Therefore, we can see that the 'records' of these kings are no obstacle to the conclusion that Aeneas was a figure of the eighth century BCE. They only appear in the first century BCE, and bear all the indications of being invented to fill a perceived chronological gap. In reality, we must accept the extensive testimony from far earlier records that the founder of Rome was just one, two or maybe three generations removed from Aeneas.

The Earlier Rome

With this in mind, an important question arises that deserves answering. How does the aforementioned conclusion tie in with the mid-eighth-century BCE date for the founding of Rome? After all, we have established 705–695 BCE as the era of the Trojan War. So if Aeneas or one of his descendants founded Rome after travelling to Italy after the fall of Troy, this would mean that Rome could only have been founded after the beginning of the seventh century BCE. Part of the answer to this conundrum lies in the archaeology of Rome.

It is accepted that the traditional date of the founding of Rome is broadly supported by archaeology. On the Palatine Hill, which was supposedly the original settlement of Rome, archaeologists have uncovered evidence of an eighth-century BCE settlement. However, archaeology has actually revealed that the settlement predates the traditional date of the founding of Rome, going back to at least as early as the ninth century BCE.[238] This fits neither the c. 1200 BCE date for the Trojan War nor the traditional date for the founding of Rome. So what can explain these archaeological finds?

There is some fascinating information provided by Dionysius of Halicarnassus that likely explains these discoveries. He reports that according to Antiochus of Syracuse, a historian of the fifth century BCE with a reputation for excellent accuracy, there was a Rome that existed even before the Trojan War.[239] This, according to Dionysius, seems to have been the most ancient one. A Roman historian named Ateius Philologus, of the first century BCE, also attests to there having already been a settlement on the Palatine Hill, which he says was originally called Valentia but then had its name changed to 'Rome' in the time of Evander (an older contemporary of Aeneas).[240] Other records report that Evander founded a city named Pallantium on the site that would later become Rome.[241] Evidently, 'founded' in this insistence means that he built up an existing settlement, the Valentia of Ateius' record. Therefore, it is very likely that these settlements – Valentia and Pallantium, or whatever reality they preserve the memory of – are likely to be the settlements which archaeologists have dated to the eighth and ninth centuries BCE. In line with the fact that Evander was a Greek king, archaeology has revealed evidence of a Greek colony by the Palatine Hill in the eighth century BCE.[242]

The Seven Kings of Rome

Now, what about the later founding by Aeneas or one of his descendants? Many of the records ascribe him a descendant named Romus, Romulus or something similar. In some records this is his son, in others it is a grandson or great-grandson, and in other records it is a combination of the two – he had a son named Romulus, who in turn had a grandson named Romus. It is impossible to know for certain what the truth is, or whether there even ever really was a man by that name. Perhaps there was a figure who occupied the place of Romulus in the legends, but he was known by a different name and was just given the name 'Romulus' in later records due to him being the founder of Rome.

In any case, this would mean that Romulus, as a son or grandson of Aeneas, was a seventh-century BCE individual rather than an eighth-century BCE individual. Is there any evidence that the seventh century saw a significant expansion of the existing site of Rome, indicating a new 'founding' of the city? Indeed there is. For example, the Roman Forum appears to have been established in the seventh century BCE, which, according to *A Companion to the Archaeology of the Roman Republic*, changed 'the configuration of Rome from a cluster of hills to a unified whole with a civic center'.[243] Another modern reference work states that 'excavations have established that from 630/620–580 BC there was a phase of systematic reorganisation of the Forum area, including the earliest evidence of paving and the construction of public buildings'.[244] In harmony with this, the earliest known temple remains in Rome date from the late seventh century BCE.[245] This is especially significant in view of the fact that Romulus was said to have built a temple to Jupiter. Thus, the archaeology would appear to place Romulus in the seventh century BCE.

Another example is the Regia, which was one of the royal residences of the kings of Rome. Incidentally, the existence of kings in Rome in this period is confirmed by the discovery of an artefact here with the word 'rex' (king) written on it, dating from the sixth century BCE. To return to the main point, it was at the end of the seventh century – perhaps

c. 625 BCE – that a brick building was first built at the site.[246] This is therefore accepted as the archaeologically established date for its true founding. Significantly, the Regia was said to have been built by Numa Pompilius, the second king of Rome. Thus, if the archaeology indicates that his achievements took place in the late seventh century BCE, and his predecessor Romulus' achievements also took place in the seventh century BCE, then the probability is that Romulus and Numa were both kings of the seventh century BCE, with Numa living near the end of the century in particular.

These conclusions are supported even by the textual information about these kings. It has been noted by scholars that the length of time covered by the seven kings of Rome seems to be implausibly long. The time between the start of Romulus' reign (753 BCE) and the end of the seventh king's reign (509 BCE) is 244 years. That gives an average of just under thirty-five years per king. This is very implausible. On the other, a more realistic average of twenty to twenty-five years per king would result in a total of 140–175 years for the seven kings of Rome. Counting back from 509 BCE (the end of the final king's reign) would take us back to 684–649 BCE for the start of Romulus' reign. This would then place the reign of Numa Pompilius, the second king, in the mid- to late seventh century. This is in line with the archaeological evidence concerning the founding of the Regia, as already discussed. Some modern scholars have even speculated that all seven kings belonged to the sixth century BCE, though this seems too extreme to be plausible and is seemingly based on outdated archaeological information.[247] But it illustrates the point that moving Romulus to the mid-seventh century BCE rather than the mid-eighth century is a perfectly reasonable conclusion, and it is supported by the most up-to-date archaeological research.

With this in mind, let us present some estimated dates for the seven kings of Rome, using an average of twenty-two years per generation. Bear in mind that these are just averages; undoubtedly they did not all reign for exactly the same number of years.

Romulus	c. 663–641 BCE
Numa Pompilius	641–619 BCE
Tulius Hostilius	619–597 BCE
Ancus Marcius	597–575 BCE
Tarquinius Priscus	575–553 BCE
Servius Tullius	553–531 BCE
Tarquinius Superbus	531–509 BCE

The Founding of Rome

Explanations for the Mid-eighth Century Date

But if the start of Romulus' reign really was in the mid-seventh century BCE, then why did later Roman writers place its founding in the eighth century BCE? There are at least two possible reasons for this.

Firstly, it is possible that the 'founding' referred to by the Romans was not actually the founding of the city by Romulus. It may be that the founding they referred to, perhaps without always realising, was the earlier founding by Evander. Recall that he was said to have founded the city of Pallantium about sixty years before the Trojan War. According to Dionysius of Halicarnassus, this was not his own conclusion, but rather, he states that this is what the Romans say. So this claim has some degree of legitimacy, though we cannot be sure how far back it goes. We also cannot learn what exactly the time difference was supposed to have been between the founding of Pallantium and the Trojan War, since Dionysius merely says that it was 'about' sixty years. This would place its founding 'about' 765 BCE. We also cannot establish for certain if the original claim was actually dated from the start of the war or from the fall of Troy ten years later. If it was the latter, then the date of the founding would have been about 755 BCE. In either case, this is an approximate match for the date given by Roman historians for the founding of Rome. The fact that Evander's city could, at times, be considered the same as Rome itself and not just its precursor is seen by Strabo's statement that some claim that Rome was a Greek city, founded by Evander.[248] So it may well be that the traditional date of Rome's founding is actually a reference to the founding of Evander's city.

An alternative possibility is that the date of the founding of Rome was calculated based on the reign lengths of the seven kings. If those reign lengths became exaggerated, which they evidently did, that would take the founding of Rome back to 753 BCE. However, the earliest surviving dates given for the founding of Rome long predate the earliest surviving records of the reign lengths of the seven kings, so there is no definitive evidence that there were any records of reign lengths circulating for those Roman historians to use in their calculations. On the other hand, the seven kings themselves are attested from an early date, so it may be that the Roman historians just used an estimate for the average reign length and then based their calculations on that. As we discussed in a previous chapter, ancient historians had a tendency to exaggerate generational lengths, so if an estimate was used in this case, there is every reason to believe that it would have been excessive. As we saw previously, the time span covered by the seven kings gives an average reign length of almost exactly thirty-five years. This is the case when the last year of the final king is fixed at 509 BCE, and it is entirely possible that this year was not so precisely fixed in earlier times. Moving it by just one year, to 508 BCE, would make the average reign length of the seven kings equal exactly thirty-five years. The imprecision of this final year may well be the cause of the variation among dates given for the founding of Rome, most being a few years either side of 750 BCE.

So far, we have seen that there is good evidence that Romulus was a seventh-century BCE king rather than an eighth-century BCE king. This is supported by the textual evidence and also by the archaeological evidence. We have also seen that the earliest evidence indicates that Romulus was a close descendant, possibly even a son, of Aeneas. In fact, for chronological reasons he must have been a grandson at most. He was certainly not a descendant who lived hundreds of years later, as popularly claimed from the first century BCE onwards. But if the Trojans under Aeneas really did migrate from Troy shortly after 695 BCE and arrived in Italy and founded Rome a few decades later, is there any surviving evidence of this? In fact, there is considerable evidence that this really did take place.

Etruscans and Their Anatolian Origin

The key to perceiving the evidence for the Trojan migration to Italy is realising the connection between the Trojans and the Etruscans, as well as the origin of the Etruscans. According to Herodotus, the Etruscans migrated from Lydia in western Anatolia to Italy centuries before his own time. According to Dionysius of Halicarnassus in the first century BCE, many other ancient writers agreed with this origin.[249] So the predominant view among the ancient Greeks was definitely that the Etruscans came from western Anatolia – the same general region as Troy. Although it has become popular to dismiss this Anatolian origin of the Etruscans, it is supported by the evidence.

A number of genetic studies have found strong connections between the Etruscans and the inhabitants of Anatolia, using both modern samples and ancient samples. Studies using cattle samples have also found the same connection. However, more recent research has indicated that these connections date back to many thousands of years ago, long before the Trojan War. They are apparently the result of large-scale migrations from Anatolia that spread out all over Europe. Thus, they cannot be used to support

The Founding of Rome

the supposed migration of the Etruscans from Anatolia to Italy in more recent times.

Does this mean that the genetic evidence does not support the supposed Etruscan migration from the Near East? Not at all. Firstly, it needs to be highlighted that most invasions and conquests do not result in the complete removal of the native population. For example, consider the Roman conquest of Britain, or the Norman conquest of Britain. Both of these historical events could be soundly 'disproved' on the basis of genetic evidence, since both groups only ever formed an elite class, contributing next to nothing to the genetic makeup of Britain. The legend of the Etruscans migrating to Italy can easily be understood in the same way: an elite class that came to dominate the native population. This being the case, we would only expect a small part of the population of the ancient Etruscans in Italy to have come from the Near East.

As it happens, this is supported by the most recent genetic studies. One from 2021, which was focused on the Etruscans, examined forty-eight samples dating to between 800 and 1 BCE. Of these forty-eight individuals, one was found to have Near Eastern ancestry, most similar to 'Iranian Neolithic farmers'. If this percentage were generalised to the population as a whole, then this would mean that about 2 per cent of the Iron Age population of Etruria was composed of individuals of Near Eastern descent, which would be significant in view of the size of the entire population. Of course, this sample size is too small to be able to generalise it in this way.

However, this evidence is supported by a study from 2019 which examined central Italy as a whole, though with a focus on Rome. Rome is known to have been extensively connected to the Etruscans from an early time, both culturally and ethnically, as we will examine later. This 2019 study examined eleven individuals dating to between 900 and 200 BCE. These samples indicated a notable influx of Iranian Neolithic DNA compared to the preceding eras. Two of these individuals were specifically noted to be best explained as a cross between the local Italic population and either Bronze Age Armenian or Iron Age Anatolian populations.

In other words, both the 2021 study focusing on the Etruscans and the 2019 study focusing on Rome found evidence of the presence of individuals of Near Eastern descent in the Iron Age. In Rome, this presence was particularly strong, while it only accounts for 2 per cent of the Etruscan samples (in both cases, though, the sample sizes were much too small to be able to make firm generalisations, so the paucity of evidence from Etruria may simply be due to a lack of samples). Approximately 20 per cent of the Roman samples may well give evidence of coming from Iron Age Anatolia in particular.

In addition, we will go on to see later in this chapter that the Etruscan migration involved more people than just the Lydians, who were native to Anatolia. In fact, it seems to have involved many peoples who originated in Europe, from the area of Greece in particular. This is consistent with findings from the 2021 Etruscan study that found that much of the Etruscan DNA from their data set (covering 800 to 1 BCE) could be attributed to Iron Age populations from southern Europe, such as Greece. Although this is usually interpreted as evidence *against* the Anatolian origin of the Etruscans, it is actually perfectly consistent with it when the legend of the Etruscans' origin is properly understood, as will be explained shortly.

Regarding archaeology, it has been noted that the Etruscan civilisation shows evidence of continuity with the earlier inhabitants of the region, supposedly indicating that the Etruscans simply developed out of the culture that already existed there. The problem with this conclusion is the same as the conclusion derived from genetic studies. It is based on a deceptive 'all-or-nothing' mindset, a false dichotomy. Unless the Anatolian immigrants completely wiped out the native population, of course there would be evidence of continuity with the existing culture. To expect anything else would be, quite frankly, bizarre. Therefore, this archaeological evidence for continuity does not in any way contradict or disprove the Anatolian origin of the Etruscan civilisation.

What we would expect is a sudden influx of cultural elements that can be linked to the Near East. For example, there might be new burial practices, styles of art and pottery, or house designs. Archaeologists claim to have noted no particular similarities between the Etruscans – or rather, the 'proto-Etruscans' who inhabited Italy since the beginning of the Iron Age – and the Lydians, but this is hardly surprising. This migration was supposed to have happened at around the time of the Trojan War, so archaeologists have looked in the era around 1200 BCE. Of course, nothing has been found. On the other hand, when we look at the era around 700 BCE, a considerable amount of evidence for this migration is discernible from the archaeological data.

Firstly, this is the era in which the Etruscan civilisation suddenly expanded. Archaeologists today generally consider it to be a development of the Villanovan culture, which dates back to 900 BCE. Thus, they consider the Etruscan civilisation to have started in

900 BCE. However, the Etruscan civilisation in its true sense began in 700 BCE – hence why archaeologists had long debated whether the preceding Villanovan culture could really be classed as part of it or not. It is widely recognised that the end of the eighth century BCE (which, remember, is an imprecise date due to being established by archaeology) is when true, fortified Etruscan cities first started appearing in Italy.[250] The earliest examples of Etruscan writing also date from 700 BCE.[251] The exact same can also be said about monumental Etruscan tombs.[252] The style of art that characterised the Etruscans also came into existence in c. 700 BCE.[253] Sculpture, likewise, only came into existence in Etruria at this time.[254]

Not all of these changes display evidence of necessarily having originated in the east, but they all demonstrate that there was general social upheaval and development in Etruria at this time, whatever the cause. This has been noted by scholars; one reference book refers to the 'cultural shift that occurred in Etruria after 700 BCE'.[255] Of particular note is the sudden emergence of monumental tombs. This has been understood by some, such as the respected archaeologist Kristian Kristiansen, to indicate the emergence of a new aristocracy ruling over the land at the time.[256] However, beyond a social shift and indications of a new aristocracy in a general sense, many things about the development of the Etruscan civilisation in 700 BCE can be tied to the Near East, and often to Anatolia in particular. In fact, the period of Etruscan history starting in 700 BCE is specifically called the 'Orientalising period' by modern historians, due to the sudden wave of influence from the Near East starting at this time.[257]

One example of this is the practice of using the liver for divination, which was common among Near and Middle Eastern peoples, including those of Anatolia. Outside of this region, evidence for liver divination is *only* found among the Etruscans.[258] Passing trade might explain Near Eastern art styles, but the intricacies involved in the practice of liver divination require a stronger connection with the east. This does not, in itself, prove the movement of peoples, but it strongly indicates it. Furthermore, if trade were responsible, then why was it only the Etruscans who adopted the practice?

Many other aspects of Etruscan religion can also be tied to the Near East. For example, the practices involved in the New Year festival of the Etruscans, which was later adopted by the Romans, have been linked by some scholars to New Year festivals in Anatolia.[259] Furthermore, the Etruscans worshipped a group of gods called the Kabeiroi (also spelled 'Cabeiri' in modern sources). This is archaeologically proven by discoveries from the Etruscan descendants on Lemnos.[260] It is also supported by the testimony of Myrsilus of Lesbos, a historian of the early third century BCE. He claimed that the Etruscans (using the Greek name for them, 'Tyrrhenians'), when they were under a period of great hardship, had promised to make offerings to Zeus, Apollo and the Kabeiroi on the condition of their deliverance.[261] This is significant, for the Kabeiroi originated in Asia Minor.[262] It is often stated that they were likely Phrygian in origin, as the Greeks themselves believed, placing them specifically in western Asia Minor.[263] It is true that they were also worshipped in Greece, but this was only in later centuries, so the Etruscans could not have adopted the worship of the Kabeiroi from the Greeks.[264]

Another example of something which specifically points to the region of Lydia as the origin of the Etruscans are their monumental graves. These have been noted to be similar to the style of monumental Lydian graves.[265] The only Etruscan grave ever described in antiquity is the grave of Lars Porsena, a famous Etruscan king of the late sixth century BCE. His tomb is described by the Roman writer Marcus Varro of the second century BCE. The tomb was described as being very intricate and enormous in size, but one significant feature was that above the tomb there were said to be five pyramids – four on each corner and one in the centre. This bears an affinity to the tomb of Alyattes, an early sixth-century BCE king of Lydia whose tomb was described by Herodotus as being made up of an enormous mound of earth with five pillars atop it.

Although the grave of Lars Porsena has never been found (while the grave of Alyattes has), archaeologists have noted that the tombs they have discovered in Etruria that date from the Early and Middle Orientalising period display similarities to those from Phrygia and Lydia.[266] For example, one scholar notes that 'Etruscan tumuli share with Lydian burial monuments a stone basement decorated with moldings in the form of circular rings'.[267] Other similarities between Etruscan and Anatolian tombs include the presence of benches, parapets and headrests.[268] Funerary statues in Etruscan tombs also closely resemble those produced in Anatolia.[269] Once again, the style of tombs is not the sort of cultural element that one would expect to be transmitted through trade, and is therefore more indicative of the movement of peoples.

An additional aspect of their culture which indicates their origin in Lydia is their use of the double-axe symbol. This double-axe symbol has been found in early Etruscan contexts, and it was also used in Anatolia. In fact, according to Plutarch, it was a symbol that was used by the kings of Lydia until the early seventh century BCE.[270] Although its exact usage among the Etruscans is uncertain due to a lack of clear evidence, the later Roman fasces was a symbol of the authority and power of a ruler. Given that the fasces is widely accepted as having an origin in the Etruscan double-axe symbol, this indicates that the Etruscan double-axe was likewise a symbol of political power or authority, thus linking its usage to the usage of the double-axe in Lydia.[271]

But regarding things which might be considered to be the result of trade, such as art styles, the oriental influence among the Etruscans is striking indeed. One modern reference work states:

> The Oriental influences in Etruria are not of the same order as the contemporary Orientalizing phase in Greece. Although there are obvious resemblances, the process in Etruria was much more sudden in its inception, and far deeper-rooted in its effects.[272]

This is supported by the *Encyclopaedia Britannica*, which refers to the 'profound Oriental influence on Etruscan culture'. In fact, it then refers to the process that occurred during the Orientalising period of Etruscan history as an 'Oriental inundation', testifying to its powerful impact. As archaeologist Jodi Magness explained, 'Near Eastern influence is evident on almost all aspects of Etruscan life, including art, clothing, chariots, military equipment and warfare, hairstyles, dining habits, religion or cult, and technology.'[273] The idea that this can be attributed to trade is peculiar, for why would the Etruscans have received a deeper-rooted Oriental influence than Greece, the nation which had been trading with the east for longer and was geographically closer? Relying on trade to explain the sudden and deep-rooted Oriental nature of Etruscan culture is simply not convincing.

With this in mind, why do some reject the obvious archaeological evidence of a Near Eastern connection when considering whether or not the Etruscans really did come from Anatolia? The reason is nicely explained by the portion of the *Encyclopaedia Britannica* referred to earlier. Here is the passage in full:

> The argument [on where the Etruscans originated from] began, in fact, in antiquity with the statement by Herodotus that the Etruscans

migrated from Lydia in Anatolia shortly after the time of the Trojan War; their leader was Tyrsenos, who later gave his name to the whole race. Supporters of this 'Eastern' theory pointed above all to the archaeological evidence of profound Oriental influence on Etruscan culture, such as in monumental funerary architecture and exotic luxury goods of gold, ivory, and other materials. But chronologically the Oriental inundation occurred nearly 500 years too late for the Herodotean migration.[274]

So in other words, the primary reason for rejecting the Anatolian origin of the Etruscans is because the archaeological evidence for such an origin dates from 500 years later than the era in which Herodotus' story about their Lydian origin is supposedly set. Rather than conclude that Herodotus had his chronology off by 500 years, scholars apparently would prefer to just dismiss the entire story. This is merely another example of the problems caused by the misdating of the Trojan War. When it is brought forward five centuries to *c.* 700 BCE, Herodotus' story is exactly in line with the archaeological evidence.

A migration as recent as *c.* 700 BCE, as well as the migration in itself, is supported by archaeological evidence found on the island of Lemnos. This is an island just off the coast of north-west Anatolia, barely 50 miles from Troy. Famously, several inscriptions from the sixth century BCE written in a language almost identical to Etruscan have been discovered on that island. In fact, this is allegedly the only place outside of Italy where written texts displaying affinities with Etruscan have been found.[275] Not only the language, but the iconography on the stele is identifiably Etruscan.[276] This has long been used by supporters of the Anatolian theory, for good reason. That the Etruscans did inhabit Lemnos is now widely accepted.[277] The Greek historian Thucydides of the fifth century BCE also testifies to the Etruscans having once inhabited that island (it appears that they were displaced from the island by the end of the sixth century BCE).[278] Strabo specified that the Etruscans stopped off at Lemnos on the way from Anatolia to Italy.[279]

The evidence from Lemnos absolutely supports this tradition. The language on the surviving inscriptions is very similar to Etruscan, but it is not exactly identical. They are more like different dialects of the same language. If, as some scholars claim, these inscriptions come from Etruscan colonists who had just recently arrived on Lemnos from Etruria, then we would expect the language to be identical to that found in Etruria in the sixth century BCE. The fact that it is not identical shows that these inscriptions must have been written by colonists who had split off from the rest of the Etruscans some time prior to the sixth century BCE – long enough for them to develop a distinct dialect. Yet, it is not as different as we would expect if these colonists had been separated from the others for many centuries. Sybille Haynes, an expert on the Etruscans, concludes that those on Lemnos had been 'separated from their people for several generations'.[280] This is consistent with placing the migration from Anatolia to Lemnos to Italy just after 700 BCE. The fact that the Etruscans on Lemnos were not the remains of a colony sent out *from* Etruria is evident from the fact that there is no evidence at all that the Etruscans had become a powerful seafaring nation that travelled as far as western Anatolia as early as 700 BCE.

Additional evidence that the Etruscans travelled from east to west, rather than from west to east, comes from records that speak of the Etruscans in Anatolia before the emergence of their civilisation in Italy in 700 BCE. According to Conon, a Greek writer in the first century BCE, the north-western Anatolian town of Cyzicus was inhabited by the Tyrrhenians (the Greek name for the Etruscans) until they were expelled and replaced by the Milesians, the inhabitants of the Greek city of Miletus on the western coast of Anatolia.[281] The Milesians are generally held to have settled Cyzicus in the eighth century BCE.[282] This being so, this record places the Tyrrhenians, or Etruscans, in north-west Anatolia *before* the emergence of their civilisation in Italy in *c.* 700 BCE.

In short, we can see that there is written, genetic and archaeological evidence for a migration from western Anatolia to Etruria in Italy in about 700 BCE or just after. They did not wipe out the native population, but they evidently intermingled with them to a large degree and at the same time became the new ruling aristocracy. This quotation regarding the blend of the pre-existing Villanovan culture with the influx of Oriental culture explains the situation perfectly:

> The ensuing hybrid culture may best be explained, in complete accordance with the views of Herodotus, by the arrival on the western coasts of Etruria and Latium of immigrants from Western Asia Minor, who took over the Villanovan world as a ruling minority and made certain substantial modifications.[283]

However, be that as it may, how does this relate to the Trojans and the legend of them migrating to Italy under Aeneas and founding Rome?

Etruscans and the Trojans

One reason why it is so important to establish that the Etruscans really did come from western Anatolia is because it helps to see the connection between the Etruscans and the Trojans. Although surprisingly few researchers have connected the Etruscans with the Trojans, there are a few notable scholars who have. For example, the late Robert Beekes, who was a firm advocate of the Anatolian origin of the Etruscans, believed that the legend of Aeneas sailing from Troy to Italy was likely connected with the Etruscan migration from Anatolia. But in what way could the two groups be connected? The almost unanimous testimony of the ancient Greeks was that the Etruscans came from Lydia. They never explicitly mentioned Troy in connection with the Etruscans. So how can the two groups be connected?

One important fact to bear in mind is that, as we have already considered, many nations on both sides were said to have been involved in the Trojan War. The Trojans had numerous allies from all over western Anatolia. Among them were the Lydians. The final year of the war involved all the allies from both sides once again united in opposition at Troy. Thus, at the climax of the Trojan War when the Greeks finally overcame the city of Troy and the Trojan army was completely defeated, there must have been troops from Lydia there as well, along with other allies of the Trojans. In addition, the city of Troy itself was not the only loser in the war, for as we saw previously, the Greeks had conquered and raided dozens of other sites in western Anatolia. This means that many of the allies of Troy would have been in similar positions to the inhabitants of that city. It would be no surprise at all if many of the survivors of the war, not just from the city of Troy but from their allies as well, had banded together under Aeneas to find another home.

Who would have kept a record of this? Well, if most of the inhabitants of Troy were massacred and those who survived migrated to another land, then there certainly would be no surviving tradition at Troy itself. This is supported by the archaeology of Troy, which indicates a complete abandonment in '*c.* 650 BCE' and a totally new material culture in *c.* 625 BCE when new settlers evidently arrived. So this tradition could only have been preserved among those who remained, such as the main population of those who were allies with

Troy. For example, if many Lydians decided to join their Trojan allies and sail to a new land, then the Lydians who remained in Anatolia would be the ones who preserved that tradition. Lydia was one of Troy's most important allies, together with Phrygia. By far the majority of the other allies of Troy mentioned in Homer's Trojan Battle Order left no lasting mark or legacy, so there is no surprise that we do not find many other traditions of migrations to Italy among the inhabitants of Anatolia.

As we stated before, it is possible that Gyges' conquest of the Troad was part of the events of the Trojan War, meaning that Troy would have been within the state of Lydia by the end of that war. This is admittedly uncertain, but even if Gyges' conquests occurred just after the fall of Troy, the boundaries of the state of Lydia must have already been very close to that city by the time it fell. This helps us to see why the city of Troy would have had a strong connection to Lydia, and why many Lydians would have joined themselves under the leadership of Aeneas after the Trojan War, especially when much of their own country had likewise been ravaged by the Greeks.

In addition to this, in case it need be mentioned, there is some evidence of Lydians in the north-west of Anatolia from an even earlier time. For example, Herodotus claims that the Mysians, who lived just to the east of the Troad, were settlers from Lydia.[284] Strabo gives a fuller version of this story, reporting that according to Xanthus of Lydia, a historian of the fifth century BCE, the Lydians sent out colonists to the region of Mount Olympus in Mysia. This account is explicitly set prior to the time of the Trojan War, because Strabo states that the Lydians were already there when the Phrygians arrived in Asia Minor from Thrace, which was obviously before the Trojan War (for the Phrygians are depicted as having an established kingdom in Asia Minor at the time of the war). The Mysians, Strabo then says, are the descendants of those Lydians.[285]

Thus, according to the written testimony, at the time of the Trojan War there were Lydians living much closer to Troy than they did in Classical times. This harmonises with the evidence we saw previously about the Tyrrhenians living in Cyzicus, which is on the north-east coast of Anatolia. Of course, that does not necessarily mean that the Lydians did not also live where they did in Classical times. But it appears that, if they did, they spanned a larger area from an earlier time than is often acknowledged. Thus, the Lydians were both allies of the Trojans during the war and close neighbours for a period of time. It is no wonder that they may have migrated together. In fact, there is every possibility that they had intermingled to a degree in the generations leading up to the Trojan War. So Herodotus' account, which was written centuries after the event in question took place, was likely distorted at least in part by the difference between the distribution of Lydians at the time of the Trojan War and the borders of Lydia at the time he was writing. Further support for the idea that the migration of Lydians to Italy was connected to Aeneas's Trojan migration is seen from the fact that at least some versions of the legend of the Lydian migration place it precisely at the time of Aeneas's journey, immediately after the Trojan War.[286]

But if Aeneas really did lead a migration of Troy and some of its allies, then it is worth asking the question: were the Lydians the only allies of Troy about whom there were traditions of a migration to Italy at this time? No, there is at least one other nation which fits this description: the Pelasgians. This is a rather enigmatic group, and there are a multitude of theories about them, but what can be said based on the weight of the ancient literary evidence is that they were apparently the indigenous inhabitants of Greece. However, some Pelasgians also lived in the vicinity of Troy. This is seen from the earliest reference to them, which comes from Homer's *Iliad*. Although the exact placement of their home is uncertain, they seem to have lived in the Troad itself.[287]

While they were regularly placed in Greece by ancient poets and historians, they were also connected to the Etruscans ('Tyrrhenians' to the Greeks). For example, Thucydides refers to the inhabitants of an area of Chalcidice, a region of northern Greece along the north coast of the Aegean Sea, as being 'Pelasgic, of those Tyrrhene nations that once inhabited Athens and Lemnos'.[288] Other translations render the phrase used here as 'Tyrrheno-Pelasgians'. So the Pelasgians are associated with the Etruscans, apparently being viewed as synonymous with them in this context. As we have seen, Lemnos certainly was inhabited by Etruscans (though ones that had been cut off from those in Italy for at least several generations). The term 'Tyrrhenian' is also used with 'Pelasgian' in this way in the writings of Sophocles, a poet of the fifth century BCE.[289]

Dionysius of Halicarnassus indicates that the reason these two names were often used interchangeably was because of the Pelasgians living with the Tyrrhenians.[290] This harmonises with a tradition that the Pelasgians travelled with Tyrrhenus, the eponymous founding hero of the Tyrrhenians, during his journey from Anatolia to

Italy.²⁹¹ Hellanicus of Lesbos, of the fifth century BCE, reports the following:

> The Pelasgians were driven out of their country by the Greeks, and after leaving their ships on the river Spines in the Ionian Gulf, they took Croton, an inland city; and proceeding from there, they colonized the country now called Tyrrhenia.²⁹²

Thus, the Pelasgians were believed to have founded Tyrrhenia – that is, Etruria. And they were believed to have done so due to being driven out of their land by the Greeks, which lends credence to associating this event with the Trojan War. Granted, this particular account presents the Pelasgians as being driven from Greece, rather than Asia Minor, but given that the Pelasgians were most common in Greece, this would be an easy mistake to make. According to Strabo, the early third-century BCE historian Anticleides stated that it was the Pelasgians who settled in the region of Lemnos and Imbros (an island even closer to the coast of Troy than Lemnos) who sailed with Tyrrhenus on his journey to Italy.²⁹³ These would logically be the Pelasgians mentioned in the *Iliad*, who lived very near the Troad.

There is additional evidence that these Pelasgians really did migrate to Etruria in Italy. The two Pelasgian leaders mentioned in the *Iliad* are described as the sons of Lethos. This name, 'Lethos', has been noted as being peculiar because it is *only* found here in Homer's story. It is not a Greek name, and it does not appear anywhere else. Or rather, it does not appear anywhere apart from in Etruria, as pointed out by scholar Robert Beekes.²⁹⁴ The fact that this name only appears among the Pelasgians in the *Iliad* and among the Etruscans in Italy is strong evidence of a connection between the two peoples. It may also, perhaps, indicate that the mysterious language of the Etruscans actually came from the Pelasgians (for it was definitely not Greek, Phrygian, Lydian, or any other Indo-European language). But this is just indicative, as it may instead have been a name that was adopted by the Etruscans from the Pelasgians. In this case, it may simply be that the Etruscan language was the language spoken by the inhabitants of Troy and its surrounding region, having been adopted by the Greek settlers when they intermingled with the local inhabitants a century or so before the Trojan War.²⁹⁵

In any case, this evidence that the Pelasgians migrated to Etruria is consistent with the conclusion that Aeneas' migration to Italy involved some of Troy's battered allies, such as the Lydians (evidently a branch of them called Tyrrhenians) and the Pelasgians. And what of the Phrygians? Well, the Phrygians were associated so strongly with the Trojans that they were often viewed as one and the same. Strabo, for example, noted that 'the tragic poets' called the Trojans by the term 'Phrygians'.[296] So there is no reason to expect to find a separate tradition about the Phrygians migrating to Italy, as that would have, by definition, been viewed simply as the same as the Trojan migration to Italy.

So far, we can see that there is good reason to connect the Etruscan migration from 'Lydia', or Lydian territory, to the Trojan migration on the basis that this Lydian migration was allegedly made in conjunction with a migration of Pelasgians, who were also allies of the Trojans just as the Lydians were; to this we can also add the evidence from the versions of the legends mentioned earlier which place the event immediately after the Trojan War. Thus, the extensive evidence that the Etruscans migrated from western Anatolia to Italy can also, by extension, be taken as evidence that the Trojan migration to Italy was a historical event, for it was really the same event as the Etruscan migration.

Additional evidence for the Etruscan migration being the same as the Trojan migration can be seen from their art. Fascinatingly, one of the most common individuals depicted in Etruscan art was Aeneas. Well over a dozen vase paintings from the late sixth century to the early fifth century BCE depict Aeneas in battle at Troy, and an even larger number depict his flight from Troy. Small statues have also been found in Etruria, possibly from the same time period or perhaps a little later, depicting Aeneas carrying his father Anchises from the city of Troy after the war. Interestingly, these scenes were far more popular in Etruria than they were elsewhere.[297] Why were the Etruscans so interested in Aeneas and especially in his flight from Troy? Could it be that he was an important figure in their history? This would be consistent with the rest of the evidence for their origin.

Furthermore, a seventh-century BCE Etruscan wine jug has been found which depicts two horsemen exiting a labyrinth. This is thought to be connected to Virgil's description of a performance held by the Trojan Romans in their commemoration of the death of Aeneas' father Anchises. The performance itself was said to have been taught to the Trojans by Anchises. It involved intricate movements from horse riders, said to invoke the twisting paths of the famous labyrinth on Crete. Significantly, the design of the labyrinth on the Etruscan wine jug is essentially identical to the depiction of the Cretan labyrinth seen on ancient artefacts. The performance described by Virgil was called the 'Troy Game'. In line with this, the Etruscan wine jug has the word 'Troia' inscribed on it, almost certainly a reference to Troy.

Another piece of evidence for the connection between the Etruscans and the Trojans may be seen in their chief god. It is well known that Apollo acts as the protector of the Trojans in Homer's *Iliad*, and this is likely connected to the fact that the god of the ancient inhabitants of Wilusa (Troy) is recorded in Hittite records as being called Apaliunas, considered to be an early form of 'Apollo'. The Etruscans definitely did worship Apollo, though they also worshipped essentially all the gods in the Greek pantheon. Therefore, Zeus would have been the highest god of the pantheon, and he appears in Etruscan mythology under the name 'Tinia'.[298] However, that does not necessarily mean that Zeus, or Tinia, was the god whom they venerated the most. The Etruscan version of Apollo, whose name was usually spelled Apulu or Aplu, was frequently depicted in Etruscan art.[299] And in addition, in Virgil's *Aeneid*, one of the Etruscan characters, Arruns, cries out to the heavens as he rushes into battle, and he directs his words to Apollo, specifically calling him the chief god and the one whom they worship the most. Given that it is an Etruscan character who says these words, this would indicate that the chief god of the Etruscans was Apollo. This harmonises perfectly with the conclusion that they were closely associated with the Trojans.[300] Archaeology has confirmed that Apollo 'was certainly widely worshipped'.[301]

An additional piece of evidence for the fact that the migration of the Lydians/Pelasgians was the same as the migration of the Trojans is the fact that both groups were said to have arrived at the same city in Italy. As mentioned earlier, Hellanicus of Lesbos claimed that the Pelasgians arrived in Italy and founded Tyrrhenia. Specifically, he states that they first took the city of Croton, believed to be modern-day Cortona in the ancient territory of Etruria. Interestingly, when Aeneas is told in the *Aeneid* to sail to Italy to reach the new home of the Trojans, he is specifically told to reach Corythus.[302] This city is generally identified with Cortona as well.[303] Thus, both groups are specifically associated with arriving at the same city, and it was a city in Etruria. This is especially significant in view of the fact that Cortona is not a coastal city, so there is nothing inherently logical about a group of travellers arriving there first.

In summary, we can see that there are very good reasons for concluding that the Etruscans were closely associated with the Trojans. It appears, really, that the Etruscan civilisation was formed out of a joint migration of Trojans, Lydians, Pelasgians and perhaps other allies of the Trojans who had suffered during the war. They were evidently led by the Trojans, most likely under the leadership of Aeneas exactly as claimed by the legends. This is heavily indicated by the fact that the Etruscans seem to have had a fascination with Aeneas and regularly depicted his flight from Troy. Most likely, the Etruscan language was the native language in use in north-west Anatolia, the language of the Trojans.[304] Regarding the genetic studies examined earlier, it should be noted that the Trojans and Pelasgians both originally came from Greece, and the Phrygians came from that same part of Europe too, though not Greece itself. Of the main groups that appear to have engaged in this migration to Italy, the Lydians were the only ones who were actually native to Anatolia.

Etruscans and the Founding of Rome
However, the Trojans were said to have founded the city of Rome. If the Trojans formed part of the Etruscans, and the arrival of the Etruscans and the emergence of their civilisation corresponds to the arrival of the Trojans in Italy, then in what sense can it be said that the Etruscans founded Rome? Let us examine what is historically known about the early development of Rome and the influence that the Etruscans had on it.

The Etruscan influence on Rome's early growth is immense. Scholars are continuing to learn more about their impact, for new evidence continues to come to light. One basic example is their architecture. Much of Roman architecture is taken directly from the Etruscan styles. For example, the designs of their temples and houses were taken from the Etruscans.[305] The first truly monumental buildings in Rome are actually considered to have been built directly by the Etruscans.[306] The famous hydraulic engineering of the Romans was also taken from the Etruscans.[307] Regarding religion, many of the Roman gods were taken from the Etruscan gods, such as Juno, who came from the Etruscan Uni. Many of their religious ceremonies had an Etruscan origin. There was even an Etruscan priesthood in Rome which continued to function there for many centuries.

Many cultural practices were adopted from the Etruscans too. For example, the gladiatorial games, which we think of as characteristic of the Romans, had their origins in Etruria.[308] Furthermore, as mentioned

The Founding of Rome

previously, the Roman fasces – a symbol of the authority and power of a ruler – was adopted from the Etruscan double-axe symbol.[309] The toga, as well, was originally Etruscan.[310] Roman law was also heavily influenced by the Etruscans.[311] And of course, one more vital area of Etruscan influence on the Romans was their alphabet. The Romans' Latin alphabet was taken directly from the Etruscan alphabet in the seventh century BCE.[312]

Furthermore, numerous prominent Roman families were originally Etruscan. For example, the Herminia gens, the Lartia gens, the Tarquitia gens, the Verginia gens and the Volumnia gens were all families of high status during the early years of the Roman civilisation, and they are all thought to be of Etruscan origin. Archaeology also reveals an Etruscan presence at Rome at least as early as the late seventh century BCE.[313]

The result of all this is that we can see that the Etruscans had an enormous part to play in the early development of Rome. Interestingly, Dionysius of Halicarnassus stated that 'many of the historians have taken Rome itself for a Tyrrhenian [Etruscan] city'.[314] This is consistent with all the archaeological evidence that we have just considered. Now, how does this tie in with the legends about the Trojans founding Rome?

The majority of ancient records that refer to the founding of Rome by the Trojans do not go into any detail. The most detailed account is found in Virgil's *Aeneid*. Livy, a contemporary of Virgil, also presents a relatively detailed account of this event. However, both of these first-century BCE accounts are evidently significantly corrupted from the genuine history, because they present Rome as being a kind of successor city to Alba Longa, centuries after the arrival of the Trojans. Yet at least two dozen earlier records state that Rome was founded in the time of Aeneas or just after. Therefore, the detailed accounts from Livy and Virgil must be used with great caution. Nonetheless, it is important to note that Virgil's account calls the natives of the country Latins, and distinguishes them from the Trojans. It is only later that both groups are said to be known by the same term, Latins.

This shows that the Latins were not simply supposed to have been descendants of the Trojans. It was not as simple as that. Rather, the Latins were a tribe that already existed in Italy. They were the 'Aborigines' of Livy's account. But when the Trojans arrived, many of the newcomers joined the Latins and at least some of them formed part of the new ruling class. What seems to have happened is that the Trojans dominated the natives of Etruria upon their arrival and formed their new civilisation there, the Etruscan civilisation, and then in the time of Aeneas' probable son Romulus a branch of the Trojans, led by this son, split off and joined the Latins to form the Roman civilisation.

However, there is reason to believe that there might have been two influxes of the Trojans to the Latin peoples. One evidently occurred when Romulus founded Rome in the mid-seventh century BCE. Yet it appears that the unification of some of the Trojan immigrants with the Latin peoples referred to by Virgil and Livy was actually a later event that they have misplaced in time.

Duplicated and Misplaced History

As noted earlier, tales of the Lydian migration to Etruria state that the Lydians were led by a man named Tyrrhenus, from whom the nation received its name. In all likelihood, this was a fictional eponymous founder created to explain the name of the nation. However, legends of this migration also mention a brother of Tyrrhenus named Tarchon. He too travelled to Etruria and was one of the leaders of the nation. Strabo states that Tarchon was put in charge of founding the Etruscan cities.[315] Virgil's *Aeneid* describes Tarchon as a king of the Etruscans, and he allies himself with Aeneas in his war against a leader of the Latins named Turnus.

It appears that these accounts are the result of a duplication and misplacement of real historical events. It has long been noted that the name 'Tarchon' is most likely connected to the Latin name 'Tarquinius', the name of a Roman gens with Etruscan origins. However, many overlook the similarities in the accounts of Tarchon's life and the life of one of the Tarquins of Roman history – specifically, Lucius Tarquinius Superbus, an Etruscan and the final king of Rome. What appears to have happened is that accounts of Tarchon, the early leader of the Etruscans and ally of Aeneas, became confused with accounts of this later king of Rome, thus leading to the stories of Tarchon and Aeneas as they appear in the accounts of Virgil and Livy.

Lucius Tarquinius Superbus is recorded as waging war against the Rutuli, a particular tribe of the Latins, just as Tarchon and Aeneas are reported to have waged war against them. Tarquinius was victorious in this campaign, just as the Rutuli are defeated in the account of Tarchon against the Rutuli. Both Virgil and Livy explain that this war started due to jealousy on the part of Turnus, the leader of the Rutuli, because Aeneas became engaged to a woman whom Turnus had been supposed to marry. This woman was Lavinia, the princess of the Latins. This was likely derived from a famous conflict between the historical Lucius Tarquinius Superbus and a man named Turnus Herdonius. Early on in his reign, Tarquinius arranged a meeting to discuss the bonds between Rome and the Latin nations. There was talk of Tarquinius receiving supreme power among the Latins, but one man, Turnus, spoke up and argued against such an outcome. He is reported to have argued the following:

> Even supposing that his own countrymen did well to entrust him with supreme power, or rather that it was entrusted and not seized by an act of parricide, the Latins ought not, even in that case, to place it in the hands of an alien.[316]

In other words, Turnus found it objectionable that such power should go to a foreigner. This is very similar to the motive given to the Turnus who was said to have gone to war against Aeneas and Tarchon. As Livy put it:

> Lavinia had been betrothed to him [Turnus] before the arrival of Aeneas, and, furious at finding a stranger preferred to him, he declared war.[317]

It could well be that this romance episode had its origin in the political intrigue born of Turnus' anger at Tarquinius, a foreigner, receiving supreme power over the Latins. In such a case, Lavinia the princess of the Latins would have originally been a figurative character, essentially representing the nation as a whole. Tarquinius was then reported to have conspired to have Turnus framed for plotting his murder. Convincing the other Latin leaders of this, Tarquinius had Turnus put to death. It is very likely that this event, along with the war against the Rutuli (which was originally a separate event), was mistakenly placed in accounts of the earlier Tarchon, the ally of Aeneas, hence bringing Aeneas into the story and placing the events in that earlier setting.

In addition, the unification between the Trojans (though in reality, only the portion of them that founded Rome) and the Latins that supposedly occurred soon after this defeat of Turnus in the *Aeneid* is evidently the same as another event described by Livy. He reports that soon after the death of Turnus Herdonius, the other Latin states accepted Tarquinius as their supreme leader and combined the Roman army with their Latin armies. So we can see that the basic events described by Virgil (and several other Roman historians, including Livy himself in an earlier part of his history of Rome) were actually distorted accounts of the activities of Tarquinius Superbus, accounts which were accidentally misplaced onto the life of Tarchon, ally of Aeneas. This distortion and misplacement evidently happened before the lifetimes of Livy and Virgil, and in Livy's account Tarchon has been dropped, while he is preserved in Virgil's *Aeneid*.

However, outside of Livy's and Virgil's accounts, Tarchon was claimed to have been one of the founders of the Etruscan League of Twelve Cities.[318] This appears to be a genuine tradition about the earlier Tarchon, the contemporary of Aeneas. Although there is not universal agreement about when the Etruscan League really was founded, and on the basis of the legend some sources claim that they were founded in about 1100 BCE (because of the popular date for the Trojan War), one recent academic book states the following:

> Twelve city-states emerged by the seventh century B.C., allied in a religious league and sharing a vivid and distinctive culture.[319]

Thus, this fits in well with the placement of Tarchon, and therefore Aeneas, in the early seventh century BCE.

Conclusion

In summary, we can see that the vast majority of ancient sources placed the founding of Rome just after the Trojan War, not centuries after it. We have also seen that there is good reason to believe that the real founding of Rome occurred in the mid-seventh century BCE, not the mid-eighth century. This is seen from the archaeology of Rome as well as calculations based on more realistic reign lengths for the kings of Rome.

In addition, we have seen that there is very good evidence to conclude that the Etruscans, or at least their ruling elite, did come from western Anatolia and established themselves in Italy just after 700 BCE. This is seen both from records about this event, as well as from archaeology. The sudden inundation of profound Oriental influence after that year strongly indicates that the Orientalising period of Etruscan history was not primarily due to trade, but rather the influence of this Near Eastern ruling elite. We can see this from their religious practices, their tomb designs, their clothing, their art, and many other aspects of their culture. Their Anatolian origin is supported by the Lemnos stele and the reference to the Tyrrhenians in north-west Anatolia *before* the emergence of the Etruscan civilisation proper in 700 BCE.

The Founding of Rome

We have also seen that this Anatolian origin of the Etruscans ties in with the legend of the Trojan migration to Italy after the Trojan War. There is good reason for viewing the Etruscans as a mixture of Trojans, Lydians, Pelasgians and other allies, led by the Trojans under the command of Aeneas.

Furthermore, it has been shown that the Etruscans had a large part in establishing Rome, as seen from the numerous elements of Roman civilisation which were taken directly from the Etruscans, as well as the many aristocratic families in the early history of Rome who had an Etruscan origin. This ties in with the legends of the Trojans founding Rome, inasmuch as the Etruscans were the Trojans. In short, we have seen that the evidence completely supports the legends about the Trojans leaving their devastated home in north-west Anatolia and migrating to Italy, where they founded Rome some decades later.

7

Brutus of Britain

Now that we have seen that the evidence fully supports the legends of the Trojans migrating to Italy and founding Rome, what can be said regarding the legends of Brutus, several generations later, leading a migration from there to Britain? Does the evidence support this? Well, before we can examine the migration, we need to examine Brutus himself. While some independent researchers consider him to have been a real figure, academics universally dismiss him as a fictional character. However, with the new information we have available to us – that is, that the Trojan War actually occurred in *c.* 700 BCE rather than *c.* 1200 BCE – we have a totally new corpus of evidence to investigate. Therefore, in this chapter we will analyse the available evidence concerning the era in which Brutus actually would have lived, and we will see how the legend is confirmed by the historical facts.

The Genealogy of Brutus
To discover the historical figure behind the legendary Brutus, we can do no better than to simply read what the earliest source says about him. This is the *Historia Brittonum*, written in *c.* 830 CE. It is a very useful source in many respects. One key aspect that makes it so useful is that the writer was not creating one continuous narrative, as in Geoffrey of Monmouth's *Historia Regum Britanniae*. Rather, the writer of the *Historia Brittonum* (whom we will follow tradition in calling 'Nennius') was compiling a record of various different traditions, many of which conflicted with each other. This means that we get a much more comprehensive view of the different traditions that existed in Britain in the ninth century CE. This is much more

useful when it comes to establishing the truth than just having a single narrative account.

In the case of Brutus, it means that Nennius provided many details about Brutus that are not contained in Geoffrey's *HRB*. One significant detail is the matter of his genealogy. In the *HRB*, Brutus is described as the son of Silvius, son of Ascanius, son of Aeneas. A similar genealogy is presented in one part of the *Historia Brittonum*. The section that deals with this version is internally inconsistent in a few ways, undoubtedly due to Nennius trying to record multiple different traditions at the same time. What does appear to be consistent is that Ascanius and Silvius are presented as brothers rather than father and son. The Britons are said to have been descended from Silvius, son of Aeneas, yet are also specified as having been descended from the family of Brutus; therefore, Brutus was evidently a descendant of this Silvius. Yet just after this, an account is presented of Ascanius marrying and his wife bearing a son. This son is Brutus, who is then described as travelling to Britain and being the forefather of the Britons. This would make Brutus the son of Ascanius rather than Silvius. However, some manuscripts do read 'Silvius' in this account, rather than 'Ascanius', which would make it consistent with the immediately preceding statements that the Britons were the descendants of Silvius, son of Aeneas, through Brutus.

As an aside, this section provides fascinating evidence that truly ancient traditions were preserved in Britain from antiquity. Nennius reports here that Aeneas 'obtained the kingdom of the Romans'. Yet from the first century BCE onwards, as we have mentioned before, it had become widely believed that Rome was founded centuries after the arrival of Aeneas in Italy. Virgil's *Aeneid*, which contains this claim, became extremely popular throughout the Roman Empire and continued to be popular throughout the medieval era. Yet here in the *Historia Brittonum*, we find the statement that Aeneas obtained the kingdom of the Romans, which is in line with the more ancient statements found in the centuries before the publication of the *Aeneid* and Livy's history. This indicates that at least some of the information in this account was not taken from recently created traditions, but originated from traditions long predating Virgil and Livy.

In any case, after the account of Brutus' birth, Nennius presents a brief list of the early rulers of the Latins along with their reign lengths, starting with Aeneas. Ascanius follows, and then Silvius is listed. Perhaps this list (which obviously existed in some form prior to Nennius compiling it) led to the belief that Silvius, the father of Brutus, was the son of Ascanius rather than his brother. In any case, it is this basic tradition that we find in Geoffrey's *HRB*. Given that Aeneas actually lived in the late eighth and early seventh centuries BCE, this would place Brutus in the late seventh century BCE.

However, this is not the only genealogy for Brutus that we find in the *Historia Brittonum*. Another version is the following:

> The first man that dwelt in Europe was Alanus, with his three sons, Hisicion, Armenon, and Neugio. Hisicion had four sons, Froncus, Romanus, Alamanus, and Brutus.

This genealogy is derived from a sixth-century CE document known as the *Frankish Table of Nations*. In this document, we find the following:

> Istio brought forth the Romans, Britons, Franks, Alamans.

Other manuscripts spell the name 'Hisitio' and many other variations. He is obviously the 'Hisicion' of the genealogy found in the *Historia Brittonum*. The Istio, or Hisitio, of the *Frankish Table of Nations* was said to have been the forefather of the Romans, the Britons, the Franks and the Alamans (the Alemanni, a collection of Germanic tribes). Somewhere along the line between the composition of this Frankish source and the composition of the *Historia Brittonum*, these nations emerging from Istio were turned into individual founding figures of those nations, thus producing 'Romanus', 'Brutus', 'Froncus' and 'Alamanus'. This does not mean that Brutus was not a real individual, but the Brutus of this specific record was evidently an artificial construction. However, after recording this tradition, Nennius presented a genealogy which is evidently a combination of this fictional founding figure named Brutus with the genealogy of the very real (as we will go on to see) founding figure named Brutus. The genealogy is as follows:

> Brutus was the son of Hisicion, Hisicion was the son of Alanus, Alanus was the son of Rhea Silvia, Rhea Silvia was the daughter of Numa Pompilius, Numa was the son of Ascanius, Ascanius of Eneas.

So according to this, Brutus's father Hisicion was the great-great-great-grandson of Aeneas. This makes Brutus the sixth-generation descendant of Aeneas, rather than just his grandson or great-grandson. This would place Brutus in the latter half of the sixth century BCE rather than the late seventh century BCE. Although this genealogy involves the fictional son of Hisicion, it is clearly not simply a combination of the record found in the *Frankish Table of Nations* with the tradition of Brutus the son of Silvius son of Aeneas. For one thing, this descent is made to go through Ascanius rather than Silvius. However, that may just be due to the conflicting traditions regarding Brutus' father – whether Silvius or Ascanius – discussed earlier. More significant is the fact that, if that were the case, we would expect Hisicion to be placed much closer to Aeneas than he is. We might expect, for example, Hisicion's father Alanus to be made the son of Silvius or Ascanius. Instead, we find Alanus separated from Ascanius by Rhea Silvia and Numa Pompilius.

The presence of these two apparently random characters from Classical sources suggests the presence of a third tradition. This third tradition evidently made Brutus a great-great-grandson of Numa Pompilius, or perhaps just an unspecified descendant of his. Numa Pompilius, for his part, presumably was recorded as the son of Ascanius, son of Aeneas, as we see here in the *Historia Brittonum*. To merge this descent of Brutus with the other claimed descent from Alanus, the scribe evidently took the most famous child of Numa Pompilius that they knew from Classical sources and used that figure to connect the two lineages. However, the scribe evidently confused Numa Pompilius with Numitor, a similarly named character from Roman records, and quite a famous one too. Thus, the scribe took Rhea Silvia, by far the most famous child of Numitor in Roman records, and inserted her in the list to connect Alanus with Numa Pompilius. This would appear to be the best explanation for the otherwise seemingly random presence of Numa Pompilius and Rhea Silvia.

In short, we can see that this genealogical list is quite a mess. Yet, nonetheless, it appears to preserve a tradition that Brutus was a descendant of Numa Pompilius. This being the case, the more famous lineage that simply makes Brutus a grandson or great-grandson of Aeneas may well actually come from an abbreviated version of a longer pedigree that went through Numa Pompilius. Therefore, it is likely that the earliest genealogical lists would have placed Brutus at some point between the late seventh and late sixth centuries BCE.

This is supported by subsequent pedigrees going back to Brutus from later historical figures. For example, there is such a pedigree contained in the record known as *Hanes Gruffydd ap Cynan*, which documents the life of a king of Gwynedd in the late eleventh/early twelfth century CE. This document was likely written in the decades following that king's death. It contains a genealogy of Gruffydd going back to Brutus and beyond. The earliest figure in his genealogy who can be securely dated is Cunedda, who left many descendants and is generally believed to have been born in *c.* 370 CE.[320] There are forty generations between Brutus and Cunedda. Using an average generation length of twenty to twenty-five years, this would take us back to about 430–630 BCE for the birth of Brutus. This is consistent with the dates derived from counting forward from Aeneas, and, in particular, placing him after Numa Pompilius, who lived in the late seventh century BCE.

Interestingly, this record describes Brutus as a prince of Rome. This is consistent with the fact that Rome was founded only a few decades at most after Aeneas arrived in Italy, long before Brutus was born. Just like in the *Historia Brittonum*, this indicates a tradition of genuine antiquity, dating back to before Virgil's *Aeneid* and Livy's history popularised the idea that Aeneas was separated from the founding of Rome by many centuries. At the same time, this detail also indicates that the Brutus of this record dates to before the monarchy of Rome was abolished, which was in *c.* 510 BCE.

False Genealogies
However, although the pedigree in *Hanes Gruffydd ap Cynan* indicates that Brutus lived at this time, the genealogy in Geoffrey of Monmouth's *Historia Regum Britanniae* extends back much further. Although the relationship between one king and the next is not always clear, this record appears to place about fifty generations between Brutus and Heli, whose position as the father of the historical Cassivellaunus would place his birth in *c.* 100 BCE. Attributing twenty to twenty-five years to a generation, this would take Brutus' birth back to about 1350–1100 BCE, in line with the traditional date for the Trojan War.

The explanation for this is undoubtedly that extra kings have been added to this list to reach *c.* 1200 BCE for the Trojan War. The belief that it took place at that time would have been perfectly well known to the medieval Britons. Thus, a scribe who was attempting to write a full history of the Britons from Brutus to the medieval era could reasonably have been compelled to attempt to 'fix' the apparently deficient genealogy actually found in the records. The fact that this really did take place is evident from two observations.

Firstly, a copious amount of names – often grouped together – in Geoffrey's king list are also found in the records of later kings, indicating that they have been taken from those records and transplanted into the pre-Roman period by the writer of Geoffrey's source. A great deal of them seem to have been taken from the kings and princes of an area that the ancient Britons called 'the Old North' (broadly northern England and southern Scotland) from roughly 400 to 600 CE. For example, we find Elidurus and Peredurus together, listed as brothers. In the available lists of kings of the medieval era, such as in the tenth-century *Harleian MS 3859*, we find the father and son Elidir and Peredur in the mid-sixth century. One of their relatives, also from the North, was Garbanion, also spelled Garmonion (in archaic Welsh, the letter 'm' and the letter 'b' are often interchanged). He is presented as another brother of the pre-Roman Peredurus and Elidurus in the *Historia Regum Britanniae*. Just a few kings after Peredurus in Geoffrey's pre-Roman king list, we find a certain Enniaunus. This is probably Einion, another relative of the historical Peredur and Elidir. Separated from this pre-Roman 'Enniaunus' by just one king, we then come to Runo, who is almost certainly the historical Rhun, son of the aforementioned Einion of the post-Roman era. His supposed brother Morgan in Geoffrey's pre-Roman king list is presumably drawn from one of the several Morgans of the Old North between 400 and 600 CE; the most likely candidate is either Morgan Fwlch, the famous slayer of Urien Rheged, or his grandson of the same name.

Returning to an earlier point in Geoffrey's list of pre-Roman kings, we find a king named Gorboduc. Although this is different from the king Geoffrey later calls Gorbonianus, Welsh versions of his work use the same Welsh name to represent both of them, indicating that Geoffrey's 'Gorboduc' is actually a corruption of 'Gorbonian' (also spelled 'Garbonian' and 'Garmonion' among other variations). Interestingly, while this Gorboduc is said to have been succeeded by a son named Porrex, the next king listed after Porrex is Dunvallo Molmutius, and after him is Brennius. In the historical records of the post-Roman kings, we find a Garbanion who was the father of Dyfnwal Moelmud, father of Bran. This is almost the exact same sequence we find in Geoffrey's pre-Roman king list, apart from the presence of Porrex between Gorboduc and Dunvallo. Without doubt, the historical kings Garbanion, Dyfnwal and Bran – kings of the North within the period between 400 and 600 CE – have been taken from their true historical context and placed in the pre-Roman era.

Some other kings who appear to be taken from the historical kings of the North between 400–600 CE include Geoffrey's Urianus, who is likely the same as the famous Urien Rheged. A few generations previously in Geoffrey's pre-Roman king list, we find a certain Catellus. It is possible that he was taken from Urien's historical son

Cadell. Another king of the North who might have been transported into the pre-Roman era is Rhydderch Hael of the sixth century CE, who may well be Geoffrey's Rederchius. It is also possible that Geoffrey's pre-Roman Eldol comes from Eidol, a figure of the North who lived towards the end of the sixth century, mentioned in an early Welsh poem called *Y Gododdin*. Yet another example might be the pre-Roman king Caph, who might really be Cof ap Caw, a prince of the North in the sixth century.

A few kings seem to have been taken from historical kings from other regions of Britain. For example, two kings near the end of the list of pre-Roman kings are Pir and Capoir. These are very unusual names, and there appears to be only one pair of historical figures whom these could have come from. In a line of otherwise unknown princes (so it is impossible to date them) who ruled Penllyn in Wales, we find a certain Pybyr ap Caper.[321] It appears that Geoffrey's 'Capoir' comes from this 'Caper', and his 'Pir' comes from a shortening of 'Pybyr'. The names have been flipped, for Geoffrey presents Capoir as coming after Pir, whereas Caper actually came before Pybyr. But the flipping of father-and-son pairs was not unusual in medieval records.

Another father-and-son pair can be identified in Merianus and his son Bledudo. A medieval document called *Bonedd y Saint* records a line of ancestry which includes 'Bleiddud ap Meirion' in the fifth century CE. Geoffrey's pre-Roman kings Merianus and Bledudo are clearly taken from this historical Meirion and his son Bleiddud. They were descendants of a famous founder of many dynasties named Cunedda, who lived in the early fifth century CE. He, too, seems to appear in Geoffrey's list of pre-Roman kings, though much earlier in the list. He is mentioned as 'Cunedagius', a Latinised form of the earliest attested spelling of Cunedda, which is 'Cunedag', found in the *Historia Brittonum*. Geoffrey's Cunedagius is made the son of 'Henwinus', most likely taken from the historical son of Cunedda named Einion; this is evidently another example of a father-and-son pair being flipped.

The list of pre-Roman kings in the *Historia Regum Britanniae* also mentions a certain Gurguint Barbtruc, whose name was evidently taken from a king of Meirionnydd in the sixth century CE whose name is recorded as 'Guurgint Barmbtruch' in the *Harleian* genealogies. Another king who can clearly be identified due to his epithet is Geoffrey's Samuil Penissel. We find him very clearly in the *Harleian* records as 'Samuil Pennissel'. He was a king of the sixth century CE, though his exact kingdom is somewhat uncertain.

Another king who can be identified as a historical post-Roman figure is Ebraucus. According to Geoffrey of Monmouth, he had an extraordinary number of sons, daughters and wives. This figure would appear to be Brychan, a historical king in the early post-Roman era. In reality, the medieval records about Brychan appear to confuse at least two, and probably even three, different figures.[322] Geoffrey's Ebraucus is seemingly a duplicate of this combined Brychan, not of any one historical Brychan in particular. Partly due to being a combination of multiple people, the medieval records of Brychan present him as having an extraordinary number of sons and daughters and also many wives, just like Geoffrey's Ebraucus.

As stated already, this is the first observation that leads us to conclude that Geoffrey's pre-Roman king list has been artificially extended – the fact that many of the kings are clearly identifiable as historical figures from records concerning later eras. All of the kings who have been identified here as later historical kings are notably *not* included in the shorter genealogical record going back to Brutus in the *Hanes Gruffydd ap Cynan* that we considered earlier. For example, the beginning of Geoffrey's genealogy is as follows:

Brutus→Locrinus→Maddan→Mempricius→Ebraucus→Brutus Greenshield→ Leil→Rud Hud Hudibras→Bladud→Leir→Regan→Cunedagius→Rivallo

By comparison, the shorter genealogy, found in the *Hanes Gruffydd ap Cynan*, presents this same sequence but omits both Ebraucus and Cunegadius, the two kings from this section who are clearly taken from later historical figures. The same can be said regarding the rest of the list as well. A full presentation of Brutus' most plausible genealogy is presented in Appendix Two, 'The Descent from Brutus'. It is shown that many more kings than just the ones discussed here were also taken from later records.

The second observation that leads us to conclude that the list from Brutus to the kings of the first century BCE has been artificially expanded is seen from looking at the portion of the descent from Brennius onwards. It was mentioned earlier that Brennius, the son of Dunvallo Molmutius, was taken from Bran ap Dyfnwal Moelmud of the sixth century CE. However, this figure from the post-Roman era was actually combined with a genuine pre-Roman historical figure. The account Geoffrey provides about Brennius is taken directly from the activities of Brennus, a historical ruler of parts of Gaul in the early fourth century BCE. Geoffrey presents

Brennius as leading a successful sack of Rome, which is exactly what the historical Brennus did. This occurred in about 387 BCE. There are some thirty generations listed between Brennius and Heli, the father of Cassivellaunus. This last king fought against Julius Caesar in the middle of the first century BCE, so his father Heli must have been born just before the turn of the first century BCE. Using twenty to twenty-five years per generation, the thirty generations from Heli back to Brennius would bring us to about 700–850 BCE. This is many centuries too early for the historical Brennus. This is direct, explicit evidence that the line of descent has been expanded. Logically, there is no reason to believe that it is only the part of the list after Brennius that has been expanded; the part of the descent before Brennius would logically have been expanded too. Ebraucus, Cunedagius, Dunvallo and Gorboduc are examples of this.

In summary, we can see that the list of pre-Roman kings in the *Historia Regum Britanniae* has been greatly expanded so as to reach the traditional date of the Trojan War. In reality, the *Hanes Gruffydd ap Cynan* is undoubtedly much closer to the truth. As noted already, this genealogy takes us back to 430–630 BCE for the birth of Brutus. Geoffrey's king list is compatible with this when the duplicated kings are removed, as explained fully in Appendix Two. Knowing when Brutus was born is immensely helpful in being able to correctly identify him, which we will now demonstrate.

The Historical Brutus

Many pieces of information about the legendary Brutus make a lot more sense when he is placed into his correct era. For example, consider a few more vital details about Brutus that are revealed in the *Historia Brittonum*. The very first mention of Brutus is found at the beginning of the author's description of Britain:

> The island of Britain derives its name from Brutus, a Roman consul.

So Brutus, apparently, was a Roman consul. This is completely inconsistent with the traditional date for Brutus, *c.* 1100 BCE, because the first Roman consuls lived in the late sixth century BCE. However, once we place Brutus into the correct era of 430–630 BCE, this makes sense. Brutus could well have been a Roman consul if he was born anywhere within the second half of that range. We get even more direct information from a later section of the *Historia Brittonum*. In this later section, the scribe reports a legend about the Scots first migrating to Ireland. Their arrival into Ireland is stated to have occurred 1,002 years after the Egyptians were lost in the Red Sea – that is, after the Exodus. As we saw previously, the Exodus occurred in roughly 1500 BCE. Therefore, the arrival of the Scots into Ireland supposedly occurred around 500 BCE, according to this legend. The *Historia Brittonum* then goes on to say:

> At that period, Brutus, who first exercised the consular office, reigned over the Romans.

According to this record, Brutus was the first person to hold the consular office in Rome, and this allegedly was in the period around 500 BCE. What does history reveal?

The first consul of Rome in historical records is recorded as setting up the position and taking power in *c.* 510 BCE, and his name was Lucius Junius Brutus – a perfect match for the legend. It is difficult to overstate just how important this is. Brutus of Britain, the figure who is widely claimed to be totally fictional, is in fact easily identifiable as this historical figure, Lucius Junius Brutus. He fits the estimated range for Brutus' birth as established by *Hanes Gruffydd ap Cynan*; he fits the position as a close descendant of Aeneas, when the latter is placed into his correct time period of *c.* 700 BCE; and he fits these details found in the *Historia Brittonum* about Brutus living about 1,000 years after the Exodus and being the first Roman consul. Without doubt, Lucius Junius Brutus was the Brutus of these records.

Why This Identification Has Been Overlooked
If this is so obvious, then why has this identification been apparently missed by virtually all researchers? Why is this not more widely recognised? Well, this identification *has* been made in the past, but it is extremely rare to find such acknowledgements. Controversial researchers Alan Wilson and Baram Blackett made this identification as early as 1980. More recently, Miles Russell referred to Lucius Junius Brutus in a discussion of the origin of the legend of Brutus, yet he thinks that the Brutus of the *Historia Brittonum* is not the historical Lucius Junius Brutus, but that such a connection *would have* been logical on the part of the scribe to make.[323] Apparently Miles Russell did not consider the details provided by the *Historia Brittonum* clear enough to perceive that Lucius Junius Brutus is, in fact, the Brutus of the account. The absence of any mention of the chronological

placement of Brutus in the *Historia Brittonum* (such as being placed 1000 years after the Exodus or being placed after Numa Pompilius) in his discussion suggests that he missed these vital details.

Astonishingly, even Anthony Adolph's 2015 publication *Brutus of Troy and the Quest for the Ancestry of the British*, which deals extensively with Brutus, completely failed to make the identification of Brutus with Lucius Junius Brutus. This is even more remarkable due to the fact that this publication did bring the latter historical figure into the analysis, yet still managed to not identify him as the Brutus of the *Historia Brittonum*.

The reason for this unfortunate mass oversight can be traced back to one influential work. One demonstration of this is Peter Bartrum's swift dismissal (in *A Welsh Classical Dictionary*) of the origin of Brutus as being a subject which was explained by Bruce.[324] The Bruce to whom he referred was James Douglas Bruce, a historian in the early twentieth century. He wrote a hugely influential work entitled *The evolution of Arthurian romance from the beginnings down to the year 1300*, which was published in 1923. In this work, Bruce summarised a theory which was not original to him, but because of the influence his book subsequently had, it grew in prominence considerably. According to this theory, the origin of the idea that Brutus founded Britain lies in the *Chronicon*, a work produced by Jerome in the fourth century CE which was still in use in the medieval period. This reports that 'Brutus subjugated Spain as far as the ocean'. This is a reference to Decimus Junius Brutus, a consul of Rome who did subjugate part of Spain in 138 BCE. According to Bruce and others, this is the origin of the following claim in the *Historia Brittonum*:

> Brutus was consul when he conquered Spain, and reduced that country to a Roman province. He afterwards subdued the island of Britain, whose inhabitants were the descendants of the Romans.

This is found embedded within the passage that discussed Brutus' descent from Aeneas and how he was the forefather of the Britons. Bruce claims that the writer of the source for this claim, which was then included by the compiler of the *Historia Brittonum*, found the reference to Brutus conquering Spain in the *Chronicon* and, due to the similarity between 'Britain' and 'Brutus', decided to expand it to say that he also conquered Britain and that Britain was named after him. Thus was born the idea that Brutus was the founder of Britain.

It is quite possible that this specific statement about Spain in the *Historia Brittonum* does come from the *Chronicon*. But that does not mean that the Brutus figure as a whole comes from Decimus Junius Brutus. As we have already seen – and as Bruce acknowledges – part of the Brutus figure in the *Historia Brittonum* is a fictional eponymous figure taken from the *Frankish Table of Nations*. There is no reason why the primary figure behind Brutus must be Decimus Junius Brutus when the reality is that he only explains one small part of the account. The primary figure who makes up the character of Brutus is the one who was a near descendent of Aeneas, though Bruce obviously could not reasonably be expected to have realised that the Trojan War occurred in *c.* 700 BCE. This is the character whose life story is presented in the *Historia Brittonum*, with the reference to him conquering Spain simply being one small part which most likely was taken from Decimus Junius Brutus. But the Brutus who lived a few generations after Aeneas and who was the first Roman consul, as the *Historia Brittonum* says, was Lucius Junius Brutus.

In actuality, it seems that Bruce did at least partially point out Lucius Junius Brutus' role in this British legend. He stated:

> The author of ch. 10–11 in the *Historia* … identifies Brutus, the first Roman consul … with the Brutus after whom, according to ch. 7, already Britannia had been named.

So Bruce noticed the reference to Brutus being the first Roman consul, and thus Bruce is logically referring to Lucius Junius Brutus in this quotation, although he does not give his full name. Yet, he states that this earlier Brutus was identified with the later one – Decimus Junius Brutus – thus holding to the later individual as the primary person making up the Brutus figure, with the earlier Lucius Junius Brutus simply being added on. In this, Bruce was surely incorrect. The earlier historical Brutus was the one who lived just a few generations after Numa Pompilius (a detail in the *Historia Brittonum* which Bruce does not even acknowledge, much less explain) and Aeneas. It was the earlier historical Brutus whose life formed the origin of the majority of the account in the *Historia Brittonum*, as we will go on to see.

Nonetheless, Bruce did acknowledge that Lucius Junius Brutus formed part of the Brutus figure in this British legend. Yet it is easy to miss, since it is only in this one line that he referred to this individual, and he also did not refer to him by his full name. For these reasons, it appears that virtually all subsequent scholars have either ignored or missed this detail. As the decades have gone on, fewer and fewer researchers have consulted Bruce's work directly. Rather, they have consulted academic books based on Bruce's publication, or books which are even further removed from that original founding work. It is viewed as an accepted fact now that Decimus Junius Brutus was the ultimate origin of Brutus, with all reference to Lucius Junius Brutus being completely lost and forgotten.

From History to Legend

Contrary to what Bruce argued, the primary figure behind the Brutus of the *Historia Brittonum* was not Decimus Junius Brutus with Lucius Junius Brutus tacked on. Rather, it was the other way around. In this section, we will see how the account about Brutus was ultimately derived, almost entirely, from the life of Lucius Junius Brutus.

Firstly, the very first statement about Brutus, that he was a Roman consul, is explained by Lucius Junius Brutus being the first Roman consul. The associated claim that Britain was named after him is, as modern scholars believe, probably just folk etymology, similar to the *HRB* claiming that Gloucester was named after Claudius; for one thing, there is evidence that the name of Britain was originally spelt with a 'P', not a 'B'.[325] Yet, needless to say, this folk etymology is not any better explained by Decimus Junius Brutus than it is by Lucius Junius Brutus.

Incidentally, in the *Hanes Gruffydd ap Cynan*, Brutus is described as a prince of Rome. Lucius Junius Brutus is the only Brutus in history who was both a consul and a prince of Rome, fitting both the description in the *Historia Brittonum* and the description in the *Hanes Gruffydd ap Cynan*.

The next statement, somewhat later on in the *Historia Brittonum*, is about Brutus conquering Spain, which does seem to be taken from Decimus. The rest of this passage, which describes the Britons being descended from Brutus, is not easily attributable to either Decimus or Lucius, but it will be shown in the next chapter that this does derive from events involving Lucius Junius Brutus. There is no evidence whatsoever for a migration from Italy to Britain in the time of Decimus, whereas there is evidence for such a migration in the time of Lucius.

Within this same passage is the claim that Brutus was the son of Silvius, although elsewhere, as we have seen, he is said to have been descended from Ascanius. In either case, he was supposedly a descendant of Aeneas. Was Lucius Junius Brutus a descendant of Aeneas? According to Virgil's *Aeneid* in the first century BCE, this Brutus was at least *believed* to have been a descendant of Aeneas.[326] What the exact lineage was supposed to have been is more difficult to establish.

His mother is recorded as being Tarquinia, the daughter of Lucius Tarquinius Priscus.[327] He was the fifth king of Rome. However, he was not a son of the previous king, Ancus Marcus, so he seemingly did not descend directly from the line of kings established by Romulus, the probable son of Aeneas. However, both Priscus' mother and his wife were Etruscan noblewomen. In particular, his wife Tanaquil was said to have come from a powerful family of Tarquinia, which was one of the mightiest and most important Etruscan cities of the time. Thus, it is conceivable that Priscus' mother, or perhaps more likely his wife, was descended from Aeneas, in view of the Trojans and their allies under Aeneas being the historical founders of the Etruscan civilisation just after 700 BCE, as established previously. However, the Romans do not seem to have had any legends about Aeneas founding Etruria, so it is difficult to see how Virgil's claim about Brutus being descended from Aeneas could have had anything to do with his descent through his Etruscan grandmother or great-grandmother. On the other hand, it is conceivable that the memory of Brutus' descent from Aeneas was preserved, while the details of that descent were forgotten.

Regarding the males in this line, Priscus' father was a Greek named Demaratus, so Brutus' Trojan descent cannot be through him. Thus, through Brutus' mother, the only possible lines of Trojan descent would be either through Lucius Tarquinius Priscus' wife (Brutus' grandmother) or his mother (Brutus' great-grandmother).

What about through Brutus' father? Not much is known about him, but most sources call him Marcus Junius. He was said to have been a wealthy man of noble descent who was murdered by Tarquinius Superbus.[328] This raises an interesting possibility. Recall that Brutus' mother was Tarquinia, a daughter of Lucius Tarquinius Priscus. Other records speak of Tarquinia the daughter of Lucius Tarquinius Priscus as being the wife of Servius Tullius, the king of Rome who came immediately after Priscus. This would lead us to believe that Servius Tullius was the father of Brutus, were it not for the records naming Brutus' father as Marcus Junius. Of course, it may be that Tarquinia remarried, perhaps after the death of Servius. Or it may be that there were two different Tarquinias, one married to

Servius and one married to Marcus Junius. It was Roman custom at this time to give daughters the same primary name, so two daughters both recorded as Tarquinia would not be unusual. Yet, the fact that Brutus' father was allegedly of noble descent, a man of great wealth, and was murdered by Tarquinius Superbus is intriguing, for this description also matches Servius Tullius. The fact that the only surviving records about these figures were written down hundreds of years after the events in question means that a great deal of confusion can be reasonably expected.

If we entertain the possibility that Servius was actually the father of Brutus, this could explain one of the lineages given to Brutus in the *Historia Brittonum*. The very first passage describing Brutus indicates that he was the son of Silvius, son of Aeneas. This Silvius appears in ancient Roman legend, so he is not a creation of the British sources. If Brutus was, in fact, the son of Servius Tullius, then it would be within reason to suggest that the name 'Servius' was confused for 'Silvius' as the story was repeated through oral tradition. After all, the letters 'r' and 'l' are often confused or swapped in many languages. This would allow for Brutus' father Servius to be confused for Silvius the son of Aeneas. In addition, the mother of Servius Tullius was said to have been a woman named Ocrisia. By coincidence, this is similar to Creusa, the name of one of Aeneas' wives according to the legends. This would have encouraged the equation of Servius with Silvius. Even if Servius Tullius was not actually the father of Brutus, perhaps he was erroneously viewed as such due to the fact that his wife Tarquinia would be easily mistaken for Tarquinia, mother of Brutus.

But we must question whether or not this scenario would allow for Brutus to have been considered a descendent of Aeneas by the first century BCE, when the *Aeneid* described him as such. It is possible, but the way in which that record presents things would lead us to believe that it was common knowledge that Brutus was descended from Aeneas. Yet, there is no record around that time of Servius being the father of Brutus, even if some details in the records indicate that he may have been (although it may be that Servius' parentage of Brutus was forgotten, but Brutus' prestigious descent from Aeneas was preserved). In addition, these sources from the first century BCE certainly did not believe that Brutus lived just a few generations from the Trojan War, so there is no possibility that the idea of Brutus' Trojan descent in Virgil's *Aeneid* came from a mistaken concept of Brutus being the son of Silvius (as a mistake for Servius), son of Aeneas. Nonetheless, this may well be the explanation for one of Brutus' lineages in the *Historia Brittonum*, although it does not explain his supposed Trojan ancestry in the *Aeneid*.

Putting aside the idea that Brutus' father may have been identical to Servius Tullius, Dionysius of Halicarnassus related how Brutus' father, Marcus Junius, was 'ranked among the most illustratious of the Romans'.[329] He also explains that he was a descendant of one of the colonists who came from Troy with Aeneas. This appears incompatible with the idea that Brutus was a descendant of Aeneas himself, unless the ancestor of Brutus referred to by Dionysius was the wife of Aeneas. Or, he could have been referring to one of Aeneas' adult sons who travelled from Troy to Italy with him. But in either case, it would seem peculiar for Dionysius to have not simply said that Marcus Junius was a descendant of Aeneas himself. A more likely harmonisation of Dionysius' words with Virgil's claim is that Marcus Junius was a descendant of one of Aeneas' companions on his father's side, while he was directly descended from Aeneas through his mother's side. For instance, it may be that Marcus Junius' mother or grandmother was the daughter of Numa Pompilius.

Alternatively, perhaps Dionysius' report simply testifies to there having been more than one tradition about Brutus' ancestry in the first century BCE. Perhaps one tradition claimed that Brutus was descended through his father from a companion of Aeneas, while another claimed that he was descended from Aeneas himself. It is impossible to know for sure what exactly was believed about him in the first century BCE, and it is even harder to ascertain what the truth actually was. But nonetheless, we can see that there is a plausible explanation for the *Historia Brittonum*'s claim that Brutus was the son of Silvius son of Aeneas. This specific tradition may well have come from the possibly mistaken belief that Brutus was the son of Servius Tullius. Due to the similarity between his name and the name of Aeneas's son Silvius, as well as the similarity between the name of Servius' mother and the name of Aeneas' wife, Servius was misunderstood to be Silvius the son of Aeneas. Thus, Brutus was made the son of Silvius, son of Aeneas, as we see in one section of the *Historia Brittonum*.

As for the other tradition we discern from the *Historia Brittonum*, which makes Brutus the descendant of Numa Pompilius, son of Ascanius, son of Aeneas, this is likely a tradition that comes from otherwise unknown records concerning Brutus' alleged descent from Aeneas, of which we see a hint in the *Aeneid* and also in another form through Dionysius of Halicarnassus. The fact that this preserves a memory which split off from Roman sources very early on (much earlier than the first century BCE) is indicated by the fact that it presents Numa Pompilius as a grandson of Aeneas. This only matches the earliest known records of the founding of Rome by Aeneas, which generally made Romulus (Numa's traditional father) the son of Aeneas rather than his distant descendant. Therefore, this testifies to the antiquity of this particular tradition.

Incidentally, the fact that Numa is here described as the son of Ascanius, son of Aeneas, whereas in the ancient Roman sources he is described as the son of Romulus (originally presented as a son of Aeneas), may well indicate that 'Romulus' the founder of Rome was actually Ascanius; he may have been given the name 'Romulus' in later records in honour of the city he founded.

How else does Lucius Junius Brutus explain the Brutus of the *Historia Brittonum*? In the passage about Brutus' birth in that work, we find some interesting information. The account relates how when Brutus' mother was pregnant with him, a magician was summoned to make a prediction about the child. The magician foresaw that the child would be a boy, and interestingly, he prophesied that the boy would grow up to become 'the most valiant among the Italians'. Significantly, a similar prophesy was said to have been made about Lucius Junius Brutus. According to Roman historian Livy, Lucius Junius Brutus was brought to see the Oracle of Delphi by his uncle, King Lucius Tarquinius Superbus, along with his cousins, the king's sons. The Oracle foretold that the one who was the first to kiss his mother would 'hold supreme sway in Rome'. Brutus understood the Oracle to not mean 'mother' in the literal sense, so he pretended to stumble and kissed the ground as he fell, in line with the viewpoint that the earth was the common mother of them all.[330] Although this story is clearly fanciful, it could easily have been created within his own lifetime after he became the first consul of Rome. This story could quite plausibly have evolved into the story that we find in the *Historia Brittonum* more than 1300 years after the events in question.

Something else that the magician in the *Historia Brittonum* was said to have prophesied is that Brutus would cause the deaths of his mother and father. In the story, this transpires when Brutus' mother died while giving birth to him, and then later when Brutus accidentally shot his father with an arrow on a hunting trip when he was a teenager. After this, he was exiled from Italy. There is clearly some confusion in the British records concerning this. If things really transpired as claimed, then Brutus could not have become a consul, nor could he have become 'the most valiant among the Italians'. So whatever origin this part of his life story has, we need to accommodate him becoming the ruler of the Romans as the first consul. Therefore, this part as it appears in the *Historia Brittonum* and later records has evidently been seriously distorted.

What may well be its origin is the fact that, after he became the first consul of Rome, Lucius Junius Brutus was said to have been directly responsible for the deaths of two immediate family members. His two sons were alleged to have been involved in a conspiracy to restore the monarchy, and in response he had them, along with other conspirators, executed.[331] Although this is very different to the account in the *Historia Brittonum*, we have already established that the *HB*'s account *must* be seriously distorted, for it does not allow for Brutus' role as the ruler of the Romans as consul. The Roman accounts about Lucius Junius Brutus, on the other hand, do allow for it. Thus, it does appear that reports of Brutus killing two family members evolved into a tradition that he had killed his parents, which then gradually evolved into the account that we now see in the *Historia Brittonum*. Perhaps the deaths were made accidental so as to preserve a favourable image of Brutus.

Another way in which Lucius Junius Brutus explains the legendary character of Brutus is with his relatives. In the *Historia Regum Britanniae*, Brutus is said to have had a nephew named Turnus. Recall that Lucius Junius Brutus was from the family of the Tarquins on his mother's side. Therefore, he had a number of relatives with the name 'Tarquinius', which could certainly have been distorted into 'Turnus' by the time the *Historia Brittonum* was written down. For example, he had three cousins, sons of King Lucius Tarquinius Superbus, with that name. However, they are portrayed in Roman legend as Brutus' enemies, whereas the Turnus of British legend was one of Brutus' companions. A more likely candidate for Turnus is Lucius Tarquinius Collatinus. He was another of Brutus' relatives, and they were close associates. According to Livy, they both served jointly as consuls of Rome at first, until Collatinus was pressured to step down for political reasons. Although we cannot blindly trust all the details of this late account, this does indicate that one of Brutus' relatives named Tarquinius was also one of his close associates, meaning that this is likely the origin of the legend in Geoffrey of Monmouth's *HRB* of Brutus being accompanied by a relative named Turnus.

According to the *HRB*, the eldest son of Brutus was named Locrinus. He was the one who succeeded Brutus to the kingship of the territory roughly equivalent to what is now England. In the *HRB*, this territory is said to have been named 'Loegria' after Locrinus. This region was historically known in Welsh records as 'Lloegyr'. Modern scholars universally reject the idea that this place name came from 'Locrinus'. But much like with Claudius and 'Gloucester', along with Brutus himself and 'Britain', it could easily be that Locrinus was still a real person, even if his name had nothing to do with the origin of the name 'Lloegyr'. As it happens, Lucius Junius Brutus did have an associate with a name very similar to 'Locrinus'. His co-consul Lucius Tarquinius Collatinus had been married to a woman named Lucretia. She was the daughter of a man named Spurius Lucretius Tricipitinus. This man, Lucretius, directly succeeded Brutus as consul of Rome after the latter was overthrown in battle.[332] This likely formed the origin of the British legend of Brutus having a son, his successor, named Locrinus.

It is true that Lucius Junius Brutus is described as dying during the aforementioned battle in which he was overthrown. This, of course, would not be compatible with the British legends of him travelling to Britain. But the Roman records that describe his death were all written many centuries after the events in question. Livy, for example, was writing about five centuries after Brutus lived. A record of him being overthrown and driven out of Italy could easily have become distorted into records of him dying, similar to how some scholars believe that the Brythonic king Togodumnus was not actually killed by the Romans in 43 CE, as the available records claim, but was merely overthrown (and then made into a client king).[333]

Conclusion

In summary, we can see that the Brutus of British legend was not a fictional character. He was a composite figure, seemingly made up of two real personages from history and one fictional figure. However, he was primarily Lucius Junius Brutus, the first consul of Rome in the sixth century BCE. Seemingly, the conquest of Spain was taken from the life of Decimus Junius Brutus, and one version of his lineage is partially taken from records of a fictional eponymous founder of the Britons, Brutus, son of Hisicion. Yet the major part of the Brutus figure in the British legends is Lucius Junius Brutus. From him derived the legendary descent from Aeneas, the prophecy about becoming a mighty man in Italy, the deaths of two close family members, and his depiction as a prince of Rome as well as its first consul. His legendary nephew Turnus appears to be identical to Lucius Tarquinius Collatinus, a relative and close associate of Lucius Junius Brutus, and his legendary son and successor Locrinus appears to be identical to Spurius Lucretius Tricipitinus, the immediate successor of Lucius Junius Brutus in Rome.

However, what about the supposed migration from Italy to Britain? How does Lucius Junius Brutus fit into this part of the legend? Is there any evidence for this event? The following chapter will outline the copious archaeological and literary evidence for this event and will consider what role Brutus may have had in it.

8

The Migration from Italy

Before we go on to examine the evidence for the migration of Trojan descendants to Britain, let us review what we have established so far. Firstly, there is clear evidence that Geoffrey of Monmouth's *Historia Regum Britanniae* was exactly what he claimed it was: a translation of an existing book, not the work of Geoffrey's own mind and imagination. So there is every reason to view his account of Brutus as a genuine tradition, as valuable as any other record from the medieval era. Equally important is the fact that the *HRB* contains accurate information which is not found in any other surviving source, showing that although it is not perfect, it is a valuable source of information about the past.

We have also seen that the evidence as a whole points to the Trojan War having occurred in about 700 BCE rather than 1200 BCE. This dovetails perfectly with the earliest records about the founding of Rome, which describe it as being founded in or just after the time of Aeneas, especially when the chronology of the kings of Rome is adjusted to more closely reflect the archaeology of the site and more realistic reign lengths. Furthermore, we have seen that there is good evidence linking the Etruscans to the Trojans. In fact, the Etruscan civilisation that emerged just after 700 BCE appears to have been formed from an amalgamation of Trojans, Phrygians, Pelasgians, Lydians and perhaps others.

Finally, as we saw in the previous chapter, this revised chronology ties in exactly with the earliest information about Brutus, placing him a few generations after Aeneas and yet as the first consul of Rome in about 500 BCE. This is also supported by later genealogical records of Brutus, such as that found in *Hanes Gruffydd ap Cynan* and also the *Historia Regum Britanniae* after the duplicate kings are removed.

The Migration from Italy

What is the significance of all this? Well, scholars have universally rejected the historicity of the story of Brutus and other Trojan descendants migrating to Britain on the basis that there is no archaeological evidence for such a migration in *c.* 1100 BCE, when the legend is generally believed to be set. However, when the chronology of these events is correctly established, we can see that the migration to Britain is really supposed to have occurred in *c.* 500 BCE. Little wonder, then, that no archaeological evidence for this event has been found in the era around 1100 BCE. This is like looking for evidence for a Norman conquest of Britain in 466 CE rather than 1066 CE and, failing to find any evidence for it then, declaring that it never happened.

But when we look for evidence of the Trojan migration to Britain in *c.* 500 BCE rather than *c.* 1100 BCE, the archaeological evidence is so obvious and striking that it is hard to miss. Before we examine that evidence, though, let us examine in closer detail the story of Brutus' migration from Italy to Britain, so as to see what the legend actually claims.

The Legend of the Migration

The account of the migration in the *Historia Brittonum* broadly agrees with the story found in Geoffrey's *Historia Regum Britanniae*, although the former only gives an overview, whereas the latter goes into considerable detail. Here is the account found in the *Historia Brittonum*:

> He [Brutus] was, for this cause [accidentally killing his father], expelled from Italy, and came to the islands of the Tyrrhene sea, when he was exiled on account of the death of Turnus, slain by Æneas. He then went among the Gauls, and built the city of the Turones, called Turnis. At length he came to this island, named from him Britannia, dwelt there, and filled it with his own descendants, and it has been inhabited from that time to the present period.

So according to this, Brutus first travelled to 'the islands of the Tyrrhenian Sea', but was exiled due to his ancestor Aeneas having slain Turnus the king of the Latins generations previously. Then Brutus went to Gaul where he founded the city now known as Tours, and then he settled in Britain. The account in the *HRB* is similar, but more detailed and with some differences. The account of Brutus' early life, from his birth to the deaths of his two parents, is essentially identical, but when he leaves Italy the accounts begin to diverge.

In the *HRB* version, Brutus does not go to the islands of the Tyrrhenian Sea. Rather, he travelled to Greece. While in Greece, he joined several thousand Trojan descendants who were being held captive by a Greek king named Pandrasus. Over the years, Brutus rose through the ranks of these Trojans and eventually became their leader. This subjected nation pleaded with Brutus to free them from the Greeks. Brutus agreed to this request. He first withdrew the Trojans to the woods and then sent a letter to the king requesting that they be allowed to either live there in freedom or simply leave the country. In response, Pandrasus set out to wage war against the Trojans. However, Brutus was able to lead his men in a surprise attack on the Greeks, slaying many of them.

After this, Pandrasus besieged a town where many of the Trojans were still living – apparently the main town out of a set of three mentioned earlier in the account. Brutus then devised a plan to lead a large portion of the Greek army into the woods, where they would then be ambushed. This plan worked, and then the Trojans were able to sneak into the camp of the rest of the Greek army and slaughter them. Pandrasus was preserved by Brutus, who then demanded that he officially grant their freedom. Finally, Pandrasus relented and allowed the Trojans to leave the country with enormous quantities of wealth and other resources. Brutus, for his part, was given Ignoge, daughter of Pandrasus, as his wife.

From Greece, the first location that Brutus and his wandering nation of Trojan refugees arrived at was an island called Leogetia. This is undoubtedly the island of Leucadia, now known as Lefkada, just a short distance from mainland Greece. On this island, which is said to have been uninhabited, Brutus found an abandoned temple to Diana. Brutus performed an act of worship to the goddess, and then she appeared to him in a dream that night. In this dream, she told him of an island beyond Gaul which he could have as his new home. From that point on, Brutus and his people had a clear destination in mind.

Sailing from Lefkada, Brutus and the wandering Trojans headed west through the Mediterranean. The account notes that they came to the Philenean Altars, which stood where Ras Lanuf is now, on the north coast of Africa just to the west of the ancient city of Cyrene. The Trojans are next said to have arrived at a place called Salinae, which is possibly a reference to the famous salt lakes in Tunisia. Next, they are described as sailing between 'Ruscicada and the mountains of Azara'. At this point in the story, Brutus and his men encounter some pirates. The latter are defeated, and the Trojans enrich themselves from the spoils.

Ruscicada is clearly Skikda in northwest Algeria, known in Roman times as Rusiccade. The mountains of Azara are possibly a reference to mountains on the island of Sardinia, which is north of Skikda. The basis for this suggestion is that one of the ancient tribes inhabiting Sardinia was called the Aesaronenses, which name might have given rise to 'Azara'. However, this is uncertain. In any case, if this account is accurate, the general region must be correct, for the 'Ruscicada' of the account is certainly the Rusiccade of ancient times, and so the mountains on the other side of a sailor travelling past Rusiccade could only conceivably be mountains of Sardinia, since there is nothing else in that region of the sea.

An alternative explanation is based on the idea that this journey was originally performed on foot, not through the seas. We will see the reasoning behind this suggestion later, but if it is correct, then this would mean that the reference to these travellers going 'between Ruscicada and the mountains of Azara' would actually mean that they travelled overland between Rusiccade and the Aures Mountains just to the south of that settlement. These mountains were known to the Romans as the Mons Aurasius. Perhaps this name evolved into 'Azara' by the time Geoffrey wrote in the twelfth century CE. This does seem more logical than the suggestion that the mountains in question were mountains on Sardinia.

Next, the wandering nation is said to have passed the Malua River and arrived at Mauretania. This river is now known as the Moulouya River, and in Roman times was called the Malva. Once Brutus and his men reached Mauretania, they went ashore and 'laid waste the whole country', collecting resources for themselves after they almost ran out of provisions. They then set sail again and headed towards the Pillars of Hercules – the two mountains on either side of the Strait of Gibraltar, marking the exit of the Mediterranean. However, as they were about to pass through the Pillars of Hercules, they were attacked by monstrous sirens, forcing them to turn back. Thus, they sailed to the Tyrrhenian Sea. This presumably corresponds to the statement in the *Historia Brittonum* that Brutus travelled to the Tyrrhenian Sea after leaving Britain.

Geoffrey of Monmouth's account then says that the Trojans landed on the shores of the Tyrrhenian Sea, though it does not actually tell us which particular island it was that they landed on. In any case, in this unspecified location, Brutus and his people met up with another group of Trojan descendants. They were led by Corineus, whom the account implies was a descendant of Antenor, a prince of Troy. The two groups merged into one, and then Brutus continued leading the Trojan descendants to the island awaiting them beyond the Gallic Sea.

The next part of Geoffrey's account is somewhat confusing. He states that Brutus then led the wandering nation to Aquitaine. In ancient times, this region was larger than it was in later medieval times. This is important to note, for it makes sense of the account's next statement: arriving at Aquitaine, the Trojans entered the mouth of the Loire and cast anchor there. This would mean that Brutus and his men arrived in Gaul by way of the ocean, for the mouth of the Loire is on the western coast of Gaul. This is peculiar, for it would suggest that they were able to sail out of the Mediterranean and around the coast of Spain and Portugal. There is no explanation for how they were able to get past the sirens this time. An overland route from the Tyrrhenian Sea through Gaul might be more logical, but that does not appear to be what the account actually describes.

In any case, the Trojans then encountered a king of the area named Goffarius Pictus. He was the king of the 'Pictavians', known as the Pictones to ancient Roman historians. This historical tribe inhabited the region immediately to the south of the Loire, so they are correctly placed in the story. Corineus and his men began hunting in the region in which they had landed, unwittingly killing the king's animals. Messengers from the king confronted him about this, sparking a war between the Trojans and the Pictavians. The Trojans were eventually victorious and drove the natives back. However, King Goffarius called upon many other Gallic kings from the surrounding regions. These kings then started gathering a large army in preparation to attack the Trojans again.

In the meantime, Brutus and the Trojans had plundered the whole area of Aquitaine and had worked their way as far into Gaul as the city of Tours (though the city itself had not yet been built, according to the account). Brutus then established his camp there. Eventually, the coalition of Gallic nations arrived and attacked the Trojans. The battle was fierce and difficult, and the Trojans were almost overwhelmed, but an effective strategy devised by Brutus and Corineus resulted in the Trojans winning the war.

Geoffrey's account then suggests that Brutus and the Trojans continued on their journey to Britain more or less straight after this victory, due to fear that the Gauls would return and inflict yet more losses on them. However, earlier in the account we are told that Brutus later built the city of Tours (said to have been named after Brutus' nephew Turnus, who had been killed in the fighting against the Gauls).

The Migration from Italy

For Brutus to have constructed this city, he must have remained in that region for quite some time. Therefore, either the time between Brutus arriving in that area and the Gallic kings making their attack on the Trojans was longer than the account seems to suggest, or the extra time should be placed after the defeat of the Gallic kings. But in any case, Brutus and the Trojans must have settled in that region for a considerable time – enough time to establish a city.

After this, the Trojans finally arrived in Britain. They are said to have landed at Totnes, in what is now Devon, in the south-west. The island was scarcely inhabited, with only a few giants remaining on the island. The Trojans defeated them, and then Brutus established his kingdom there. The Trojans are described as spreading out over the whole island, but Brutus himself established his capital city on the shores of the Thames. He named it Troia Nova (New Troy), which name eventually evolved into Trinovantum. This, according to the account, was the original city of London. And the name of the whole island, Britain, was taken from Brutus himself.

Historical Evidence for the Migration

The account we have just considered was, for a long time, broadly accepted. Yet for the past few centuries, this has been rejected as mere fiction. It is now considered so obviously fictional that it is not even worth entertaining. But as we have already seen, the same has long been said of Brutus himself, yet a closer examination of the literary evidence reveals that the Brutus of British legend is merely a distorted version of the historical Lucius Junius Brutus. Therefore, could it be that there actually is evidence of a Trojan migration to Britain?

What this section will demonstrate is that there is copious archaeological and literary evidence for this migration. There are two central issues that have caused this evidence to be missed. Firstly, the Trojan War has long been misdated. Placing it in *c.* 1200 BCE rather than *c.* 700 BCE means that Brutus' migration was believed to have occurred in *c.* 1100 or 1000 BCE, rather than the correct date of *c.* 500 BCE. Secondly, the connection between the Etruscans and the Trojans has generally been missed. This itself is largely due to the misdating of the Trojan War, since the archaeological evidence that supports the Etruscans coming from western Anatolia does not fit the traditional date of the Trojan War. But once the date is correctly established, the evidence for their Near Eastern origin is clearly seen.

The exact same principle applies to the migration to Britain. When the chronology of this event is correctly placed in the time of Lucius

Junius Brutus, roughly 500 BCE, the evidence for it becomes readily obvious. But this is only the case when we also recognise that the Trojans became the Etruscans after they arrived in Italy.

The War in Greece

Let us examine the first part of the legendary migration. Brutus was said to have joined up with many Trojan descendants in Greece. Where exactly in Greece is this story set? Well, we saw previously that the very first island the Trojans arrived at after leaving Greece was almost certainly Lefkada, which is just off the western coast of Greece. Therefore, it is likely that the story is set somewhere near that island. The account in the *HRB* helpfully names the major river in the location in which the story is set. It is called the Akalon River, which is almost certainly the Acheron River. This runs through Epirus, the territory of Greece just next to the island of Lefkada.

Evidence that the account is based on real events is seen from some of the place names in the account. For example, the main settlement described in the account is called Sparatinum. Interestingly, the region as a whole in which the account is based was anciently called Thesprotia, or Thesprotis. One can see how the placename 'Sparatinum' might have evolved from 'Thesprotia' over the centuries. The beginning would have been dropped, leaving 'Sprotia'. It could then have been slightly expanded by being pseudo-Latinised into 'Sparatinum', a form which would have looked correct and accurate to Geoffrey of Monmouth.

Another example is seen from the fact that the account states that there were three castles being held by the Trojans in that area, which they were trying to defend against the Greeks. In that very area, just next to the Acheron River as described in the *HRB*, is an ancient settlement called 'Trikastro'. This placename means 'three castles'. Yet this is a minor, local placename. The site was not of any national importance and certainly does not appear on any medieval maps that Geoffrey of Monmouth could have accessed. Unless the match between the reference to the Trojans having three castles in that area and the name of this ancient settlement is a coincidence, this strongly indicates that the story could not have simply been invented in later times. It indicates that it preserves a genuine tradition about events in that location. Additionally, the settlement of Trikastro is believed to have been built in the Pre-Classical Era at the earliest, lending extra support to the fact that these events occurred in *c.* 500 BCE, and not centuries earlier.[334]

The Migration from Italy

Is there any evidence for Trojans in that area? Well, let us remember that the Trojans formed the Etruscan nation after the Trojan War, having travelled from Troy to Lemnos and then Italy, along with a number of allies. These allies evidently included the Lydians, Phrygians and Pelasgians. We have already noted that ancient Greek writers sometimes used the term 'Pelasgian' to mean 'Etruscan'. Therefore, it may well be significant that both Homer and Strabo indicate that there were 'Pelasgians' living in Dodona, Greece.[335] This is exactly the region of Epirus in which Trikastro is located. If these 'Pelasgians' were actually Etruscans, this would perfectly correspond to the Brutus legend placing a community of Trojan descendants in that region.

Although there is no direct, independent record of the event described in the *HRB*'s account, there are many records of conflicts between the Etruscans and the Greeks throughout the sixth and fifth centuries BCE. For example, in the western Mediterranean, the Etruscans and Carthaginians fought against the Greeks in the Tyrrhenian Sea in *c.* 540 BCE.[336] Some years later, in *c.* 524 BCE, the Etruscans attempted to invade the Greek lands of southern Italy.[337] So the basic idea of there being a conflict between the Greeks and the Etruscans at the end of the sixth century BCE is perfectly consistent with the historical situation at that time.

However, there is a record which may well have something to do with the actual event described in the *HRB*. This record is a Homeric hymn which seems to date to the latter half of the end of the sixth century BCE.[338] It describes Etruscan pirates kidnapping the god Dionysus from the shore of Greece. They did not realise who he was at first, and in punishment for their deed, the god turned all but one of them into dolphins. It is generally believed that this myth was created to represent the apparently common Etruscan piracy around Greece in the eastern Mediterranean in that era.[339] Ancient Greek references to Etruscan piracy are plentiful, though there are rarely any details provided about specific events or what exactly was involved. But this myth would seem to indicate that they did, at times, go ashore to collect spoil. This is also shown by ancient references to a raid on Attica by Pelasgians from Lemnos (i.e. Etruscans) in the same era.[340] This would be consistent with the idea that some Etruscans went ashore in Thesprotia, where their kinsmen were living (going by the reference to 'Pelasgians' in Dodona, within the ancient kingdom of Thesprotia). There, they could have engaged in some battles or raids against the Greeks, before then withdrawing along with many of their kinsmen who had already been living in that territory.

This is not to say that the Homeric hymn about the Etruscans kidnapping Dionysus from the shores of Greece is directly about this event described in the *HRB*. As scholars believe, it is probably not about any single event, but it is likely a parody representing events which were common in that era. The important point is that this shows that such events were common in precisely the era and location in which the story in the *HRB* is set. Therefore, the aforementioned scenario of Etruscan pirates raiding the area of Dodona and then withdrawing with a large group of the 'Pelasgians' who were already living there is perfectly plausible and consistent with the historical facts.

The rest of this part of the narrative is on much shakier ground in terms of historical backing. There is no known record of King Pandrasus, and unfortunately there is no information at all from ancient records about the king of the Thesprotians, or the king of Epirus, or the king of any other sub-region involved in the account in the late sixth century BCE. Therefore, it is impossible to even attempt to identify him with any historical figure. Similarly, the existence of his daughter Ignoge and the marriage between her and Brutus can also not be confirmed, but nor can it be refuted either. Nonetheless, the idea of Etruscans taking women from mainland Greece is not remarkable, for the same thing occurred during the 'Pelasgian' raid on Attica mentioned earlier.

Lefkada

Brutus and the rest of his Trojans are then described as travelling to the island of Leogetia, that is, Lefkada. This is a perfectly logical first stop after leaving Thesprotia in Greece, given that it is just off the coast. While on this island, Brutus is said to have found an abandoned temple dedicated to Diana. After performing an elaborate ritual, the goddess later appeared to him in a dream and inspired him to go to the island in the Gallic Sea, Britain. What can we say about the historical origin behind this story?

First of all, was Britain even known by the nations in the central and eastern Mediterranean at such an early date? Yes. In fact, as early as the Mycenaean era, it seems that there was trade between Britain and the Near East, for tin ingots found in Israel dating to this era have been found to have likely originated in Cornwall.[341] It is likely that there was trade with Britain in later centuries as well, particularly by the ancient Phoenicians. This is indicated, though not explicitly confirmed, by the words of Herodotus. Other ancient writers after him are more explicit, such as Strabo and Diodorus. It is also understood that the Etruscans in particular imported tin from Britain.[342]

In any case, the story of Diana coming to Brutus in a dream to tell him to travel to Britain is obviously fanciful. It is very unlikely that this group of Etruscans specifically set out to settle in Britain. This part of the story is evidently a much later addition to give divine backing to the migration and settlement of the island. This would be similar to how the *Aeneid* contains a passage where it is 'foretold' that Aeneas would found a nation that would eventually come to rule the world. Given that this text was composed in the time of Augustus, the first emperor of Rome, it is obvious that this is a later addition. The vision of Diana in the *HRB* is simply another example of this.

Nonetheless, as we have acknowledged, the idea that this group of Etruscans first stopped off at Lefkada after raiding part of Thesprotia is perfectly logical. And even though the story of Diana appearing to Brutus is clearly fictional, could there have been an abandoned temple to Diana on the island? After all, this would explain *why* the account places the fictional vision at Lefkada, rather than at any other part of Brutus' wanderings. Firstly, it needs to be mentioned that Diana was actually a Roman goddess. She was the equivalent of the Greek goddess Artemis. Thus, the reference to 'Diana' in the *HRB* is the result of the name in the account being changed from the Greek name to the Roman name. This change in the account likely occurred during Britain's Roman era.

In any case, the point is that we are actually looking for a temple of *Artemis* on Lefkada. As it happens, we know from the ancient poet Callimachus, who lived in the third century BCE, that there was indeed a temple of Artemis on Lefkada.[343] This is very interesting, for we can hardly imagine that Geoffrey of Monmouth thoroughly searched through ancient texts for information on Lefkada until he finally found this obscure reference by Callimachus. In addition to the obvious unlikelihood of such a discovery by Geoffrey, Callimachus goes into extensive detail about a statue of the goddess on the island, yet no statue is mentioned in the *HRB*. This strongly indicates that Geoffrey did not take his information about Lefkada from the obscure reference by this ancient poet, yet this ancient reference does prove that Geoffrey was accurate about there being such a temple on the island. This is a very strong piece of evidence that the account is genuine, and was not invented in later times.

The Trojan Kings of Britain

The Journey along the African Coast

The next part of the *HRB*'s account tells us that Brutus sailed along the north coast of Africa. He passed the Philenean Altars – just to the west of the ancient city of Cyrene – before passing some salt lakes (possibly those of Tunisia), then he sailed past Rusiccade in what is now Algeria, and then he reached the Strait of Gibraltar. However, there is reason to believe that this entire account has been lifted from an account of a separate event and placed onto this narrative of Brutus' life.

In the *Historia Brittonum*, there is a legend about the origin of the Scots, the natives of Ireland. We are told that there was a certain Scythian family living in Egypt at the time of the Biblical Exodus. After the Exodus, due to the weakened state of Egypt at that time, the Egyptians expelled the Scythian family in case they intended to seize the opportunity to take over the country. The family is then described as wandering through Africa until they finally reached the Pillars of Hercules at the entrance of the Mediterranean. From there, they are said to have passed over to Spain, where they settled for a long time, multiplying greatly. Eventually, this nation of Scythian descendants journeyed to Ireland and became the Scots. The description of the journey through Africa bears more than a few passing similarities to the account in the *HRB* about Brutus. Here is the description from the *Historia Brittonum*:

> He wandered forty-two years in Africa, and arrived, with his family, at the altars of the Philistines, by the lake of Osiers [*lacum salinarum*]. Then passing between Rusicada and the hilly country of Syria, they travelled by the river Malva through Mauritana as far as the Pillars of Hercules.

The 'altars of the Philistines' is an obvious error for the Philenean Altars, given the location in North Africa. After these altars, we see the mention of a salt lake, just as in Geoffrey's *HRB*.[344] Likewise, the group is next mentioned as passing between Rusiccade and another area noted for its mountains, or hills. Here in the *Historia Brittonum*, this area is called 'Syria', whereas in the *HRB*, it is called 'Azara'. 'Syria' is an obvious mistake, since Syria is not even in Africa. The account in the *HRB* almost certainly preserves a form closer to the original word. Given the location of Rusiccade and the fact that the account in the *Historia Brittonum* is clearly describing an overland journey, it is evident that the mountains in question are the Aures Mountains, or the 'Mons Aurasius', just south of Rusiccade.

The Migration from Italy

Just as in the *HRB*, the account in the *Historia Brittonum* next lists the River Malva, Mauretania and the Pillars of Hercules. Thus, it is clear that the description of this part of Brutus' journey has been lifted from this account of the migration of the Scots to Ireland. The fact that it was taken from the story about the Scots and placed into the story about Brutus, and not vice versa, is discerned from the issue concerning the group passing between Rusiccade and the hilly or mountainous location. Given that the inland route (by which the 'Azara Mountains' are identical to the Aures Mountains) is far more credible than the oversea route (which requires the Azara Mountains to be mountains on the distant island of Sardinia), it is evident that this route originally came from an overland journey, not a voyage through the sea. It makes no logical sense in the account of Brutus, though a writer who did not know what or where the 'Azara Mountains' were would not realise that the account did not make sense in the context of Brutus' sea voyage.

To be clear, this is not to say that the compiler of the text which Geoffrey translated took this part of the route directly from the *Historia Brittonum* and applied it to his account of Brutus' journey. As has already been noted, the *HRB*'s account evidently preserves an earlier form of the name of the mountains. Therefore, this route must have been taken from a record which also, independently, came to be used by the compiler of the *Historia Brittonum*. But evidently the latter compiler was using a later, more corrupted version, with the more accurate version being preserved in the *HRB* (yet misapplied there to Brutus).

As to why this journey along the coast of North Africa was misapplied to Brutus, this may have something to do with the fact that Brutus himself is actually mentioned in the account. After describing the Scots finally reaching Ireland after their long journey, the *Historia Brittonum* tells us:

> Thence, a thousand and two years after the Egyptians were lost in the Red Sea, they passed into Ireland. At that period, Brutus, who first exercised the consular office, reigned over the Romans.

So according to this, the Scots passed from Spain into Ireland at about the time in which Brutus was consul over the Romans, in c. 510 BCE. Of course, this is not actually the era in which the journey across North Africa is set; that is actually based shortly after the Exodus, 1,000 years earlier. However, a careless reading of the account could cause that detail to be easily missed, so a scribe might have misunderstood that Brutus was involved in these events, especially since he too was known for having journeyed from the Mediterranean to Britain.

Regardless of the reason for this journey being misapplied to Brutus, the key point is that this part of the account should be removed from the narrative of the Trojan migration. Rather, it appears that Brutus travelled directly from Lefkada to the Tyrrhenian Sea, on the western side of Italy.

The Tyrrhenian Sea

At this point in the account in the *HRB*, we are at the same part referred to by the *Historia Brittonum* when it states that Brutus arrived at the islands of the Tyrrhenian Sea. There are roughly a dozen notable islands in the Tyrrhenian Sea, but by far the biggest three are Sicily, Sardinia and Corsica. Sicily was heavily inhabited by the Greeks at the time this story is set. This might make sense of the statement in the *Historia Brittonum* that Brutus was exiled from there on account of the fact that his ancestor Aeneas had slain Turnus. In some ancient texts, the Turnus supposedly slain by Aeneas is given a Greek ancestry.[345] Therefore, it could make logical sense that Brutus would be expelled from the Greek-inhabited island of Sicily due to his ancestor's actions against a prominent Greek.

However, this seems far more likely to be a later interpolation. After all, the account in the *HRB* makes no mention of this whatsoever. Generally speaking, as seen from their respective accounts of the Roman era of Britain, the *HRB* is more accurate than the *HB*. To give just one example among many, the *Historia Brittonum* contains the bizarre and unhistorical reference to British emperors just after the account of Claudius' invasion. Additionally, Turnus actually being of Greek descent is very doubtful. Therefore, given the complete absence of this supposed exile from the Tyrrhenian Sea in the *HRB*, it is probably just an interpolation that made its way into the text for some reason or another.

One possible explanation is that there may have been a reference to Brutus purposely not going to the island of Sicily but going to one of the other islands in the region due to the fact that Etruscans and Greeks were enemies. Naturally, Brutus would not want to disembark on an island inhabited by his foes. Perhaps, if such a statement had been transmitted in the tradition, someone may have decided to expand this statement into something more personal, as we see in the *Historia Brittonum*.

In any case, it is almost certain that this particular episode never actually happened. What this shows is that it is perfectly possible for a story of an exile to be invented – and not just the exile itself, but the circumstances leading up to it. This helps us to see how the Brutus of British legend is the same as Lucius Junius Brutus, even though the historical figure was evidently never exiled for killing his parents.

What the account in the *HRB* tells us is that once Brutus and his wandering Trojans reached 'the shores of the Tyrrhenian Sea', they encountered other groups of Trojan descendants. This ties in with the historical facts. Corsica, one of the three main islands of this sea, was dominated by the Etruscans from the latter part of the sixth century BCE.[346] Sardinia also had strong connections with the Etruscans. In fact, it appears that one of the tribes inhabiting the eastern coast of the island – the Aesaronenses – were actually of Etruscan origin.[347] So of the three largest islands of the Tyrrhenian Sea, two of them were extensively inhabited by Etruscans during the time in which the Brutus story is set. Elba, the largest of the smaller islands in that sea, was also inhabited by the Etruscans in antiquity.[348]

Thus, we can see that there were Etruscans living all over the Tyrrhenian Sea in the sixth century BCE. With this in mind, the claim that Brutus came across fellow Trojan descendants on the shores of the Tyrrhenian Sea is very logical. It fits in perfectly with the historical reality of the shores of that sea at the time in which the account is set.

A part of the story which does not have such an obvious historical basis is the description of these separate groups of Trojans being led by a man named Corineus. There is a character by that name (or rather, 'Corynaeus') who appears in Virgil's *Aeneid*. It has been claimed that this cannot possibly be the same as the contemporary of Brutus, because the Corynaeus of the *Aeneid* is made a contemporary of Aeneas, several generations before the time of Brutus. However, it may be that there was more than one Corynaeus in the *Aeneid*. One of them is the priest who presides over Misenus' funeral, while the other appears to be a separate character who participates in the war against Turnus and the Rutuli in Italy. As we saw previously, the war against Turnus and the Rutuli seems to be taken from historical events which actually occurred in the reign of Tarquinius Superbus, but which were then mistakenly placed onto the life of Tarchon, the ally of Aeneas, in the early seventh century BCE. Tarquinius Superbus was a contemporary of Brutus, ruling from about 531 to 509 BCE. The events involving Turnus occurred right at the beginning of Tarquinius' reign, while the campaign against the Rutuli occurred near the end. The Corynaeus mentioned in Virgil's *Aeneid*, if he was a real person, was more likely involved in the war against the Rutuli than the downfall of Turnus Herdonius. The reason for saying this is that Corynaeus is presented in the *Aeneid* as a warrior fighting in battle.

This would mean that there apparently was a historical figure named Corynaeus at the end of the sixth century BCE. Could he have been the Corineus who appears in the *HRB* as a contemporary of Brutus? It is certainly possible. However, Corynaeus is placed in Italy, whereas Corineus was supposedly met by Brutus on one of the islands of the Tyrrhenian Sea. Of course, there is no reason why Corynaeus could not have travelled from Italy to one of these islands, such as Sardinia, since there was regular trade between the Etruscans in Italy and those in Sardinia (and other islands in that area). Therefore, there is a distinct possibility that the Corineus of the *HRB* is the same as the Corynaeus of the *Aeneid*.

Another possibility that has been suggested is that the character of Corineus comes from the Celtic god Cernunnos. He is attested by name in Gaul, and iconography of his appears in Britain. However, there are virtually no similarities at all between the characteristics of Corineus and Cernunnos, so this theory is not very convincing. An alternative possibility that gives Corineus a divine origin is that he comes from the early Roman god Quirinus. He was the god of war, which is very fitting for Corineus, who is presented in the *HRB* as a mighty warrior. Many Greek and Roman legends present real people as interacting with divine beings, so it is conceivable that the tale of Brutus coming to Britain may have presented the god Quirinus as being involved in the events. This is a far more likely theory than the one which attributes his origin to the Celtic god Cernunnos. Yet, whether this theory is correct or not is another matter. In the absence of additional evidence, it remains an open question whether Corineus was the apparently historical figure of Corynaeus from the *Aeneid*, or a historicised version of the early Roman god Quirinus.

Up until this point in the legend, Brutus has stayed within regions in which the Etruscans were regularly active in that era of history. So although the 'migration' to Britain could be counted as starting from either the moment Brutus left Italy or the moment he left Greece, there is nothing remarkable about these travels in the story so far. The situation we have here is a perfectly unremarkable one of a group of Etruscans travelling from Italy to Thesprotia in Greece, from there to nearby Lefkada, and then to the islands of the Tyrrhenian Sea. There is nothing implausible or even particularly notable about such travels, for these were regions the Etruscans regularly frequented. However, at this point in the legend, the characters finally go outside the area in which the Etruscans are normally placed by modern historians. Let us now examine the journey from the Tyrrhenian Sea to Gaul and then Britain.

9

The Migration to Gaul and Britain

As stated before, Brutus and the rest of the Trojan descendants, now with Corineus and his companions too, are said to have travelled to the region of Aquitaine. This is not the pre-Roman region known by that name, for that region did not include the mouth of the Loire, where the Trojans are said to have arrived. Rather, the use of the name 'Aquitaine' for this region evidently comes from the Roman province of Aquitaine, which did encompass the Loire. Evidently this place name in the legend was provided at some point during the Roman era. How exactly the Trojans were supposed to have arrived in Aquitaine is not totally clear, but as we have already seen, the most likely conclusion is that they were supposed to have left the Mediterranean and sailed to Gaul by way of the Atlantic Ocean, around the coast of Spain and Portugal. Otherwise, they would not have arrived at the mouth of the Loire.

Is there any evidence of a migration of Etruscans from the Tyrrhenian Sea to Gaul? Yes, there is indeed. Evidence has been found at Lattes, in southern France, of a probable Etruscan community dating to *c.* 500 BCE.[349] This is likely where Brutus and his followers settled for a brief period early on their journey west from the Tyrrhenian Sea.

Further west than Lattes, there is some evidence of an Etruscan presence at Pech Maho, southern France, dating to the early fifth century BCE. This evidence has been interpreted as showing that 'Etruscans were integrated to some degree with the people of the region'.[350] The evidence found here may be another trace of Brutus' migration. Slightly further west along the coast of the Mediterranean, within the borders of modern Spain, evidence for an Etruscan presence has been found at Ampurias. It is dated to 'the end of the sixth century'.[351] It is possible that this is just from trade, but equally, it could be a trace of Brutus' migration. The same can be said about Etruscan evidence found at Ullastret, just south of Ampurias, as well as evidence found even further along the coast of Spain, in the vicinity of Alcanar.[352]

We continue to find evidence of an Etruscan presence as we look further along the coast of the Mediterranean. Etruscan goods have been found 'remarkably on both the Mediterranean and Atlantic façades of the Straits of Gibraltar: to the east at Malaga and in the west at Huelva'.[353] As with the other evidence in Spain, it is possible that this is evidence left behind merely by traders from Etruria, rather than by Brutus' migration. Nonetheless, there is a distinct possibility that at least some of this evidence was left by Brutus. This is supported by the fact that Stephanus of Byzantium claimed that some Etruscans actually settled in Spain, rather than just trading there.[354] Diodorus Siculus even reports an account of Etruscan sailors travelling beyond Spain, into the Atlantic, in hopes of colonisation, although he does not describe what ultimately became of them beyond mentioning a skirmish with the Phoenicians.[355] He places this during the period in which the Etruscans were the 'masters of the sea', which would fit the time of Brutus. Therefore, this account may well be a description of Brutus' migration.

From there, Brutus supposedly sailed around the Atlantic coast of Spain and France until he reached the mouth of the Loire. This is what the account in the *HRB* leads us to believe. And as we have seen, there are some archaeological and historical reasons to give weight to the scenario of a group of Etruscans migrating from the Tyrrhenian Sea to outside the Mediterranean. However, an alternative scenario is that Brutus and his followers simply travelled up through the Rhone valley into Gaul. The Etruscan community founded at Lattes in Gaul, dating to *c.* 500 BCE, is surely a trace of his migration, but Lattes is at the mouth of the Rhone. If Brutus had intended to travel into Gaul, then surely the most logical route would be through the Rhone valley. Archaeology makes it clear that this was an established trade route, and it is even mentioned by Diodorus.[356]

So if Brutus had intended to travel to central Gaul, then there is no reason why he would have travelled outside the Mediterranean, all the way around the coast of Spain and Portugal, to get there. But if he did not set out to travel to that region, and he was simply making his way along the northern coast of the Mediterranean as the leader of a band of travellers or pirates until he came across the mouth of the Loire and decided to head inland, then why do we not find archaeological traces of the Etruscans along the Atlantic coast of Spain and Gaul? The only way in which this Atlantic route could possibly make sense in view of the archaeological evidence is if Brutus did not specifically intend to travel to Gaul at first. Perhaps he was indeed simply travelling along the coast of the Mediterranean with no specific destination in mind. Then, once he got to the south of Spain, he would have had direct interactions with the Phoenician traders there, from whom he could easily have learned about the parts of Gaul further north and west than he was previously familiar with. Thus, from southern Spain, he could have decided specifically to sail to the Loire, so as to take advantage of the valuable tin deposits of north-western Gaul.[357] This would harmonise with the archaeological evidence, and it is a fairly plausible scenario. Still, there remains the possibility that, from the settlement established at Lattes, he simply travelled directly through the Rhone valley.

Regardless of how he got there, does evidence exist for a strong Etruscan presence in Gaul, and in the region of Tours in particular (as claimed by the *Historia Brittonum* and the *Historia Regum Britanniae*)? Yes, indeed it does. There is copious archaeological evidence for an Etruscan ruling elite establishing themselves in Gaul in exactly the time in which this legend is set. This evidence is essentially synonymous with the emergence of the La Tène culture among the Celts of Gaul. So, what exactly was this 'La Tène' culture?

The La Tène Culture in Gaul

The La Tène culture is the name given to the material culture that appears in Celtic lands from about 500 BCE onwards (although some modern reference works give the date as *c.* 450 BCE).[358] It is distinctive for its strong Greek and especially Etruscan influences. One example of Etruscan influence is seen from the use of chariots at this time. It is widely agreed that the Celts' use of chariots was adopted directly from the Etruscans.[359] The distinctive La Tène art style is also understood to have been derived primarily from the Etruscan world.[360]

Beyond simply the material culture of the Celts from 500 BCE onwards showing strong Etruscan influences, even their burial customs are virtually direct copies of Etruscan burial practices. Shortly after the Anatolian elite arrived in Etruria just after 700 BCE, the Etruscans developed a distinctive and very impressive type of burial – the chariot burial. This could be done in several different ways, but the key element in this type of burial was that the corpse was buried along with a two-wheeled chariot. These types of burials are famous for their extremely impressive nature. They undoubtedly mark the graves of the elite, not average citizens of Etruria.

Over in Gaul, almost identical two-wheeled chariot graves are found from about 500–450 BCE onwards, corresponding to the onset of the La Tène culture.[361] Not only did the Celts of this era imitate this basic Etruscan concept, but they also imitated another aspect of Etruscan burial customs. The Etruscans developed a custom of placing a life-size statue of the deceased above or outside their tombs.[362] The Celts of the period between 500 and 450 BCE did likewise.[363] Furthermore, the tombs of the Etruscans were designed to imitate the houses of the living. One of the most intriguing aspects of La Tène chariot burials – along with burials that did not include a chariot, for that matter – is the fact that they used square burial chambers, rather than circular ones like most nations throughout ancient history used. This peculiar feature of La Tène chariot burials would be easily explained if they were intended to invoke the Celtic houses of that period, which were rectangular.[364] It should also be noted that although the La Tène barrows are usually called 'square', many of them are actually rectangular.[365]

What explains this sudden emergence of Etruscan artefacts, art designs and burial customs in Gaul from *c.* 500 BCE onwards? Well, the Celts did start interacting with the Etruscans from about that time. This interaction occurred in northern Italy. Could it be the case that Etruscan culture spread simply by means of cultural diffusion to the Celts in Gaul? That is, could this simply be a case of one group's culture being adopted by their neighbours, and then by the neighbours' neighbours, and so on? No, that is impossible. Archaeology shows that La Tène culture did not spread gradually from Etruria, through northern Italy and then to Gaul. Rather, it appeared suddenly in central eastern Gaul and then spread out from there (including back towards Italy). Therefore, cultural diffusion is not a viable explanation in view of the archaeological evidence.

A more common explanation for the emergence of Le Tène culture is that it came about through trade. The Greeks had established a colony in southern Gaul called Massalia (present-day Marseille) in 600 BCE, and from that time on, the Greeks and other nations of the Mediterranean began trading extensively with the Gauls. This is usually understood to be what led to the emergence of the La Tène culture. However, this theory is flawed for a similar reason to the idea of cultural diffusion. We do not find a gradual spread of La Tène culture going from Massalia outwards. Of course, there are many elements of Mediterranean trade discernible across southern Europe in that era, but not to the profound degree found among the La Tène culture of central Gaul.

Of particular note are the Etruscan-style burials. How exactly are these supposed to have been spread through trade? What kind of traders would be distributing elite burial customs? Traders spread pots, bowls, wine jugs, fine materials, etc. But they do not spread elite burial customs. Are we to believe that some traders from Etruria felt compelled, for some reason, to share with the inhabitants of central Gaul – but only central Gaul, and none of the peoples closer to them – how their ruling elite were buried? Or alternatively, are we to believe that some Celtic traders from central Gaul – and again, only from central Gaul – travelled to Etruria and asked how the ruling elite were buried? And then they travelled back to their homes in central Gaul and convinced their own elite class to start burying themselves like that?

Both of these scenarios are wholly unconvincing. With no preconceived notions, the most logical and natural explanation for the Etruscan-style burials associated with the La Tène culture is that there was a migration of an Etruscan elite class to central Gaul. This scenario best fits the fact that La Tène culture 'appeared rather suddenly, coinciding with some kind of societal upheaval that involved a shift of the major centers to the northwest'.[366] After this migration, the new culture that developed then spread out from where they had settled in central Gaul, as archaeologists discern regarding the La Tène culture. So in other words, the archaeological evidence clearly supports the notion of a group of Etruscans travelling to central Gaul and setting themselves up as rulers there in *c.* 500 BCE, exactly as the legend of Brutus states.

Granted, the area in which La Tène culture first appeared is somewhat to the east of Tours, where the legend places Brutus. We must appreciate that the geography of Geoffrey of Monmouth's *Historia Regum Britanniae* is not always reliable. For example, the account of Caesar's first invasion of Britain states that he arrived at the mouth of the River Thames. In reality, he arrived along the coast of Kent. This is not a huge mistake, since the mouth of the Thames is in the same general region of the country in which Caesar did land – the south-east. This is just one of many examples of geographical errors found in the *HRB*. Therefore, the fact that there is not a perfect correspondence between the location in the legend and the location

The Migration to Gaul and Britain

in which the La Tène culture historically first emerged should not be overly concerning. The general region is still the same.

There may well be a specific reason why Tours was singled out as the location that Brutus was associated with during his stay in Gaul. According to the *HRB*, during one of the battles between Brutus and Goffarius Pictus, a nephew of Brutus named Turnus was killed. According to the legend, the city of Tours, whose ancient Roman name was Civitas Turonorum, was named in his honour. As we saw earlier, this character was likely based on a real relative of Lucius Junius Brutus with the name 'Tarquinius'. Obviously, the city of Tours was not really named after anyone called Tarquinius or Turnus; it was named after the tribe called the Turones. This is hardly surprising, for it was not uncommon for a historical figure to be erroneously presented as the eponymous founder of a town or region. As we have seen, the *HRB* similarly claimed that Gloucester was named for Claudius. This is incorrect, although Gloucester really was founded in the general era of Claudius' visit to Britain, and the general location is consistent with where Claudius did visit: the south of what is now England.

In a similar way, it may well be that there were reports of Brutus and his companions (possibly including a specific mention of 'Turnus', or Tarquinius) travelling inland through the Loire, towards the centre of Gaul. It would have been quite natural for medieval scribes – who were generally all too eager to identify eponymous founders of locations and peoples – to conclude that Brutus' companion with a name similar to the ancient name for Tours must have given his name to that city. Thus, it is likely that the general region (central Gaul) was narrowed down to a specific location (the city of Tours) due to this false association. Although this cannot be proven definitively, it seems to be a reasonable explanation for why that specific city was singled out in the story.

Nonetheless, the emergence of the La Tène culture corresponds very well to the legend of Brutus. He is presented as entering the Loire and travelling east some way through the country. If we discount the specific connection to Tours in particular, the general idea of an invading force sailing up through the Loire and then making their way east through the country is reflected in the archaeological record. Here is what *The Oxford Encyclopedia of Ancient Greece and Rome* has to say about the emergence of the La Tène culture:

> The western Hallstatt chiefdoms collapsed in the mid-fifth century BCE, with the destruction of many of the hillforts causing an end to the

chiefly burials in the area from Burgundy to Bohemia ... The demise of the western Hallstatt culture is thought to be the result of a warrior society in northern Gaul, particularly at the Marne and Hunsrück-Eifel areas, that developed into what is referred to as La Tène.[367]

The Burgundy and Marne areas of France are precisely the areas where the Loire stops going east into the continent and curves to the south. Thus, we can easily imagine an invading force sailing up the Loire and then disembarking once it had taken them about as far east as it would. There, they fought fiercely against the local tribes, as per the legend in the *Historia Regum Britanniae* and as preserved by the archaeological evidence of destruction of the Hallstatt chiefdoms in Burgundy. They evidently then established themselves in the nearby Marne region, but then at least some of them continued campaigning east, as shown by the archaeological evidence for the rapid destruction of Hallstatt hillforts from there to Bohemia. Scholars do believe that the early La Tène centre in Bohemia was established *after* the ones in France and Germany, supporting this idea of a west-to-east movement.[368]

Therefore, although the archaeological evidence indicates that the real events took place over a much larger region than the *HRB*'s account claims, it fully supports the general concept of an Etruscan elite entering the Loire and then travelling east through Gaul, overthrowing the local rulers and establishing themselves as the new ruling class, thus resulting in the emergence of the highly-Etruscanised La Tène culture.

Across to Britain
The legendary account in the *HRB* and also the *Historia Brittonum* reports that Brutus and his wandering nation then continued on their journey to Britain, evidently after having spent more than a fleeting visit in Gaul. What does the archaeological evidence reveal? As it happens, the archaeological evidence shows that the La Tène culture spread to Britain almost immediately after it emerged in Gaul. The dates for the earliest La Tène remains in Gaul are placed at about 500 BCE. At present, the earliest La Tène remains in Britain are dated to about 450 BCE.

The specific site which is given this date is a chariot burial found in Edinburgh. It is known as the Newbridge Chariot Burial. Most chariot burials in Britain have been found in Yorkshire, within the territory of the Parisi tribe. The vast majority of those discovered in Yorkshire are dated to the fourth century BCE onwards, but it is thought that the chariot burial culture in this region (called the Arras culture) may date back to the fifth century BCE.[369] This would place it in the same general era as the Newbridge Burial, although probably not quite as early. Nonetheless, there is a distinct possibility that archaeology will one day uncover a chariot in Yorkshire which dates back to the same date as the Newbridge Burial.

Although almost all the chariot burials in Britain have been found in Yorkshire, aerial photography indicates that there may be chariot burials far further south than currently realised. The reason for saying this is that, as mentioned before, the type of barrow associated with the La Tène chariot burials is the square barrow. Most barrows, or burial mounds, throughout history have been round, but the Celts of the La Tène period used square barrows. These have been found on the continent, and they also spread to Britain in the first half of the fifth century BCE. Relatively few of them have been found to contain chariots, but virtually all chariot burials are in square barrows. Therefore, square barrows are indicative of the possible presence of a chariot burial. Although these square barrows have been most readily discovered in Yorkshire, aerial photography has revealed that they can actually be identified in many different regions of Britain, including at least as far south as East Anglia.[370] If these square barrows were excavated, there is every possibility that they would yield chariot burials as well.

In any case, square barrows themselves are characteristic of the early La Tène culture.[371] Therefore, with or without chariots, the presence of square barrows down almost the entire eastern side of Britain demonstrates the spread of La Tène culture from the continent. And as we have already noted, the earliest dated grave shows that this spread occurred at least as early as *c.* 450 BCE, shortly after the emergence of the La Tène culture in Gaul in *c.* 500 BCE.

Current academic thinking acknowledges that the La Tène burials in Britain may well have been brought from Gaul by means of a small-scale migration.[372] Some scholars accept the evidence for this without any issues, such as Christopher R. Fee and David Adams Leeming.[373] However, other scholars view the migration model as less likely than other options, though often on inadequate grounds. One archaeologist explains that these burials 'could well have been adopted through the "conversion" of a small but dominant ruling group by "missionaries" or envoys of a related group from the Continent ... without any element of immigration whatsoever'.[374] This is hardly the most natural explanation. There is then an attempt at justifying it by saying that this would account for the fact that the Yorkshire chariot burials are different from the continental ones in a few key ways. But this does not follow. If there was a small-scale migration of a group who brought their burial practices to Britain, then the only way they would perfectly preserve their customs from the continent would be if they did not mingle at all with the natives. This would be very unusual; the natural conclusion would be that there must have been a measure of exchange between the two cultures, even if the immigrants did force themselves upon the natives as overlords.

In addition, the chariot burials in Yorkshire are not the earliest ones which have been found in Britain, as we have already noted. The Newbridge Burial is the earliest example yet discovered. Notably, the Newbridge Burial is decidedly more similar to the continental burials than the Yorkshire ones are. The chariot was buried intact rather than being dismantled. The Ferrybridge Burial, which seems to be the oldest of all the Yorkshire ones, dating back to the end of the fifth century BCE or the very beginning of the fourth, also contains an intact chariot. This demonstrates that the practice of chariot burials in Britain gradually became more dissimilar to their continental parallels over time, rather than starting off that way.

Therefore, the archaeological evidence is perfectly consistent with the idea that a relatively small group of Etruscans, perhaps numbering in the thousands, migrated from Gaul to Britain and set themselves up as a new elite class. In reality, it is the most natural explanation. In the words of historian Christopher Snyder, 'all but the most sceptical archaeologists admit to some movement of warrior groups from northern Gaul to eastern Britain, where they may have intermarried with the native aristocracy'.[375]

But does this mean that the Etruscan elite class that moved from Gaul to Britain at some point between 500 and 450 BCE only settled in Yorkshire? No. As we have already noted, the earliest known chariot burial was found in Scotland, far from Yorkshire. Renowned scholar Barry Cunliffe suggested that the first-generation immigrants may have been spread quite widely, but that 'it was only in Yorkshire that the tradition [of chariot burials] was taken up and became an enduring part of the local culture'.[376] Furthermore, as mentioned, aerial photography gives us reason to believe that this practice may have been performed at least as far south as East Anglia. This being the case, it may have been preserved over a much wider area than first realised. Even so, the principle behind Cunliffe's words is likely still correct. The first-generation immigrants may have been spread out over a much wider area, with the practice of chariot burials only being preserved along the eastern side of Britain. In support of this is the fact that a number of La Tène-style items, dated to the fifth century BCE, have been found across Britain, in places as far apart as Northumberland and Wiltshire.[377]

Other Archaeological Evidence

Other changes occurred in Britain and Gaul around this time. One of these changes is, in fact, intricately connected to the La Tène culture, but it is a general change rather than anything related to specific art styles or customs. In c. 500 BCE, as the La Tène culture emerged and spread throughout Europe from central Gaul, the use of iron became widespread. It had already begun to be used during the preceding Hallstatt culture, but its use was limited. It was only after 500 BCE that the use of iron became more extensive and actually replaced the old bronze weapons and tools.[378]

Although it does not require it, this is consistent with a migration of people who were already regularly using iron. This would include the Etruscans. Given that the commonplace use of iron coincides, precisely in the La Tène culture, with Etruscan-style chariot burials and other Etruscan designs and artefacts, it is very likely that it was due to this Etruscan influence that the use of iron became widespread. In other words, this is yet more supporting archaeological evidence for the arrival of an Etruscan elite in Gaul in c. 500 BCE.

There is also some evidence of this from the architecture that developed in Celtic lands at this time. Over in Italy, the Etruscans mostly built their settlements on hilltops.[379] By the sixth century BCE (the time of Brutus), many of them were fortified with stone walls, although the Etruscans sometimes made use of earth ramparts and palisades.[380] Over in Celtic lands, both in Gaul and in Britain, hill forts had been in use for centuries by this time, so the use of hill forts in itself is no evidence of a connection between the Etruscans and the Celts. However, in the La Tène era, the Celts suddenly began building up their hill forts far more than they had previously. Their fortifications became more impressive and substantial, and they made extensive use of stone, even constructing vertical stone walls around the perimeters of their settlements in some cases.[381] The entrances to the forts became far more complex, and there is evidence that these forts began to be used as permanent settlements of large communities, rather than for specific activities or purposes as it appears they had been before the La Tène era, in the Hallstatt culture.[382]

This happened at about the same time – the start of the La Tène era – in both Gaul and Britain. One notable example of this from Britain is Maiden Castle. This hill fort was rather small and unremarkable during the Hallstatt era, but in *c.* 450 BCE it underwent a major expansion that practically tripled its size.[383] For comparison, this made it almost equal in size to the major Minoan settlement of Akrotiri on the island of Thera in the Bronze Age. Another example is Crickley Hill in Gloucestershire. In approximately 500 BCE, this modest abandoned hill fort underwent extensive reconstruction and expansion. A massive vertical stone wall, 5 or 6 meters high, was constructed around the perimeter of the settlement. Stone guard towers stood on either side of the entrance, which comprised large wooden gates with a walkway above them.[384]

This dramatic architectural change that occurred with the onset of the La Tène culture is elegantly explained by the arrival of an Etruscan elite. It is true that we do not find any evidence of large public spaces akin to the agora or forum of the Greek and Roman world. However, these public features were lacking in Etruscan towns as well, so their absence in the Celtic hill forts of the La Tène era is not significant.[385] Furthermore, we would not expect them to exactly replicate the cities that they had built in Etruria, for the environment of Gaul was different to that of Etruria. In addition, if it was just a ruling class that arrived, then we would logically expect a merging of the native architecture with the Etruscan architecture rather than a total replacement. And this is exactly what we find with the hill forts of the La Tène culture.

The use of statues is another piece of evidence in support of an Etruscan migration to Gaul. The oldest known Iron Age statue of a person anywhere north of the Alps is the Warrior of Hirschlanden, a funerary stone statue found in Germany and generally dated to *c.* 500 BCE.[386] Some sources assign it a date in the fifth century BCE.[387] Other carved sculptures had been made in the Hallstatt era, but this is the earliest known bona fide statue. This is life-size, just like the statues produced by the Etruscans. It is highly notable that the Celts suddenly started making life-size statues of people exactly when Brutus allegedly led a migration from Italy to Gaul. And beyond just this general similarity of concept, the Italic influence in this Celtic statue has long been noted. It has similarities to the Greek 'kouros' style, which was the style of statue used by the Greeks in this era.

However, there are significant differences, and the statue is actually far more similar to the Etruscan versions of the Greek kouros style.[388] Yet, there are also elements which appear to have come from native Celtic designs, consistent with the merging of an Italic elite with the local population.

Furthermore, the statue is shown with unnaturally raised shoulders. Some scholars have interpreted this as indicating that the figure whom this statue represents was buried upright, supported by spears underneath his armpits. This was an early Italic funerary custom, supporting the connection to the Etruscans.[389] Additionally, the placement of the left hand diagonally on the upper chest and the right hand diagonally just above the waist is paralleled exactly by many figures that have been found in Etruria.[390]

The archaeological record also reveals a change in grave goods at this time. In the latter part of the Hallstatt era, most graves contained nothing more than a four-wheeled cart and a dagger. But La Tène culture graves regularly contained, beyond the two-wheeled Etruscan-style chariot discussed previously, arms and armour, such as helmets, swords and other weapons.[391] This is consistent with the arrival of an Etruscan warrior elite introducing their customs to the land. In addition, the actual designs of some of these items are indicative of this migration. For instance, the Celts of the La Tène era used plumed helmets, just like the Greeks and Etruscans, and they have even been described as 'Italo-Greek'.[392] The general design of their bronze helmets has also been understood by scholars to be an example of Italic influence.[393] Furthermore, it has been noted that there is Italic influence on early La Tène shields.[394]

Regarding their armour, it is known that the Celts at times used metal cuirasses, while at other times they used armour made from leather or some other organic material. This is seen from another early Celtic life-size statue, the Glauberg Warrior. This statue dates to *c.* 450 BCE. Just like the slightly earlier Hirschlanden statue, this statue displays clear Etruscan influence, both in general design and in the placement of the hands.[395] However, more pertinent to the current point is the fact that the warrior is shown wearing what appears to be armour made from leather.[396] The Etruscans are known to have worn leather armour from at least as early as the sixth century BCE.[397] This Etruscan armour had broad shoulder straps just like those seen on the statue of the Glauberg Warrior.

The metal cuirasses of the Celts are also notable. The Celts had been using these from before the emergence of the La Tène culture, but at some point in the sixth century BCE, their design changed. They became more similar to the bell cuirass used by the Greeks and the Etruscans during the Archaic Era, with the lower part extending out from the body slightly. In addition, these cuirasses contained some rudimentary representations of the human torso, which is also clearly taken from the Greco-Etruscan design.[398] However, it should be noted that it might be the case, depending on the exact dating of these metal Celtic cuirasses, that this design was introduced slightly before the time of Brutus' legendary migration. If so, then this could be explained by trade (particularly through the Greek colony of Massalia) in line with the traditional explanation. The exact evidence regarding the dating of these cuirasses is not totally clear, so no definitive statement can be made in this regard.

Scale armour was also used by the Etruscans.[399] Although there does not appear to be any direct evidence of this type of armour being used by the Celts, it is known that the Celts did use chain mail by about as early as 400 BCE, and they are generally accepted as the inventors of that type of armour. Given that it has been speculated that chain mail was inspired by scale armour, it could be the case that the invention of chain mail by the Celts by about 400 BCE is indirect evidence for the presence of scale armour among the Celts in the immediately preceding era.[400]

Of course, it is known that not all of the Celts used armour. After all, some groups were even famous for going into battle naked (perhaps simply meaning without armour), and this has persisted as a modern stereotype. However, this was not the case with all Celts. It is true that armour was apparently only used by the higher-status warriors, but this is compatible with the concept of an Etruscan warrior elite establishing themselves over the Celts, which is certainly not the same as saying that the Celts as a whole were Etruscans.[401]

Linguistic Evidence
What about the language of this elite class of Etruscans? Does this mean that the mysterious language of the Etruscans was actually the language that led to Gaulish and Brythonic? No. The Greeks and the Romans were well aware of the Celtic languages, and they clearly tell us that the language of the Etruscans was not like any other language with which they were familiar. Not that the testimony of those ancient writers is necessary, for the Etruscans themselves left countless inscriptions for us to examine today. Although the Etruscan language is famous for still being a mystery, it must be emphasised

The Migration to Gaul and Britain

that the alphabet is not. It is the same basic alphabet as that used by the Greeks, the Phrygians, the Phoenicians and Hebrews, and other nations. So there is no doubt as to which letters are represented by which characters on the Etruscan inscriptions.

This means that it is perfectly possible to create a romanised transcription of ancient Etruscan writings. They can be 'read', just not understood. This is why there is such certainty that Etruscan is not related to any other known language. It is definitely not Gaulish, Brythonic or any other Celtic language; it is not even Indo-European.

With this in mind, how can the idea that Etruscans became the new ruling class over parts of Gaul and Britain be reconciled with these linguistic facts? Why did Etruscan not start to be spoken in Gaul and Britain? Well, it is certainly true that when a foreign ruling class arrives in a new territory, their language will often be adopted by the general populace. However, this is most certainly not always the case. For example, although the Romans ruled Britain for about three and a half centuries, Latin never replaced Brythonic among the general populace. In fact, it has been perfectly common throughout history for the ruling class to actually adopt the language of the general populace. For example, although Latin did not replace Brythonic in Britain, it did replace Gaulish in Gaul. When the Franks then came to rule over Gaul, they started speaking Latin rather than Frankish. Another example can be seen from the Lombards in Italy. After they came to dominate that country, they too started speaking Latin instead of their original Germanic language. After the Vikings conquered a part of France and became the Normans, they began speaking a form of French in place of their own Germanic language. Countless more examples could be given from all over the world. The point is that there is nothing unusual about the idea of the Etruscan elite that migrated to Gaul and then Britain adopting a Celtic language, as opposed to them introducing Etruscan to the natives.

However, it appears that there may well be some linguistic evidence actively supporting the presence of Etruscans in Gaul at this early date. First, it needs to be explained that the Celtic languages are fundamentally divided by scholars into two main categories: Q-Celtic and P-Celtic. These two branches of the language family are so called because of the fact that the latter uses the letter 'p' where the former has a 'k' sound. One example of this is the word for 'head'. In Welsh, which is a P-Celtic language, this is 'pen'. In Irish, a Q-Celtic language, this word is 'ceann'. Another example is the word for 'son', which is 'map' in Welsh but 'mac' in Irish. Ancient Brythonic and Gaulish were P-Celtic languages, while Celtiberian and ancient Gaelic were Q-Celtic languages (in ancient times, the pertinent sound in this branch was similar to the English 'qu', usually displayed as k^w in modern books). It is widely believed that Q-Celtic came before P-Celtic.[402]

The exact mechanism that caused some groups to shift to using a 'p' sound rather than a 'k^w' sound is unknown. However, there is one interesting theory regarding this which ties in well with the legend of Brutus. According to at least one researcher, Martin Counihan, the emergence of P-Celtic may well have come about through Etruscan influence.[403] The logic behind this goes that Etruscan speakers could not easily pronounce the Celtic 'k^w' sound, since they did not have it in their own language. Therefore, they substituted it for 'p'. One supposed example of this is the Etruscan word 'pupluna', the origin of the Latin 'populus' and ultimately the English 'people'.[404] According to Counihan, this Etruscan word was likely a borrowing from the Proto-Indo-European root '$k^w ok^w lo$-'. If so, this demonstrates the transition from a 'k^w' sound to a 'p' sound among Etruscan speakers. This would then lend credence to the idea that Etruscan influence was behind this shift among the Celtic languages.

Additional evidence of this is seen from the fact that Osco-Umbrian (a language group in Italy, related to Latin) also went through a '$k^w \rightarrow p$' shift.[405] Given that this language group was definitely within the sphere of Etruscan influence, this supports the idea that the reason for this shift is to do with Etruscan.

Further support for this idea can be seen from Lepontic. This was a Celtic language spoken around the border of northern Italy. It is the earliest attested P-Celtic language.[406] The earliest inscriptions, dating from the sixth century BCE, are written in an alphabet derived directly from the Etruscan alphabet.[407] The alphabet proves conclusively that there was Etruscan influence in the use of written language among the Lepontic speakers. Could the Etruscans have also influenced the spoken language too, leading to it experiencing the $k^w \rightarrow p$ shift? According to Counihan, this is the most natural explanation.

This is not to suggest that this possible Etruscan influence in Lepontic is evidence of Brutus' migration from Italy to Britain. After all, the earliest Lepontic inscriptions appear to predate the migration by at least a few decades, and northern Italy does not factor into the account of the journey. However, the point is that if it happened with Lepontic (and the use of the Etruscan alphabet does suggest that this explanation is correct), then the $k^w \rightarrow p$ shift in other Celtic

The Migration to Gaul and Britain

languages, principally Gaulish, can be taken as evidence of their presence there as well. Therefore, independently of their influence on Lepontic speakers, the fact that Gaulish went through a $k^w \rightarrow p$ shift supports the conclusion that Etruscan rulers became established over the inhabitants of Gaul.

Of course, the idea that the $k^w \rightarrow p$ shift is attributable to Etruscan influence is, by necessity, a very speculative theory. Therefore, it cannot be taken as strong evidence in itself. Nonetheless, whether or not this is what *did* happen among the Celtic languages, it appears reasonable to conclude that this *could* be the origin of P-Celtic, meaning that the linguistic evidence is, at the very least, consistent with this theory about an Etruscan ruling elite arriving in Gaul and then Britain, even if it does not require it.

Similarly, there are a number of words in Celtic languages which may well be loanwords from Etruscan, which is also consistent with this theory. For instance, consider the modern Welsh word 'llythyr'. This word means 'letter', and it evolved directly from Brythonic, the language of the ancient Britons. The Brythonic form, in turn, is understood to have been borrowed from the Latin word 'littera', which has the same meaning.[408] Significantly though, the Latin 'littera' is believed to be an Etruscan loanword.[409] Thus, although the traditional explanation that it came from Latin is acceptable, it could easily be the case that this is actually an example of a loanword directly from Etruscan into Brythonic. Supporting this alternative explanation is the fact that a form of this word was also used in Old Irish. It is known that La Tène culture reached Ireland, but the Romans did not conquer Ireland or even visit it apart from possibly once in the first century CE. Thus, it is surely more likely that the word spread to both Britain and Ireland through the migration of Celtic groups – as evidenced by the spread of La Tène culture – rather than as a result of the Roman conquest, which never reached Ireland. Crucially, the Romans had no significant interactions with the La Tène Celts until long after the La Tène culture had already spread to Ireland, yet there is demonstrably plenty of Etruscan influence from the very start of that culture. This indicates that the word owes itself to the Etruscans rather than the Romans.

A similar argument can be made about the Latin word 'populus', which is also believed to have an Etruscan origin.[410] This word, supposedly, spread from Latin to the Celtic languages, where it appears in Brythonic as 'pobl' and Old Irish as 'popul'. Again, the fact that it appears in Irish argues against it spreading from the Romans during their occupation of Britain, since they never occupied Ireland. And it is unlikely to have spread through trade, because the word refers to a basic concept ('people'), rather than some technical process or object that might require a loanword. Given that the Latin word was actually an Etruscan word, a more convincing explanation is that it passed into the Celtic languages through Etruscan influence in the La Tène culture, which definitely did spread to Ireland, unlike the Romans.

Another word of Etruscan origin which can be found in all the Celtic languages, including Old Irish, is the word for 'tower'. This word ('tŵr' in Modern Welsh, 'tor' in Modern Irish) is 'turris' as it appears in Latin. This Latin word is widely agreed to have come from Etruscan.[411] Once again, the fact that it appears in all the Celtic languages indicates that it did not spread to them through the Romans, who did not go to Ireland, but through the Etruscans by means of the La Tène culture, which did spread to Ireland.

The Latin word for window, 'fenestra', is also believed to have come from Etruscan.[412] This is found in Welsh as 'ffenestr'. This is generally considered to have been taken from Latin through Roman influence, but it could instead have been taken directly from Etruscan, in harmony with the evidence for Etruscan influence within the La Tène culture. As with the previous examples, this word appears in Old Irish, where it had the form 'senester'.[413] This supports the notion that this was not actually borrowed from Latin, but rather was borrowed directly from Etruscan.

A similar example is the Welsh word 'milwr' (meaning 'soldier'), which is generally stated to have come from Latin 'miles'. However, the Latin word itself is an Etruscan loanword.[414] Therefore, we can speculate that this is actually a direct borrowing from Etruscan rather than through Latin. It is true that this word does not appear in any of the Irish languages, which might appear to weaken this case. However, the word which is used in Irish is 'saighdiúir', which derives from the Old Irish word 'saiget' (meaning 'arrow' or 'javelin') combined with the suffix '-óir', which was added onto the end of words to indicate a person who performs the action described. Thus, to the Irish, a soldier was referred to by the idea of someone who shot arrows or threw javelins. Significantly, this word 'saiget' is believed to have come from a Latin word which, like 'miles', is also thought to be an Etruscan loanword.[415] Thus, although the Britons appear to have expressed the concept of a soldier in a slightly different way to how the Irish expressed it, they both used terms ultimately derived from Etruscan.

The Migration to Gaul and Britain

To these examples we might also add the Gaulish god 'Esus', also recorded as 'Aisus'. The name of this god might have come from the generic Etruscan word for a god, which was 'ais'.

These examples of linguistic connections between Celtic languages and Etruscan do not necessarily *require* an Etruscan elite to have imposed themselves over the Celts and caused the emergence of the La Tène culture, although, in the case of words with an Etruscan origin that appear in Irish as well as Welsh, it certainly seems more likely that they derived from Etruscan rather than Latin as is commonly suggested. In any case, whether these could be explained through a migration or simply through trade or cultural exchange, these examples demonstrate that the linguistic evidence is at least *consistent* with the migration theory, even if it does not *require* it. At the very least, it refutes any potential 'absence of evidence' argument against an Etruscan elite ruling over Celtic lands.

Cultural Evidence

If an Etruscan elite really did migrate from Italy to Gaul and Britain, it would be fair to expect that this elite influenced, to one degree or another, the general culture of the Celts in the areas to which they migrated. One clear example of this comes from the use of chariots. In commentaries of Homer's *Iliad*, it has often been claimed that one piece of evidence for the fact that Homer was writing about events long in the past is the fact that he did not seem to have any understanding of how chariots were used. His description of how the Greeks and Trojans used chariots during their warfare is supposedly nothing like how they were actually used. This is then taken as evidence that the events were just a distant memory in the time of Homer.

In reality, this reasoning is completely incorrect. Homer's description of the use of chariots is not unique in the ancient world. First, let us consider what exactly that description is and how it differs from the traditional use of chariots.

In most ancient warfare, the chariots would be used as weapons in their own right. A line of chariots would charge towards the enemy troops and plough through them. A warrior on the chariot would then use a spear or a bow and arrow to fight from the vehicle itself. This is the traditional way of using them in the open battlefield. However, Homer's description is quite different. Rather than the chariots themselves being used as weapons to attack the enemy, they are used primarily as methods of transportation for the soldiers. The driver of the chariot would swoop into the battlefield, the soldier would jump off and engage in battle, and the driver would then take the chariot back out of harm's way and wait on the sidelines until the soldier needed to be recovered again.

The claim that this description is not how chariots were historically used is incorrect. What is true is that the Mycenaean Greeks did not use them this way, but that simply ties in with the fact that the Trojan War did not really take place in Mycenaean times. What we can say definitively, however, is that certain other ancient nations did use chariots in the manner described in the *Iliad*. For example, the people of Cyrene are said by the historian Xenophon to have used their chariots in the manner of the Trojans.[416] Therefore, although it was very rare, Homer's description is not fictional – it is an accurate description of one ancient use of chariots.

Significantly, Homer's description of how the Greeks and Trojans used their chariots almost exactly matches Caesar's description of how the ancient Britons used chariots. In his eyewitness account in *De Bello Gallico*, Caesar explains how the Britons would charge their chariots into the battlelines, the warriors would jump off and engage in battle on foot, and the charioteers would withdraw to the sidelines until needed again. In other words, they used them just like how the Greeks and Trojans used them in the *Iliad*. Modern researchers are not the only ones who have noticed this; the ancient historian Diodorus explicitly stated that 'in their battles they [the Britons] use chariots in the same manner as it is reported the ancient Greek heroes fought in the Trojan War'.[417]

It is already widely accepted that the Celts of the La Tène era started using chariots in imitation of the Etruscans. However, this evidence regarding the *manner* in which they used them supports the notion that the use of chariots came to them through an elite class descended from the Homeric world. This ties in perfectly with the idea that the Etruscans were descended from the Trojans, and thus when they migrated to the land of the Celts and introduced their chariots there, the Celts began using them in the way in which the Trojans used them in the *Iliad*.

The connection between the Etruscans and the La Tène Celts is also supported by the manner in which javelins were thrown. In most of the world, when a particular device (beyond simply one's own hand) was used to throw a javelin, a 'spear-thrower' was used. This was an open shaft with a partially enclosed end in which the end of the spear or javelin was placed. The warrior would grasp the spear-thrower rather than the spear or javelin itself, and he would use that to hurl the weapon through the air, achieving a greater velocity than he would be able to by merely throwing the weapon normally. However, in Greece and Italy (including Etruria), a different method was used. A strap called an 'amentum' was tied around the middle of the javelin. The warrior would hold onto the strap and then throw the javelin; again, this resulted in a greater velocity than one could achieve by throwing the javelin directly.

It appears that this method of javelin throwing was originally unique to the Greeks and the inhabitants of Italy. However, we also find it among the La Tène Celts. This is proven by ancient depictions of Gallic warriors, and also by the fact that it is mentioned in Irish mythology. It is also known to have been used in Denmark, after the La Tène culture had spread to that territory. The Celtiberians are also described in historical sources as using this same method. Yet, it seems to have been completely unknown outside of these areas.[418] Thus, similar to the use of chariots, this aspect of the warfare of the La Tène Celts seems to be paralleled only in the Greco-Etruscan world.

Another notable custom that the Celts had in warfare was that of having single combat challenges between warriors. This was commonly done as two armies approached each other. A strong warrior would step forward from the battlelines and challenge the enemy army to send forth their best warrior to fight him.[419] The *Iliad* is famous for its single combat challenges, which occur throughout the poem. Historian Adrian Goldsworthy even specifically noted regarding the Celts that, in many respects, 'this type of battle is close to the Homeric pattern'.[420] This was by no means unique to the Trojans, though, so it is of limited value in showing the connection between the two cultures. Nonetheless, it is a point worth mentioning. This is especially so because we can perceive a clear transmission of this type of warrior culture all the way from Troy to Rome and to the Celts. Single combat appears frequently in histories of ancient Rome. This is seen right back at the beginning of their history, for Romulus is reported to have duelled a king named Acro in single combat.[421] Therefore, it is notable that this is later seen to form a large part of Celtic culture in warfare.

In summary, we can see that the way that the La Tène-era Celts used chariots in warfare, the way they threw javelins, and their tendency to engage in single combat before pitched battles all point to Trojan/Etruscan influence in their culture.

Religious Evidence
Another piece of evidence for the connection between the ruling class of the ancient Britons and the Trojans is seen in their religious beliefs.

As we have already noted, the chief god of the Trojans was Apollo. Appropriately, Apollo was frequently depicted by the Etruscans and is explicitly stated to have been their chief god in the *Aeneid*. What about the Britons and the Gauls? Is there evidence that Apollo was an important god for them too?

Diodorus Siculus presented his own account of Britain and the peoples living there. But elsewhere, he related an account from a Greek traveller of the fourth century BCE, Hecataeus of Abdera, which was probably also about Britain. This account refers to an island said to be off the coast of Gaul and no smaller than Sicily. This is surely a reference to Britain, as is generally accepted.[422] Significantly, the account includes this description:

> Apollo is honoured among them above all other gods; and the inhabitants are looked upon as priests of Apollo, after a manner, since daily they praise this god continuously in song and honour him exceedingly.[423]

So, according to this account from the fourth century BCE, the chief god of this island, which can almost certainly be identified as Britain, was Apollo. This firmly supports the notion that the inhabitants of Britain were descended from the inhabitants of Troy, whose chief god was Apollo. However, this account is found in the works of Diodorus Siculus, a Greek writer. Therefore, was the 'Apollo' in question really named Apollo, or did Diodorus Siculus (or Hecataeus, from whom this account originates) simply use that name because they considered the Brythonic god in question to be the equivalent of the Greek Apollo? After all, it was very common for Greek and Roman writers to use the names of their own gods when describing the gods of other nations.

To a large degree, the answer to this question is not important. It may well be that the god had a Celtic name, rather than the name 'Apollo'. Nevertheless, it is evident that this Celtic god must have been sufficiently similar to the Greek Apollo for the Greek writers to make the connection between the two. This is important because if the Greek writers could make the connection, then evidently the reverse is true as well; Celtic peoples who came into contact with the worship of Apollo could have identified him with one of their own gods who was sufficiently similar, regardless of their native name for such a god. But significantly, this Apollo-like god was the chief deity of the Britons at least as early as the fourth century BCE. There is nothing remarkable in itself about the fact that the Britons had an Apollo-like god, because virtually every polytheistic culture would have had a god that shared certain characteristics with at least one god from another culture. But what is significant is that this Apollo-like god was their *chief* god. This supports the notion that Trojan descendants arrived in Britain and introduced the worship of Apollo to the natives. Even if he was equated with a native Celtic god and the name of that native god was used instead of the Mediterranean name, the Mediterranean influence would be seen from the fact that the god in question then began to be worshipped as their chief god.

However, there is even evidence that the inhabitants of Gaul and Britain did use the name 'Apollo', albeit in a slightly evolved form. In the Aquitaine region of Gaul, a god named 'Abellio' is attested. His name is elsewhere spelt 'Abelio' and 'Abelionni'. There is evidence that this god was identical to Apollo. The Greek god Apollo was referred to in some dialects as 'Apello'. This form was found in Italy, among other places.[424] In Crete and a few other regions, Apollo was called 'Abelios', an almost identical form to the Gallic 'Abellio' or 'Abelio'.[425] The Gallic god is believed by some scholars to have been a sun god, which would also match the Greek Apollo.[426] Although very little has been written about Abellio in recent years, a number of scholars in the past believed that he was, in fact, identical with the Greek Apollo.[427] Julius Caesar mentioned the worship of Apollo among the Gauls, and some have identified this Gallic Apollo with Abellio.[428] According to Caesar, in his time Apollo was one of the chief gods of the Gauls.[429]

However, there is no evidence that the worship of Abellio was widespread throughout Gaul, since inscriptions mentioning him have only been found in the southern part of the region. There is another Celtic god whose worship is much more widely attested who may well be equivalent to both Abellio and the Greek Apollo. This god is Belenus. Inscriptions testify to the worship of this god all over Celtic lands, including all of Gaul and in Britain as well. It is obvious that he was one of the chief gods of the Celts. In Greek and Roman inscriptions, Belenus is directly equated with Apollo.[430] The consensus opinion is that this is the god to whom Caesar was referring when he described Apollo as being one of the chief gods of the Gauls.[431]

The scholars mentioned earlier, who argued that the Gallic Abellio is identical to the Apollo mentioned by Caesar, also suggested that Abellio is identical to Belenus as well.[432] Evidence for this can be seen through the name of the god. Belenus' name was variously spelt 'Belenus', 'Bellenus', 'Belanus', 'Belinus' or even 'Belis'. Recall that

Abellio's name was also written 'Abelionni'. The removal of the 'a' sound at the beginning would not be a remarkable occurrence, especially if the first syllable was unstressed. This would leave 'Belioni' or 'Belionus'. A linguistic simplifying of this name would result in 'Belinus' or something similar, like the other spellings of Belenus.

Consider how this connects to the Etruscans. Being descendants of the Trojans, one of their chief gods was Apollo, written as 'Apulu' and 'Aplun' in their inscriptions.[433] Either directly from their form of the name or from a Greek dialect version (perhaps from the Etruscans who had been living in Thesprotia in Greece), this god came to be worshipped in Gaul as 'Abellio' and 'Abellioni'. The name of this god then evolved into 'Belinus' and other variations, with the more original forms only being preserved in parts of southern Gaul. Independently of a connection to Abellio, some scholars have suggested that 'Belenus' and 'Apollo' come from the same root.[434]

Even if this theory is incorrect and the name 'Belenus' is etymologically unrelated to the name 'Apollo', there is good evidence that the origin of the god Belenus does come, at least in large part, from Apollo. One piece of evidence for this is seen from the associations that Belenus had. It was not a case of Belenus simply being a solar god and therefore identified with Apollo, also a solar god. Rather, their similarities are deeper than that. Not only was Belenus associated with the sun, but he was also associated with healing, just like Apollo.[435] There is no inherent connection between these two concepts. Countless sun gods from cultures around the world were not connected with healing. So the fact that Belenus and Apollo were both connected with the sun and with healing is significant. Therefore, even without any etymological connection, the evidence suggests that the Etruscans introduced the worship of their prominent god Apollo to the Celts, thus accounting for the importance of Belenus in Gaul and Britain and also accounting for Belenus' specific associations with the sun *and* with healing.

Another example of religious evidence for the connection between the Britons and the Trojans is their respective concepts of the afterlife. A concept that appears among the Greeks, at least as early as Homer's time, was the idea that the departed souls of the dead lived on an island to the west, called Elysium.[436] This was not a common concept in the ancient world. Thus, it is notable that this very same concept appears in ancient Celtic mythology.[437] It is preserved in Irish and Welsh mythology, and it is also described by the Byzantine scholar Procopius of Caesarea when discussing the afterlife of the ancient Gauls.[438]

The Migration to Gaul and Britain

To summarise, we can see that it is probable that the worship of the god Apollo was brought to Gaul, where the name became 'Abellio' or 'Abelionni'. This may have then evolved into 'Belionus' and then 'Belinus', thus leading to Belenus, the famous god of the Gauls and the Britons. Even if the name 'Belenus' is unrelated to the name 'Apollo', the similarities between the two gods strongly indicates that the worship of Belenus was influenced by the worship of Apollo. Therefore, regardless of the etymology of the names, the evidence supports the conclusion that the worship of Apollo was introduced to ancient, pre-Roman Gaul. And the fact that this Apollo-like god was one of the primary gods of the Celts – *the* chief god of the Britons as early as the fourth century BCE, in fact – strongly indicates that it was introduced by a migration of Etruscans, Trojan-descendants, to whom Apollo was extremely important. Furthermore, the concept of the afterlife found among the ancient Celts is strikingly similar to the concept found in the Homeric world – the idea that it was an island to the west.

DNA Evidence

As we saw in the case of the Etruscan migration from western Anatolia, it should not be expected that a migration from one country to another would cause a complete change in the genetic makeup of the second country. In the case of an elite class, it may well be the case that the newcomers only make a small impact on the genetics of the region, or possibly even no discernible impact at all. Therefore, we should not necessarily expect to see a significant trace of this migration in the genetic makeup of Gaul and Britain.

Furthermore, by the time of the migration from Italy to Gaul and then to Britain, somewhat less than 200 years had passed since the initial migration from Anatolia to Italy. It is unclear, then, how many of the Etruscan followers of Brutus were actually descended from the original immigrants from Anatolia. It may be that many of them were the native Villanovan inhabitants of Etruria rather than the actual Anatolian elite class. We would not expect the DNA of this elite class to have spread through intermarriage to all of the natives of Etruria after just two centuries of their having resided there. Thus, depending on who exactly made up Brutus' collection of followers, it may be that very little in the way of Anatolian DNA would have reached Gaul.

An additional fact that is hugely important to recognise is that many of the groups who migrated under Aeneas and formed the new Etruscan elite class were not actually native to Anatolia. The

The Trojan Kings of Britain

Trojans themselves (their ruling aristocracy, at least) were Greeks, the Pelasgians seem to have originally come from Greece, and the Phrygians also came from the Balkans.

When we take into account these three points – that an elite class rarely makes a significant impact on the native population; that many of Brutus' followers may have been native Villanovan inhabitants with no genetic connection to the Etruscan elite class; and that only a small portion of the groups making up the original Etruscan elite class themselves were actually native to Anatolia – it is reasonable to expect that there would be very little, if any, DNA evidence in Britain and Gaul of this migration from Anatolia.

Yet, it does appear that there is a small amount of perceptible genetic evidence for these Near Eastern arrivals. A recent comparison of DNA from thirty different samples from Bronze Age Gaul with DNA from eleven different samples from Iron Age Gaul has revealed something interesting. This analysis compared how much of the DNA of the samples came from various different regions around the world, divided into the following sections: Gedrosia (roughly equivalent to southern Pakistan); Siberia; North West Africa; South East Asia; Atlantic Mediterranean; North Europe; South Asia; East Africa; South West Asia; East Asia; Caucasus; Sub-Saharan Africa.

Both the Bronze Age and the Iron Age samples are composed mostly of Atlantic Mediterranean and North European DNA. In fact, the averages from both groups are almost exactly identical for each one of these world regions. However, there are two regions where the Iron Age samples have a slightly higher percentage than the Bronze Age samples: South West Asia and the Caucasus. These two regions are the most representative of Anatolia on the list. Bearing this in mind, it is interesting to note the slight increase. The Bronze Age samples have an average of 1.73 per cent of their DNA from South West Asia, while the La Tène-era samples have an average of 3.17 per cent of their DNA from that region. Regarding the Caucasus, the Bronze Age samples have an average of 7.55 per cent of their DNA from there, while the La Tène-era samples have an average of 10.18 per cent.

This is a small difference, but considering that almost all the other regions are represented by almost the exact same percentage (or a smaller one), this small increase may well be significant. This is especially so when we consider both the increase in the Caucasus DNA and the South West Asian DNA together, since they are both broadly indicative of Anatolia. It is a combined increase of over 4 per cent. Although this is small, it is consistent with the presence of an elite group of Etruscans who were, themselves, only partially descended from Anatolian peoples.

Regarding Britain, it does not appear that a comparable study of paleo-DNA has yet been performed. Therefore, we cannot do the same kind of analysis with Britain as we have done with Gaul. However, there was a study in 2018 which has provided some potentially very significant information. This analysed the change in genetics of the inhabitants of Britain from Neolithic times until Roman times. A fascinating discovery was made. When the 'Beaker people' arrived in Britain at the beginning of the Bronze Age, they appear to have completely replaced the Neolithic population. However, as highlighted by Professor David Reich, a sudden change occurred many centuries later. In the south-eastern quarter of Britain, DNA similar to the earlier Neolithic population suddenly became widespread again. The exact date in which this change occurred has proven difficult to establish, leading to three suggested explanations.

The first explanation suggests that the Beaker people did not completely eliminate the native population, but that small pockets of Neolithic communities survived in Britain through to later times, when they then became populous again. The second theory suggests that this Neolithic DNA was reintroduced by the arrival of Celtic tribes from central Gaul during the Iron Age. A third explanation is that it came from the Romans, and that they evidently made more of an impact on the genetic makeup of Britain than previously thought.

The first explanation is the weakest. There is no evidence from archaeology that Neolithic communities continued in any part of Britain through the Bronze and Iron Ages. In addition, given that the Beaker people came from the continent, the south-east of Britain is the last place we would expect to find surviving communities of the population that was replaced by these continental arrivals. They would be more likely to survive on the fringes of Britain, far away from the continent, such as in the northern or western corners. Thus, the resurgence of Neolithic DNA in the south-eastern quarter of Britain is unlikely to be explained by surviving Neolithic communities from before the arrival of the Beaker people.

The second and third explanations are more plausible. However, there is a fourth explanation which is equally conceivable, and it is somewhat of a combination of the two aforementioned ones. Just as the Romans from Italy would have preserved the pertinent Neolithic DNA (since the Beaker people never spread to Italy), the Etruscans likewise would have preserved that DNA in their genetic makeup.

Thus, the resurgence of Neolithic DNA in the south-east of Britain is perfectly concordant with an Etruscan migration to Gaul and then to Britain, bringing their own Neolithic DNA along with that of whatever Celts joined them after they briefly established themselves in Gaul.

In summary, we can see that there was a small increase in DNA from the Caucasus and South West Asia – which regions are the most representative of Anatolia out of all those used in the study – in La Tène-era Gallic Celts compared to Bronze Age Gallic Celts. This is consistent with a relatively small group of Anatolian descendants among a population of, perhaps, several thousand Etruscans travelling with Brutus to Gaul and some of them settling there. Furthermore, the resurgence of Neolithic DNA in the south-east of Britain possibly as early as the Iron Age Celtic migration to Britain (i.e. 500 BCE) is consistent with an Etruscan migration to that region from Gaul in *c*. 500 BCE.

Written Evidence

So far, we have seen archaeological, linguistic, cultural, religious and genetic evidence for the connection between the ancient Britons (along with the inhabitants of Gaul) and the Trojans (through the Etruscans). What about written evidence? This may seem like a hopeless endeavour, since it is widely accepted that the earliest record of the legend of Trojan descendants coming to Britain is in the ninth-century *Historia Brittonum*. Although this is commonly stated to be the case, the reality is that there is written evidence for this migration from as early as the fourth century BCE.

Before we go so far back, let us first examine a source which is closer in date to the *Historia Brittonum*. The sixth-century *Frankish Table of Nations*, as explained in an earlier chapter, states that a certain 'Istio' was the forefather of the Romans, the Franks, the Britons, and the Alemanni. Although the specific genealogy presented in this table is fictional, it does reveal what was believed in that era about those nations. It reveals that those four nations were believed to be kinsmen. Why is that significant? Well, the Romans were famously said to have been descended from the Trojans. The Franks, too, were already claiming descent from the Trojans in this era.[439] It thus makes sense that the Romans and Franks are portrayed as kinsmen in this record. The Franks and the Alemanni were closely related Germanic peoples, so it is no surprise that the Alemanni are also placed in this group. However, what this means is that the Britons were also believed to share a descent with the Romans and the Franks. Since the Romans and Franks were both believed to be descended from the Trojans, the logical conclusion is that the Britons were likewise believed to be of Trojan descent – otherwise, they would not be included here as kinsmen of the Romans and Franks.

So, we can see that it is very likely that the Trojan descent of the Britons is attested in this sixth-century document. Now, let us go back a few centuries to the writings of Ammianus Marcellinus, a Roman writer of the fourth century CE. In his famous *Roman History*, he recorded some very helpful information about the ancient Gauls. He specifically stated that this information came from a Greek historian named Timagenes, who lived in the first century BCE.[440] The following quotation is very pertinent for our discussion:

> Some again maintain that after the destruction of Troy, a few Trojans fleeing from the Greeks, who were then scattered over the whole world, occupied these districts.[441]

Thus, according to this record from the first century BCE, some Trojans migrated to Gaul after the destruction of Troy. This ties in perfectly with the legend of Brutus, yet the significance of this appears to have been completely missed. Although this does not describe the whole migration process, it supports the legend of Brutus right up to the point that they arrive and settle in Gaul. The only missing part is the final step from Gaul to Britain.

This Trojan migration to Gaul is supported by slightly later records concerning specific tribes which claimed descent from Troy. For example, the Roman poet Lucan, from the first century CE, reported that the Arverni tribe claimed descent from the Trojans, although he himself did not believe their claim.[442] Sidonius Apollinaris of the fifth century CE also referred to this claim.[443] In addition, the Aedui tribe, just next to the Arverni, appear to have also claimed descent from the Trojans.[444] This is indicated by the fact that Caesar stated that this tribe was 'often hailed by the Senate as brethren and kinsmen'.[445] Perhaps the reason that the Aedui's claim was accepted while the Arverni's claim was not was that the Aedui tribe was pro-Roman very early on, causing the Romans to have a more favourable view of them. Some scholars have also argued that the Remi, a Belgic tribe in north-east Gaul, likewise claimed a shared descent with the Romans.[446]

Therefore, these ancient records, going back to the first century BCE, support the claim that some Trojans ended up migrating to Gaul and becoming prominent there, with the Arverni, the Aedui, and the Remi being singled out by later sources. The Aedui, incidentally, lived in central Gaul. Thus, they were positioned close to where the *HRB* indicates that the Trojans settled, and they also lived quite close to the heartland of the early La Tène culture. Their territory was near the bend in the Loire where the La Tène elite class appears to have first overthrown the Hallstatt chiefdoms, as discussed earlier. Thus, everything supports the conclusion that the Aedui's supposed descent from Troy ties in with the legend of Brutus' migration to Gaul and with the emergence of the La Tène culture. This connection is seen even more firmly in the case of the Remi, who inhabited the Marne region, precisely the area in which the La Tène culture first emerged.

Yet, the connection to Brutus' migration is even stronger than just this. Accepting that Trojans did migrate to Gaul and become rulers there, as the ancient testimonies claim, it is an inevitability that Britain would have also been inhabited by Trojans from an ancient period. Why? Because the Celts of Gaul are believed to have migrated to Britain in pre-Roman times. This is the reason why the Britons and the Gauls spoke Celtic languages. It is generally believed that the Celtic language emerged on mainland Europe and then, through migrations, spread to Britain. Although different scholars hold different opinions, this is usually believed to have occurred in roughly the middle of the first millennium BCE. Historian Janet Davies wrote:

> The distinguished Irish historian Myles Dillon argued that Celtic speakers reached Britain and Ireland as early as 2,000 BC, but the most generally held opinion tends to date their arrival to the centuries following 600 BC.[447]

The *Encyclopaedia Britannica*, similarly, states that 'it is hardly likely that the Celtic invasions of those islands began much before 500 BC'.[448] These dates are, by necessity, only approximate, since they are based on comparing the differences between Insular Celtic and Continental Celtic in the first century BCE and then estimating how far back they must have separated to have arrived at those differences by the first century BCE. Therefore, the estimated date for the Celtic language being brought to Britain, which by its nature is only an approximate estimate, is compatible with our date of *c.* 500 BCE for Brutus' migration to Britain. This approximate date ties in with the spread of La Tène chariot burials discussed earlier, which archaeology shows spread from Gaul to Britain somewhere between 500 and

The Migration to Gaul and Britain

450 BCE. This is the only evidence of any kind of migration from Gaul to Britain in this general era.

In recent years, some scholars have proposed an alternative theory regarding the spread of Celtic languages, suggesting that they actually originated in Western Europe and spread eastward. However, the general consensus is still that the Celts migrated from central Europe to Britain in the Iron Age, at around 500 BCE or so according to most estimates.

Therefore, if some Trojans did migrate to Gaul and set themselves up as the new leaders of the Gallic tribes, and then a migration from Gaul to Britain occurred around 500 BCE or so, then this would mean that Trojans migrated to Britain at that time. Rather than being some radical idea, this is actually the natural consequence of combining what the ancient records actually say about the Gallic tribes with the modern understanding of how the Celts spread to Britain. In fact, we do not even have to bring that modern understanding into the matter at all. Even in ancient times, it was believed – at least by some – that the Britons were descendants of the Gauls. For example, while the Roman historian Tacitus was describing the peoples of Britain, he noted the following:

> Those who are nearest to the Gauls are also like them, either from the permanent influence of original descent, or, because in countries which run out so far to meet each other, climate has produced similar physical qualities. But a general survey inclines me to believe that the Gauls established themselves in an island so near to them.[449]

In other words, Tacitus believed that the Britons who lived in the south of Britain were descendants of Gauls who had 'established themselves' in the island. Other records reflect the same belief. For example, the first-century BCE writer Parthenius of Nicaea recorded the following story:

> Hercules, it is told, after he had taken the kine of Geryones from Erythea, was wandering through the country of the Celts and came to the house of Bretannus, who had a daughter called Celtine. Celtine fell in love with Hercules and hid away the kine, refusing to give them back to him unless he would first content her. Hercules was indeed very anxious to bring the kine safe home, but he was far more struck by the girl's exceeding beauty, and consented to her wishes; and then, when the time had come round, a son called Celtus was born to them, from whom the Celtic race derived their name.[450]

The Trojan Kings of Britain

In summary, the Celts were supposedly descended from the daughter of a king named Bretannus. This Bretannus, surely, is supposed to be the eponymous ancestor of the Britons. Yet in this account, he is definitely placed in 'the country of the Celts', in Gaul. So although this story does not reveal the way in which the Britons were believed to have come to inhabit the island of Britain, it does reveal that they were believed to have shared an origin with the Celts of Gaul, and that their ancestor was believed to have lived there, similar to what Tacitus wrote. In the medieval era, we find the same view expressed by Bede; he wrote that the inhabitants of the southern half of Britain had migrated from Armorica, the north-west region of Gaul.[451]

Thus, the idea that the inhabitants of Britain were descendants of the Celts of Gaul is not a modern theory – it was also a view that existed in ancient and medieval times. When we combine this traditional view with the fact that the Trojans were believed to have migrated to Gaul, we see that the belief that the Trojans migrated to Britain does, in fact, extend back to ancient times, even though no surviving ancient source explicitly puts it in those words. Despite the fact that there is no explicit written evidence of this belief *in full* from the Roman era or before, some scholars have suggested that it does date back to the first century CE, although these scholars use different reasoning to arrive at that conclusion.[452]

However, since there are these ancient records of the Trojans settling in Gaul, and since both ancient sources and modern scholars claim that a migration from Gaul to Britain occurred in pre-Roman times, why have more researchers not made the obvious connection between these facts and the legend of the Trojan migration to Britain?

Once again, the answer lies in the matter of chronology. Since the Celtic migration to Britain is usually placed in roughly 500 BCE, while Brutus' migration to Britain is usually placed in about 1100 or 1000 BCE, it appears at first glance that the Celtic migration could not possibly have anything to do with the Brutus story. Even so, obviously Trojan descendants would have spread to Britain *eventually*, during the Celtic migration, although this could not possibly have anything to do with Brutus according to the commonly accepted date of the Trojan War. It is for this reason that these records of the Trojans migrating to Gaul and the modern theory of the Celtic migration to Britain were not connected to Brutus. It is only when the chronology of Brutus is properly established that these events logically link together.

As stated before, there is actually written evidence for this Trojan migration to Britain going back all the way to the fourth century BCE.

The Migration to Gaul and Britain

Let us now consider that evidence. It was mentioned earlier that Diodorus Siculus related a report from Hecataeus of Abdera regarding an island at least as big as Sicily beyond Gaul, which is clearly a reference to Britain. This is the report which mentioned Apollo being their chief god. This record contains another truly fascinating piece of information about the inhabitants of that island. It mentions a city dedicated to Apollo on the island, where there was a 'spherical' temple. This is often taken to be a reference to Stonehenge, though it could actually be a reference to any one of the many sacred stone circles in Britain.[453] In any case, a few lines later, Diodorus' account (reporting the testimony of the fourth-century BCE explorer Hecataeus, remember) states that 'the kings of this city and the supervisors of the sacred precinct are called Boreadae, since they are descendants of Boreas'.[454]

So, according to this source, the kings of this particular city in Britain were descendants of Boreas. Now, who was Boreas? Boreas was the Greek god of the north wind. Significantly, he was believed to have lived in Thrace.[455] Although he was a god, the Greek legends present him as having children within a specific chronology, some of whom were also known as the 'Boreadae', just like the kings of this city in Britain. One of Boreas' daughters, Cleopatra, married a certain Phineus, the king of Thrace.[456] This country was just next to the Troad, being separated from it only by the Dardanelles. And the Thracians, it should be noted, were allies of the Trojans according to the *Iliad*. Furthermore, according to some traditions, one of Phineus' sons was Mariandynus, the eponymous forefather of the Mariandyni tribe in north central Anatolia, not too far from Troy. Therefore, the descendants of Boreas were closely associated with the Trojans.

However, the connections between Boreas' descendants and the Trojans are stronger than just this. In fact, Phineus, king of Thrace – the son-in-law of Boreas – is recorded as having a daughter named Olizone. These records further state that this Olizone was the great-great-great-grandmother of Priam of Troy by virtue of her marriage to King Dardanus.[457] Thus, the descendants of Boreas intermarried with the dynasty of Troy. And further still, Priam's daughter Creusa was the wife of Aeneas of Troy and mother of Ascanius, making her an ancestor of Brutus.[458] Thus, according to what the ancient Greeks believed, Brutus would, in fact, have been a descendant of Boreas. Even if we just take the general descent from Boreas, this fourth-century BCE account tells us that some of the kings of Britain originally came from Thrace, just across from Troy. This is immensely significant. It demonstrates that it is *not* the case that the *Historia Brittonum* was the first record to claim that the kings of Britain migrated from the Near East. Nor was the *Frankish Table of Nations*. No, long before those records, in the fourth century BCE, we have this claim that some of the kings of Britain descended from a dynasty based in Thrace, the homeland of Boreas. And, as we have seen, this is completely compatible with the claim regarding Brutus, since he was allegedly a descendant of Aeneas, whose wife Creusa was held to be a descendant of Boreas.

But why would the account mention Boreas, instead of mentioning Brutus, or Aeneas, or Priam, or Dardanus, or some other prominent figure in the line of descent from Boreas to Brutus? The reason is evidently because this island was viewed by the Greeks who visited it (apparently Hecataeus, in this case) as 'Hyperborea'. This place name, 'Hyperborea', was a flexible term which was used by the Greeks to apply to a number of different places to the north. The word means 'beyond the north wind', Boreas himself being the north wind. Therefore, sometimes this term was applied to the area beyond Thrace, to the north, and sometimes to other places. As we have seen, in this particular account recorded by Diodorus Siculus, it is most likely a reference to Britain. It is likely because of a desire to focus on this concept of the land being 'Hyperborea' that the one recounting what they learned about the kings of the island decided to focus on the fact that they were descended from Boreas, rather than focusing on any other individual from the line of descent.

To be clear, it is unlikely that the British kings themselves would have mentioned Boreas. But they may well have described being descended from Aeneas of Troy (since it is clear that the Etruscans definitely remembered his role in their history), or some other figure from Troy. The Greek traveller, knowing what their own mythology said about the ancestry of the dynasty of Troy and being motivated by the concept of this distant land being 'Hyperborea', would have then made the connection to Boreas.

However, some might try to argue that the only reason why this account claims that the kings of the city were descended from Boreas is actually *because* this land was considered to be Hyperborea. But this is not a convincing explanation. Hyperborea is mentioned in numerous other Greek texts, in contexts which show that it is referring to places other than Britain, and none of these describe the inhabitants of those Hyperboreas as being descended from Boreas. The Greeks considered Boreas to have had definite, specific children; it was certainly not the case that the Greeks considered the inhabitants of any land they called 'Hyperborea' to be his descendants. Such a claim is *only* found here, in this account about Britain. Furthermore, the account does not say that these Hyperboreans (of Britain) were all descended from Boreas. Rather, its claim is very specific. According to Diodorus' account, Hecataeus related specifically that the kings of that particular city were his descendants, suggesting that the common people there were not believed to be descended from him.

Thus, it is definitely not the case that the claim regarding these kings being descended from Boreas simply comes from the fact that this place was viewed as Hyperborea. The evidence we have just considered strongly indicates that there was a much more specific reason, and that it thus genuinely did have something to do with the alleged ancestry of those kings. If the legend of Brutus is true, this would offer a satisfying explanation as to how these kings were connected to Boreas.

Conclusions

In summary, we have seen that the legend of the Trojan migration to Britain is supported by copious amounts of evidence. The accounts in the *Historia Brittonum* and Geoffrey of Monmouth's *HRB* give evidence of having genuinely ancient origins, rather than being medieval inventions (seen, for example, by the description of Aeneas receiving the kingdom of the Romans rather than founding Alba Longa, and the *HRB*'s mention of a temple to Diana on Lefkada). It has been shown that the story of Brutus' travels is logical, given the evidence of Etruscan settlements in all the locations in which Trojan descendants were said to have been found by Brutus, along with evidence of Etruscans raiding the shores of Greece itself, in line with Brutus' alleged war against the Greeks.

In addition, it has been shown that there is written evidence for this migration going back to the first century BCE – with records of Trojans migrating to Gaul, combined with the modern understanding of Gallic tribes having migrated to Britain in the Iron Age, which itself is also found in traditions dating back to at least as early as the first century BCE – and even as far back as the fourth century BCE, with the claim that some of the kings were descended from Boreas of Thrace, whose descendants included the dynasty of Troy.

It has also been highlighted that there is some potential linguistic evidence for the settlement of Etruscans (Trojan descendants) among the Gauls and the Britons, in the form of the linguistic shift that occurred among those peoples which could potentially be explained by Etruscan influence. The presence of Etruscan loanwords in Celtic languages, including the word for such a basic concept as 'people', adds support to this argument.

Furthermore, the culture of the Gauls and the Britons displays evidence of their Trojan origin. We saw that Apollo was one of their chief gods by the time the Romans interacted with them and documented their beliefs around the first century BCE onwards, and he was apparently *the* chief god in Britain as early as the fourth century BCE. In addition, their Trojan origin is supported by the way in which they engaged in warfare, including their use of chariots, their technique for throwing spears, and their practice of single combat.

However, the most important and most convincing evidence of all is the archaeological evidence. It is as clear as it can possibly be that in *c.* 500 BCE, Etruscan settlers established themselves in Gaul. Whether we want the Brutus legend to be true or not, this is genuinely the most natural explanation for the sudden appearance of Etruscan-style chariots, Etruscan-style burial practices, Etruscan-style pottery and artwork, Etruscan-style architecture and sculpture, and Etruscan-style armour and weaponry in central Gaul at that time. And again, whether we like it or not, archaeology clearly shows that this elite class – or a part thereof – migrated to Britain shortly afterwards. The archaeological evidence alone makes this clear enough, but when this is combined with the other evidence, the conclusion is inescapable: in the time of Lucius Junius Brutus, a group of Trojan-descendants migrated from Italy to central Gaul, and then on to Britain, exactly as the legend of Brutus claims.

APPENDIX 1

A Small Adjustment in Assyrian and Egyptian Chronology

As Chapter 2 establishes, a comparison between the currently accepted chronology of the Near and Middle East with the continuous chronological framework found in the Bible supports the conclusion that the currently accepted chronology is, indeed, broadly correct. This comparison indicates that any revised chronology which would bring forward the chronology of nations such as Egypt by several centuries must be wrong. However, this does not necessarily mean that the conventional chronology is perfect. It could potentially be off by a few years or even a few decades. This becomes important when comparing the Greek legends with specific people and events that are placed in the era around 700 BCE. As Chapter 4 shows, legendary pharaohs of Egypt from around the time of the Trojan War can be identified with historical pharaohs of that time period. Memnon can also be understood as a military general involved in Assyria's historical invasion of Egypt and in the excursion into Anatolia to support Lydia, one of Troy's allies, in the same year.

For these reasons, it is important to establish the exact year in which events in Egyptian and Assyrian history occurred. The relative chronology between these two nations is not an issue, because the chronologies of Egypt and Assyria are intricately linked. Therefore, if one of them can be shown to require an adjustment, then the other one will automatically have to be adjusted by the same amount. The issue, then, is when it comes to the absolute chronology of these nations, because that is what will enable us to determine how it relates to the Greek legends and the chronology indicated by the Greek records.

Working from a Definitive Year

To do this, it is best to work backwards from a clearly established year. As before, the Bible's straightforward, continuous chronological record can be used to determine the exact dates of certain events before that clearly established year. One such year that we can use is the year in which Babylon was overthrown by the Persian armies of Cyrus the Great. This is universally accepted as having occurred in 539 BCE. There is strong support for this date. For example, it is found in the *Canon of Kings*, also known as *Ptolemy's Canon*, the work of Claudius Ptolemy of the second century CE. Other historians such as Diodorus, Africanus and Eusebius affirm that Cyrus' last year was in the second year of the sixty-second Olympiad, which would cover the second half of 531 to the first half of 530 BCE. According to ancient cuneiform tablets, Cyrus ruled over Babylon for nine years. Thus, counting nine years back from 531 or 530 BCE would take us to 540 or 539 BCE, supporting the 539 BCE date claimed by *Ptolemy's Canon*. The contemporary Nabonidus Chronicle informs us that this event, the overthrow of Babylon by the Persians, occurred in October. Thus, October 539 BCE is almost certainly the date in which Cyrus overthrew Babylon.[459]

With this in mind, we can see that Cyrus' 'first year' would have begun in the spring of 538 BCE. This is because of the ancient custom of differentiating between the accession year and the regnal year. The accession year began from the day the king took the throne until the end of the year (which, to the Babylonians, was in the spring). Thus, Cyrus' accession year lasted from October 539 until the spring of 538 BCE. Then his first proper year, or his first 'regnal year', began. Thus, although he conquered Babylon in 539 BCE, 'the first year of Cyrus' would generally refer to the year lasting from the spring of 538 to the spring of 537 BCE.

The reason that this is important is that the Biblical record states that Cyrus gave a decree permitting the Jews in Babylon to return to their land in his first year, most likely meaning his first regnal year. Thus, Cyrus' decree could not have been made before the spring of 538 BCE. In Ezra 3:1, the record tells us that the Jews were settled in their cities by the seventh month of the calendar year, which corresponds roughly to the second half of September and the first half of October. Ezra 7:9 indicates that the journey from Babylon to Jerusalem took about four months. If Cyrus' decree was made right at the beginning of his first regnal year, in the spring of 538 BCE, then it would be just about possible for the Jews to have travelled the four-month journey to Jerusalem before the seventh month of the year, roughly mid-September. However, this would not leave much time for the extensive preparations that would have been necessary for the Jews to leave the lives that they had established in Babylon. Therefore, a more likely scenario is that Cyrus' decree was made later on in his first regnal year, perhaps in late 538 or early 537 BCE. The Jews then would have had several months to make the necessary preparations for the journey, and then they could have arrived in Judah after a four-month journey and settled in their cities by roughly mid-September, as the Biblical narrative claims.

Length of the Babylonian Captivity

Thus, from the clearly established year of 539 BCE for the fall of Babylon, we can arrive at 537 BCE for the year in which Judah was resettled by the Jews after their captivity in Babylon. From this date, we can begin to work backwards through to the era relevant to the Trojan War. The Jews had been in captivity in Babylon for a number of decades, after the Babylonian king Nebuchadnezzar invaded and destroyed their land, including their capital, Jerusalem. If we know how long this captivity lasted, we can count back from 537 BCE to determine the year in which Jerusalem fell, which occurred in the eighteenth regnal year of Nebuchadnezzar's rule.

It is commonly claimed that the Jews were in captivity for fifty years, from 587 until 537 BCE.[460] This date for the fall of Jerusalem is established largely on the basis of *Ptolemy's Canon* showing how many kings reigned – and how long their reigns were – between Nebuchadnezzar and Nabonidus, the last king of Babylon before Cyrus conquered it. However, this chronicle is far from perfect. For instance, it is known that it omits certain kings, even ones who ruled for a significant length of time. Ptolemy's list of kings of Babylon between Kandalanu and Nabonidus places just four kings between them, but earlier documents, such as the Uruk King List, record seven kings between those rulers. Another ruler who is not mentioned even in the Uruk King List is known to have existed based on contemporary records. His name was Ashur-etil-ilani, and he is known to have reigned for four years. Yet he, too, does not appear in *Ptolemy's Canon*. Therefore, it is unquestionable that this chronicle is far from perfect.

Records from earlier historians are also used to support the conventional chronology of the kings of Babylon found in *Ptolemy's Canon*. One notable example is the Babylonian historian Berossus, who wrote the *Babyloniaca* in about 281 BCE. As an example of his inaccuracies, he claimed that King Sennacherib succeeded his brother, that his son ruled for eight years, and that his son, in turn, ruled for twenty-one years.[461] Every one of these details is inaccurate. It is now known and accepted, on the basis of earlier documents, that Sennacherib actually succeeded his father, not his brother, and that his son's reign lasted twelve years, not eight, and that his grandson ruled for twenty years, not twenty-one years. Notably, many later Greek historians made use of Berossus' writings; in fact, Berossus' writings are only known to us through references to them by later historians.

Therefore, it is clear that the literary sources available to us simply cannot be used to establish a definitive chronology of the kings of Babylon, including the period encompassing the Jewish captivity. On the other hand, the Biblical record states very clearly that the desolation of Jerusalem would last for seventy years (for example, at Daniel 9:2 and 2 Chronicles 36:21). If the Jews returned in 537 BCE, then that would place Nebuchadnezzar's destruction of Jerusalem in 607 BCE, not 587 BCE as per the conventional chronology based on the writings of ancient historians. Could the conventional chronology really be out by twenty years?

The available cuneiform tablets concerning the Babylonian kings of this period directly support the conclusion that the period spanning the Jewish captivity needs to be expanded from the traditional fifty years. For example, business tablets include a precise date, mentioning the day, month and year of the current monarch. These tablets show that Nebuchadnezzar was still reigning in the tenth month of his forty-third year, which is widely understood to have been his final year.[462] Tablets have also been found dating to the accession year (the remaining part of the year after the previous king had died) of his successor Amel-Marduk. Interestingly, these tablets are dated to the fourth and fifth months.[463] It is impossible for Amel-Marduk to have been ruling in the fourth and fifth months of the year during his accession year if Nebuchadnezzar's last year of reign continued until at least the tenth month of the year. Amel-Marduk's predecessor must have died before the fourth month of the year at the latest for Amel-Marduk's accession year to include that month.

Thus, either Nebuchadnezzar's reign actually lasted beyond his forty-third year and he died before the fourth month of a later year, or there was an otherwise unattested king between Nebuchadnezzar and Amel-Marduk who succeeded the former after the tenth month of his forty-third year (thus preserving Nebuchadnezzar's traditional reign length) and died before the fourth month of his final year (thus accounting for Amel-Marduk already being king in the fourth month of his accession year). Given the provable omission of certain kings in records such as *Ptolemy's Canon* and the Uruk King List, it is entirely possible that this latter suggestion is the correct one.

A similar 'issue' has been noted concerning the transition between Amel-Marduk and his successor, Neriglissar. There is a business tablet dated to the seventh month of Amel-Marduk's second year (his final year), and another one is dated to the tenth month.[464] Yet, a tablet has been found which dates to the second month of Neriglissar's accession year, showing that his predecessor must have died before the second month of their final year, which is clearly not the case with Amel-Marduk (unless he ruled for longer than two years).[465] This indicates that there may have been another king between those two monarchs as well. No objection to this can be made on the basis that these hypothetical extra kings and their activities do not appear in the Babylonian chronicles, for those records only cover thirty-five years of the Neo-Babylonian Empire, despite the fact that the empire is believed to have lasted for eighty-eight years. Thus, the Babylonian chronicles present a very incomplete record, easily allowing for unattested kings. In fact, direct evidence for one of these otherwise unattested kings is seen from a tablet referring to Neriglissar as the son of Bêl-shum-ishkun, referring to this figure explicitly as 'king of Babylon'.[466] It is virtually certain, then, on the basis of this tablet and the discrepancy between the months covered by Amel-Marduk's final year and those covered by Neriglissar's accession year, that this otherwise unknown Bêl-shum-ishkun reigned for an unknown period of time between Amel-Marduk and Neriglissar.

Astronomical tablets can also be used to establish when these Babylonian kings ruled. Concerning Nebuchadnezzar, whose reign is most relevant to establishing the date of the fall of Jerusalem, there is an astronomical tablet dated to the thirty-seventh year of his reign. It is known as VAT 4956. This tablet contains thirteen lunar observations along with the dates on which they were made. According to the conventional chronology, Nebuchadnezzar's thirty-seventh year ran from the spring of 568 to the spring of 567 BCE. However, the problem for supporters of the conventional chronology is that the thirteen lunar observations do not all match the reality of the moon's positions in 568/567 BCE. On the other hand, there is a perfect correspondence between all thirteen observations and the moon's positions on those dates exactly twenty years earlier, in 588/587 BCE.[467] This strongly supports the conclusion that Nebuchadnezzar's reign should be dated twenty years earlier than the conventional chronology places it.

This twenty-year discrepancy between the conventional dates and the actual dates can be applied consistently back through the reign of Nabopolassar, the predecessor of Nebuchadnezzar. The Biblical record places Nabopolassar's defeat of the Egyptians at the Battle of Carchemish in the fourth year of the reign of Judean king Jehoiakim, which was in 625 BCE according to the Bible's clear and continuous chronology (counting back from Jerusalem's destruction in 607 BCE).[468] According to a Babylonian chronicle, this occurred in Nabopolassar's twenty-first year. The conventional chronology places Nabopolassar's twenty-first year in 605 BCE, exactly twenty years later than the Biblically established date. This is very useful to know, as the following example illustrates: Nabopolassar's reign notably interacted with Assyrian history when he seized control of Babylon from Assyrian king Sinsharishkun. The conventional date for this is 626 BCE, meaning that the true date for this event must have been exactly twenty years earlier, 646 BCE.

A Further Adjustment

This being the case, we can see that all of the Babylonian, Assyrian and Egyptian kings prior to Nabopolassar should also be moved back by at least twenty years, at least insofar as they are dated relative to each other (which is usually, though not strictly always, the case) and insofar as the currently understood succession periods and reign lengths are correct. However, there is evidence that a further adjustment of eleven years is necessary as we go further back through the history of the Middle Eastern kings and their Egyptian contemporaries. Once again, it is vital to bear in mind that the current chronology is built on an analysis of cuneiform tablets, inscriptions, chronicles and descriptions by later historians. As we saw earlier, the fragmentary and imperfect nature of these records makes any chronology derived from them potentially flawed.

On the other hand, the Biblical records provide us with one continuous chronology, and no inscriptions have been found from Israel mentioning any kings who are not mentioned in the Bible, indicating that the Bible's chronology is reliable. Thus, it is a very valuable resource. With this in mind, when we count back to the reign of King Hezekiah, we see that his reign began in 745 BCE.[469] The Assyrian siege of Jerusalem – which is recorded in Assyrian as well as Biblical records – took place in the fourteenth year of Hezekiah,

A Small Adjustment in Assyrian and Egyptian Chronology

or 732 BCE, as per 2 Kings 18:13. However, the conventional chronology places this siege in 701 BCE. Assyrian records show that it occurred in Sennacherib's fifth year. When we apply the twenty-year adjustment necessary according to the true date of Jerusalem's fall to the Babylonians, in 607 BCE rather than 587 BCE, this takes Sennacherib's fifth year back to 721 BCE. Yet, that still leaves a gap of eleven years between this date and the Biblical date of 732 BCE. Thus, it appears that somewhere between Sennacherib's reign and the start of Nabopolassar's reign, there are another eleven years of extra history that should be added. This can likely be accounted for by a combination of certain kings ruling a little longer than commonly believed and the existence of a few short-lived usurpers who left no trace in the historical record.

The important question is *where*, between Sennacherib's reign and Nabopolassar's reign, these eleven years should be placed. The succession between Sennacherib and his son Esarhaddon is well recorded in contemporary inscriptions; Sennacherib was murdered by two of his sons, but then their brother, Esarhaddon, pursued and executed them, taking over as king. Thus, it is likely that Esarhaddon's reign can also be moved quite simply by thirty-one years, meaning that he reigned between 712 and 700 BCE.

The transition between Esarhaddon and his son Ashurbanipal also seems to be quite well recorded, meaning that it is unlikely that there are missing years to be found there. In fact, the most likely period for them is the period just after Ashurbanipal. The final years of his reign and the transition to the next king of Assyria is known for being shrouded in mystery. There is dispute as to when exactly he died. One common suggestion is 627 BCE (note that this is the conventional date, without any adjustment). This is based on an ancient inscription found in the city of Harran, made by the mother of King Nabonidus of Babylon, which records that Ashurbanipal ruled for forty-two years.[470] However, it is claimed that this is impossible because Assyria lost Babylon to Nabopolassar in '626' BCE (actually in 646 BCE, in line with the twenty-year adjustment of Nabopolassar's reign) and never regained it, yet inscriptions made by two of Ashurbanipal's successors have been found in Babylon, covering a span of several years. This indicates that Ashurbanipal must have died earlier, allowing time for two of his successors to rule in Babylon for several years before it was taken by Nabopolassar in '626' BCE.[471] Evidence that his death should be moved further back is the fact that the reign lengths of his successors, when added together, indicate that Ashurbanipal's final year came in '631' BCE, and no later.[472]

It is assumed that the inscription that appears to place Ashurbanipal's death in '627' BCE is in error. However, an equally obvious solution is that his reign actually started several years earlier, allowing his reign to last for as long as the inscription claims (forty-two years), while still ending well before '626' BCE (actually 646 BCE), thus allowing his successors plenty of time to rule Babylon and erect inscriptions covering several years there before Assyria lost control of that territory for the last time.

This partially helps to explain the extra eleven years between Ashurbanipal's reign and Nabopolassar's reign. By allowing Ashurbanipal the reign of forty-two years, as the inscription claims, four out of the eleven years are explained, leaving seven years still unaccounted for. Given the acknowledged uncertainty surrounding this period, it is likely that these extra seven years can be attributed to one or more unattested rulers or usurpers between Ashurbanipal and Ashur-etil-ilani (generally assumed to be his immediate successor), or between Ashur-etil-ilani and Sinsharishkun (again, assumed to be the former's immediate successor). Alternatively, Ashur-etil-ilani's reign may have lasted longer than commonly understood. It could, of course, be a combination of these reasons. The period being poorly recorded allows for such a conclusion.

To summarise so far, Sennacherib's reign can be securely placed in 736–712 BCE, thirty-one years earlier than the conventional dates, since the siege of Jerusalem occurred in 732 BCE and was, according to the Assyrian records, in his fifth year. It appears that the dates of his successor, Esarhaddon, can similarly be moved back by exactly thirty-one years, placing his reign in 712–700 BCE. His successor, Ashurbanipal, does appear to have followed Esarhaddon as commonly believed, meaning the start of his reign was in 700 BCE rather than 669 BCE. However, rather than his reign ending in 662 BCE, in line with a thirty-one-year adjustment from the commonly-stated year of 631 BCE, it appears that his reign actually ended four years later, which would be 658 BCE, in line with the reign-length given on the inscription made by Nabonidus' mother. In 646 BCE, only *twenty* years before the conventional date, Nabopolassar seized control of Babylon. This is twelve years after Ashurbanipal's death, whereas the conventional chronology places it only five years after. That leaves seven years of unattested history. Therefore, it is evident that the two Assyrian kings who reigned between Ashurbanipal's death and the capture of Babylon by Nabopolassar actually reigned for longer than previously thought, or there were one or more unrecorded rulers or usurpers within this gap, or both, thus accounting for the seven years.

The Egyptian Kings
During this period of history, Egyptian and Assyrian affairs were closely connected. Thus, whatever adjustments are necessary for one nation almost certainly apply to the other. So, what can be said for Egyptian chronology during this period?

In Chapter 4, Shebitku is identified with the legendary King Sesostris of Egypt, who was believed to have lived shortly before the Trojan War. It has long been believed that Shebitku was preceded by Shabaka, but it is now known that the reverse is true.[473] Shebitku's reign is placed in the years 713 to 704 BCE, which should be corrected to 744–735 BCE.[474] However, his reign must actually have continued until at least 732 BCE, in view of his role in the events involving Assyria's siege of Jerusalem in that year. His successor, Shabaka, must have then ruled for at least fourteen years, on the basis of contemporary inscriptions. This would presumably take his reign from 732 (if not slightly later) until at least 718 BCE. He was succeeded by Taharqa, whose reign lasted for twenty-six years. That would take his reign from 718 to 692 BCE.

However, there is a slight problem with these figures. The reader may note that these figures are only twenty-eight years earlier than the commonly assigned dates for Taharqa, not thirty-one years earlier. The reason for this is the three-year adjustment necessary in the case of Shebitku, who is known to have been reigning at the time of the Assyrian siege of Jerusalem even though his reign is commonly stated to have ended three years before that siege. When we extend his reign by three years to encompass the siege, this moves the subsequent dates forward by three years. But the problem here lies in the fact that Egyptian history is firmly intertwined with Assyrian history in this period. The last year of Taharqa is known to correspond to the first year of Psamtik (based on an inscription concerning the birth and death of an Apis bull).[475] Notably, Psamtik was appointed king after the death of Necho I, who died during a Kushite rebellion in Egypt against the Assyrians. Assyrian king Ashurbanipal crushed the rebellion and appointed Psamtik as king in place of Necho. Assyrian records confirm that this occurred in the year commonly given in modern sources as

664 BCE, which, as we have already seen, should be corrected by thirty-one years to 695 BCE.

Therefore, 695 BCE was Psamtik's first year and thus Taharqa's final year, not 692 BCE. This means that there is a three-year discrepancy between this date and the date derived when counting forward from Shebitku's final year. Thus, it is evident that there must have been a coregency at some point between Shebitku's reign and Taharqa's reign. Either Shebitku had a brief, three-year coregency with Shabaka, or Shabaka had a coregency with Taharqa. In the past, some scholars claimed for unrelated reasons that there was a coregency between Shebitku and Shabaka. Although this is now generally rejected, the existence of this three-year discrepancy indicates that this may well have been the case.

Thus, it appears that the following dates are the true dates of the Egyptian and Assyrian kings relevant to this period:

Upper Egyptian Kings
Shebitku: 744–732 BCE
Shabaka: 735–721 BCE
Taharqa: 721–695 BCE
Tantamani: 695–684 BCE

Lower Egyptian Kings
Ammeris: *c.* 734–716 BCE
Tefnakht II: *c.* 716–709 BCE
Necho I: 709–695 BCE
Psamtik I: 695–641 BCE

Assyrian Kings
Sennacherib: 736–712 BCE
Esarhaddon: 712–700 BCE
Ashurbanipal: 700–658 BCE
Possible unrecorded ruler/s
Ashur-etil-ilani: *c.* 654–650 BCE
Possible unrecorded ruler/s
Sinsharishkun: 647–632 BCE

APPENDIX 2

The Descent from Brutus

In Chapter 7, it is explained that the legendary Brutus of Britain can be identified with Lucius Junius Brutus, the historical or semi-legendary first consul of Rome. He lived in the sixth century BCE. Yet, the genealogy of Brutus contained in Geoffrey of Monmouth's *Historia Regum Britanniae* contains a record of names which would take us back to about 1350 to 1100 BCE for the birth of Brutus, using an average of twenty to twenty-five years per generation. This is consistent with the traditional date of the Trojan War, *c.* 1200 BCE, given that Brutus was said to have been the close descendant of Aeneas, a prince of Troy at the time of the Trojan War. However, as is thoroughly shown in the third, fourth and fifth chapters of this book, the Trojan War actually occurred in *c.* 700 BCE. This harmonises well with the identification of Aeneas' close descendant Brutus with Lucius Junius Brutus of the sixth century BCE. But how can we explain the fact that the genealogical record of Brutus found in the *HRB* goes back to the traditional date?

In reality, it is clearly not a coincidence that the genealogy provided in the *HRB* takes us back to the traditional date. There is clear evidence that this record has been tampered with for that very purpose. Chapter 7 of this book explains that figures from the Roman period and the post-Roman period have been taken and inserted into Brutus' genealogical record. Twenty-two examples of this were provided in that chapter, with nineteen of them representing distinct generations. However, those are not the only examples. This appendix will present a full analysis of the genealogical list of pre-Roman kings in the *HRB*, along with the most likely genuine line of descent from Brutus.

The Trojan Kings of Britain

The Genealogy of Brutus in the HRB

Brutus was said to have had three sons: Locrinus, Albanactus and Kamber. The *HRB* follows the line from Locrinus, since he is presented as the senior king of Britain. Here is the record from Locrinus onwards:

Locrinus
↓
Maddan
↓
Mempricius
↓
Ebraucus
↓
Brutus Greenshield
↓
Leil
↓
Rud Hud Hudibras
↓
Bladud
↓
Leir
↓
Regan
↓
Cunedagius
↓
Rivallo
↓
Gurgustius
↓
Sisillius I
↓
Kinmarcus
↓
Gorboduc
↓
Porrex
↓
(Civil war leading to the rise of a sub-branch of Brutus' dynasty)

Dunvallo Molmutius
↓
Belinus
↓
Gurguint Barbtruc
↓
Guithelinus
↓
Sisillius II
↓
Danius
↓
Morvidus
↓
Elidurus
↓
Gerennus
↓
Catellus
↓
Coillus
↓
Porrex II
↓
Cherin
↓
Andragius
↓
Urianus
↓
Eliud
↓
Cledaucus
↓
Clotenus
↓

Gurgintius
↓
Merianus
↓
Bledudo
↓
Caph
↓
Oenus
↓
Sisillius III
↓
Archmail
↓
Eldol
↓
Redion
↓
Rederchius
↓
Samuil Penissel
↓
Pir
↓
Capoir
↓
Digueillus
↓
Heli
↓
Caswallon

The Descent from Brutus

This last king, Caswallon, is identical to Cassivellaunus, the historical king who fought against Caesar in his invasion of Britain in 54 BCE. Therefore, we can conclude that his father, 'Heli' according to the *HRB*, was born in *c.* 100 BCE. Fifty generations back to Brutus would place his birth in *c.* 1350-1100 BCE. This means that a span of at least 550 years needs to be removed from this genealogical list, given that the historical Brutus was actually born around *c.* 550 BCE. Therefore, there are around thirty generations too many in this list. It should actually be around twenty names long rather than fifty names long.

The following names can be removed with certainty on the basis of their epithets, clearly identifying them as kings from the post-Roman era: Dunvallo Molmutius, Samuil Penissel and Gurguint Barbtruc.

These are the kings who can be definitely removed on the basis of a sequence of names matching, or nearly matching, a sequence from the post-Roman era: Gorboduc and Brennius (from the sequence 'Bran ap Dyfnwal ap Garbanion'), Merianus and Bledudo (from the sequence 'Bleiddud ap Meirion'), Pir and Capoir (from the sequence 'Pybyr ap Caper'), Cledaucus and Clotenus (from the sequence 'Clydog ap Clydwyn') and Cunegadius and Henwinus (from the sequence 'Einion ap Cunedda').

More pre-Roman figures can be removed on these two bases, such as Enniaunus and his second successor Runo (almost definitely Einion and his successor Rhun), but these are not part of the main genealogical sequence. So, from the main genealogical sequence, we can see that twelve generations (not thirteen, due to Henwinus not being part of the main list) can be definitely removed, due to their epithets and the sequences of names. This brings the total down to thirty-eight generations.

The following names can be removed on the basis that their names are relatively distinctive, and also often on the basis of their associates: Elidurus (Elidir, the father of Peredur, presented as his brother in the *HRB*), Urianus (Urien Rheged), Catellus (probably Cadell son of Urien), Coillus (probably Coel Hen), Caph (probably Cof, son of Caw), Rederchius (Rhydderch Hael), Eldol (possibly Eidol, a prince of the Old North mentioned in *Y Gododdin*), Archmail (either the sixth-century king of part of Glywysing, or an earlier king of that name in the ancestry of Gwrgan Fawr of Ergyng), Redion (Rheidon, father of Ceindrech), Gerennus (probably Geraint, son of Erbin, king of Dumnonia), Kinmarcus (Cynfarch the father of Urien Rheged) and Guithelinus (Gwidolin the grandfather of Vortigern).

To add to these, Ebraucus is certainly Brychan; they are both assigned a shockingly high number of wives, son and daughters, and 'Ebraucus' is reasonably explained as a Latin version of 'Brychan', also

The Trojan Kings of Britain

influenced by the desire to connect the name to the origin of the place name 'Caerebrauc' (Eboracum). This connection is confirmed by the fact that several of Ebraucus' daughters have names which are only shared by some of Brychan's recorded daughters.[476]

This leaves us with twenty-four generations between Brutus and Heli. The list is now close to being accurate, although it is still too long. Starting from *c.* 100 BCE, counting back twenty-four generations would bring us to 700–580 BCE. Clearly, another four generations or so need to be removed for the chronology to work. As pointed out in Chapter 7, a genealogical list which is evidently much closer to the truth than the *HRB*'s list is found in the *Hanes Gruffydd ap Cynan*. This presents only twenty names between Brutus and Beli (the Welsh equivalent of Geoffrey's 'Heli'). This perfectly takes us back to Lucius Junius Brutus when using an average of about twenty-two or twenty-three years per generation. Scholar Peter Bartrum stated in *A Welsh Classical Dictionary* that this list is probably 'a pre-Geoffrey pseudo-history'.[477] Whether it is 'pseudo'-history or not is clearly a matter for debate, but the key point here is that Bartrum acknowledged that this list is likely from before the *HRB*, even though the document itself was written afterwards.

The first parts of both lists are very similar, although there are two highly interesting differences. Here is the beginning of the genealogical list as found in the *HRB*:

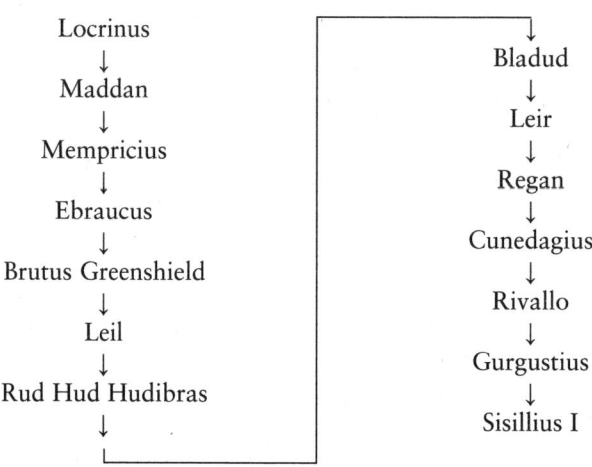

The Descent from Brutus

In the *Hanes Gruffydd ap Cynan*, the beginning of the list is very similar, although with two very notable differences:

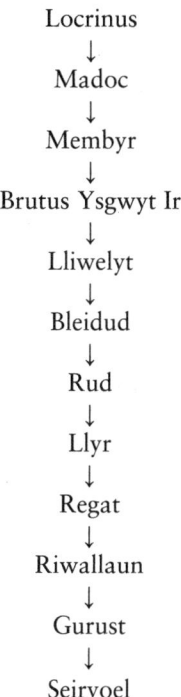

Locrinus
↓
Madoc
↓
Membyr
↓
Brutus Ysgwyt Ir
↓
Lliwelyt
↓
Bleidud
↓
Rud
↓
Llyr
↓
Regat
↓
Riwallaun
↓
Gurust
↓
Seiryoel

Many of the names are spelt differently, although there is nothing unusual in that. Also, Rud and Bladud in the *HRB* are seen in the reverse order in the *Hanes Gruffydd ap Cynan*. This is peculiar, but similar reverses are seen in other genealogical records. The two most notable differences by far are the absence of both Ebraucus and Cunedagius. These two figures appear in the *HRB*, but they do not appear in this alternative list. As we saw, Ebraucus and Cunedagius were the two characters from this section who were clearly taken from records about post-Roman figures. The fact that they are not included in this alternative list supports its accuracy, indicating that it really does preserve a more authentic genealogical record. With that in mind, let us now compare the rest of both lists (overleaf):

The Trojan Kings of Britain

Porrex
↓
(Civil war leading to the rise of a sub-branch of Brutus' dynasty)
↓
Sisillius II
↓
Danius
↓
Morvidus
↓
Porrex II
↓
Cherin
↓
Andragius
↓
Eliud
↓
Gurgintius
↓
Oenus
↓
Sisillius III
↓
Digueillus
↓
Heli

Note that this version of the list has the spurious insertions from the post-Roman era already excluded, hence why it is much shorter than the earlier presentation of the list from Porrex onwards. Now, here is the equivalent list in the *Hanes Gruffydd ap Cynan*:

Antonius
↓
Aet Mawr
↓
Prydein
↓
Dyvynarth
↓
Kryton
↓
Kerwyt
↓
Eneit
↓
Manogan
↓
Beli Mawr

The Descent from Brutus

As can be seen, this is four names shorter than the version from the *HRB*. The list as a whole is also very different from the equivalent list from the *HRB*. In fact, at first glance, it looks like the lists share almost no similarities at all. However, it is possible to connect them. At the end, of course, we can see Heli and Beli Mawr, who are clearly identical (and 'Beli Mawr' is indeed the name used in Welsh records instead of 'Heli'). The father of this character is called 'Manogan' in the second list, but as Chapter 1 explains, this is demonstrably the result of a series of scribal mistakes. The *HRB* evidently preserves the genuine name of this figure. Interestingly, Julius Caesar stated that within living memory of *c.* 55 BCE, the most powerful man of Gaul was a king named Diviciacus, who ruled not only over much of Gaul but also over parts of Britain as well.[478] The *HRB*'s 'Digueillus' is a perfect chronological match for Diviciacus, and the similarity of their names supports the conclusion that they are one and the same.

Before Digueillus, the *HRB* lists (going in reverse chronological order) Sisillius, Oenus and Gurgintius. It appears that two of these three figures can be identified with the two figures preceding Manogan in the list from *Hanes Gruffydd ap Cynan*: Eneit and Kerwyt. Although the Welsh translations of the *HRB* use 'Owain' for Geoffrey's 'Oenus', that is completely different from the form Geoffrey uses for a figure who genuinely was known by the Welsh name 'Owain'. When Geoffrey referred to that figure, Owain ap Urien, he spelt his name 'Eventus'. On that basis, it seems reasonable to suggest that Geoffrey's 'Oenus' is not actually a form of the name 'Owain'. Rather, it may well be a garbled form of the 'Eneit' found before Manogan (or 'Eneit' may be a garbled form of the original Brythonic name of which 'Oenus' is a Latin version).

The list in the *Hanes Gruffydd ap Cynan* places 'Kerwyt' before Eneit. It seems likely that he can be identified with the 'Gurgintius' who appears before Oenus in the version from the *HRB*. Consider the fact that the similar name 'Gurgustius' is written as 'Gorust' in the Welsh versions of Geoffrey's account, showing the disappearance of the middle 'g'. In fact, the Welsh versions used 'Gorwst' in exchange for 'Gurgintius' as well, again showing the disappearance of the middle 'g'. Let it be noted, though, that Geoffrey's spelling definitely does not contain an 's', unlike 'Gurgustius'. This indicates that the true Welsh name of which Geoffrey's 'Gurgintius' is a Latin version may have become something like 'Gorwt' rather than 'Gorwst'. Given that the letter 'n' was quite frequently transformed into the letter 'u' (and vice versa) by careless scribes, the disappearance of the 'n' is not surprising. Therefore, 'Kerwyt' could easily be a corruption of the Brythonic name that 'Gurgintius' is an attempt to Latinise.

With 'Oenus' tied to 'Eneit' and 'Gurgintius' linked to 'Kerwyt', that leaves five preceding generations in the *Hanes* list that need to be connected to some of the eight preceding names in the *HRB* list (evidently 'Sisillius III' is an insertion from a later period – either Seisyll ap Clydog of the seventh century CE or Seisyll ap Euddyn Ddu of the fifth century CE). Working forward this time, from the Antonius of the *Hanes* list, the closest apparent match within this section of the *HRB* list is Danius. It appears that the first part of the name 'Antonius' has been clipped, just like how the last part of the name 'Lliwelyt' (seen earlier in the *Hanes* list) was clipped to create the 'Leil' that appears in the *HRB*, as seen from the earlier comparison of the first part of both lists. This shorter 'Tonius' was then evidently transformed into the more familiar 'Danius'. This would indicate that the two names before Danius – Sisillius II and Porrex – are insertions from later periods. Sisillius II must be either Seisyll ap Clydog or Seisyll ap Euddyn Ddu (whichever one Sisillius III was not taken from).

Porrex is far more difficult to identify. The closest name in Peter Bartrum's *A Welsh Classical Dictionary* is Peris. However, he is recorded as a saint and does not seem to have any known connections to any royal family. All of the other spurious names that we have seen so far have been taken from royal families, meaning that this identification is unlikely. A more likely possibility is Peirio. He is also recorded as a saint, but he was supposedly the son of Caw, a king of part of the North, meaning that Peirio would have been a northern prince just like numerous other figures whose names were inserted into the pre-Roman era in the *HRB*.[479]

In any case, moving forwards from Antonius, the next person in the *Hanes* list is Aet Mawr. This figure is usually recorded in modern sources with the spelling 'Aedd Mawr'. He appears in other sources as the father of Prydain (as shown in the *Hanes* list as well), about whom more is said in the sources. But nothing more is known about Aedd Mawr himself. However, it has been suggested that his name derives from 'Addedomarus', the name of a historical pre-Roman king whose name appears on some coins found in Britain. This historical

The Descent from Brutus

king cannot be identical to Aedd Mawr, for chronological reasons, but there is nonetheless a definite similarity between the names. It is reasonable to conclude that Aedd Mawr's historical name probably was identical to the name of this genuine pre-Roman king, although he was not the same person. However, how does he connect to Geoffrey's list of pre-Roman kings? Well, Aedd Mawr appears after Antonius in the *Hanes* list. If Antonius was Danius, then perhaps Aedd Mawr was simply the king who appears after Danius – that is, Morvidus. This does seem like the most likely solution. The name 'Morvidus' is likely a garbled Latin version of the second part of the name 'Aedd Mawr'. Although 'Mawr' is actually a title and not a name, if the original form was 'Addedomarus', then the second part *was* actually part of the name. Thus, just like how the name 'Freothulf' was shortened into 'Ulf', the name 'Addedomarus' could have been shortened into simply 'Marus', which was then expanded into the garbled Latin form 'Morvidus'.

That now leaves just three names in the *Hanes* list to be connected to some of the four remaining names in the version from the *HRB*. The three names in the *Hanes* list are, in chronological order, Prydein, Dyvynarth and Kryton. The four names in the version from the *HRB* are Porrex II, Cherin, Andragius and Eliud. Out of these, the first names in both groups seem to be a match – Porrex and Prydain. They both begin with 'P', then followed by an 'r' (although 'Porrex' has a vowel in between), and then the 'r' is followed by a vowel. Although they are otherwise quite dissimilar, other names in the *HRB* are also peculiarly dissimilar from their original forms. For example, the brother of Urien Rheged was called 'Arawn' in Welsh sources, yet the *HRB* refers to him as 'Augusel'. Thus, the name 'Porrex' could well be Geoffrey's distorted form of 'Prydain'. Additionally, it needs to be born in mind that 'Prydain' is the Welsh name for 'Britain'. In fact, the character 'Prydain ap Aedd Mawr' appears in certain Welsh records as a founding figure in the history of Britain, the one who gave his name to the island. Given that this directly contradicts the narrative in the *HRB* about Brutus giving his name to Britain, it may well be that Geoffrey intentionally obscured the name of this character so as to avoid this contradiction.

As to who Prydain actually was and why he had a name which is simply the Welsh form of 'Britain', it appears that he really was an important founding figure in the history of Britain. But rather than him giving his name to the island, it appears that he was given the name 'Prydain' in the records specifically because of his role as a founding figure. Evidently his true name was something else. This would be similar to how Aulus Plautius came to be known in legend as 'Lelius Hamo', the second part coming from the mistaken belief that he died at Southampton.

In Irish legend, Prydain appears as 'Britain Mael'. He is portrayed as the son of Fergus Red-Side, the son of Nemed. 'Britain Mael' appears in Irish legend as the founder of Britain, just like Prydain in Welsh legend. In the Irish version, Nemed sails from the Near East and arrives in Ireland. His migration party is eventually all but slaughtered after besieging a tower, and one surviving part of his family (led by Britain Mael) travels to Britain and populates that country.

Interestingly, the earliest version of this legend is actually found not in an Irish record but in the *Historia Brittonum*. It is not exactly the same, but it is very similar. Nemed appears as 'Nimech'. He is said to have travelled from Spain to Ireland, but then after some time, he and his followers returned to Spain. Some time later, the sons of an unnamed Spanish soldier travelled to Ireland. In the sea, they encountered a tower and decided to besiege it. However, just like in the Irish version, the attackers were slaughtered, with only a few small groups surviving. This part of the account then concludes:

> Ireland, however, was peopled, to the present period, from the family remaining in the vessel which was wrecked. Afterwards, others came from Spain, and possessed themselves of various parts of Britain.

The 'others who came from Spain' and migrated to Britain just after this slaughter at the tower clearly corresponds to the part of the Irish version that tells of Britain Mael leading a small group of survivors to the island of Britain after the slaughter at the siege of the tower. The only major difference between the two versions is that the earliest version, from the *Historia Brittonum*, does not directly connect the group that migrated to Britain with the survivors of the slaughter at the tower – though they are still part of the same overall group from Spain – whereas the Irish version does directly connect them. But whether the settlers migrated directly from Spain or went with the other group to Ireland first and then travelled to Britain after the slaughter at the tower, they are clearly both relating the same basic tale. Thus, the line in the *Historia Brittonum* that 'others came from Spain, and possessed themselves of various parts of Britain' is a direct reference to the legend of Britain Mael. To put it another way, this is a reference to the legend of the migration of Prydain ap Aedd Mawr.

It seems that this migration also appears in the *HRB*. Recall that, although it is not presented this way in the *HRB* itself, the evidence indicates that Geoffrey's Morvidus actually came immediately before Porrex. Thus, Morvidus is identified with Aedd Mawr and Porrex is identified with Prydain. The Irish version of the legend explicitly makes Britain Mael the son of a man named Fergus, not Aedd Mawr. Even in the Welsh version, the very fact that he was said to have migrated to Britain indicates that he was not part of the existing line of kings descended from Brutus. Evidently he was 'ap Aedd Mawr' in the sense that he was actually his successor, not his son. This being the case, let us return to the point about this migration appearing in the *HRB*. Geoffrey's account of Morvidus' life ends with a description of him being killed by a 'monster' that came from the Irish Sea. This story may well originate with a figurative account of the migration and subsequent conquest by the group that came from Ireland (or that came from Spain but was associated with the group that went to Ireland, as the version in the *Historia Brittonum* presents it).

When in history did this take place? Given that Prydain appears six generations before Beli Mawr, whose birth can be placed in *c.* 100 BCE, Prydain should have been born somewhere between 250 and 220 BCE. If we assume that he was about twenty-five years old at the time of his migration to Britain, we can see that this migration apparently occurred in the final quarter of the third century BCE. This appears to correspond to the second wave of La Tène culture arriving in Britain and Ireland, which occurred in *c.* 200 BCE and brought with it more of the stylistic elements which, for unknown reasons, did not make any impact during the first wave of *c.* 500–450 BCE.[480] The La Tène culture had already spread to Spain, albeit to a limited degree, by 200 BCE, so a migration to Ireland and Britain at that time would logically have brought that culture along with it, and that is exactly what we see in the archaeology of those two islands at that time.

Although this is substantially later than the Irish legends place it, it appears that these Irish legends suffer from the same problem as the *HRB*; the early part of Ireland's history has been artificially extended. In reality, the earlier version found in the *Historia Brittonum* supports this late date, by placing it 'long after' the time in which Brutus was governing the Romans (*c.* 500 BCE). In fact, it is actually the first legendary migration of Scots that was said to have taken place 'long after' Brutus, with the one led by Nimech (the Nemed of Irish legend) that resulted in a settlement of Britain being the second legendary migration. Thus, the *Historia Brittonum* places this settlement by Britain Mael, or Prydain, considerably later than 500 BCE, the time of Brutus. A date towards the end of the third century BCE is consistent with this.

Interestingly, Geoffrey mentions another interesting incident in the life of Morvidus (Aedd Mawr), just before the story of him being killed by the 'monster' from the Irish Sea (evidently Prydain's invasion). Geoffrey describes how Morvidus fought off an invasion by the king of the Morini that occurred in Northumberland. The Morini was a Belgic tribe. Therefore, this account portrays an invasion by a Belgic tribe in the final part of the third century BCE. It is known, based on coinage evidence, that Belgic tribes first started settling in the south of Britain in *c.* 200 BCE.[481] There is no historical evidence for Belgic tribes settling in the north of the country at any period. However, the account in the *HRB* presents this incident as a raid, not anything that established a permanent settlement – in fact, the account makes it clear that the Morini were driven out of that region immediately after they arrived. But the key point is that the idea of a Belgic raid into Northumberland is plausible in the era in which the Belgae first started settling in the south of the country, which was *c.* 200 BCE, exactly when the corrected chronology in the *HRB* indicates that this story is set.

To move on from Prydain, we are left with two figures from the *Hanes Gruffydd ap Cynan* list that need to be identified with people from Geoffrey's list. These two figures are Dyvynarth and Kryton. The three figures in the equivalent part of the *HRB*'s list that still need to be identified are Cherin, Andragius and Eliud. One of these names must be taken from later times, and the most likely option is Eliud. This name was probably taken from a prince of Powys in the late sixth century CE named Eiludd ap Cynan Garwyn. The remaining two figures in each list can presumably be identified with each other, although the names seem to indicate that the situation is not quite as simple as that. Given the complete dissimilarity between

'Dyvynarth' and 'Cherin', and between 'Kryton' and 'Andragius', it appears that one of these pairs has been swapped. As noted before, it is not too unusual to see father-and-son pairs being swapped around accidentally. In fact, we saw this earlier, where the *HRB* has Rud and Bladud in the reverse order as that found in the *Hanes* list. It appears that the same thing has occurred here.

Therefore, the *HRB*'s Cherin appears to match the Kryton of the *Hanes* list – the names are clearly similar enough to allow for one to be a corruption of the other, or for both to be slight corruptions of the original form. On the other hand, 'Andragius' is not particularly similar to 'Dyvynarth'. It is possible that the final part of the latter name is linked to the first part of the former name. However, this is not a strong connection. It is possible that these are just alternative names given to represent the same person, for whatever reason, just as the father of Heli is called Digueillus in the *HRB*, while he is called Manogan in the *Hanes* list (and other examples of isolated name changes are found in many other genealogical records). In any case, they can be understood to refer to the same figure.

It is known that many of the tribes of the south of Britain by the time of Caesar's invasion were actually Belgic tribes. This includes the Catuvellauni, the tribe whose kings include the final individuals in the list of descent from Brutus.[482] Thus, one of the rulers prior to Cassivellaunus must have been unrelated to the previous dynasty, with the 'ap' simply denoting their place as a successor, not a son, just as how we saw earlier that Prydain was evidently not actually the son of Aedd Mawr. It is impossible to know which king between Prydain and Caswallon established this new Belgic dynasty. However, the earliest Belgic ruler who is known to have been powerful in Britain is Diviciacus, the historical king mentioned by Caesar as being the most powerful king in living memory and as ruling parts of Britain and Gaul. His name and the chronology clearly identify him as the Digueillus of the *HRB*. In the absence of any clear evidence of significant Belgic power in Britain before then, we can consider Digueillus to be the founder of this new Belgic dynasty, even though this cannot be confirmed.

One final correction that needs to be made is the removal of Locrinus right at the start of the list. Rather than actually being Brutus' son, he appears to be a misplaced version of the historical figure Spurius Lucretius Tricipitinus, as explained in Chapter 7. With all of this in mind, the following would seem to be the true

The Trojan Kings of Britain

list of descent and succession from Brutus, using the names found in the *Historia Regum Britanniae* and providing their approximate birth years:

Maddan	*c.* 496 BCE
Mempricius	*c.* 474 BCE
Brutus Greenshield	*c.* 452 BCE
Leil	*c.* 430 BCE
Bladud	*c.* 408 BCE
Rud Hud Hudibras	*c.* 386 BCE
Leir	*c.* 364 BCE
Regan	*c.* 342 BCE
Rivallo	*c.* 320 BCE
Gurgustius	*c.* 298 BCE
Sisillius	*c.* 276 BCE
Danius	*c.* 254 BCE
Morvidus	*c.* 232 BCE
Porrex	*c.* 232 BCE (not the son of the former, but the founder of a new dynasty from the continent)
Cherin	*c.* 210 BCE
Andragius	*c.* 188 BCE
Gurgintius	*c.* 166 BCE
Oenus	*c.* 144 BCE
Digueillus	*c.* 144 BCE (not the son of the former, but the founder of a new dynasty from the continent)
Heli	*c.* 122 BCE

Notes

1. Stirling, Brent, *Do Fences Make Good Neighbors? What History Teaches Us about Strategic Barriers and International Security* (Washington, DC: Georgetown University Press, 2009), pp. 92, 93.
2. The *HB*'s Constantius, along with the *HRB*'s Constantine, have commonly been assumed to be poor descriptions of the historical usurper Constantine III. However, this is unlikely; as scholar Peter Bartrum noted in *A Welsh Classical Dictionary*, the literary characters bear virtually no similarities at all to the historical usurper of the fifth century.
3. Ashley, Mike, *A Brief History of King Arthur* (London: Constable & Robson Ltd, 2010).
4. Brewer, Douglas, *The Archaeology of Ancient Egypt: Beyond Pharaohs* (New York: Cambridge University Press, 2012), p. 16.
5. Mandzuka, Zlatko, *Demystifying the Odyssey* (Bloomington: AuthorHouse UK Ltd, 2013), p. 115.
6. *Insight on the Scriptures* Volume I (New York: Watchtower Bible and Tract Society of New York, 2018), pp. 776, 777.
7. Kaiser, Walter, *History of Israel* (Tennessee: Broadman & Holman Publishers, 1998), p. 62.
8. Lawrence, Paul, *The Books of Moses Revisited* (Oregon: Wipf & Stock, 2011), p. 44.
9. Hoffmeier, James, *Israel in Egypt: Evidence for the Authenticity of the Exodus Tradition* (New York: Oxford University Press, 1999), p. 68.
10. Bar, Shay; Khan, Daniel; and Shirley, JJ, *Egypt, Canaan and Israel: History, Imperialism, Ideology and Literature: Proceedings of a Conference at the University of Haifa, 3-7 May 2009* (Leiden: Koninklijke Brill, 2011), p. 30.

11. *The Watchtower* March 2020 (New York: Watchtower Bible and Tract Society of New York, 2019), p. 30.
12. Hoffmeier, James, *Israel in Egypt: Evidence for the Authenticity of the Exodus Tradition* (New York: Oxford University Press, 1999), p. 61.
13. Hoffmeier, James, *Israel in Egypt: Evidence for the Authenticity of the Exodus Tradition* (New York: Oxford University Press, 1999), p. 87.
14. Hess, Richard; Klingbiel, Gerald; and Ray Jr, Paul, *Critical Issues in Early Israelite History* (Pennsylvania: Eisenbrauns, 2008), p. 91.
15. Kitchen, Kenneth, *On the Reliability of the Old Testament* (Michigan: Wm. B. Eerdmans Publishing Company, 2003), pp. 149, 150.
16. There are a minority of scholars, notably Israel Finkelstein, who argue that these casemate systems actually date from the time of King Omri in the ninth century BCE. However, the majority opinion, headed by renowned Egyptologist and Biblical scholar Kenneth Kitchen, is still that these structures date from Solomon's time.
17. Hoffmeier, James, *Israel in Egypt: Evidence for the Authenticity of the Exodus Tradition* (New York: Oxford University Press, 1999), p. 87.
18. Dever, William and Gitin, Seymour, *Symbiosis, Symbolism, and the Power of the Past: Canaan, Ancient Israel, and Their Neighbors from the Late Bronze Age through Roman Palaestina* (Pennsylvania: Eisenbrauns, 2003), p. 124.
19. Ibid.
20. Melchert, Craig, *The Luwians* (Leiden: Brill, 2003), p. 67.
21. Schofield, Louise, *The Mycenaeans* (London: The British Museum Press, 2007), p. 194.
22. Herodotus 2.145.4.
23. Kokkinos, Nikos, *Ancient Chronology, Eratosthenes and the Dating of the Fall of Troy – Ancient West & East* Volume 8 (Leiden: Brill, 2009), p. 44.
24. Compare Diodorus 2.22.2 with 2.23.1 (note that Diodorus was recounting Ctesias' account of Assyrian history).
25. Compare Diodorus 2.21.8 (in the original Greek) with 2.22.2.
26. The total for the Median kings who came before Cyrus recorded by Ctesias as found in Diodorus 2.32.6 and 34.1.6, along with Herodotus' figure for the final reign length which is otherwise lost, comes to 317 years. Adding that onto Ctesias' date of 590 BCE for Cyrus' accession takes us back to 907 BCE for the start of the first Median king's reign, which corresponds by definition to the Fall of Nineveh.
27. Kokkinos, Nikos, *Ancient Chronology, Eratosthenes and the Dating of the Fall of Troy – Ancient West & East* Volume 8 (Leiden: Brill, 2009), pp. 44-46.

Notes

28. Finkelstein, Jacob and Greenberg, Moshe, *Oriental and Biblical Studies: Collected Writings of E. A. Speiser* (Philadelphia: University of Pennsylvania Press, 1967), p. 51.
29. Parker, Robert and Steele, Philippa, *The Early Greek Alphabets: Origin, Diffusion, Uses* (Oxford: Oxford University Press, 2021), p. 89.
30. Herodotus placed the fall of Nineveh in 710 BCE, and he assigned 520 years to the Assyrian Empire, thus placing its start in the thirteenth century BCE. This would place Ninus, supposedly the first king of the Assyrian Empire, in the very same century as Tukulti-Ninurta I.
31. Connor-Linton, Jeff and Fasold, Ralph, *An Introduction to Language and Linguistics: Second Edition* (Cambridge: Cambridge University Press, 2014), p. 436.
32. Ogden, Daniel, *The Oxford Handbook of Heracles* (New York: Oxford University Press, 2021), p. 414.
33. Johnston, Sarah, *Ancient Greek Divination* (Chichester: Wiley-Blackwell, 2008), p. 62.
34. Wilson, Nigel, *Encyclopedia of Ancient Greece* (Oxford: Routledge, 2010), p. 116.
35. Livy 45.9.
36. Herodotus 8.137.
37. Thucydides 2.100.2.
38. Roisman, Joseph and Worthington, Ian, *A Companion to Ancient Macedonia* (Chichester: Wiley-Blackwell, 2010), p. 128.
39. Herodotus 8.138.
40. *Epitome of the Philippic History of Pompeius Trogus* 7.1, 2.
41. Pausanias 2.13.1, 2.
42. Bachvarova, Mary, *From Hittite to Homer: The Anatolian Background of Ancient Greek Epic* (Cambridge: Cambridge University Press, 2016), p. 435, 436.
43. Gagarin, Michael and Fantham, Elaine, *The Oxford Encyclopedia of Ancient Greece* Volume I (New York: Oxford University Press, 2010), p. 89.
44. Henry, Roger, *Synchronized Chronology: Rethinking Middle East Antiquity* (New York: Algora Publishing, 2003), p. 122.
45. Herodotus 6.127.
46. Pausanias 2.19.2.
47. Buckley, Terry, *Aspects of Greek History 750-323 BC: A source-based approach* (London: Routledge, 1996), p. 55.
48. Diodorus 7.17.1.
49. Diodorus 4.49.1.
50. Norwich, John, *The Middle Sea: A History of the Mediterranean* (London: Vintage Books, 2007), p. 54.

51. Manning, Joseph, *The Open Sea: The Economic Life of the Ancient Mediterranean World from the Iron Age to the Rise of Rome* (New Jersey: Princeton University Press, 2018), p. 243.
52. Powell, Anton, *A Companion to Sparta* Volume I (Chichester: Wiley-Blackwell, 2018), p. 62.
53. Bradford, James, *International Encyclopedia of Military History* (New York: Routledge, 2006), p. 864.
54. Conon *Narrations* 13.
55. Hammond, Nicholas, *A History of Macedonia: Historical Geography and Prehistory* (Oxford: Clarendon Press, 1972), p. 426.
56. Strabo 6.1.15.
57. Domenico, Roy, *The Regions of Italy: A Reference Guide to History and Culture* (Connecticut: Greenwood Press, 2002), p. 38.
58. Wood, Jeryldene, *Ippolita Maria Sforza: The Renaissance Princess Who Linked Milan and Naples* (North Carolina: Mcfarland & Company, 2020), p. 96.
59. Fragoulaki, Maria, *Kingship in Thucydides: Intercommunal Ties and Historical Narrative* (Oxford: Oxford University Press, 2013), p. 314.
60. Ibid.
61. Hughes, Jessica and Buongiovanni, Claudio, *Remembering Parthenope: The Reception of Classical Naples from Antiquity to the Present* (Oxford: Oxford University Press, 2015), p. 22.
62. Gagarin, Michael and Fantham, Elaine, *The Oxford Encyclopedia of Ancient Greece* Volume I (New York: Oxford University Press, 2010), p. 184.
63. Murray, Carrie, *Diversity of Sacrifice: Form and Function of Sacrificial Practices in the Ancient World and Beyond* (New York: State University of New York Press, 2016), p. 104.
64. López-Ruiz, Carolina and Doak, Brian, *The Oxford Handbook of the Phoenician and Punic Mediterranean* (New York: Oxford University Press, 2019), p. 142.
65. Appian *The Punic Wars* I
66. Strabo 12.8.7
67. Kirby, Mayson, *History of Civilizations* (Waltham Abbey: ED-Tech Press, 2018), p. 70.
68. Thucydides 1.12, 13
69. Parker, Victor, *A History of Greece: 1300 to 30 BC* (Chichester: John Wiley & Sons, 2014), p. 53.
70. Stillwell, Richard and Macdonald, William, *The Princeton Encyclopedia of Classical Sites* (New Jersey: Princeton University Press, 1976), p. 91.
71. Hansen, Mogens and Nielsen, Thomas, *An Inventory of Archaic and Classical Poleis* (Oxford: Oxford University Press, 2004), p. 693.
72. *Argonautica Orphica*, 143

Notes

73. Morgan, Catherine, *Early Greek States Beyond the Polis* (London: Routledge, 2003), p. 103.
74. Brown, Jonathan, *In Search of Homeric Ithaca* (Canberra: Parrot Press, 2020), p. 14.
75. Ibid.
76. De Jong, Irene, *Homer: Critical Assessments* Volume II – *The Homeric World* (London: Routledge, 1999), p. 14.
77. Wilson, Nigel, *Encyclopedia of Ancient Greece* (Oxford: Routledge, 2010), p. 91.
78. Brown, Jonathan, *In Search of Homeric Ithaca* (Canberra: Parrot Press, 2020), p. 14.
79. Cooke, Tim, *The New Cultural Atlas of the Greek World* (New York: Marshall Cavendish, 2010), p. 59.
80. *The New Encyclopaedia Britannica* Volume I (Illinois: Encyclopaedia Britannica, 2005), p. 546.
81. Miller, Molly, *The Sicilian Colony Dates* (New York: State University of New York Press, 1970), p. 230.
82. van Wees, Hans, *The Homeric Way of War: The Iliad and the Hoplite Phalanx (II) – Greece & Rome*, Second Series, Volume 41, Issue 2 (Cambridge: Cambridge University Press, 1994), pp. 143-145.
83. van Wees, Hans, *The Homeric Way of War: The Iliad and the Hoplite Phalanx (II) – Greece & Rome*, Second Series, Volume 41, Issue 2 (Cambridge: Cambridge University Press, 1994), p. 131.
84. Taylor, Richard, *The Greek Hoplite Phalanx: The Iconic Heavy Infantry of Classical Greece* (Yorkshire: Pen & Sword History, 2021), p. 12.
85. Connolly, Peter, *The Ancient Greece of Odysseus* (Oxford: Oxford University Press, 1999), p. 32.
86. Kagan, Donald and Viggiano, Gregory, *Men of Bronze: Hoplite Warfare in Ancient Greece* (New Jersey: Princeton University Press, 2013), p. 99.
87. De Jong, Irene, *Homer: Critical Assessments* Volume II – *The Homeric World* (London: Routledge, 1999), p. 16.
88. Cleland, Liza; Davies, Glenys; and Llewellyn-Jones, Lloyd, *Greek and Roman Dress from A to Z* (Abingdon: Routledge, 2007), p. 10.
89. van Wees, Hans, *The Homeric Way of War: The Iliad and the Hoplite Phalanx (II) – Greece & Rome*, Second Series, Volume 41, Issue 2 (Cambridge: Cambridge University Press, 1994), p. 135.
90. De Jong, Irene, *Homer: Critical Assessments* Volume II – *The Homeric World* (London: Routledge, 1999), p. 16.
91. van Wees, Hans, *The Homeric Way of War: The Iliad and the Hoplite Phalanx (II) – Greece & Rome*, Second Series, Volume 41, Issue 2 (Cambridge: Cambridge University Press, 1994), p. 138.
92. van Wees, Hans, *The Homeric Way of War: The Iliad and the Hoplite Phalanx (II) – Greece & Rome*, Second Series, Volume 41,

Issue 2 (Cambridge: Cambridge University Press, 1994), pp. 138, 152.
93. van Wees, Hans, *The Homeric Way of War: The Iliad and the Hoplite Phalanx (II) – Greece & Rome*, Second Series, Volume 41, Issue 2 (Cambridge: Cambridge University Press, 1994), p. 146.
94. De Jong, Irene, *Homer: Critical Assessments* Volume II – *The Homeric World* (London: Routledge, 1999), p. 17.
95. Ibid.
96. Rose, Charles, *The Archaeology of Greek and Roman Troy* (New York: Cambridge University Press, 2014), p. 52.
97. Grainger, John, *The Straits from Troy to Constantinople: The Ancient History of the Dardanelles, Sea of Marmara & Bosporos* (Yorkshire: Pen & Sword History, 2021), p. 30.
98. Muscarella, Oscar, *The Date of the Destruction of the Early Phrygian Period – Ancient West & East*, Volume II, No. 2 (Leiden: Koninklijke Brill, 2003), p. 248.
99. Diodorus 2.22.2.
100. Plato *Laws* 685c.
101. De Jong, Irene, *Homer: Critical Assessments* Volume II – *The Homeric World* (London: Routledge, 1999), p. 18.
102. Ibid.
103. De Jong, Irene, *Homer: Critical Assessments* Volume II – *The Homeric World* (London: Routledge, 1999), p. 19.
104. Diogenes *Lives of the Eminent Philosophers* 1.38.
105. Susemihl, Franz and Hicks, Robert, *The Politics of Aristotle: A Revised Text: Books I-V* (London: Macmillan and Co, 1894), p. 353.
106. Budelmann, Felix and Phillips, Tom, *Textual Events: Performance and the Lyric in Early Greece* (Oxford: Oxford University Press, 2018), p. 195.
107. Kuiper, Kathleen, *Classical Authors: 500 BCE to 1100 CE* (New York: Britannica Educational Publishing, 2014), p. 17.
108. Watrous, Livingston; Hadzi-Vallianou; and Blizter, Harriet, *The Plain of Phaistos: Cycles of Social Complexity in the Mesara Region of Crete* (Los Angeles: Cotsen Institute of Archaeology Press, 2004), p. 347.
109. Strabo 1.2.9.
110. De Jong, Irene, *Homer: Critical Assessments* Volume II – *The Homeric World* (London: Routledge, 1999), p. 3.
111. Mutschler, Fritz-Heiner, *The Homeric Epics and the Chinese Book of Songs: Foundational Texts Compared* (Newcastle: Cambridge Scholars Publishing, 2018), p. 33.
112. Kim, Lawrence, *Homer Between History and Fiction in Imperial Greek Literature* (Cambridge: Cambridge University Press, 2010), p. 25.
113. Ibid.

Notes

114. Tatian *Address to the Greeks* 36.1.
115. Saïd, Suzanne, *Homer and the Odyssey* (Oxford: Oxford University Press, 2011), p. 16.
116. Diodorus 7.1.
117. Graziosi, Barbara, *Inventing Homer: The Early Reception of Epic* (Cambridge: Cambridge University Press, 2002), p. 100.
118. Saïd, Suzanne, *Homer and the Odyssey* (Oxford: Oxford University Press, 2011), p. 16.
119. De Temmerman, Koen, *The Oxford Handbook of Ancient Biography*, (Oxford: Oxford University Press, 2020), p. 318.
120. Ibid.
121. Swift, Laura and Carey, Chris, *Iambus and Elegy: New Approaches* (Oxford: Oxford University Press, 2016), p. 110.
122. Grant, Michael and Hazel, John, *Who's Who in Classical Mythology* (London: Routledge, 2002), p. 252.
123. Graziosi, Barbara, *Inventing Homer: The Early Reception of Epic* (Cambridge: Cambridge University Press, 2002), p. 99.
124. Wade-Grey, Theodore, *The Poet of the Iliad* (Cambridge: Cambridge University Press, 2013), p. 27.
125. Herodotus 6.53.
126. Herodotus 2.43.
127. Lloyd, Alan, *A Companion to Ancient Egypt* Volume I (Chichester: Wiley-Blackwell, 2010), p. 135; Moyer, Ian, *Egypt and the Limits of Hellenism* (Cambridge: Cambridge University Press, 2011), p. 109.
128. Bard, Kathryn, *Encyclopedia of the Archaeology of Ancient Egypt* (Abingdon: Routledge, 1999), p. xxix.
129. Bromiley, Geoffrey, *The International Standard Bible Encyclopedia – Volume Three: K-P* (Michigan: Wm. B. Eerdmans Publishing Company, 1986), p. 191.
130. Villing, Alexandra, *Greece and Egypt: Reconsidering Early Contact and Exchange – Regional Stories Towards a New Perception of the Early Greek World* (Volos: University of Thessaly Press, 2017), p. 565.
131. Mellink, Machteld, *Troy and the Trojan War: A Symposium Held at Bryn Mawr College, October 1984* (Bryn Mawr: Bryn Mawr Commentaries, 1986), p. 14.
132. Venit, Marjorie, *Visualizing the Afterlife in the Tombs of Greco-Roman Egypt* (New York: Cambridge University Press, 2016), p. 6.
133. Vavouranakis, Giorgos; Kopanias, Konstantinos; and Kanellopoulos, Chrysanthos, *Popular Religion and Ritual in prehistoric and ancient Greece and the eastern Meditarranean* (Oxford: Archaeopress Publishing, 2018), p. 113.
134. Villing, Alexandra, *Greece and Egypt: Reconsidering Early Contact and Exchange – Regional Stories Towards a New Perception of the Early Greek World* (Volos: University of Thessaly Press, 2017), p. 565.

135. Larson, Jennifer, *Understanding Greek Religion* (Abingdon: Routledge, 2016), p. 103.
136. Pausanias 9.37.3.
137. Ritner, Robert, *The Libyan Anarchy: Inscriptions from Egypt's Third Intermediate Period* (Atlanta: Society of Biblical Literature, 2009), p. 443.
138. Apollodorus 2.7.8.
139. Apollodorus 3.9.1.
140. Apollodorus 3.14.3.
141. Hyginus *Fabulae* 56.
142. Moore, Karl and Lewis, David, *The Origins of Globalization* (Abingdon: Routledge, 2009), p. 105.
143. Apollodorus 2.5.1.
144. Pausanias 5.4.5, 6.
145. Grabbe, Lester, *'Like a Bird in a Cage' – The Invasion of Sennacherib in 701 BCE* (London: Sheffield Academic Press, 2003), p. 135.
146. Lieu, Judith and Rogerson, John, *The Oxford Handbook of Biblical Studies* (Oxford: Oxford University Press, 2006), p. 95.
147. Strabo 15.1.6.
148. Bennett, James, *The Archaeology of Egypt in the Third Intermediate Period* (Cambridge: Cambridge University Press, 2019), p. 9.
149. Burton, Anne, *Diodorus Siculus, Book I: A Commentary* (Leiden: E. J. Brill, 1972), p. 183.
150. Moyer, Ian, *Egypt and the Limits of Hellenism* (Cambridge: Cambridge University Press, 2011), p. 232.
151. Ruffini, Giovanni and Harris, William, *Ancient Alexandria Between Egypt and Greece* (Leiden: Koninklijke Brill, 2004), p. 260.
152. Bennett, James, *The Archaeology of Egypt in the Third Intermediate Period* (Cambridge: Cambridge University Press, 2019), p. 10.
153. Odyssey 4.126.
154. Speake, Graham, *Encyclopedia of Greece and the Hellenic Tradition – Volume I: A-K* (Abingdon: Routledge, 2019), p. 67.
155. Strabo 13.3.3.
156. Bryce, Trevor, *The Routledge Handbook of the Peoples and Places of Ancient Western Asia: The Near East from the Early Bronze Age to the Fall of the Persian Empire* (Abingdon: Routledge, 2009), p. 175.
157. Strabo 13.1.3.
158. *The New Encyclopaedia Britannica* Volume 9 (Illinois: Encyclopaedia Britannica, 2003), p. 408.
159. Venable, Shannon, *Gold: A Cultural Encyclopedia* (California: ABC-CLIO, 2013), p. 200.
160. Diodorus 3.67.2.
161. Frazer, James, *The Golden Bough* Volume 7 (Frankfurt am Main: Books on Demand, 2020), p. 157.
162. Justin 7.1.1-11.

Notes

163. Bane, Theresa, *Encyclopedia of Mythological Objects* (North Carolina: McFarland & Company, 2020), p. 78.
164. Jerome *Chronicle*.
165. Pomponius Mela 1.88.
166. Sweeny, Naoíse, *Foundation Myths and Politics in Ancient Ionia* (Cambridge: Cambridge University Press, 2013), p. 113.
167. John Tzetzes *Lycophron* 427.
168. Strabo 14.5.16.
169. Astour, Michael, *Hellenosemitica: An Ethnic and Cultural Study in West Semitic Impact on Mycenaean Greece* (Leiden: E. J. Brill, 1967), p. 56.
170. Jennings, Victoria and Katsaros, Andrea, *The World of Ion of Chios* (Leiden: Brill, 2007), p. 65.
171. Rose, Charles, *The Archaeology of Greek and Roman Troy* (New York: Cambridge University Press, 2014), p. 53.
172. Strabo 14.2.28.
173. Pausanias 1.42.3.
174. Herodotus 5.54.
175. Diodorus 2.22.1-3.
176. *Homeric Hymn to Aphrodite* 218.
177. Diodorus 4.75.4.
178. Shaw, Ian, *The Oxford History of Ancient Egypt* (Oxford: Oxford University Press, 2003), p. 353; Bard, Kathryn, *Encyclopedia of the Archaeology of Ancient Egypt* (Abingdon: Routledge, 1999), p. 66.
179. Yar-Shater, Ehsan, *Encyclopedia Iranica* Volume II, Issues 5-8 (London: Routledge & Kegan Paul, 1982), p. 805.
180. Redford, Donald, *The Oxford Encyclopedia of Ancient Egypt: G-O* (Oxford: Oxford University Press, 2001), p. 138.
181. Aruz, Joan and Seymour, Michael, *Assyria to Iberia: Art and Culture in the Iron Age* (New York: The Metropolitan Museum of Art, 2016), p. 242.
182. Alexandridou, Alexandra, *The Early Black-Figured Pottery of Attica in Context (c. 630-570 BCE)* (Leiden: Brill, 2011), p. 98.
183. Mellink, Machteld, *Troy and the Trojan War: A Symposium Held at Bryn Mawr College, October 1984* (Bryn Mawr: Bryn Mawr Commentaries, 1986), p. 14.
184. Rose, Charles, *The Archaeology of Greek and Roman Troy* (New York: Cambridge University Press, 2014), p. 50.
185. Lycophron *The Alexandra* 1308.
186. Dionysius 1.61.1-4.
187. Dionysius 1.61.1.
188. Dowden, Ken and Livingstone, Niall, *A Companion to Greek Mythology* (Chichester: Wiley-Blackwell, 2014), p. 435.
189. Rose, Charles, *The Archaeology of Greek and Roman Troy* (New York: Cambridge University Press, 2014), p. 53.

190. Price, Roberto, *Homeric Whispers: Imitations of Orthodoxy in the Iliad and Odyssey* (San Antonio: Scylax Press, 2006), p. 251.
191. Lemos, Irene and Kotsonas, Antonis, *A Companion to the Archaeology of Early Greece and the Mediterranean* Volume I (New Jersey: Wiley-Blackwell, 2020), pp. 954, 955.
192. Dowden, Ken and Livingstone, Niall, *A Companion to Greek Mythology* (Chichester: Wiley-Blackwell, 2014), p. 436.
193. Ibid.
194. *Iliad* 16.715.
195. Wood, Michael, *In Search of the Trojan War* (London: BBC Books, 2005), p. 27.
196. Thucydides 1.11.
197. *Iliad* 9.328.
198. Apollodorus *Epitome* 3.33.
199. Thucydides 1.10.
200. Ibid.
201. Turner, Barry, *The Stateman's Yearbook: The Politics, Cultures and Economies of the World – 2010* (Hampshire: Palgrave Macmillan, 2009), p. 1235.
202. *The New Encyclopaedia Britannica: Part 1* (Chicago: Encyclopaedia Britannica, 1974), p. 823.
203. Graham, Alexander, *Collected Papers on Greek Colonization* (Leiden: Brill, 2001), p. 123.
204. Kagan, Donald and Viggiano, Gregory, *Men of Bronze: Hoplite Warfare in Ancient Greece* (New Jersey: Princeton University Press, 2013), p. 181.
205. Bury, John, *A History of Greece* (Cambridge: Cambridge University Press, 1900), p. 111.
206. Rose, Charles, *The Archaeology of Greek and Roman Troy* (New York: Cambridge University Press, 2014), p. 53.
207. Aslan, Carolyn, *New evidence for a destruction at Troia in the mid 7th century B.C. – Studia Troica*, 18 (Pennsylvania: INSTAP Academic Press, 2009), p. 37.
208. de Boer, Jan, *The 'Western Cimmerians' and the first Greek settlers in the Troad – The Greeks and Romans in the Black Sea and the Importance of the Pontic Region for the Graeco-Roman World (7th Century BC-5th Century AD): 20 Years On (1997-2017): Proceedings of the Sixth International Congress on Black Sea Antiquities (Constanţa – 18-22 September 2017)* (Oxford: Archaeopress Publishing, 2021), pp. 21, 22.
209. Grant, Michael and Hazel, John, *Who's Who in Classical Mythology* (London: Routledge, 2002), p. 503.
210. Steiner, Margreet and Killebrew, Ann, *The Oxford Handbook of the Archaeology of the Levant* (Oxford: Oxford University Press, 2013), pp. 806, 807.

211. Stillwell, Richard and Macdonald, William, *The Princeton Encyclopedia of Classical Sites* (New Jersey: Princeton University Press, 1976), p. 675.
212. Tsetskhladze, Gocha, *Greek Colonisation: An Account of Greek Colonies and Other Settlements Overseas – Volume Two* (Leiden: Brill, 2008), p. 247.
213. Brown, John, *Israel and Hellas* Volume II (Berlin: De Gruyter, 2000), p. 195.
214. Alexandridou, Alexandra, *The Early Black-Figured Pottery of Attica in Context (c. 630-570 BCE)* (Leiden: Brill, 2011), p. 103.
215. Dionysius 1.31-33.
216. McColl, R.W., *Encyclopedia of World Geography* (New York: Facts on File, 2005), p. 572.
217. Orlin, Eric, *A Social and Cultural History of Republican Rome* (New Jersey: Wiley-Blackwell, 2022), p. 270.
218. Apollodorus *Epitome* 6.15.
219. Too, Yun, *The Idea of the Library in the Ancient World* (Oxford: Oxford University Press, 2010), p. 139.
220. Herodotus 4.150-158.
221. Osborne, Robin, *Greece in the Making, 1200-479 BC – Second Edition* (Abingdon: Routledge, 2009), p. 15.
222. Montanari, Franco; Rengakos, Antonios; and Tsagalis, Christos, *Homeric Contexts: Neoanalysis and the Interpretation of Oral Poetry* (Berlin: De Gruyter, 2012), p. 335.
223. Herodotus 2.152.
224. Dionysius 1.52.
225. Gleba, Margarita, *Textile Production in Pre-Roman Italy* (Oxford: Oxbow Books, 2008), p. 21.
226. Alcock, Susan and Osborne, Robin, *Classical Archaeology – Second Edition* (Chichester: Wiley-Blackwell, 2012), p. 365.
227. King, Russell; Proudfoot, Lindsay; and Smith, Bernard, *The Mediterranean: Environment and Society* (Abingdon: Routledge, 2014), p. 60.
228. Galinksy, Karl, *Aeneas, Sicily, and Rome* (New Jersey: Princeton University Press, 1969), p. 74.
229. Pausanias 2.5.4.
230. Lemos, Irene and Kotsonas, Antonis, *A Companion to the Archaeology of Early Greece and the Mediterranean* Volume I (New Jersey: Wiley-Blackwell, 2020), p. 733.
231. Horsfall, Nicholas, *Virgil's Roman Chronography: A Reconsideration – The Classical Quarterly*, Volume 24, No. 1 (Cambridge: Cambridge University Press, 1974), p. 111.
232. Plutarch 2.2.
233. Dionysius 1.72.1.

234. Sanders, Henry, *The Chronology of Early Rome – Classical Philology*, Volume 3, No. 3 (Illinois: University of Chicago Press, 1908), pp. 317–19
235. Blackie, John, *Homer and the Iliad – Homeric Dissertations* Volume I (Edinburgh: Edmonston and Douglas, 1866), p. 59.
236. Froude, James, *Fraser's Magazine* Volume 52, July to December (London: John W. Parker and Son, West Strand, 1855), p. 463.
237. Beard, Mary, *SPQR: A History of Ancient Rome* (London: Profile Books, 2015), p. 77.
238. Holleran, Claire and Claridge, Amanda, *A Companion to the City of Rome* (Chichester: Wiley-Blackwell, 2018), p. 101.
239. Dionysius 1.73.4.
240. Wiseman, Timothy, *Remus: A Roman Myth* (Cambridge: Cambridge University Press, 1995), p. 167.
241. For example, Dionysius 1.89.2.
242. Kneale, Matthew, *Rome: A History in Seven Sackings* (New York: Simon and Schuster, 2017), p. 12.
243. Evans, Jane, *A Companion to the Archaeology of the Roman Republic* (Chichester: Wiley-Blackwell, 2013)
244. Cooley, Alison, *A Companion to Roman Italy* (Chichester: Wiley-Blackwell, 2016), p. 295.
245. Stamper, John, *The Architecture of Roman Temples: The Republic to the Middle Empire* (Cambridge: Cambridge University Press, 2005), p. 6.
246. Cornell, Tim, *The Beginnings of Rome: Italy and Rome from the Bronze Age to the Punic Wars (c. 1000-264 BC)* (Abingdon, Routledge, 1995), p. 239.
247. Venning, Timothy, *A Chronology of the Roman Empire* (New York: Continuum International Publishing Group, 2011), p. 32.
248. Strabo 5.3.3.
249. Dionysius 1.27, 28.
250. Waldman, Carl and Mason, Catherine, *Encyclopedia of European Peoples* (New York: Facts on File, 2006), p. 244.
251. Ibid.
252. Bell, Sinclair and Carpino, Alexandra, *A Companion to the Etruscans* (Chichester: Wiley-Blackwell, 2016), pp. 343, 344.
253. Bonfante, Larissa, *Etruscan Life and Afterlife: A Handbook of Etruscan Studies* (Michigan: Wayne State University Press, 1986), p. 163.
254. Bell, Sinclair and Carpino, Alexandra, *A Companion to the Etruscans* (Chichester: Wiley-Blackwell, 2016), p. 344.
255. Middleton, John, *World Monarchies and Dynasties – Volume 1-3: A-Z* (Abingdon: Routledge, 2015), p. 288.
256. Kristiansen, Kristian, *Europe Before History* (Cambridge: Cambridge University Press, 1998), p. 140.

Notes

257. Scarre, Christopher and Fagan, Brian, *Ancient Civilizations – Third Edition* (Abingdon: Routledge, 2016), p. 279.
258. Naso, Alessandro, *Etruscology* Volume I (Berlin: De Gruyter, 2017), pp. 341-343.
259. Versnel, Henk, *Triumphus: An Inquiry into the Origin, Development and Meaning of the Roman Triumph* (Leiden: E. J. Brill, 1970), p. 300.
260. Burkert, Walter, *Greek Religion* (Massachusetts: Harvard University Press, 1985), p. 281.
261. Thomas, Rosalind, *Polis Histories, Collective Memories and the Greek World* (Cambridge: Cambridge University Press, 2019), pp. 268, 269.
262. *Britannica Encyclopedia of World Religions* (Chicago: Encyclopaedia Britannica, 2006), p. 174.
263. Fowler, Robert, *Early Greek Mythography – Volume 2: Commentary* (Oxford: Oxford University Press, 2013), p. 39.
264. Hard, Robin, *The Routledge Handbook of Greek Mythology* (London: Routledge, 2004), p. 220.
265. Man, John, *Alpha Beta: How 26 Letters Shaped the Western World* (New York: John Wiley & Sons, 2001), p. 247.
266. Turfa, Jean, *The Etruscan World* (Abingdon: Routledge, 2013), p. 665.
267. Bell, Sinclair and Carpino, Alexandra, *A Companion to the Etruscans* (Chichester: Wiley-Blackwell, 2016), p. 344.
268. Lufrani, Riccardo, *The Saint-Etienne Compound Hypogea (Jerusalem): Geological, architectural and archaeological characteristics: A comparative study and dating* (Göttingen: Vandenhoeck & Ruprecht, 2019), p. 66.
269. Bell, Sinclair and Carpino, Alexandra, *A Companion to the Etruscans* (Chichester: Wiley-Blackwell, 2016), p. 344.
270. Plutarch *Quaestiones Graecae* 45.
271. Versnel, Henk, *Triumphus: An Inquiry into the Origin, Development and Meaning of the Roman Triumph* (Leiden: E. J. Brill, 1970), p. 298.
272. Higgins, Reynold, *Greek and Roman Jewellery – Second Edition* (Berkeley: University of California Press, 1980), p. 135.
273. López-Ruiz, Carolina, *Phoenicians and the Making of the Mediterranean* (Massachusetts: Harvard University Press, 2021), p. 152.
274. *The New Encyclopaedia Britannica: Macropaedia: Knowledge in Depth* (Chicago: Encyclopaedia Britannica, 2003), p. 276.
275. Haynes, Sybille, *Etruscan Civilization: A Cultural History* (California: Getty Publications, 2000), p. 1.
276. McInerney, Jeremy, *A Companion to Ethnicity in the Ancient Mediterranean* (Chichester: Wiley-Blackwell, 2014), p. 406.

277. Demetriou, Denise, *Negotiating Identity in the Ancient Mediterranean: The Archaic and Classical Greek Multiethnic Emporia* (Cambridge: Cambridge University Press, 2012), p. 68.
278. Thucydides 4.109.
279. Strabo 5.2.4.
280. Haynes, Sybille, *Etruscan Civilization: A Cultural History* (California: Getty Publications, 2000), p. 2.
281. Conon *Narrations* 41.
282. Rutherford, Ian, *Hittite Texts and Greek Religion: Contact, Interaction, and Comparison* (Oxford: Oxford University Press, 2020), p. 74.
283. Higgins, Reynold, *Greek and Roman Jewellery – Second Edition* (Berkeley: University of California Press, 1980), p. 135.
284. Herodotus 7.74.
285. Strabo 12.8.3.
286. Dionysius 1.28.
287. Bryce, Trevor, *The Routledge Handbook of the Peoples and Places of Ancient Western Asia: The Near East from the Early Bronze Age to the Fall of the Persian Empire* (Abingdon: Routledge, 2009), p. 409.
288. Thucydides 4.109.
289. Dionysius 1.25.4.
290. Dionysius 1.29.1, 2.
291. Strabo 5.2.4.
292. Dionysius 1.28.3.
293. Strabo 5.2.4
294. Beekes, Robert, *The prehistory of the Lydians, the origins of the Etruscans, Troy and Aeneas – Bibliotheca Orientalis* 59 (Leiden: NINO, 2002) pp. 205–241.
295. There are about as many different theories regarding the origin of the Etruscan language as there are scholars who study the subject, so there is little use in using arguments based on linguistics to attempt to prove the origin of the Etruscans. Nonetheless, it is worth noting that Robert Beekes, who was primarily a linguist rather than a historian, agreed with the viewpoint that Etruscan shows the most signs of being influenced by Lydian (such as the presence of some loanwords).
296. Strabo 12.8.7.
297. Evans, Jane, *The Art of Persuasion: Political Propaganda from Aeneas to Brutus* (Michigan: University of Michigan Press, 1992), p. 35.
298. Turfa, Jean, *The Etruscan World* (Abingdon: Routledge, 2013), p. 434.
299. de Grummond, Nancy, *Etruscan Myth, Sacred History, and Legend* (Pennsylvania: University of Pennsylvania Museum of Archaeology and Anthropology, 2006), p. 130.

Notes

300. The idea that the Etruscans took their worship of Apollo from Troy might be disputed on the basis that the form of his name used by the Etruscans was 'Apulu', or 'Aplu'. Since the Greek form of the name was 'Apollon' (similar to the 'Apaliunas' form seen from Hittite accounts of Wilusa), the fact that the Etruscan form contains no 'n' at the end has been used as evidence that the Etruscan Apulu was not taken directly from the Greek Apollon (and similarly, this could be used as evidence that it could not come from 'Apaliunas'). Thus, it is believed that it came from the Latin form, 'Apollo'. However, the obvious flaw in this way of thinking is that there is no evidence at all, or any reason to believe, that the evolution of the name had to have gone 'Apollon', 'Apollo', and then 'Apulu'. The Etruscan form could easily have come before the Latin form. If the 'n' could be dropped from the name when it was adopted into the Latin language, why could the same not have occurred first in Etruscan, or even in both languages independently? Furthermore, the name of this god *has*, in fact, been found written as 'Aplun' on Etruscan bronze mirrors, though this appears to have been forgotten. Yet, this fact is recorded on page 846 of *Über Die Sprache Der Etrusker*, Volume I.
301. Jannot. Jean-René, *Religion in Ancient Etruria* (Wisconsin: University of Wisconsin Press, 2005) p. 146.
302. Aeneid 3.167-71.
303. Denecke, Wiebke, *Classical World Literatures: Sino-Japanese and Greco-Roman Comparisons* (New York: Oxford University Press, 2014), p. 128.
304. Although it has been claimed that the language in Troy was Luwian on the basis of artefacts found at the site, there is really no evidence that this is due to anything other than that Luwian was used as the lingua franca of that region. It does not prove that it was the native language of the Trojans.
305. Adkins, Lesley, *Handbook to Life in Ancient Rome – Updated Edition* (New York: Facts on File, 2004), p. 164.
306. Sear, Frank, *Roman Architecture* (Abingdon: Routledge, 1998), p. 10.
307. Orlin, Eric, *A Social and Cultural History of Republican Rome* (New Jersey: Wiley-Blackwell, 2022), p. 223.
308. Polizzotti, Mark, *Etruscan Art in the Metropolitan Museum of Art* (New York: The Metropolitan Museum of Art, 2013), pp. 171, 172.
309. Ibid.
310. Ibid.
311. Ibid.
312. Campbell, George, *Compendium of the World's Languages – Second Edition – Volume II: Ladakhi to Zuni* (London: Routledge, 2000), p. 966.
313. Jones, Prudence and Pennick, Nigel, *A History of Pagan Europe* (Abingdon: Routledge, 1995), p. 31.

314. Dionysius 1.29.2.
315. Strabo 5.2.2.
316. Livy 1.50.
317. Livy 1.2.
318. Strabo 5.2.2.
319. McIntosh, Jane, *Handbook to Life in Prehistoric Europe* (New York: Oxford University Press, 2006), p. 84.
320. Bartrum, Peter, *A Welsh Classical Dictionary* (Aberystwyth: The National Library of Wales, 1993), p. 172.
321. Bartrum, Peter, *A Welsh Classical Dictionary* (Aberystwyth: The National Library of Wales, 1993), p. 112.
322. Bartrum, Peter, *A Welsh Classical Dictionary* (Aberystwyth: The National Library of Wales, 1993), p. 73.
323. Russell, Miles, *Arthur and the Kings of Britain: The Historical Truth Behind the Myths* (Stroud: Amberley Publishing, 2017).
324. Bartrum, Peter, *A Welsh Classical Dictionary* (Aberystwyth: The National Library of Wales, 1993), p. 69.
325. Cunliffe, Barry, *Britain Begins* (Oxford: Oxford University Press, 2013), p. 4.
326. *Aeneid* 6.756-823.
327. McAuley, Mairéad, *Reproducing Rome: Motherhood in Virgil, Ovid, Seneca, Statius* (Oxford: Oxford University Press, 2016), p. 29.
328. Dionysius 4.68.1, 2.
329. Ibid.
330. Livy 1.56.6-12.
331. Livy 2.4, 5.
332. Livy 2.8.4, 5.
333. Mattingly, David, *Imperialism, Power, and Identity: Experiencing the Roman Empire* (New Jersey: Princeton University Press, 2011), p. 90.
334. *Castles and fortresses in Prefecture of Preveza* (Rhodes: CEST2017, 2017), p. 3.
335. Gruen, Erich, *Rethinking the Other in Antiquity* (New Jersey: Princeton University Press, 2011), p. 241.
336. Waldman, Carl and Mason, Catherine, *Encyclopedia of European Peoples* (New York: Facts on File, 2006), p. 243.
337. Kuiper, Kathleen, *From Romulus and Remus to the Visigoth Invasion* (New York: Britannica Educational Publishing, 2011), p. 206.
338. Naso, Alessandro, *Etruscology* Volume I (Berlin: De Gruyter, 2017), p. 144.
339. Demetriou, Denise, *Negotiating Identity in the Ancient Mediterranean: The Archaic and Classical Greek Multiethnic Emporia* (Cambridge: Cambridge University Press, 2012), p. 67.
340. Herodotus 6.138.

Notes

341. Berger, Daniel; Soles, Jeffrey; Giumlia-Mair, Alessandra, Brügmann, Gerhard; Galili, Ehud; Lockhoff, Nicole; Pernicka, Ernst, *Isotope systematics and chemical composition of tin ingots from Mochlos (Crete) and other Late Bronze Age sites in the eastern Mediterranean Sea: An ultimate key to tin provenance?* Volume 14, Issue 6, (California: PloS One, 2019)
342. Moffett, Marian; Fazio, Michael; Wodehouse, Lawrence, *A World History of Architecture* (London: Laurence King Publishing, 2003), p. 111.
343. Harder, Annette, *Callimachus: Aetia – Volume I: Introduction, Text, Translation, and Commentary* (Oxford: Oxford University Press, 2012), p. 171.
344. If the wording in the *Historia Brittonum* is accurate when it describes the Philenean Altars as being 'next to the *lacum salinarum*', then the lake in question is probably the Sabkah al Kabirah, which is a salt lake near Ras Lanuf, where the ancient altars used to stand. On the other hand, if the wording in the *HRB* is correct in listing 'the place called Salinae' as the next location on the journey along from the altars, then the salt lakes of Tunisia must be the correct location.
345. *Aeneid* 7.371-372.
346. Camporeale, Giovannangelo, *The Etruscans Outside Etruria* (Los Angeles: The J. Paul Getty Museum, 2004), p. 277.
347. Turfa, Jean, *The Etruscan World* (Abingdon: Routledge, 2013), p. 241.
348. Dunstan, William, *Ancient Rome* (Plymouth: Rowman and Littlefield Publishers, 2011), p. 10.
349. Stoddart, Simon, *Historical Dictionary of the Etruscans* (Plymouth: Scarecrow Press, 2009), p. 110.
350. Camporeale, Giovannangelo, *The Etruscans Outside Etruria* (Los Angeles: The J. Paul Getty Museum, 2004), p. 89.
351. Turfa, Jean, *The Etruscan World* (Abingdon: Routledge, 2013), p. 337.
352. Turfa, Jean, *The Etruscan World* (Abingdon: Routledge, 2013), p. 339.
353. Turfa, Jean, *The Etruscan World* (Abingdon: Routledge, 2013), p. 384.
354. Demetriou, Denise, *Negotiating Identity in the Ancient Mediterranean: The Archaic and Classical Greek Multiethnic Emporia* (Cambridge: Cambridge University Press, 2012), p. 67.
355. Diodorus Siculus 5.20.
356. Diodorus Siculus 5.22.
357. Fowler, Chris; Harding, Jan; and Hofmann, Daniela, *The Oxford Handbook of Neolithic Europe* (Oxford: Oxford University Press, 2015), p. 712.
358. Birx, Harry, *Encyclopedia of Anthropology: 1* (California: Sage Publications, 2006), p. 457.

359. Cunliffe, Barry, *Britain Begins* (Oxford: Oxford University Press, 2013), p. 308.
360. Lavin, Patrick, *The Shaping of the Celtic World: And the Resurgence of the Celtic Consciousness in the 19th and 20th Centuries* (Bloomington: iUniverse, 2011), p. 42.
361. Cunliffe, Barry, *Britain Begins* (Oxford: Oxford University Press, 2013), p. 316.
362. Haynes, Sybille, *Etruscan Civilization: A Cultural History* (California: Getty Publications, 2000), p. 295.
363. Gosden, Christopher; Crawford, Sally; Ulmschneider, Katharina, *Celtic Art in Europe: Making Connections* (Oxford: Oxbow Books, 2014), p. 122.
364. Green, Miranda, *The Celtic World* (Abingdon: Routledge, 1995), p. 591.
365. Harding, Dennis, *The Iron Age in Lowland Britain* (Abingdon: Routledge, 2015), p. 108.
366. Jacey, Joann, *History of Art and Architecture* Volume I (Sugar Creek: Joann Lacey, 2021), p. 564.
367. Gagarin, Michael and Fantham, Elaine, *The Oxford Encyclopedia of Ancient Greece* Volume I (New York: Oxford University Press, 2010), p. 89.
368. Haywood, John, *The Celts: Bronze Age to New Age* (Abingdon: Routledge, 2014), p. 18.
369. Harding, Dennis, *The Iron Age in Northern Britain: Celts and Romans, Natives and Invaders* (Abingdon: Routledge, 2004), p. 35.
370. Bradley, Richard, *The Prehistory of Britain and Ireland: Second Edition* (Cambridge: Cambridge University Press, 2019), p. 316.
371. Bradley, Richard, *The Past in Prehistoric Societies* (London: Routledge, 2002), p. 130.
372. Eaton, Jonathan, *An Archaeological History of Britain: Continuity and Change from Prehistory to the Present* (Barnsley: Pen and Sword Archaeology, 2014), pp. 46, 47.
373. Fee, Christopher, *Gods, Heroes, and Kings: The Battle for Mythic Britain* (New York: Oxford University Press, 2001), p. 63.
374. Harding, Dennis, *Rewriting History: Changing Perceptions of the Archaeological Past* (Oxford: Oxford University Press, 2020), p. 115.
375. Snyder, Christopher, *The Britons* (Oxford: Blackwell Publishing, 2003), p. 17.
376. Cunliffe, Barry, *Britain Begins* (Oxford: Oxford University Press, 2013), p. 318.
377. Harding, Dennis, *The Archaeology of Celtic Art* (Abingdon: Routledge, 2007), p. 141.
378. Kenney, Jane, *A Welsh Landscape Through Time: Excavations at Parc Cybi, Holy Island, Anglesey* (Oxford: Oxbow Books, 2021), p. 18.

379. Grimbly, Shona, *Encyclopedia of the Ancient World* (Illinois: Fitzroy Dearborn Publishers, 2000), p. 83.
380. Steingräber, Stephan, *The Process of Urbanization of Etruscan Settlements from the Late Villanovan to the Late Archaic Period (End of the Eighth to the Beginning of the Fifth Century B.C.): Presentation of a Project and Preliminary Results – Etruscan Studies* Volume 8, Article 1 (Berlin: De Gruyter, 2001), pp. 18, 20.
381. Haywood, John, *The Celts: Bronze Age to New Age* (Abingdon: Routledge, 2014), p. 35.
382. Mountain, Harry, *The Celtic Encyclopedia* Volume I (California: Universal-Publishers, 1998), p. 86.
383. Lepage, Jean-Denis, *British Fortifications Through the Reign of Richard III* (North Carolina: McFarland and Company, 2012), p. 30.
384. Harding, Dennis, *The Iron Age in Lowland Britain* (Abingdon: Routledge, 2015), p. 61.
385. Girdwood, Peter, *On the Edge of History: How the Modern Reception of Etruscans and Celts has Been Shaped Through a Roman Reality* (Southampton: University of Southampton, 2011), p. 21.
386. Koch, John; Minard, Antone, *The Celts: History, Life, and Culture – Volume 1: A-H* (California: ABC-CLIO, 2012), p. 38.
387. Friedland, Elise; Sobocinski, Melanie; and Gazda, Elaine, *The Oxford Handbook of Roman Sculpture* (New York: Oxford University Press, 2015), p. 476; Green, Miranda, *Symbol and Image in Celtic Religious Art* (London: Routledge, 1989), p. 111.
388. Armit, I. and Grant, P., *Gesture politics and the art of ambiguity: the Iron Age statue from Hirschlanden – Antiquity* Volume 82, Issue 316 (Cambridge: Cambridge University Press, 2015) pp. 409-22
389. Ibid.
390. Ibid.
391. Maier, Bernhard, *Dictionary of Celtic Religion and Culture* (Woodbridge: The Boydell Press, 1997), p. 229.
392. Hubert, Henri, *The Rise of the Celts* (New York: Routledge, 1996), p. 94.
393. Pare, C., *Fürstensitze, Celts and the Mediterranean World: Developments in the West Hallstatt Culture in the 6th and 5th Centuries BC – Proceedings of the Prehistoric Society* Volume 57, Issue 2 (Cambridge: Cambridge University Press, 2015), p. 198.
394. Ibid.
395. Bonfante, Larissa, *The Barbarians of Ancient Europe: Realities and Interactions* (New York: Cambridge University Press, 2011), p. 266.
396. Waddell, John, *Myth and Materiality* (Oxford: Oxbow Books, 2018), p. 72.
397. D'Amato, Raffaele and Salimbeti, Andrea, *The Etruscans: 9th-2nd Centuries BC* (London: Bloomsbury Publishing, 2018), p. 56.

398. Esposito, Gabriele, *Armies of Celtic Europe: 700 BC to AD 106* (Yorkshire: Pen & Sword Military, 2019)
399. Grotowski, Piotr, *Arms and Armour of the Warrior Saints: Tradition and Innovation In Byzantine Iconography (843-1261)* (Leiden: Brill, 2010), p. 134.
400. Krebs, Robert and Krebs, Carolyn, *Groundbreaking Scientific Experiments, Inventions, and Discoveries of the Ancient World* (Connecticut: Greenwood Press, 2003), p. 309.
401. Haywood, John, *The Celts: Bronze Age to New Age* (Abingdon: Routledge, 2014), p. 35.
402. Koch, John, *Celtic Culture: A Historical Encyclopedia* (California: ABC-CLIO, 2006), p. 372.
403. Counihan, Martin, *An Etruscan solution to a Celtic problem* (2009).
404. Janda, Richard; Joseph, Brian; and Vance, Barbara, *The Handbook of Historical Linguistics* Volume II (Chichester: Wiley-Blackwell, 2021), p. 589.
405. Koch, John, *Celtic Culture: A Historical Encyclopedia* (California: ABC-CLIO, 2006), pp. 372, 373.
406. Ibid.
407. Koch, John, *Celtic Culture: A Historical Encyclopedia* (California: ABC-CLIO, 2006), p. 1142.
408. Stokes, Whitley, *Celtic Declension* (Göttingen: Vandenhoeck & Ruprecht, 1886), p. 47.
409. Bonfante, Giuliano and Bonfante, Larissa, *The Etruscan Language: An Introduction – Second Edition* (Manchester: Manchester University Press, 2002), p. 73.
410. Baldi, Philip, *The Foundations of Latin* (Berlin: Mouton de Gruyter, 1999), p. 166.
411. Ostler, Nicholas, *Ad Infinitum: A Biography of Latin* (London: HarperPress, 2007), p. 37.
412. Ibid.
413. Fisiak, Jacek, *Linguistic Reconstruction and Typology* (Berlin: Mounton de Gruyter, 1997), p. 139.
414. McInerney, Jeremy, *A Companion to Ethnicity in the Ancient Mediterranean* (Chichester: Wiley-Blackwell, 2014), p. 26.
415. *The Babylonian and Oriental Record: A Monthly Magazine of the Antiquities of the East – Volume Sixth – from July, 1892, to June, 1893* (London: Luzac and Co, 1893), p. 86.
416. Xenophon *Cyropedia* 6.27.
417. Diodorus 5.21.5.
418. *The Journal of Hellenic Studies* Volume 27 (London: Macmillan and Co, 1907), pp. 255-257.
419. Diodorus 5.29.2.
420. Goldsworth, Adrian, *The Roman Army at War: 100 BC-AD 200* (Oxford: Clarendon Press, 1996), p. 274.

Notes

421. Valerius Maximus 3.2.3-5.
422. Waldman, Carl and Mason, Catherine, *Encyclopedia of European Peoples* (New York: Facts on File, 2006), p. 165.
423. Diodorus 2.47.2.
424. Fisher, Jay, *The Annals of Quintus Ennius and the Italic Tradition* (Maryland: John Hopkins University Press, 2014), p. 13.
425. Smith, William, *A Dictionary of Greek and Roman Biography and Mythology* Volume I (London: John Murray, 1873), p. 2.
426. Begg, Ean, *The Cult of the Black Virgin* (London: Arkana Publishing, 1985), p. 71.
427. Davis, Joseph and Thurnam, John, *Crania Britannica: Delineations and Descriptions* Volume I (London: Taylor and Francis, 1865), p. 129.
428. Smith, William, *A Dictionary of Greek and Roman Biography and Mythology* Volume I (London: John Murray, 1873), p. 2.
429. *De Bello Gallico* 6.17.
430. Jordan, Michael, *Dictionary of Gods and Goddesses: Second Edition* (New York: Facts on File, 2004), p. 48.
431. Cotterell, Arthur, *Mythology of the Celts: Myths and Legends of the Celtic World* (London: Southwater Publishing, 2007), p. 19.
432. Smith, William, *A Dictionary of Greek and Roman Biography and Mythology* Volume I (London: John Murray, 1873), p. 2.
433. See note 300.
434. Macbain, Alexander, *Celtic Mythology and Religion* (Inverness: A. & W. MacKenzie, 1885), p. 36.
435. Jordan, Michael, *Dictionary of Gods and Goddesses: Second Edition* (New York: Facts on File, 2004), p. 48.
436. Manuel, Frank and Manuel, Fritzie, *Utopian Thought in the Western World* (Massachusetts: Harvard University Press, 1979), p. 77.
437. Freitag, Barbara, *Hy Brasil: The Metamorphosis of an Island: From Cartographic Error to Celtic Elysium* (Amsterdam: Rodopi, 2013), p. 103.
438. Procopius *History of the Wars* 8.20.42.
439. Geary, Patrick, *The Myth of Nations: The Medieval Origins of Europe* (New Jersey: Princeton University Press, 2002), p. 117.
440. Ammianus 15.9.2.
441. Ammianus 15.9.5.
442. Lucan 1.427-8.
443. Derks, Ton and Roymans, Nico, *Ethnic Constructs in Antiquity: The Role of Power and Tradition* (Amsterdam: Amsterdam University Press, 2009), p. 221.
444. Ibid.
445. *De Bello Gallico* 1.33.

446. Derks, Ton and Roymans, Nico, *Ethnic Constructs in Antiquity: The Role of Power and Tradition* (Amsterdam: Amsterdam University Press, 2009), p. 221.
447. Davies, Janet, *The Welsh Language: A History* (Cardiff: University of Wales Press, 2014), p. 6.
448. *The New Encyclopaedia Britannica: Macropedia – Volume 19* (Chicago: Encyclopaedia Britannica, 1983), p. 1065.
449. Tacitus, *Agricola 11*.
450. Parthenius *Erotica Pathemata* 30.
451. Bede 1.1.
452. Derks, Ton and Roymans, Nico, *Ethnic Constructs in Antiquity: The Role of Power and Tradition* (Amsterdam: Amsterdam University Press, 2009), p. 221.
453. Waldman, Carl and Mason, Catherine, *Encyclopedia of European Peoples* (New York: Facts on File, 2006), p. 165.
454. Diodorus 2.47.6.
455. Bridgman, Timothy, *Hyperboreans: Myth and History in Celtic-Hellenic Contacts* (Abingdon: Routledge, 2005), p. 21.
456. Roman, Luke and Roman, Monica, *Encyclopedia of Greek and Roman Mythology* (New York: Facts on File, 2010), pp. 104, 105.
457. Dictys Cretensis 4.22.
458. *Aeneid*, 2.674.
459. Yarshater, Ehsan, *Encyclopaedia Iranica: Volume 12, Part 3* (Abingdon: Routledge & Kegan Paul, 1982), p. 326.
460. Durken, Daniel, *The New Collegeville Bible Commentary* (Minnesota: Liturgical Press, 2017), p. 820.
461. Berossus *Babyloniaca* 3.2.1, 4.
462. Mansikka, Pekka, *New Chronology Using Solar Eclipses* Volume III (Norderstedt: Books on Demand, 2020), p. 23.
463. Ibid.
464. Ibid.
465. Ibid.
466. Dougherty, Raymond, *Nabonidus and Belshazzar: A Study of the Closing Events of the Neo-Babylonian Empire* (Oregon: Wipf & Stock, 2008), p. 61.
467. Neugebauer, Paul and Weidner, Ernst, *Ein astronomischer Beobachtungstext aus dem 37. Jahre Nebukadnezars II, (-567/66) – Berichte über die Verhandlungen der Königlich Sächsischen Gesellschaft der Wissenschaften zu Leipzig – Volume 67, May 1* (Leipzig: S. Hirzel, 1915), p. 41.
468. Second Kings 25:2-7 and Jeremiah 39:2-7 explain that the city of Jerusalem fell to the Babylonians in Zedekiah's eleventh year – that is, after ten full years and some months. Counting back from 607 BCE brings us to 617 BCE for the start of his reign. Second Kings 24:8 shows that Zedekiah's predecessor, Jehoiachin, only ruled for three months. Jehoiachin's predecessor, in turn, is stated at

2 Kings 23:26 to have reigned for eleven years. Thus, counting back from 617 BCE brings us to 628 BCE for the start of Jehoiakim's reign. Jeremiah 46:2 states that Pharaoh Necho of Egypt was defeated by the Babylonians at Carchemish in Jehoiakim's fourth year. His 'fourth year' would be three full years after the start of his reign, which brings us to 625 BCE.

469. Since Jehoiakim's reign began in 628 BCE, a reading of the following citations shows that Hezekiah's reign began in 745 BCE: 2 Chronicles 36:1, 2; 34:1; 33:21; 33:1; and 29:1.
470. Chen, Fei, *Study on the Synchronistic King List from Ashur* (Leiden: Koninklijke Brill, 2020), p. 121.
471. Na'aman, Nadav, *Chronology and History in the Late Assyrian Empire (631–619 B.C.) – Zeitschrift für Assyriologie* Volume 81 (1–2) (Berlin: De Gruyter, 1991), p. 246.
472. Reade, Julian, *Assyrian eponyms, kings and pretenders, 648–605 BC – Orientalia (NOVA Series)* Volume 67, Issue 2 (Rome: GBPress, 1998), p. 263.
473. Shaw, Ian and Bloxam, Elizabeth, *The Oxford Handbook of Egyptology* (Oxford: Oxford University Press, 2020), p. 707.
474. Ibid.
475. Finegan, Jack, *Archaeological History of the Ancient Middle East* (New York: Routledge, 2018), p. 140.
476. *The Transactions of the Honourable Society of Cymmrodorion* Volume 31, Session 1937 (London: Honourable Society of Cymmrodorion, 1938), p. 364.
477. Bartrum, Peter, *A Welsh Classical Dictionary* (Aberystwyth: The National Library of Wales, 1993), p. 239.
478. *De Bello Gallico* 2.4.
479. Bartrum, Peter, *A Welsh Classical Dictionary* (Aberystwyth: The National Library of Wales, 1993), p. 612.
480. Haywood, John, *The Celts: Bronze Age to New Age* (Abingdon: Routledge, 2014), p. 17.
481. Eagles, Robin, *The Rough Guide Chronicle: England* (London: Rough Guides, 2002), p. 9; Slatyer, Will, *Ebbs and Flows of Ancient Imperial Power, 3000 BC-AD 900: A Short History of Ancient Religion, War, Prosperity, and Debt* (Singapore: Partridge Publishing, 2014), p. 325.
482. Koch, John, *Celtic Culture: A Historical Encyclopedia* (California: ABC-CLIO, 2006), p. 357.

Bibliography

Alcock, Susan and Osborne, Robin, *Classical Archaeology – Second Edition* (Chichester: Wiley-Blackwell, 2012)

Bartrum, Peter, *A Welsh Classical Dictionary* (Aberystwyth: The National Library of Wales, 1993)

Beekes, Robert, *The prehistory of the Lydians, the origins of the Etruscans, Troy and Aeneas – Bibliotheca Orientalis 59* (Leiden: NINO, 2002)

Bell, Sinclair and Carpino, Alexandra, *A Companion to the Etruscans* (Chichester: Wiley-Blackwell, 2016)

Bennett, James, *The Archaeology of Egypt in the Third Intermediate Period* (Cambridge: Cambridge University Press, 2019)

Bradley, Richard, *The Prehistory of Britain and Ireland: Second Edition* (Cambridge: Cambridge University Press, 2019)

Brown, Jonathan, *In Search of Homeric Ithaca* (Canberra: Parrot Press, 2020)

Bryce, Trevor, *The Routledge Handbook of the Peoples and Places of Ancient Western Asia: The Near East from the Early Bronze Age to the Fall of the Persian Empire* (Abingdon: Routledge, 2009)

Camporeale, Giovannangelo, *The Etruscans Outside Etruria* (Los Angeles: The J. Paul Getty Museum, 2004)

Cooley, Alison, *A Companion to Roman Italy* (Chichester: Wiley-Blackwell, 2016)

Cornell, Tim, *The Beginnings of Rome: Italy and Rome from the Bronze Age to the Punic Wars (c. 1000-264 BC)* (Abingdon, Routledge, 1995)

Cotterell, Arthur, *Mythology of the Celts: Myths and Legends of the Celtic World* (London: Southwater Publishing, 2007)

Cunliffe, Barry, *Britain Begins* (Oxford: Oxford University Press, 2013)

Bibliography

de Grummond, Nancy, *Etruscan Myth, Sacred History, and Legend* (Pennsylvania: University of Pennsylvania Museum of Archaeology and Anthropology, 2006)

De Jong, Irene, *Homer: Critical Assessments* Volume II – *The Homeric World* (London: Routledge, 1999)

Demetriou, Denise, *Negotiating Identity in the Ancient Mediterranean: The Archaic and Classical Greek Multiethnic Emporia* (Cambridge: Cambridge University Press, 2012)

Derks, Ton and Roymans, Nico, *Ethnic Constructs in Antiquity: The Role of Power and Tradition* (Amsterdam: Amsterdam University Press, 2009)

Dowden, Ken and Livingstone, Niall, *A Companion to Greek Mythology* (Chichester: Wiley-Blackwell, 2014)

Eaton, Jonathan, *An Archaeological History of Britain: Continuity and Change from Prehistory to the Present* (Barnsley: Pen and Sword Archaeology, 2014)

Evans, Jane, *A Companion to the Archaeology of the Roman Republic* (Chichester: Wiley-Blackwell, 2013)

Evans, Jane, *The Art of Persuasion: Political Propaganda from Aeneas to Brutus* (Michigan: University of Michigan Press, 1992)

Friedland, Elise; Sobocinski, Melanie; and Gazda, Elaine, *The Oxford Handbook of Roman Sculpture* (New York: Oxford University Press, 2015)

Gagarin, Michael and Fantham, Elaine, *The Oxford Encyclopedia of Ancient Greece* Volume I (New York: Oxford University Press, 2010)

Geary, Patrick, *The Myth of Nations: The Medieval Origins of Europe* (New Jersey: Princeton University Press, 2002)

Gosden, Christopher; Crawford, Sally; Ulmschneider, Katharina, *Celtic Art in Europe: Making Connections* (Oxford: Oxbow Books, 2014)

Grant, Michael and Hazel, John, *Who's Who in Classical Mythology* (London: Routledge, 2002)

Graziosi, Barbara, *Inventing Homer: The Early Reception of Epic* (Cambridge: Cambridge University Press, 2002)

Grimbly, Shona, *Encyclopedia of the Ancient World* (Illinois: Fitzroy Dearborn Publishers, 2000)

Gruen, Erich, *Rethinking the Other in Antiquity* (New Jersey: Princeton University Press, 2011)

Hard, Robin, *The Routledge Handbook of Greek Mythology* (London: Routledge, 2004)

Harding, Dennis, *Rewriting History: Changing Perceptions of the Archaeological Past* (Oxford: Oxford University Press, 2020)

Harding, Dennis, *The Archaeology of Celtic Art* (Abingdon: Routledge, 2007)

Harding, Dennis, *The Iron Age in Lowland Britain* (Abingdon: Routledge, 2015)

Harding, Dennis, *The Iron Age in Northern Britain: Celts and Romans, Natives and Invaders* (Abingdon: Routledge, 2004)

Haynes, Sybille, *Etruscan Civilization: A Cultural History* (California: Getty Publications, 2000)

Haywood, John, *The Celts: Bronze Age to New Age* (Abingdon: Routledge, 2014)

Henry, Roger, *Synchronized Chronology: Rethinking Middle East Antiquity* (New York: Algora Publishing, 2003)

Higgins, Reynold, *Greek and Roman Jewellery – Second Edition* (Berkeley: University of California Press, 1980)

Hoffmeier, James, *Israel in Egypt: Evidence for the Authenticity of the Exodus Tradition* (New York: Oxford University Press, 1999)

Holleran, Claire and Claridge, Amanda, *A Companion to the City of Rome* (Chichester: Wiley-Blackwell, 2018)

Insight on the Scriptures Volume I (New York: Watchtower Bible and Tract Society of New York, 2018)

Janda, Richard; Joseph, Brian; and Vance, Barbara, *The Handbook of Historical Linguistics* Volume II (Chichester: Wiley-Blackwell, 2021)

Jordan, Michael, *Dictionary of Gods and Goddesses: Second Edition* (New York: Facts on File, 2004)

Kagan, Donald and Viggiano, Gregory, *Men of Bronze: Hoplite Warfare in Ancient Greece* (New Jersey: Princeton University Press, 2013)

Kim, Lawrence, *Homer Between History and Fiction in Imperial Greek Literature* (Cambridge: Cambridge University Press, 2010)

Koch, John, *Celtic Culture: A Historical Encyclopedia* (California: ABC-CLIO, 2006)

Koch, John; Minard, Antone, *The Celts: History, Life, and Culture – Volume 1: A-H* (California: ABC-CLIO, 2012)

Kokkinos, Nikos, *Ancient Chronology, Eratosthenes and the Dating of the Fall of Troy – Ancient West & East* Volume 8 (Leiden: Brill, 2009)

Lemos, Irene and Kotsonas, Antonis, *A Companion to the Archaeology of Early Greece and the Mediterranean* Volume I (New Jersey: Wiley-Blackwell, 2020)

Lieu, Judith and Rogerson, John, *The Oxford Handbook of Biblical Studies* (Oxford: Oxford University Press, 2006)

Lloyd, Alan, *A Companion to Ancient Egypt* Volume I (Chichester: Wiley-Blackwell, 2010)

Bibliography

McColl, R.W., *Encyclopedia of World Geography* (New York: Facts on File, 2005)

McInerney, Jeremy, *A Companion to Ethnicity in the Ancient Mediterranean* (Chichester: Wiley-Blackwell, 2014)

Naso, Alessandro, *Etruscology* Volume I (Berlin: De Gruyter, 2017)

Orlin, Eric, *A Social and Cultural History of Republican Rome* (New Jersey: Wiley-Blackwell, 2022)

Osborne, Robin, *Greece in the Making, 1200-479 BC – Second Edition* (Abingdon: Routledge, 2009)

Roman, Luke and Roman, Monica, *Encyclopedia of Greek and Roman Mythology* (New York: Facts on File, 2010)

Rose, Charles, *The Archaeology of Greek and Roman Troy* (New York: Cambridge University Press, 2014)

Saïd, Suzanne, *Homer and the Odyssey* (Oxford: Oxford University Press, 2011)

Shaw, Ian and Bloxam, Elizabeth, *The Oxford Handbook of Egyptology* (Oxford: Oxford University Press, 2020)

Shaw, Ian, *The Oxford History of Ancient Egypt* (Oxford: Oxford University Press, 2003)

Snyder, Christopher, *The Britons* (Oxford: Blackwell Publishing, 2003)

Steiner, Margreet and Killebrew, Ann, *The Oxford Handbook of the Archaeology of the Levant* (Oxford: Oxford University Press, 2013)

Sweeney, Emmet, *Gods, Heroes and Tyrants: Greek Chronology in Chaos* (New York: Algora Publishing, 2009)

Tsetskhladze, Gocha, *Greek Colonisation: An Account of Greek Colonies and Other Settlements Overseas – Volume Two* (Leiden: Brill, 2008)

Turfa, Jean, *The Etruscan World* (Abingdon: Routledge, 2013)

van Wees, Hans, *The Homeric Way of War: The Iliad and the Hoplite Phalanx (II) – Greece & Rome*, Second Series, Volume 41, Issue 2 (Cambridge: Cambridge University Press, 1994)

Venning, Timothy, *A Chronology of the Roman Empire* (New York: Continuum International Publishing Group, 2011

Villing, Alexandra, *Greece and Egypt: Reconsidering Early Contact and Exchange – Regional Stories Towards a New Perception of the Early Greek World* (Volos: University of Thessaly Press, 2017)

Waldman, Carl and Mason, Catherine, *Encyclopedia of European Peoples* (New York: Facts on File, 2006)

Wilson, Alan and Blackett, Baram, *The Trojan War of 650 BC: Fractured History* (Indiana: Trafford Publishing, 2010)

Index

Abantes 105–6
Abellio 215–17
Achilles 60, 108, 119
Aedd Mawr 244, 246–7, 249–50, 251
Aeneas 9, 154, 157, 179, 187, 191
  ally of Tarchon 154–6, 192
  ancestor of Brutus 61, 159–62, 167–9, 171–4, 176, 178, 190, 226, 239
  chronology 61, 167
  depictions by Etruscans 150
  founder of Rome 132, 135, 153, 178, 227
  legendary meeting with Dido 64–5
  migration to Italy 128, 131–4, 138, 146–52, 173, 217
  wife 225
Agamemnon 45, 47, 56, 67, 76, 79, 103–4, 118, 124
  historical identity 100–1
  kingdom 69–71
Agapenor 124

Alaksandu, king of Wilusa 46–8
Alan Wilson 167
Alba Longa 131, 153, 227
  fictional dynasty 133
Albanactus 240
Albion 9
Amel-Marduk, king of Babylon 232–3
Ammeris, king of Egypt 97–8, 116, 238
Anatolia 36, 45, 61, 65, 75, 78, 86–7, 91, 93, 96, 103–4, 108–9, 116–18, 218, 220, 225, 229
  Greek colonisation of 66, 101, 120–2
  Greek warfare in 45, 46–8, 119–20, 122, 124, 129–30
  origin of Etruscans 138–52, 156–7, 183, 196, 217–19
  visited by Heracles 114–15
Andragius, king of Britain 240, 244, 247, 250–1, 252
Anthony Adolph 168

Anysis, king of Egypt 50–1
  identified as Ammeris 96–7, 116
Apollo 69, 86–7, 115, 142
  chief god of the Trojans, Etruscans and Celts 151, 214–17, 225, 228, 267 n. 300
Archilochus 78
Archmail, king of Britain 240–1
Argonauts 56, 59, 60, 63–4, 68, 86, 104, 115
Argos 57, 59, 77, 91, 115, 118
  kingdom of Agamemnon 70–1, 101, 118
Artemis 187
Arthur, king 26, 31–3
Ascanius 133, 159–61, 170, 173–4, 225
  possibly Romulus 174
Ashurbanipal 108–9, 235–8
Ashur-etil-ilani, king of Babylon 231, 236, 238

Index

Assyrians 52–4, 75, 89–90, 95–6, 99, 107–9, 115–16, 118, 121–2
  chronology 229, 234–8, 255 n. 30
Athens 56, 75, 81–2, 148
Atreus 45, 47–8
Attarsiya 47–8
Attica 56, 185–6

Babylon 54, 118, 230–7
Bede 23, 29, 33, 224
Belenus 215–17
Belgae 221, 250, 251
Beli Mawr ap Manogan 24, 61, 242, 244–5, 249
Belinus
  ancestor of Brutus 240
  commander of Britons 13, 24–5
  king of the Britons 12–14, 22–7
Bêl-shum-ishkun, king of Babylon 233
Black Sea 62, 115, 118
Bladud, king of Britain 165, 240, 242, 243, 251, 252
Bledudo, king of Britain 164, 240–1
boar tusk helmet 71
Bocchoris, king of Egypt 90–1, 94, 116
Boreas 225–7
Brennius, king of Britain 163, 165–6, 241
Britain 28, 139, 158, 159, 166, 186, 192
  foundation legend 8–10
  genetics 139, 217–20
  identified with Hyperborea 214

name 170, 176
Post-Roman era 25, 27, 163–5
Pre-Roman kings 61, 162–6, 239–52
Roman era 12–22, 24–5, 30, 32, 34, 187, 190, 198, 199
trade with Mediterranean 186–7
Trojan migration to 29, 33, 34, 37, 128, 158–9, 168, 170, 177–183, 187, 192–228
Britons 9, 16, 18–19, 25, 160, 162–3, 170, 176, 209, 210, 250
  conflict with Anglo-Saxons 27
  conflict with Romans 12–15
  descended from Gauls 222–4
  descended from Trojans 9, 159, 168, 220–1, 227–8
  religious beliefs 213–17
  use of chariots 212
Brutus 9, 11, 158, 178–9, 208, 217–18, 227, 228
  apparent death 176
  chronology 159–62, 166–7, 178, 224
  death of parents 174–5
  father 171–3
  fictional Brutus 160–1
  genealogy 61, 158–66, 170–73, 178, 225–6, 239–252

identified as Lucius Junius Brutus 166–76
journey along African coast 188–90
migration through Mediterranean 179–81, 190–3, 227
migration to Britain 128, 130, 179, 183, 200, 228
migration to Gaul 182–3, 194–6, 204, 220–2, 228
prince of Rome 162, 170, 177
prophecy 174
Roman consul 166–7, 169–70, 174–7, 178, 189, 239
visit to Lefkada 186–7, 227
war against Greeks 184–6, 227
Brutus Greenshield, king of Britain 165, 240, 242, 252
Brythonic language 206–9, 245, 246
Busiris, king of Egypt 90–1, 92, 116

Cadmus 51, 55, 61, 80–1, 102, 113
Callimachus 187
Canaan 39–43, 93, 95
Canterbury 14, 30
Caph, king of Britain 164, 240–1
Capoir, king of Britain 164, 240–1
Caranus, fictional founder of Macedon 57
Carausius 19

281

Carians 105–6, 119, 127
Carthage 64–5, 113,
    115, 131–2
Caswallon 13–14, 15,
    61, 240–1, 251
  historical Cassivellaunus
    13–14, 15, 24–5, 30,
    61, 162, 166, 241,
    251
Catalogue of Ships 68–9,
    74
Catellus, king of Britain
    163, 240–1
Catherine Morgan 68, 74
Catleu ap Catel 32
Celtic language 206–7,
    222–3
  Etruscan influence
    207–211, 228
Celts 196–228
  adoption of La Tène
    culture 196
  chief god 214–17
  descended from
    Bretannus 223–4
  descended from
    Trojans 221–2
  genetics 217–20
  migration to Britain
    201–3, 222–4
  religion 213–17
  trade with Greeks
    197–8
  warfare 211–13
chariots 41, 211–13,
    222, 228
  Etruscan 143
  Celtic 196–7, 200–3,
    205
Cherin, king of Britain
    240, 244, 247,
    250–1, 252
Chios, island of 58–9,
    77, 104–6

Cimmerians 65–6, 75,
    78, 108
Cinyras, king of Cyprus
    91–2, 124
Claudius 15–16, 24, 27,
    190
  Gloucester supposedly
    named after 170,
    176, 199
Cledaucus, king of
    Britain 240–1
Clotenus, king of Britain
    240–1
Coillus, king of Britain
    240–1
Corineus 182
  possible identity
    191–2, 194
Corsica 190–1
Constantine the Great 19
Constantius
  father of Constantine
    the Great 19–20
  fifth-century ruler 21,
    253 n. 2
Crete 105, 116–17, 123,
    150, 215
Ctesias of Cnidus 50–6,
    75, 76, 107, 108,
    254 n. 26
Cunedagius, king of
    Britain 164–5, 166,
    240, 242, 243
Cunedda 162, 164, 241
Cunobelinus 24–5, 27
Cyme 101, 119
Cyprus 88, 91–2, 113,
    124, 128
Cyrene 79, 125–6, 180,
    188, 212
Cyrus the Great 230–1,
    254 n. 26

Danius, king of Britain
    240, 244, 246–7,
    252
Dardanus 117, 225, 226
David Rohl 34–5, 43
Decimus Junius Brutus
    168–70, 176
Demophon, king of
    Athens 56, 81
Diana, goddess 180,
    186–7, 227
Dido, princess of Tyre
    64–5, 131
Digueillus, king of
    Britain 240, 244–5,
    251, 252
Diodorus Siculus 59,
    60, 79, 82, 93, 107,
    187, 195, 212, 214,
    225–7, 230, 254
    n. 24
Dionysius of
    Halicarnassus 117,
    134, 137, 148, 153,
    173–4
  founding of Rome 132
  origin of Etruscans 138
Dodona 185–6
Dolobellus 12–14, 30
Dorians 66–7, 84, 91
Dorobernia 14, 30
  Roman Durovernum 30
Dunvallo Molmutius 163,
    165, 166, 240–1

Ebraucus, king of Britain
    165–6, 240–3
Egypt 62, 88–92, 107–9,
    110, 114–16, 188
  chronology 35–45,
    229–38, 274 n. 468
  Greek migration to
    126–8

Index

kings 35, 38, 42–4, 50–1, 84–6, 88, 93–100, 110–12
relationship with Lydia 86–7, 114
Eldol, king of Britain 164, 240, 241
Eleutherius, Pope 17–18
Elidurus, king of Britian 163, 240–1
Eliud, king of Britain 240, 244, 247, 250
Elymians 128–9
Enniaunus, king of Britain 163, 241
Eratosthenes 53, 79
Esarhaddon 235–6, 238
Eteocles 45, 48
Ethiopians 50, 95, 106–7
from the east 107
Etruscans
  alphabet 153
  Anatolian origin 138–45
  chief god 151
  descendants of Trojans 145–52
  double-axe symbol 142–3
  founders of Rome 152–4
  genetics 138–40, 152
  interest in Aeneas 150
  language 144–5, 149, 152, 206–11
  Orientalising period 141
  religion 141–2
  tombs 141
Evander, king of Pallantium 125, 134–5, 137
Evaristus, Pope 17

Exodus 38–9, 41, 43, 167–8, 188, 189

Frankish Table of Nations 160–1, 169, 220, 226
Freowulf 27, 247

Gades 124–5
Garbanion, king of Britain 163
Gaul 165, 179, 180, 182, 192–3, 194–207, 211, 214–17, 220–4, 225, 227–8, 245, 251
genetics 217–19
Geoffrey of Monmouth 9, 61, 175, 184, 189, 198
account of Brutus's genealogy 158–61, 162–6, 239–52
account of Brutus' migration 179–82
veracity of claims 11–33, 178, 167, 227
Gerennus, king of Britain 240–1
Gezer 43
Gildas 23, 25–6, 29–30, 33
De Excidio 25–6, 29
Goffarius Pictus 182, 199
Golden Fleece 56, 87, 115
Gorboduc, king of Britain 163, 166, 240–1
Greece 55, 61, 63, 68, 71, 80, 88, 93, 98, 105, 107, 118, 119, 120, 140, 148–9, 193, 213, 227
Archaic era 68, 75–6

gods of 142, 151
homeland of the Trojans 117, 152, 218
kings of 48, 69, 75–6
Mycenaean era 69, 75
Orientalising period 143
relations with Egypt 86–7, 91, 114
Trojans captive in 9, 129, 180, 184–6, 216
Greek Dark Ages 45, 71, 74
Greeks 34, 46, 63, 65, 69, 71–2, 75, 83, 103, 106, 107, 115, 123, 128, 142, 190, 206, 211, 221, 225–7
afterlife 216
alphabet 55, 113, 207
ancestors of Trojans 105, 117, 218
antiquity 52–54
collective identity 76
colonisation of Anatolia 66, 101, 119–21, 129–30, 146–7
conflict with allies of Troy 121–2
conflict with Etruscans 185
conflict with Wilusa 37, 45–6, 47, 49
defeated by Brutus 180, 184, 227
designs 204–6
identified as Ahhiyawa 37, 45, 48
in Egypt 86–7, 111–12, 126–7
migrations after Trojan War 124–128, 130

283

Mycenaean 117, 212
mythology 8, 82,
    87–8, 89, 102, 103,
    106, 185, 226
Pelasgians driven out
    by 149
trade with Celts 197
views on Etruscans
    138, 146
warfare 72–4, 212–13
Guithelinus, king of
    Britain 240–1
Guneus 125
    historical identity 125–6
Gurgintius, king of Britain
    240, 244–6, 252
Gurguint Barbtruc, king
    of Britain 164, 240–1
Gurgustius, king of Britain
    240, 242, 245, 252
Gyges, king of Lydia 78,
    86, 102, 108–9, 115,
    121–2, 127, 147

Hadrian's Wall 18
*Hanes Gruffydd ap
    Cynan* 61, 161–2,
    165–7, 170, 178,
    242–5, 250
Hans van Wees 72–4, 78
Harleian genealogies
    31–2, 163–4
Hazor 42
Hecataeus of Abdera
    214, 225–7
Hector of Troy 104–6,
    108
Helen 8, 46, 62, 63, 98,
    110–11, 126, 226
Helen by Euripides 110,
    127
Heli, king of Britain 162,
    166, 240–2, 244–5,
    251–2

Hellanicus of Lesbos 79,
    80, 82, 132, 149,
    151
Heracleion 63, 77
Heracles 55–6, 59, 61,
    77, 79, 80–1, 83,
    91–3, 94, 102–3,
    113
    historical identity
        84–91, 113–16, 126
    legendary descendants
        58, 59–60, 67
Herodotus 57, 59, 62–3,
    81, 84, 93–7, 102,
    107, 110, 115,
    125–7, 142, 147,
    187, 255 n. 30
    chronology of Trojan
        War 50–2, 54–6
    dating of Homer 81–2
    origin of Etruscans 138,
        143–4, 145, 148
Hezekiah, king of Judah
    234, 278
Historia Brittonum 9,
    28–30, 164, 196
    account of Prydain's
        arrival 248–50
    account of Scottish
        migration 188–90,
        269 n. 344
    account of Trojan
        migration 179, 181,
        190–1, 200, 220,
        227
    compared to *HRB*
        11–22, 33
    description of Brutus
        166–70, 174–5
    genealogy of Brutus
        158–62, 172–3
    not source for *HRB*
        22–5, 33

*Historia Regum
    Britanniae* 9, 158,
    175, 178
    account of Trojan
        migration 179–83,
        196, 200
    authenticity 11–33
    genealogy of Brutus
        162–6, 239–52
    unreliable geography
        198
Hittites 37, 47–9, 75, 151
Holinshed's Chronicles 9
Homer 63, 83, 99–100,
    103, 104, 105–6,
    109–10, 118,
    120–1, 126–7, 147,
    185, 216
    chronology 51, 77–82
    writings 68–77,
        109–10, 123, 148,
        149, 151, 211–12
Huelva 124, 195
Hyperborea 226–7

Iliad 47, 77, 81, 83,
    91, 104–5, 108,
    110, 117, 119,
    123, 148–9, 151,
    211–13, 225
    period described 68–77
    when written 82
Ilus 116–17, 123
Iphitos 93, 114
Irene de Jong 69, 71, 73,
    75–6, 78
Israelites 38–42
Italy 9, 25, 153, 170, 176,
    177, 185, 190, 191,
    192, 197, 203, 207,
    208, 213, 215, 219
    Brutus expelled from
        9, 174

Index

Brutus' migration from 179, 193, 204, 208, 211, 217
Greek migrations to 63, 125, 128
Trojan migration to 128, 132–4, 138–52, 156–7, 158, 159, 162, 173, 184, 185, 228
visited by Heracles 87, 91, 114

James Douglas Bruce 168
James K. Hoffmeier 40
Jason, leader of the Argonauts 56, 59, 86, 87, 115
Jerusalem 38, 43, 94–5, 230–7, 274 n. 468
Jesus Christ 16, 62
Jodi Magness 143
John Kinloch Anderson 68
Jonas Grethlein 68, 70
Joseph, patriarch 38–40, 41, 43, 44
Josephus 55–6
Julius Caesar 12–15, 22, 24–5, 29, 30, 32, 61, 166, 198, 212, 215, 221, 241, 245, 251

Kamber 240
Kinmarcus 240–1

La Tène 196–205, 209–11, 212–13, 218, 220, 222, 249
armour 205–6
chariot burials 196–7, 200–3, 205
early centres 198, 200
Etruscan influences 196–8
funerary customs 197, 204–5
spread to Britain 200–2
square barrows 201
statues 197, 204–5
use of hill forts 203–4
Laomedon 86, 115–17, 123
Lattes 194–6
Lavinia 132, 155
Lefkada 180, 184, 186–7, 190, 193, 227
Leil, king of Britain 165, 240, 242, 246, 252
Leir, king of Britain 165, 240, 242, 252
Lelius Hamo 16, 27–8, 248
historical Aulus Plautius 16, 27–8, 248
Lemnos 118
Etruscan settlement 142, 144–5, 148–9, 156, 185
Libya 125–6, 127
Linus 80–1, 102, 113–14
Livy 56, 159, 174–6
founding of Rome 131, 133, 153–6, 162
Locrinus 165, 176–7, 240, 242–3, 251
Loire River 182, 194–6, 199–200, 222
Lombards 16, 207
London 14, 183
Lucius, King 16–18
Lydia 66, 78, 86, 102, 104, 108–9, 114, 115, 118–19, 121–2, 127, 229

origin of Etruscans 138–48, 150–2, 154, 157, 178, 185

Macedon 56–8, 77, 91
Maddan, king of Britain 165, 240, 242, 252
Magna Graecia 125
Magnus Maximus 20–1, 25–6, 28, 94
Manetho 84–5, 93–4, 97–100
Manogan 24, 61, 244–5, 251
known as Minocannus 12–13, 23–5
Mary Beard 134
Mediterranean 9, 15, 35, 39, 49, 86, 104, 113, 180, 190, 196, 215
conflict within 185
entrance to 95, 181–2, 188, 194
Etruscan colonies within 194–5
genetics 218
Greek and Trojan colonies within 127, 130
trade with ancient Britain 186–7
trade with ancient Gaul 197–8
Medon
of Argos 59
of Athens 81–2
Megiddo 42
Memphis 98–100, 116
Memnon 106–9, 229
Mempricius, king of Britain 165, 240, 242, 252

285

Menelaus 45, 47, 111, 118
  visits Egypt 126–7
Mentor 110
Merianus, king of Britain 164, 240–1
Midas 100–3
Middle East 34, 87, 93, 107, 141
  chronology 35–6, 45, 49, 229, 234
Milan 25–6
Miles Russell 9, 167
Miletus 106, 145
Mopsus 103–4
Morgan, king of Britain 163
Morvidus, king of Britain 240, 244, 247, 249–50, 252
Moses 39, 41, 43–4
Mycenae 47
  ruled by Agamemnon 69–70
Mykonos 83

Nabonidus, king of Babylon 231, 235, 236
Nabopolassar, king of Babylon 234–7
Naples 63
Near East 95, 139–41, 143, 156, 183, 186, 218, 226, 248
  chronology 35, 38–9, 44–5, 49, 229
Nebuchadnezzar, king of Babylon 231–4
Necho I 98–100, 111–12, 116, 126–7, 237–8, 274 n. 468
Neriglissar 233
Nicholas Horsfall 132

Nikos Kokkinos 52
Nineveh 53–5, 108, 255 n. 30
Ninus 54, 255
Numa Pompilius 136, 160–2, 168, 169, 173–4

Oedipus 48, 56
Oenopion 59, 104–6
Oenus, king of Britain 240, 244–6, 252
Odin 61–2
Odysseus 63, 109, 110, 132
Odyssey 69, 75, 80, 109–10, 123
Olympic Games 55–6, 61, 77, 78, 84–5, 93, 114
Oracle of Delphi 56, 77, 102, 174
Orosius 23–5
Orpheus
  brother of Linus 80–1, 82, 102, 113
  student of Linus 102
Osorkon I 44
Osorkon IV 84–92, 113–16, 126

Palatine Hill 134–5
Pallantium 134–5, 137
Pandrasus, Greek king 180, 186
Paphos 124
Parian Chronicle 34, 50
Paris Alexander 8, 63, 98, 110
  supposedly King Alaksandu 45–48
Parthenope 63, 77
  lover of Heracles 91–2

Pausanias 58, 59–60, 89, 129
Pelasgians 148, 185–6, 218
  association with Etruscans 148–50, 151–2, 157, 178, 185
Perdiccas I 57–8, 60
Peredurus, king of Britian 163, 241
Persians 57, 66, 230
Peter James 34–5, 43
pharaoh, Egyptian title 41, 43, 96–7
Pheidon 59
Phemius 109–10
Pheron 96–8, 111, 116
Phoenicians 55, 64–5, 187, 195–6
  alphabet 55, 61, 76, 80, 113, 207
Phrygians 75, 100–3, 108, 118–19, 142, 147, 149–50, 152, 178, 185, 207, 218
Picts 18–17
Pillars of Hercules 95, 181, 188–9
Pir, king of Britain 164, 240–1
Piyama-Radu 46–7
Piye, king of Egypt 88–9, 114
Plutarch 77, 132, 143
Porrex I, king of Britain 163, 240, 244, 246
Porrex II, king of Britain 240, 244, 247, 249, 252
  identified with Prydain 247, 249
Priam 45–7, 55, 61–2, 63, 67, 86–7,

Index

103-4, 106, 117, 118, 223, 225-6
vassal king of Assyrians 75
Proteus 98-100, 110-12, 116, 126-7
Prydain 246-50, 251
Psamtik I 86-7, 112, 115, 127, 237-8
Pygmalion 64, 91-2, 113, 116
Pythagoras 58, 60, 77

radiocarbon dating 36, 64
Rameses the Great 35-7, 43, 44
Rederchius, king of Britain 164, 240-1
Redion, king of Britain 240-1
Regan, queen of Britain 165, 240, 242, 252
Rhea Silva 160-1
Rhone valley 195-6
Rivallo, king of Britain 165, 240, 242, 252
Robert Beekes 146, 149, 266 n. 295
Roman Empire 25, 159
Rome 16, 19, 21, 25-6, 155-6, 162, 167, 168, 170, 175-7, 213, 239
archaeology 134-6, 138, 156
chronology of founding 131-3, 134-8, 156, 159, 162, 178
emperors of 12, 62, 187
Etruscans' role in founding 152-4, 157
Evander's city 134-5, 137

Salamis 124
Samothrace 105, 118
Samuil Penissel, king of Britain 164, 240-1
Sardinia 181, 189-91, 192
Sargon 89-90, 115
Scione 63, 77
Scots 18-19
migration to Ireland 166-7, 188-9, 250
Segesta 128
Sennacherib 95, 232, 235-6, 238
Septimius Severus 18-19
Servius Tullius 136, 171-3
Sesostris, king of Egypt 93-6, 111, 116, 237
Shabaka 50-2, 54, 55, 96-7, 237-8
Shebitku 94-7, 116, 237-8
Shishak 42-4
Sicily 69, 128, 131, 190
214, 225
Silvius 159, 161, 170, 172-3
Sinsharishkun, king of Assyria 234, 236, 238

Sisillius I, king of Britain 240, 242, 252
Sisillius II, king of Britain 240, 244, 246
sacked by Brennus 166
seven kings 135-6, 137-8, 154, 171, 178
Sisillius III, king of Britain 240, 244, 246
Solomon 38, 42-4, 254 n. 16
Spain 95, 168-9, 170, 176, 182, 188, 189, 194-6, 248-9
migration of Greeks to 124-5, 128
Sparatinum 184
Sparta 63, 71, 118
Strabo 65-66, 67, 78, 93, 95-6, 100-1, 106, 137, 144, 147, 149-50, 154, 185, 187
Suetonius 23-4

Taharga 94-6, 100, 107, 127, 237-8
Tantamani 111-12, 127, 238
Tarchon 154-6, 196
Tarquinius Priscus 136, 171
Tarquinius Superbus 136, 154-6, 171-2, 174, 175, 191-2
Tawagalawa letter 48
Tefnakht 94, 97-9, 116, 238
Tenea 129
Tenedos 105, 118
Teucer
archer 124-5
founder of Troy 105, 116-17, 123
Temenus 58-60, 67
Terpander 77-8
Thaletas 77-8

Thames 12, 13, 22, 183
Thasos 105, 118
Thebes
  Grecian 45, 48, 88
  Egyptian 99-100, 127
Theoclymenus 110-12, 127
Theseus 56
Thrace 93, 95, 105, 116, 147, 225-7
Thucydides 57, 66-7, 119-21, 144, 148
Thuoris 99-100, 111
Togodumnus 27, 176
Tours 179, 182, 196
Trier 25-6
Trikastro 184
Trinovantum 13, 14, 183
Trojan Horse 8, 49, 83, 101, 123
Trojan War 8, 85, 86, 105, 110, 110, 112, 116, 138, 146-8, 229, 231, 237
  date of 34-7, 44, 83, 117, 131-4, 137, 169, 239
  historical 113, 118-23
  migrations subsequent to 65-6, 124-129, 140, 148-50, 156-7, 185
  revised chronology 54-82, 91-4, 96-104, 107-8, 115, 144, 158, 178
  traditional chronology 45-9, 50-4, 156, 162, 166, 172, 183, 224, 239
Trojans 8, 47, 101, 104-7, 121, 122, 124, 155
  ancestors of Britons 9-10
  ancestors of Etruscans 138, 146-52, 157, 171, 178
  ancestors of Norse 61
  Assyrian vassals 75
  descendants of Greeks 117
  language 117, 149, 152, 267 n. 304
  led by Brutus 180-6, 191
  migration to Britain and Gaul 194-227
  migrations after fall of Troy 128-32, 138, 152-4, 157, 158
  war with Greeks 46, 118-19
Troy 8, 37, 45-9, 56, 61, 62-3, 69, 80, 82, 98, 101, 103, 105-6, 110, 126, 129, 138, 144, 147-52, 173, 185, 213-14, 222, 225-6, 229
  archaeology 49, 87, 106, 115-18, 122-3, 130, 146
  Assyrian support of 75, 107-9
  chronology 36-7, 65
  dynasty of 75, 86, 104-6, 115, 116, 118, 128, 181, 225-7, 239
Turnus
  leader of Latins 154-5, 179, 182, 190, 191-2
  ally of Brutus 175, 177, 199
Tychius 110
Tyndareus 63, 71
Tyre 64, 92, 113
Tyrrhenian Sea 12, 13, 179-82, 185, 190-5
Tyrrhenus 148-9, 154

Urien 31, 163, 241, 245, 247

Villanovan culture 140-1, 145, 217-18
Virgil 64-5, 105, 116, 131-2, 150-1, 153-4, 156, 159, 162, 171-3, 191, 192
Vortigern 21, 241

Walter, archdeacon of Oxford 12

Zeus 84, 142, 151